Black Rights/White Wrongs

TRANSGRESSING
BOUNDARIES

Studies in Black Politics and Black Communities
Cathy Cohen and Fredrick Harris, Series Editors

Black Rights/
White Wrongs

The Critique of Racial Liberalism

Charles W. Mills

OXFORD
UNIVERSITY PRESS

OXFORD
UNIVERSITY PRESS

Oxford University Press is a department of the University of Oxford. It furthers
the University's objective of excellence in research, scholarship, and education
by publishing worldwide. Oxford is a registered trade mark of Oxford University
Press in the UK and certain other countries.

Published in the United States of America by Oxford University Press
198 Madison Avenue, New York, NY 10016, United States of America.

CIP data is on file at the Library of Congress
ISBN 978–0–19–024542–9 (Pbk); ISBN 978–0–19–024541–2 (Hbk)

11 10 9

Paperback printed by Marquis, Canada
Hardback printed by Bridgeport National Bindery, Inc., United States of America

Toward a deracialized liberalism

I have almost reached the regrettable conclusion that the Negro's great stumbling block in the stride toward freedom is not the White Citizen's Counciler or the Ku Klux Klanner, but the white moderate who is more devoted to "order" than to justice.
—Martin Luther King Jr., "Letter from a Birmingham City Jail"

A white moderate . . . is a cat who wants to lynch you from a *low* tree.
—Dick Gregory

CONTENTS

CONTENTS

ACKNOWLEDGMENTS

Many of the chapters in this book have benefited from being presented in earlier incarnations as papers at campus colloquia and at conferences over the period 2002–15. The chronological order of these presentations is as follows: at "The Moral Legacy of Slavery: Repairing Injustice" conference, Bowling Green State University (2002); at the annual Chapel Hill Colloquium in Philosophy (2002); at a conference organized by the Chicago Political Theory Group (2002); on an American Philosophical Association (APA) Central Division annual meeting symposium panel, "Race, Gender, and Public Life" (2003); at the Race and Politics Workshop, UCLA Department of Political Science (2003); at the annual meeting of the Society for Phenomenology and Existential Philosophy (SPEP) (2003); in the "Just Globalization" lecture series, Lehigh University (2003); as a lecture at Colby College (2003); at the "Women Philosophers, Sidelined Challenges, and Professional Philosophy" special session, APA Eastern Division annual meeting (2003); as a lecture as Visiting Eminent Scholar, University of Alabama at Huntsville (2004); as an opening keynote address at the "Ethics and Epistemologies of Ignorance" conference, Pennsylvania State University (2004); at the American Political Science Association annual meeting (2007); at "The Social Contract Revisited: The Modern Welfare State" workshop, Oxford University (2007); at the annual meeting of SPEP (2007); at the APA Eastern Division annual meeting (2007); as the opening keynote address at the annual Philosophy of Social Science Roundtable (2008); as one of the keynote addresses at the "Examining Whiteness: White Privilege and Racism in America" conference, Allegheny College (2008); in the "Diaspora Talk Series: Theory, Politics, and History," University of Texas at Austin (2008); at the Spindel Conference, "Race, Racism, and Liberalism in the 21st Century," University of Memphis (2008); at the Graduate School of Education, University of California Berkeley (2008); as the opening plenary address at the annual conference of the British Political Studies Association (2009); in the "Justice" series, University of Mary Washington (2009); at "Critical Refusals: The

Fourth Biennial Conference of the International Herbert Marcuse Society,"
University of Pennsylvania (2011); on an APA Eastern Division annual
meeting panel, "Philosophers Respond to Occupy Wall Street" (2011); at
the annual meeting of the Western Political Science Association (2012);
on an APA Eastern Division annual meeting panel, "African-American
Political Theory" (2014); as the Kneller Lecture at the annual meeting
of the Philosophy of Education Society (2015); at the conference "Race
in 21st Century America: Race and Democracy," James Madison College,
Michigan State University (2015); and as the Centre for Ethnicity and
Racism Studies public lecture in celebration of the United Nations
International Decade for People of African Descent, Leeds University
(2015).

I have greatly benefited from the feedback, encouragement, and criticisms I received over this time from various people, whether as organizers
of the campus colloquia and conferences to which I was invited to give pre-
sentations, or as critics, commentators, and editors. I would like to mention
in particular Linda Martín Alcoff, Kal Alston, Elizabeth Anderson, Marcus
Arvan, Alison Bailey, Lawrie Balfour, Bruce Baum, Robert Bernasconi,
Eduardo Bonilla-Silva, Bernard Boxill, Harry Brighouse, Bill Bywater,
Cheshire Calhoun, Brad Cokelet, David Copp, Harvey Cormier, Derrick
Darby, Peggy DesAutels, Eduardo M. Duarte, Samuel Fleischacker, Tyrone
Forman, Paul Gomberg, Robert Gooding-Williams, Barnor Hesse, Thomas
Hill, Nancy Holmstrom, Juliet Hooker, the late Richard Iton, Chike Jeffers,
Desmond King, Ruth Kinna, Pauline Kleingeld, Janet Kourany, Anthony
Laden, Andy Lamas, Bill Lawson, Zeus Leonardo, Amanda Lewis, Moya
Lloyd, Robert Louden, David Lyons, Michael T. Martin, Diana Meyers,
Tom Mills, Carole Pateman, John Pittman, Raymond Rocco, Salman
Sayyid, Richard Schmitt, Tommie Shelby, Falguni Sheth, Shu-mei Shih,
Anna Marie Smith, Stephen Steinberg, Curtis Stokes, Shannon Sullivan,
Shirley Tate, Winston C. Thompson, Lynda Tredway, Nancy Tuana, Jack
"Chip" Turner, Jennifer Uleman, Andrew Valls, Harry van der Linden,
Craig Vasey, Timothy Waligrow, Margaret Urban Walker, Kristin Waters,
Bill Wilkerson, Yolonda Wilson, Alison Wylie, George Yancy, Marilyn
Yaquinto, and Naomi Zack. Special thanks to Tyler Zimmer for the impres-
sive computer graphics he did for the epilogue, "Toward a Black Radical
Liberalism."

Over the course of this same period I have changed institutions
twice, moving first from the University of Illinois at Chicago (UIC)
to Northwestern University and then to my present position at the
CUNY Graduate Center. I am deeply grateful for the research support I have received from all three institutions: first as a Distinguished
Professor at UIC (2004–7), then as a John Evans Professor of Moral and

Intellectual Philosophy at Northwestern (2007–16), and now (2016–) as a Distinguished Professor at the Graduate Center. Bill Hart and Peter Hylton, as successive chairs of the UIC Philosophy Department, and Ken Seeskin and Sandy Goldberg, as successive chairs of the Northwestern Philosophy Department, were consistently supportive of my research during the years I worked on these papers and the later book manuscript, as were Charlotte Jackson and Valerie Brown (UIC) and Crystal Foster (Northwestern), office staff, and I want to express my appreciation for their help. However, after more than a quarter-century in Chicago, I have decided to embark on what I hope will be an exciting new phase of my life and philosophical career. In this connection, I wish to thank in particular then-Provost Louise Lennihan and Philosophy Department chair Iakovos Vasiliou for their vigorous 2015 recruitment effort to convince me to come to the CUNY Grad Center, and I look forward to the academic and personal challenges of my new home in what the locals assure me is the center of the known universe.

Finally, my appreciation to the two anonymous referees for Oxford University Press, whose conscientiously detailed criticisms and suggestions significantly contributed to the streamlining and improvement of the original manuscript, and to editor Kathleen Weaver for her keen editorial eye, valuable guidance on rewriting sections of the introduction and epilogue, and energetic push to get the project moving again after a long hiatus.

The author and the publisher gratefully acknowledge permission to reprint the following chapters:

"New Left Project Interview with Charles Mills" first appeared as "New Left Project: Racism and the Political Economy of Domination," by Charles W. Mills, interviewed by Tom Mills, first posted on the New Left Project website April 12, 2012. (The New Left Project ran from 2010 to 2015.)

"Occupy Liberalism!" first appeared as "Occupy Liberalism! Or, Ten Reasons Why Liberalism Cannot Be Retrieved for Radicalism (And Why They're All Wrong)," in *Radical Philosophy Review* 15, no. 2 (2012), in a "Discussion: Liberalism and Radicalism," with responses by Nancy Holmstrom and Richard Schmitt, and my reply to them.

"Racial Liberalism" first appeared in the *Publications of the Modern Language Association of America (PMLA)* 123, no. 5 (October 2008), Special Topic: Comparative Racialization, coordinated by Shu-mei Shih.

"White Ignorance" first appeared in *Race and Epistemologies of Ignorance* (Albany: State University of New York Press, 2007), edited by Shannon Sullivan and Nancy Tuana.

"'Ideal Theory' as Ideology" first appeared in *Moral Psychology: Feminist Ethics and Social Theory* (Lanham, MD: Rowman & Littlefield, 2004), edited by Peggy DesAutels and Margaret Urban Walker.

"Kant's *Untermenschen*" first appeared in *Race and Racism in Modern Philosophy* (Ithaca, NY: Cornell University Press, 2005), edited by Andrew Valls.

"Racial Exploitation" first appeared in a slightly different version as "Racial Exploitation and the Wages of Whiteness" in *America's Unpaid Debt: Slavery and Racial Justice*, Bowling Green State University Department of Ethnic Studies Working Papers Series on Historical Systems, Peoples and Cultures, nos. 14–16 (May 2003), edited by Michael T. Martin and Marilyn Yaquinto. More recently, it was reprinted in abridged form as "Racial Exploitation and the Payoff of Whiteness" in Monique Deveaux and Vida Panitch, eds., *Exploitation: From Practice to Theory* (London: Rowman & Littlefield International, 2017).

"Rawls on Race/Race in Rawls" first appeared in the *Southern Journal of Philosophy* 47 (2009) Supplement: Race, Racism, and Liberalism in the Twenty-First Century, edited by Bill E. Lawson.

"Retrieving Rawls for Racial Justice?" first appeared as "Retrieving Rawls for Racial Justice? A Critique of Tommie Shelby" in *Critical Philosophy of Race* 1, no. 1 (2013).

"The Whiteness of Political Philosophy" first appeared as "Philosophy Raced, Philosophy Erased" in *Reframing the Practice of Philosophy: Bodies of Color, Bodies of Knowledge* (Albany: State University of New York Press, 2012), edited by George Yancy.

Finally, a shorter version of the epilogue, "Toward a Black Radical Liberalism," was posted online on the PEA ("Philosophy, Ethics, and Academia") Soup discussion blog on February 23, 2015. Thanks to Brad Cokelet for the invitation.

INTRODUCTION

If any political ideology is centrally—perhaps almost definitionally—associated with modernity, it is liberalism. In all of its iterations—from its original contractarian formulation through its later utilitarian variants to its revised post-Rawlsian contractarian rebirth—liberalism was and is supposed to be emancipatory. Liberalism was the incarnation of the rationalism and egalitarianism of the emerging bright new world that was going to sweep away the darkness and irrational social hierarchies of the ancien régime. But as the Italian philosopher Domenico Losurdo has argued in his recently translated *Liberalism: A Counter-History*,[1] liberalism's actual record is far more checkered. Not merely has it been complicit with continuing discriminatory practices of the past (as with gender) but it has been vigorously active in installing nouveaux régimes of imperial racial rule with a body count far greater than the anciens régimes of class.

Thus Losurdo urges a revisionist historiography that would forsake uncritical adulation for an objective recounting of the documented history. If you add together what he calls the various "exclusion clauses" of liberalism's most celebrated manifestos, treatises, and declarations of human rights, you get a litany of oppressions rather than a list of emancipations. Even on paper, the white male working class does not get some of the rights we associate with modernity until the late nineteenth/early twentieth century, and in the case of white women and people of color, the wait has been even longer (and in some cases continues still). It is only possible to present this narrative as a triumphalist one because of the systematic erasure of these histories, and the tight focus on a small subset of the "political" population (the polis proper, so to speak): propertied white males. The most famous documents of liberal modernity are primarily about this group's liberation, not anybody else's.

So how should this story really be told? The route taken by most philosophers purifies and Platonizes liberalism into an ideal Form of itself, and then—ignoring the exclusions that in fact deprive the majority of the population of entitlement to equal liberal status—produces a conceptual history in this elevated realm that never touches down to the hard ground of reality. Liberalism as it should have been is represented as liberalism as it actually was. This is not merely bad intellectual history but is also a poor strategy for realizing the promise of liberalism. The real-life political struggles that were historically necessary to overcome liberalism's particularisms are erased by a myth of implicit potential inclusion. Better, in my opinion, to recognize these exclusions as theoretically central, admit their shaping of liberalism's array of rights and freedoms, and then confront the critics' case for discrediting liberalism altogether with the defense's arguments for how it can nonetheless be reclaimed and redeemed.

Orthodox Marxism, varieties of radical feminism and black nationalism, dominant strains of post-structuralist and post-colonial theory, exemplify the path of a principled rejection of liberalism. Essentially irredeemable in the eyes of these opponents, liberalism is to be transcended by a higher communal, post-bourgeois, sororal and decolonial social order, even if the details are too often more gestured at than worked out. By contrast, social democracy and feminist liberalism argue for a radical rethinking of liberalism that—recognizing its deficiencies—still seeks to reclaim it as a liberatory political philosophy. Rejecting mainstream liberalism's classically individualistic social ontology for an ontology of class and gender, challenging its cramped schedule of rights for a normative empowerment of the class- and gender-subordinated, these political projects affirm a more expansive vision that would take us beyond bourgeois liberalism (not a pleonasm, for this analysis) and patriarchal liberalism. Liberalism's historic complicity with ruling class and male power does not, they contend, preclude retrieving it.[2]

Class theory and feminism are well established in the disciplines of political theory and political philosophy. But the recognition and critical theorization of what I am here calling—by analogy with bourgeois and patriarchal liberalism—*racial liberalism* is much more undeveloped in these circles.[3] This collection of essays is my attempt to assemble work that brings out, from various angles, some of the key features of racial liberalism, thus expanding the parameters of the debate. Part I comprises my critiques of different dimensions of racial liberalism, Part II my critiques of Rawls, Rawlsianism, and "white" liberal political philosophy for their non-existent or at best problematic attempts to deal with race and justice. So my hope is that the framework will constitute a useful contribution to debates about liberalism in general and the theorization of race in ethics, political philosophy, and political theory in particular.

But first I must address a possible objection. One might argue that— however useful the concept—the term that I have chosen is unhelpfully ambiguous, since in the 1950s, for example, to be a racial liberal in the United

States meant being someone who opposed segregation and endorsed black civil rights. Why not just say directly and unequivocally: "racist liberalism"? The reason is that I want a phrase broad enough to encompass both overtly racist liberalism, where people of color are explicitly conceptualized as racial inferiors, and the no longer overtly racist, "color-blind" liberalism of today. In the latter variety of liberalism, illicit white racial advantage is still being secured, but now primarily through the evasions in the theory's key assumptions rather than the derogation of nonwhites. (Compare the second-wave feminist argument that the arbitrary public sphere/private sphere distinction continues to reproduce gender hierarchy, even in a putatively post-sexist period in which men and women are now supposedly treated as equals.)[4] Since most contemporary white liberals would disavow any explicitly racist sentiments, it is important to convey to them that the liberalism they are endorsing is still racialized, even if it ostensibly repudiates any racist representations of people of color.

For me, then, racial liberalism (analogous to patriarchal liberalism) is a liberalism in which key terms have been written by race and the discursive logic shaped accordingly. This position expresses my commitment to what has been called the "symbiotic" view of racism, which sees race as historically penetrating *into* liberalism's descriptive and normative apparatus so as to produce a more-or-less consistent racialized ideology, albeit one that evolves over time, rather than seeing race as being externally and "anomalously" related to it.[5] Unlike my post-structuralist and post-colonial colleagues, however, I see this penetration as contingent, not a matter of a pre-ordained logic of liberalism itself, but a consequence of the mandates for European liberal theorists of establishing and maintaining imperial and colonial rule abroad, and nonwhite racial subordination at home.[6] Hence the hope of redeeming liberalism by self-consciously taking this history into account: recognizing the historic racialization of liberalism *so as better to deracialize it*—thereby producing a color-conscious, racially reflexive, anti-racist liberalism on the alert for its own inherited racial distortions.[7] Abstract Platonized liberalism erases actual liberalism's racist history, a blinding white Form that, in pretending a colorlessness that it did not and does not achieve, obfuscates more than it illuminates. The problem is not abstraction as such but a problematic mode of idealizing abstraction that abstracts away from social oppression, and in that way both conceals its extent and inhibits the development of the conceptual tools necessary for understanding and dealing with its workings.[8] Identifying the historically hegemonic varieties of liberalism *as* racialized and white alerts us to the erasure, the whiting-out, of the past of racial subordination that current, seemingly genuinely inclusive varieties of liberalism now seek to disown.

As the title of this book signifies, then, it is an enterprise based on the inversion of the standard metaphors in which white is right and black is wrong. It urges us to recognize how the historically exclusionary rights of white liberalism (a.k.a. "liberalism"), based on the suppression of equal black rights, have left a legacy of white wrongs. These wrongs have thus been not merely material but also normative and conceptual, wrongs within the apparatus of liberalism itself—as summarized by the two famous judgments about white "moderates" (in context roughly equivalent to "liberals") made by Martin Luther King Jr. and Dick Gregory that I have used as my epigraphs. Hence the need for their black righting.

Part I of the book covers the overarching themes of epistemology, personhood, and property, all central to the liberal project, and all, in my opinion, distortionally shaped by race. Liberal enlightenment presumes an objective perception of things as they are and as they should be, factually and morally, for political communities characterized by reciprocally respecting relations among equally recognized persons in agreement on the fair terms for the appropriation of the world. But racial domination interferes with objective cognition, denies equal racial personhood, and generates rationalizations of unjust white acquisition. Thus they are all negatively transformed by the dynamic of racial liberalism.

The opening chapter sets the stage with a 2012 interview I did with Tom Mills (no relation, so far as I know) of the British New Left Project. For the benefit of a transatlantic audience less familiar with critical race theory, I explain the rationale for retaining "race" as a crucial category, suitably transformed, and what I see as its historic link with imperial domination and its relation to the conceptually distinct, if empirically overlapping, systems of gender and class. Racial liberalism is introduced as homologous with the far more familiar "patriarchal liberalism" identified by feminist theory.

Chapter 2, "Occupy Liberalism!," locates the project within the broader context of the need to transform liberalism for a progressive political agenda. Invoking the slogan of the (then) recent "Occupy!" movement, I argue—against radical orthodoxy—that liberalism has an under-appreciated radical potential that is masked by the long complicity of its hegemonic varieties with plutocratic, patriarchal, and white-supremacist structures of power. But this complicity, I argue, is a function of dominant group interests and the successful political projects of the privileged, not the consequence of any ineluctable immanent conceptual dynamic of liberalism as a political ideology. Once we pluralize liberalism into *liberalisms* (both actual and hypothetical), we should be able to see how many claims about liberalism's putatively problematic ontology and alleged incapacity to recognize and/or theorize social oppression really depend on the contingent features of its historically dominant (but not inevitable) incarnations. An emancipatory liberalism can, I contend, be reconstructed that is not theoretically constrained in these unfortunate ways.

With this background established, I go on in chapter 3, "Racial Liberalism," to make a detailed case for the usefulness of the construct. I point out the global hegemony of liberalism in a post–Cold War world and the triumph in the academy over the last few decades of Rawlsian contractarian liberalism in particular. But in the wide range of political responses to the work of John Rawls, the historic racialization of the contract apparatus and of the dominant varieties of liberalism will rarely be a topic of inquiry. Yet insofar as racism (ostensibly) violates the moral norms of modern political theory in general, liberal theorists across the spectrum, however much they disagree on other issues, should be able to converge on the necessity for purging contemporary liberal theory of its racist ancestry. Contra the exponents of color-blindness, however, I argue that this project can only be accomplished through a color-conscious investigative genealogy and reconstruction. Thus I urge a self-conscious deracializing of liberalism that would begin by recognizing the centrality of a social ontology of race to the modern world and the acknowledgment of a corresponding history of racial exploitation that needs to be registered in liberal categories and addressed as a matter of liberal social justice.

Oppositional bodies of political thought are often preoccupied with epistemological questions, in part for the simple reason that they are trying to explain how a dominant but misleading body of ideas (classist, sexist, racist) continues to perpetuate itself. One wants to understand both how the privileged can continue to deny the unfairness of their privilege and how (perhaps) one was oneself originally taken in by these ideas. I suggest that this pattern of denial and misapprehension can in the case of race be thought of as a "white ignorance," an elaboration of the concept I introduced in *The Racial Contract* of an "epistemology of ignorance."[9] Chapter 4, "White Ignorance," locates white miscognition as a structural phenomenon rather than a matter of individual white myopias. It is the result (not unavoidably, but as a strong psychological tendency) of racial location. Because of racial privilege, an inherited racialized set of concepts and beliefs, differential racial experience, and racial group interest, whites tend to get certain kinds of things wrong. As such, the chapter can be seen as a contribution from critical philosophy of race to the new "social" epistemology that has emerged in recent decades, a welcome turn away from the solipsistic Cartesian meditations that have typically characterized modern epistemology.

Chapter 5, " 'Ideal Theory' as Ideology," takes a critical look at what could be called the epistemology of normative theory, specifically the normative apparatus of "ideal theory" liberalism. Like chapter 2, it also adopts a broader perspective, reminding us that a focus on race should not exclude a concern with gender and class privilege also, all of which are indeed always in the modern world in intersection and interaction with one another. First written as a contribution to a feminist collection on moral psychology, it was then reprinted in a special symposium of the feminist philosophy journal *Hypatia*, stimulating widespread discussion. The chapter expressed a frustration I and many others at the time (as it turned out) had begun to feel with "ideal theory" in ethics and political philosophy, most notably, of course, though not exclusively, in the work of Rawls. "Ideal theory" is not just normative theory, which by definition is a prerequisite for ethics and political philosophy, but the normative theory of a perfectly just society. The rationale was that developing such a perspective was crucial to doing non-ideal justice theory properly later on. But to many of us at the time it became increasingly questionable whether this "later on" was ever going to arrive, and that in reality ideal theory—whatever its original motivation— was functioning as a way of avoiding the hard facts of class, gender, and racial oppression; how they shape the human agents enmeshed in these relations of domination; and what our normative priorities should be. So the essay was an early effort in what has since become a growing wave of criticism of ideal theory, and I would like to think that it made at least a small contribution to getting things going.

No Western Enlightenment philosopher can equal the standing of Immanuel Kant, the luminary par excellence of eighteenth-century thought, with stellar accomplishments not merely in ethics and political philosophy, but in metaphysics and aesthetics also. Yet Kant, the pre-eminent theorist of personhood, whose work through his appropriation by John Rawls and Jürgen Habermas has become central to normative political philosophy as well as ethics, has also a more dubious accomplishment to his (dis)credit: being one of the founders—or (for some theorists) *the* founder—of modern "scientific" racism. As such, he wonderfully illustrates the combination of light and darkness in the "white" Enlightenment's racial liberalism. Until recently, when the challenge from scholars of race made some response unavoidable, mainstream white political philosophers and ethicists had for the most part scrupulously avoided any mention of his racist writings in anthropology and physical geography. Now the dominant line of argument is that they are embarrassing and should of course be condemned, but they form no part of his *philosophy*. In chapter 6, "Kant's *Untermenschen*," I challenge this conceptual segregation and ask whether it would not be more theoretically fruitful to explore the possible presence in Kant's work of a philosophical anthropology of persons and sub-persons, thereby inevitably raising questions about the standard interpretations of the prescriptions of his ethics, political philosophy, and teleology.

The seeming demise of Marxism—though as I write this introduction in 2016, the worsening conditions of plutocracy, not merely in the United States but globally, must surely be fostering a rethinking[10]—has taken "exploitation" off the table as a subject for moral analysis. Exploitation is assumed to be necessarily tied to the labor theory of value, long repudiated not merely by mainstream economists but by even most contemporary Marxists. But a concept of exploitation can easily be developed that is straightforwardly condemnable by respectable liberal criteria: exploitation as the "using" of people for illicit benefit and unjust enrichment. Marx famously contrasted the transparent exploitation of slave and feudal societies with the more opaque exploitation of capitalism, which, resting as it did on "free" wage-labor and voluntary consent, generally needed theoretical work to uncover. But racial exploitation in modernity was originally as transparently exploitative as (or even more transparently exploitative than) exploitation in pre-modern systems. Racial chattel slavery, aboriginal expropriation, colonial forced labor, and so forth are paradigms of nonconsensual coercive systems directed by liberal polities at home and abroad. Yet they have not received the attention they deserve in liberal descriptive and normative theory for what they say about the actual architecture of the liberal state and its supervision of the wrongful transfer of wealth and opportunities from people of color to whites. In chapter 7, "Racial Exploitation," I argue for a revival of the concept of exploitation in philosophical discourse that could be brought into fruitful engagement with the by now large body of literature in sociology and economics on racial differentials in wealth and how they serve to perpetuate racial inequality.

Part II of the book focuses on Rawls, Rawlsianism, and white political philosophy more generally. My claim is that most of this work either exemplifies the racial liberalism I am critiquing or adopts strategies for addressing and correcting it that are, in my opinion, going to be inadequate.

Chapter 8, "Rawls on Race/Race in Rawls," examines the writings of the person generally regarded (certainly in Anglo-American analytic philosophical circles) as the most important American political philosopher of the twentieth century, and, for some, the most important political philosopher, period, of the twentieth century. I try to bring out the absurdity of the leading American philosopher of justice having nothing substantive to say over his working lifetime about what has historically been the most salient form of American *injustice*, racial domination. Moreover, by analyzing the underpinnings of Rawlsian ideal theory, I try to make the stronger case not merely that Rawls and Rawlsians *have not* addressed the issue of racism, but that the apparatus itself hinders them from doing so adequately, not merely contingently but also structurally. In the conclusion, I point the reader to my own work in my 2007 book with Carole Pateman, *Contract and Domination*, where I argue that retrieving the Rawlsian apparatus for racial justice and non-ideal theory will require radical changes in it.[11]

The natural follow-up is a look at the work of Tommie Shelby, since he— as a black philosopher at Harvard, Rawls's home institution for most of his career—is the most prominent African American representative of the position that, contra my claims, Rawls's apparatus as is can indeed be used to tackle racial injustice. In chapter 9, "Retrieving Rawls for Racial Justice?," I do a detailed analysis of one of Shelby's articles and explain why I think his attempted appropriation of Rawls (an extension to race of Rawls's "fair equality of opportunity" principle) cannot work. I should emphasize here that I do not, of course, see Shelby as *himself* an exponent of racial liberal-ism but rather as a philosopher trying, as I am, to correct it. But my conten-tion is that the racial liberalism that for me Rawls represents is more deeply embedded in the apparatus and thus requires more conceptual rethinking and reworking of that apparatus than Shelby recognizes.

Chapter 10, "The Whiteness of Political Philosophy," takes a retrospec-tive look at the evolution (and non-evolution) of the field in the many years since my graduation. Commissioned by the hyperactive (in a good way) George Yancy for a volume bringing together seventeen black and Hispanic/Latino philosophers to reflect on their experiences in the pro-fession, it offers both an account of how much progress has been made in recent decades in Africana philosophy and race as legitimate philosophical areas of research, and how far we still have to go. Though there has been a burgeoning of literature in the discipline, the low demographic numbers of black philosophers and people of color generally, and the radicalness of the challenge race poses to conventional ways of doing philosophy, somewhat temper one's optimism about its future. Using a well-known companion to political philosophy as a representative target, I point out how "white" its conceptual framework and underlying assumptions are, paying virtually no attention to the large body of work in post-colonial theory and critical race theory not just in philosophy but across many other disciplines.

Finally, in an epilogue that is simultaneously a prologue (in gesturing toward what I intend to be a future project), I sketch the contours of what I am calling a "black radical liberalism." Taxonomies of Africana political thought have traditionally opposed black radicalism and black liberalism, the latter seen as necessarily committed to mainstream white norms and assumptions, even if adjusted somewhat for racial difference. But in keep-ing with the overall line of argument of this book, I make a case here for a different variety of black liberalism, one radicalized by taking seriously (in a way that mainstream black liberalism does not) the shaping of the modern world by white supremacy. Black radical liberalism as an emancipatory ideology will of course have to be supplemented and modified by the experience of other racially subordinated communities. But given the centrality of African slavery and subsequent anti-black oppression to the making of modernity, it represents a crucial step toward the comprehensive theorization and reconstruction of the deracialized, color-conscious liberalism for which I am calling.

The promise of liberalism was famously the granting of equal rights to all individuals, destroying the old social hierarchies and establishing a new social order where everybody, as an individual, could flourish, free of "estate" membership. But the reality turned out to be the preservation, albeit on a new theoretical foundation, of old hierarchies of gender and the establishment of new hierarchies of race. Thus the struggle to realize the liberal ideal for everybody and not just a privileged minority still continues today, centuries later. If this struggle is ever to be successful, a prerequisite must be the acknowledgment of the extent to which dominant varieties of liberalism have developed so as to be complicit with rather than in opposition to social oppression. I hope that by formally identifying the ideological phenomenon of "racial liberalism" as a subject for research and critique, this book will contribute both to its analysis and its eventual dismantling, as theory and as practice.

PART I

Racial Liberalism

Epistemology, Personhood, Property

CHAPTER 1

New Left Project Interview
with Charles Mills

1. *The concept of "race" as an objective category has long been discredited by anthropology and biology, yet the social sciences show that racial disadvantage persists. How do you understand the concept of race and racism?*

On this side of the Atlantic, a lot of work has been done over the past twenty years in critical race theory to develop what could be called a "successor concept" of race. In other words, we've inherited a concept that was central to the justification of imperialism, colonialism, African slavery, Jim Crow, apartheid, the "color bar," and the "color line." And the question then is, What should anti-racist theorists and activists seeking to dismantle the legacy of these systems and practices do with it?

One obvious option is eliminativism—drop the concept from one's vocabulary and discourse altogether. On this line of analysis, "race" should be seen as comparable to "phlogiston"—a term designating an element within combustible substances supposedly released during the process of combustion. The French chemist Lavoisier showed that combustion does not actually take place by this process, and that in fact phlogiston does not exist. So "phlogiston" as a concept is scientifically refuted, is doing no work for us, and should just be dropped.

But contrast that with "witch." Witches in the sense of evil women with supernatural powers don't actually exist either, so those unfortunate women burned at the stake for this sin were not really witches. But the term is retained in contemporary usage, not just to refer to characters in fantasy novels or films (the White Witch of C. S. Lewis's Narnia novels) but also to indicate a believer in the Wiccan religion. "Witch" has been reconceived.

Now "race" is arguably more like "witch" than "phlogiston" in that many social and political theorists have contended it can still do useful work for us. So for these theorists (anti-eliminativists), it is better to retain the term. "Race" is redefined so that it is purged of its unscientific and morally pernicious associations. Instead of seeing race biologically, and as part of a natural hierarchy, one reconceptualizes it so it refers to one's structural location in a racialized social system, thereby generating a successor concept. People are "raced" according to particular rules—we shift from a noun to a verb, from a pre-existing "natural" state to an active social process—and these ascribed racial identities then tendentially shape their moral standing, civic status, social world, and life chances. In that sense, race obviously does exist, and we can talk about "whites" being privileged and "nonwhites" being disadvantaged by particular racial systems without implying any biological referent.

"Racism" has been given various competing definitions and attributed competing areas of application. I would distinguish between racism in the ideational sense (a complex of ideas, beliefs, values) and racism in the socio-institutional sense (institutions, practices, social systems). For the first sense, I would favor this definition: racism is the belief that (i) humanity can be divided into discrete races, and (ii) these races are hierarchically arranged, with some races superior to others. The second sense would then refer to institutions, practices, and social systems that illicitly privilege some races at the expense of others, where racial membership (directly or indirectly) explains this privileging.

2. *If the earlier, more overt, forms of racism (asserting the inherent inferiority of non-whites) were rooted in the political economy of chattel slavery and colonialism, what are the politico-economic factors behind racism today? In other words, what continues to drive racism?*

In a phrase, I would say it's the political economy of racialized capitalism: the legacy of these systems (chattel slavery, colonialism) both globally (as North-South domination) and in particular nations (the former colonizing powers, the former colonies, the former white settler states). White-over-nonwhite racism is not, of course, the only variety—one also has to take into account intra-Asian and intra-African racism, as well as Latin American variants where racial antagonisms affect relations between Afro-Latins and indigenous peoples. But obviously on a global scale, white domination has been the most important kind, and some of the latter examples are themselves influenced by the colonial history, as with the Belgian shaping of Tutsi-Hutu relations in Rwanda. So this inherited system of structural advantage and disadvantage, which was heavily racialized, continues to affect life chances today, thereby reproducing "race" and racial identities as crucial social categories. Where whites are a significant population, they are generally privileged by their racial membership (I say more about this under #6, below), and their resistance to giving up this privilege manifests itself in racial ideologies of various kinds. So racism is most illuminatingly seen in this social and historical context—as an ever-evolving ideology linked with group domination and illicit advantage—rather than in the framework of individual "prejudice" favored by mainstream social theory.

3. *Before we get onto the idea of "racial liberalism," could you first outline what you mean by liberalism?*

By liberalism I mean the ideology that arises in Europe in the seventeenth-eighteenth centuries in opposition to feudal absolutism, predicated on the equal rights of morally equal individuals, and having as its key figures such political thinkers as John Locke, David Hume, Immanuel Kant, Adam Smith, and John Stuart Mill. Obviously, as even this brief list indicates, there are many different strains within liberalism: contractarian versus utilitarian versions, property-and-self-ownership-based versus personhood-based versions, right-wing laissez-faire liberalism versus left-wing social-democratic liberalism. But in theory all these different variants are supposed to be committed to the flourishing of the individual.

What I call "racial liberalism" is then a liberalism in which—independent of which particular version we're considering—key terms have been rewritten by race so as to generate a different set of rules for members of different "races," R1s and R2s, because (historically) the R2s don't meet the criteria of the capacity for attaining individuality. So I am following the example of second-wave feminist liberals from the 1970s onward and arguing that we need to see liberalism as structurally shaped in its development by group privilege—in this case, white racial privilege. "Racial liberalism" as a theoretical construct is then supposed to be analogous to "patriarchal liberalism."

4. *There is little overt racism in political theory today. In what way is liberal political theory still compromised by the issue of race?*

Again, the feminist model and theoretical precedent is very useful here. Women active in the movements of the 1960s and 1970s who went into the academy and into political theory came to the realization that the "maleness" of the work of the central canonical figures ran deeper than stigmatizing references to women, though these were offensive enough. Overtly sexist patriarchal liberalism explicitly represents women as lesser creatures not deserving of equal rights, appropriately to be subjected to male authority, not permitted to vote or own property, having their legal identity subsumed into their husbands' under the doctrine of coverture, and so on. But the point second-wave feminists made was that even now, when formal gender equality has been attained and sexism is officially repudiated, liberalism remains patriarchal in its conceptualization of the official polity, its view of the individual, its division of society into public and private spheres, its exclusion of the family from the ambit of justice, and so forth. So for substantive as against merely nominal gender inclusiveness, what is necessary is a rethinking of inherited political categories from the perspective of women, a rethinking guided by the desire to achieve genuine gender inclusivity in the cartography of the political and thus facilitate the struggle for genuine gender equity in the polity itself.

You can see how this line of argument can be adopted and translated for race. My similar claim would be that liberal political theory is so shaped by the history of white domination, both national and global, that, analogously, it tacitly takes as its representative political figure the white (male) subject. The parallel is not perfect, since male domination/patriarchy already exists at the dawn of modernity, whereas European domination/white supremacy does not. So you don't get the same taken-for-grantedness of the rightness of European rule that you get for male rule—it's more contested. Jennifer Pitts's *A Turn to Empire*, for example, is subtitled *The Rise of Imperial Liberalism in Britain and France*,[1] and her point is to demarcate a transition from an early liberalism with significant anti-racist and anti-imperialist elements to a later liberalism more uniformly racist and imperialist. But the dominant variety does, of course, eventually become a liberalism that assumes the superiority of Europe as the global civilization, and the identity of Europeans as the appropriate agents of the civilizing process. John Locke invests in African slavery and justifies aboriginal expropriation; Immanuel Kant turns out to be one of the pioneering theorists of modern "scientific" racism; Georg Hegel's World Spirit animates the (very material and non-spiritual) colonial enterprise; and John Stuart Mill, employee of the British East India Company, denies the capacity of barbarian races in their "nonage" to rule themselves.

The way in which contemporary liberalism is still compromised by race is, in my opinion, in the failure to rethink itself in the light of this history. Liberalism needs to be reconceptualized as ideologically central to the imperial project; both colonial and imperial domination need to be recognized as political systems in themselves (so, as with the gender critique, the boundaries of the polity would be redrawn); liberalism's official ontology needs to officially admit races as social existents (they're already tacitly there); and above all, in normative political theory (the distinctive terrain of political philosophy), racial justice needs to be placed at center stage.

5. *What causes the "color-blindness" of liberal political theory?*

To begin with, there's just the huge weight of the European tradition's focus on the white political subject (which we're now to read as the generic colorless political subject), and the thousands of books and tens of thousands of articles over the years that take it for granted, thereby constituting an overwhelmingly hegemonic set of norms for what counts as "real" political theory. Perhaps one could also add that it's just theoretically simpler and easier to operate as if people of color can be subsumed under these categories without rethinking them. And it could be argued that group interest plays a role: the interests of a largely white profession in not having these troubling questions raised, given their disruptive implications for the social order that racial liberalism has rationalized and from which whites benefit.

6. *Radicals argue that it is impossible to realize the liberal vision of class equality within the framework of a capitalist system. Is the same true of race? How do you see race as relating to class and can racism be defeated without fundamental social change?*

One's view of the relation of race and class will obviously depend on one's larger social theory. Within the Marxist tradition, various attempts have been made to give a historical materialist explanation of race and racism, usually centering (as your second question intimated) on claims about the peculiar political economy of imperial capitalism and the articulation of modern African slavery to its workings. Class-reductionist versions would represent race as "really" being class in disguise, class in nonwhite skin— non-wage-labor in the form of slavery, or as sub-proletarianized labor. Other versions, drawing on Gramsci, would talk about race as ideology, as a particular way of being in the world and making sense of that world.

My own sympathies are with attempts to combine the materialist dynamic that is crucial for Marxism with a theorization that takes account of issues like personhood less well theorized in the Marxist tradition. In my own work, I have argued that we need to see white supremacy as a system of domination in its own right, whose dynamic—even if it is originally generated by expansionist capitalism—then attains a "relative autonomy" of its own. So when, in the United States, for example, the white working class excludes blacks from unions and joins lynch mobs, they are not just (as a top-down, bourgeois manipulation model would have it) serving capitalist interests but affirming and developing an identity that, in certain respects, pays off for them. David Roediger, inspired by E. P. Thompson, argues in his *The Wages of Whiteness* that the white American working class *makes itself as white*.[2]

In the United States, whites in general, including the white working class, benefit materially from their whiteness in numerous ways: the original expropriation of the continent from Native Americans; the diffusion within the white economy generally of the surplus from slave labor; the differential access to jobs, promotions, bank loans, transfer payments from the state; the benefits of segregated housing and consequent wealth accumulation. A 2015 online report, for example, says that because of the recession and the subprime meltdown the median wealth of white households is now (2011 figures) *sixteen times* the median wealth of black households and *thirteen times* the median wealth of Latino households.[3]

So for me it is a mistake, as the left tradition has too often done, to see only class—one's relationship to the means of production in the famous "base" of the base-and-superstructure—as material, and to only recognize class exploitation. Socialist feminists in the 1970s–1980s argued that we needed to see capitalist patriarchy as a dual system, in which gender was part of the material base also. I would claim that this needs to be extended to race. Races as social entities exist and are connected in relations of racial exploitation. So the "big three"—class, gender, race—are all part of a political economy of domination. And race is material also, both in terms of economic advantage/disadvantage and in terms of patterns of social cognition being shaped by the body. It's not a biological materiality (that would be biological determinism); it's a social materiality rooted in the relation between the individual body and the body politic that needs to be conceptually differentiated from class, even if class forces explain its origins. (That would be a point of disanalogy with gender, which predates class.)

My own view of the race/class differentiation is that race is originally the demarcator of full and diminished personhood. The white working class in capitalist modernity do attain personhood status; the Native American or Native Australian, the African slave, the colonial subject, do not.

You can see why this would immediately seem very problematic from the perspective of orthodox Marxism. I am claiming to be sympathetic to materialism and yet giving theoretical centrality to a moral category! But bear in mind that what I really mean is (in the Hegelian tradition, materialistically understood) *socially recognized* personhood. Race functions as a "materially embedded" moral category, signifying membership or non-membership in the subset of humans recognized as fully human, and linked to the materialist political economy of Euro-domination. So what we have is a triple system involving the interaction of one's relationship to the means of production, to gender structures, and to socially recognized personhood and sub-personhood.

So I would agree that "fundamental social change" is required to defeat such a system. The question is, What counts as fundamental? The original left claim would have been that the imbrication of class and race is so thorough that a socialist revolution is required to get rid of racism. But the problem today, of course, is the discrediting of the left in a "post-Marxist" world without any attractive "post-capitalist" models. So could you have "fundamental social change" in the form of a revolutionary transition from white-supremacist capitalism (the dominant variety since modernity) to non-white-supremacist capitalism? I am hoping so, since a socialist revolution in the Marxist sense no longer seems likely, and the twentieth-century history of Stalinist regimes claiming the socialist label is a depressing one. But given the points I just made about white working-class benefit from racialized capitalism, what is going to motivate the white working class to join with people of color in such a struggle? Materialism rules out moral motivation as a prime social mover, so it would have to be perceived group interest.

What would be necessary is a political project that makes a plausible case that the *long-term* group interests of poorer and working-class whites (looking ahead to the fates of their children and grandchildren) would be better served by a more egalitarian, redistributivist capitalism, and that racial division, by its weakening of the working class, has played a crucial role in enabling the development of plutocratic capitalism. I believe that one can make such a case in the United States, given the historic centrality of race to social division here and the dizzying heights to which income and wealth inequality have ascended in recent years (the highest in the Western democracies); I'm not sure about Britain.

CHAPTER 2

Occupy Liberalism!

The "Occupy!" movement, which has made headlines around the country, has raised the hopes of young American radicals new to political engagement and revived the hopes of an older generation of radicals still clinging to nostalgic dreams of the glorious '60s. If the original and still most salient target was Wall Street, a long list of other candidates for "occupation" has since been put forward. In this chapter, I want to propose as a target for radical occupation the somewhat unusual candidate of liberalism itself. But contrary to the conventional wisdom prevailing within radical circles, I am going to argue for the heretical thesis that liberalism should not be contemptuously rejected by radicals but retrieved for a radical agenda. Summarized in bullet-point form, my argument is as follows:

- The "Occupy Wall Street" movement provides an opportunity unprecedented in decades to build a broad democratic movement to challenge plutocracy, patriarchy, and white supremacy in the United States.
- Such a movement is more likely to be successful if it appeals to principles and values most Americans already endorse.
- Liberalism has always been the dominant ideology in the United States.
- Liberalism in the United States has historically been complicit with plutocracy, patriarchy, and white supremacy, but this complicity is a contingent function of dominant group interests rather than the result of an immanent conceptual logic.
- Therefore, progressives in philosophy (and elsewhere) should try to retrieve liberalism for a radical democratic agenda rather than rejecting it, thereby positioning themselves in the ideological mainstream of the country and seeking its transformation.

Let me now try to make this argument plausible for an audience likely to be aprioristically convinced of its obvious unsoundness.

PRELIMINARY CLARIFICATION OF TERMS

First we need to clarify the key terms of "radicalism" and "liberalism." While of course a radicalism of the right exists, here I refer to radicals who are progressives. But "progressive" cannot just denote the left of the political spectrum, since the whole point of the "new social movements" of the 1960s onward was that the traditional left-right political spectrum, predicated on varying positions on the question of public versus private ownership of the means of production, did not exhaust the topography of the political. Issues of gender and racial domination were to a significant extent "orthogonal" to this one-dimensional trope. So I will use "radicalism" broadly, though still in the zone of progressive politics, to refer generally to ideas/concepts/principles/values endorsing pro-egalitarian structural change to reduce or eliminate unjust hierarchies of domination.

"Liberalism" may denote both a political philosophy and the institutions and practices characteristically tied to that political philosophy. My focus will be on the former. The issue of how bureaucratic logics may prove refractory to reformist agendas is undeniably an important one, but it does not really fall into the purview of philosophy proper. My aim is to challenge the radical shibboleth that radical ideas/concepts/principles/values are incompatible with liberalism. Given the deep entrenchment of this assumption in the worldview of most radicals, refuting it would still be an accomplishment, even if working out practical details of operationalization are delegated to other hands.

In the United States, of course, "liberalism" in public parlance and everyday political discourse is used in such a way that it really denotes left-liberalism specifically ("left" by the standards of a country whose political center of gravity has shifted right in recent decades). In this vocabulary, right-liberals are then categorized as "conservatives"—in the market sense, as against the Burkean sense. On the other hand, some on the right would insist that only they, the heirs to the classic liberalism of John Locke and Adam Smith, are really entitled to the "liberal" designation. Later welfarist theorists are fraudulent pretenders to be exposed as socialist intruders unworthy of the title. Rejecting both of these usages, I will be employing "liberalism" in the expanded sense typical of political philosophy, which links both ends of this spectrum. "Liberalism" then refers broadly to the

def—

anti-feudal ideology of individualism, equal rights, and moral egalitarian-ism that arises in Western Europe in the seventeenth-eighteenth centuries to challenge the ideas and values inherited from the old medieval order, and which is subsequently taken up and developed by others elsewhere, includ-ing many who would have been explicitly excluded by the original concep-tion of the ideology. Left-wing social democrats and right-wing market conservatives, fans of John Rawls on the one hand and Robert Nozick on the other, are thus both liberals.[1]

From this perspective, it will be appreciated that liberalism is not a monolith but an umbrella term for a *variety* of positions. Here are some examples—some familiar, some perhaps less so:

VARIETIES OF LIBERALISM

Left-wing (social democratic) vs. Right-wing (market conservative)
Kantian vs. Lockean
Contractarian vs. Utilitarian
Corporate vs. Democratic
Social vs. Individualist
Comprehensive vs. Political
Ideal-theory vs. Non-ideal-theory
Patriarchal vs. Feminist
Imperial vs. Anti-imperial
Racial vs. Anti-racial
Color-blind vs. Color-conscious
Etc.[2]

It is not the case, of course, that these different species of liberalism have been equally represented in the ideational sphere or equally implemented in the institutional sphere. On the contrary, some have been dominant while others have been subordinate, and some have never, at least in the full sense, been implemented at all. But nonetheless, I suggest they all count as liberalisms and as such they are all supposed to have certain ele-ments in common, even those characterized by gender and racial exclu-sions. (My motivation for making these last *varieties* of liberalism rather than *deviations* from liberalism is precisely to challenge liberalism's self-congratulatory history, which holds an idealized liberalism aloft, untainted by its actual record of complicity with oppressive social systems.) So the initial question we should always ask people making generalizations about "liberalism" is this: What particular variety of liberalism do you mean? And are your generalizations really true about *all* the possible kinds of lib-eralism, or only a subset?

Here is a characterization of liberalism from a very respectable source, the British political theorist, John Gray:

> Common to all variants of the liberal tradition is a definite conception, distinctively modern in character, of man and society. . . . It is *individualist,* in that it asserts the moral primacy of the person against the claims of any social collectivity; *egalitarian,* inasmuch as it confers on all men the same moral status and denies the relevance to legal or political order of differences in moral worth among human beings; *universalist,* affirming the moral unity of the human species and according a secondary importance to specific historic associations and cultural forms; and *meliorist* in its affirmation of the corrigibility and improvability of all social institutions and political arrangements. It is this conception of man and society which gives liberalism a definite identity which transcends its vast internal variety and complexity.[3]

v.
nice

What generate the different varieties of liberalism are different concepts of *individualism,* different claims about how *egalitarianism* should be construed or realized, more or less inclusionary readings of *universalism* (Gray's characterization sanitizes liberalism's actual sexist and racist history), different views of what count as desirable *improvements,* conflicting normative balancings of liberal *values* (freedom, equality) and competing *theoretical prognoses* about how best they can be realized in the light of (contested) *socio-historical facts.* The huge potential for disagreement about all of these explains how a common liberal core can produce such a wide range of variants. Moreover, we need to take into account not merely the spectrum of actual liberalisms but also hypothetical liberalisms that could be generated through novel framings of some or all of the above. So one would need to differentiate dominant versions of liberalism from oppositional versions, and actual from possible variants.

Once the breadth of the range of liberalisms is appreciated—dominant and subordinate, actual and potential—the obvious question then raised is this: even if actual dominant liberalisms have been conservative in various ways (corporate, patriarchal, racist) why does this rule out the development of emancipatory, *radical* liberalisms?

One kind of answer is the following (call this the *internalist* answer): because there is an immanent conceptual/normative logic to liberalism as a political ideology that precludes any emancipatory development of it.

Another kind of answer is the following (call this the *externalist* answer): it doesn't. The historic domination of conservative exclusionary liberalisms is the result of group interests, group power, and successful group political projects. Apparent internal conceptual/normative barriers to an emancipatory liberalism can be successfully negotiated by drawing

on the conceptual/normative resources of liberalism itself, in conjunction with a revisionist socio-historical picture of modernity.

Most self-described radicals would endorse—indeed, reflexively, as an obvious truth—the first answer. But as indicated from the beginning, I think the second answer is actually the correct one. The obstacles to developing a "radical liberalism" are, in my opinion, primarily externalist in nature: material group interests, and the way they have shaped hegemonic varieties of liberalism. So I think we need to try to justify a radical agenda with the normative resources *of* liberalism rather than writing off liberalism. Since liberalism has always been the dominant ideology in the United States and is now globally hegemonic, such a project would have the great ideological advantage of appealing to values and principles that most people already endorse. All projects of egalitarian social transformation are going to face a combination of material, political, and ideological obstacles, but this strategy would at least reduce somewhat the dimensions of the last. One would be trying to win mass support for policies that—and the challenge will, of course, be to demonstrate this—are justifiable by *majoritarian* norms, once reconceived and put in conjunction with facts not always familiar to the majority. Material barriers (vested group interests) and political barriers (organizational difficulties) will of course remain. But they will constitute a general obstacle for *all* egalitarian political programs, and as such cannot be claimed to be peculiar problems for an emancipatory liberalism.

But the contention will be that such a liberalism cannot be developed. Why? Here are ten familiar objections, variants of internalism, and my replies to them.

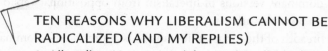

TEN REASONS WHY LIBERALISM CANNOT BE RADICALIZED (AND MY REPLIES)

1. Liberalism Has an Asocial, Atomic Individualist Ontology

This is one of the oldest radical critiques of liberalism; it can be found in Marx's derisive comments—for example, in the *Grundrisse*—about the "Robinsonades" of the social contract theory whose "golden age" (1650–1800) had long passed by the time he began his intellectual and political career:

> The individual and isolated hunter or fisher who forms the starting-point with Smith and Ricardo belongs to the insipid illusions of the eighteenth century. They are Robinson Crusoe stories . . . no more based on such a naturalism than is Rousseau's *contrat social* which makes naturally independent individuals come in contact and have

mutual intercourse by contract. . . . Man is in the most literal sense of the word a *zoon politikon*, not only a social animal, but an animal which can develop into an individual only in society. Production by individuals outside society . . . is as great an absurdity as the idea of the development of language without individuals living together and talking to one another.[4]

But several replies can be made to this indictment. To begin with, even if the accusation is true of contractarian liberalism, not all liberalisms are contractarian. Utilitarian liberalism rests on different theoretical foundations, as does the late nineteenth-century British liberalism of T. H. Green and his colleagues: a Hegelian, social liberalism.[5] Closer to home, of course, we have John Dewey's brand of liberalism. Moreover, even within the social contract tradition, resources exist for contesting the assumptions of the Hobbesian/Lockean version of the contract. Rousseau's *Discourse on the Origins of Inequality* (1755) (nowhere cited by Marx) rethinks the "contract" to make it a contract entered into *after* the formation of society, and thus the creation of socialized human beings. So the ontology presupposed is explicitly a social one. In any case, the contemporary revival of contractarianism initiated by John Rawls's 1971 *A Theory of Justice* makes the contract a thought-experiment, a "device of representation," rather than a literal or even metaphorical anthropological account.[6] The communitarian/contractarian debates of the 1980s onward recapitulated much of the "asocial" critique of contractarian liberalism (though usually without a radical edge). But as Rawls pointed out against Michael Sandel, for example, one needs to distinguish the figures in the thought-experiment from real human beings.[7] And radicals should be wary about accepting a communitarian ontology and claims about the general good that deny or marginalize the dynamics of group domination in actual societies represented as "communities." The great virtue of contractarian liberal individualism is the conceptual room it provides for hegemonic norms to be critically evaluated through the epistemic and moral distancing from *Sittlichkeit* that the contract, as an intellectual device, provides.

2. Liberalism Cannot Recognize Groups and Group Oppression in Its Ontology—I (Macro)

The second point needs to be logically distinguished from the first, since a theory could acknowledge the social shaping of individuals while denying that group oppression is central to that shaping. (So #1 is necessary, but not sufficient, for #2.) The Marxist critique, of course, was supposed to encapsulate *both* points: people were shaped by society and society (post-"primitive communism") was class dominated. The ontology was social and it was an ontology of class. Today radicals would demand a richer ontology that can accommodate the realities of gender and racial oppression also. But whatever candidates are put forward, the key claim is that a liberal framework cannot accommodate an ontology of groups in relations of domination and subordination. To the extent that liberalism recognizes social groups, these are basically conceived of as voluntary associations that one chooses to join or not join, which is obviously very different from, say, class, race, and gender memberships.

But this evasive ontology, which obfuscates the most central and obvious fact about all societies since humanity exited the hunting-and-gathering stage—that is, that they are characterized by oppressions of one kind or another—is not a definitional constituent of liberalism. Liberalism has certainly recognized some kinds of oppression: the absolutism it opposed from the seventeenth to the nineteenth century, the Nazism and Stalinism it opposed in the twentieth century. Liberalism's failure to systematically address structural oppression in supposedly liberal-democratic societies is a contingent artifact of the group perspectives and group interests privileged by those structures, not an intrinsic feature of liberalism's conceptual apparatus.

In the preface to her recent *Analyzing Oppression*, Ann Cudd makes a striking point: that hers is the first book-length treatment of the subject in the analytic tradition.[8] Philosophy, the discipline whose special mandate it is to illuminate justice and injustice for us, has had very little to say about injustice and oppression because of the social background of the majority of its thinkers. In political theory and political philosophy, the theorists who developed the dominant varieties of liberalism have come overwhelmingly from the hegemonic groups of the liberal social order (bourgeois white males). So it is really not surprising that, given this background, their socio-political and epistemic standpoint has tended to reproduce rather than challenge group privilege.

Consider Rawls, famously weak on gender and with next to nothing to say about race. Rawlsian "ideal theory," which has dominated mainstream political philosophy for the last four decades, marginalizes such concerns not contingently but structurally. If your focus from the start is principles of distributive justice for a "well-ordered society," then social oppression cannot be part of the picture, since by definition an oppressive society is not a well-ordered one. As Cudd points out, *A Theory of Justice* "leaves injustice virtually untheorized," operating on the assumption "that injustice is merely the negation of justice."[9] But radically unjust societies—those characterized by major rather than minor deviations from ideality—will be different from just societies not merely morally but also *metaphysically*. What Cudd calls "nonvoluntary social groups" will be central to their makeup.

Accordingly, Cudd contends that a conceptualization of "nonvoluntary social groups" must be central to any adequate account of social oppression: "without positing social groups as causally efficacious entities, we cannot explain oppression." Contra the conventional wisdom in radical circles, however, she is insistent that the ontology of such groups can be explained "[using] current social science, in the form of cognitive psychology and modern economic theory, and situat[ing] itself in the Anglo-American tradition of liberal political philosophy."[10] Identifying "intentionalist" and "structuralist" approaches as the two broad categories of competing theorizations of social groups, she recommends as the best option

> a compatibilist position, holding that while all action is intentionally guided, many of the constraints within which we act are socially determined and beyond the control of the currently acting individual; to put a slogan on it, intentions dynamically interact within social structures. . . . My theory of nonvoluntary social groups fits the description of what Philip Pettit calls "holistic individualism," which means that the social regularities associated with nonvoluntary social groups supervene on intentional states, and at the same time, group membership in these and voluntary social groups partly constitutes the intentional states of individuals.[11]

If Cudd is right, then, such a theorization can indeed be developed within a liberal framework, using the resources of analytic social and normative theory. But such a development of the theory is not merely permissible but should be seen as *mandatory*, given liberalism's nominal commitment to individualism, egalitarianism, universalism, and meliorism. These values simply cannot be achieved unless the obstacles to their realization are identified and theorized. Social-democratic (left) liberalism, feminist liberalism, black liberalism all historically represent attempts to take these structural realities into account for the purposes of rethinking dominant liberalism.[12] They are attempts to get right, to map accurately, the *actual* ontology of the societies for which liberalism is prescribing principles of justice. What Cudd's book demonstrates is that it is the *ignoring* of this ontology of group domination that is the real betrayal of the liberal project. A well-ordered society will not have nonvoluntary social groups as part of its ontology. So the path to the "realistic utopia" Rawls is supposedly outlining would crucially require normative prescriptions for eliminating such groups. That no such guidelines are offered is undeniably an indictment of ideal-theory liberalism, which is thereby exposed as both epistemologically and ontologically inadequate. But that does not rule out a reconceptualized liberalism, a non-ideal-theory liberalism that, starting from a different social metaphysic, requires a different normative strategy for theorizing justice.

3. Liberalism Cannot Recognize Groups and Group Oppression in Its Ontology—II (Micro)

But (it will be replied) liberalism suffers from a deeper theoretical inadequacy. Even if it may be conceded that liberal theory can recognize oppression at the macro-level, it will be argued that its individualism prevents it from recognizing how profoundly, at the micro-level, individuals are shaped *by* structures of social oppression. Class, race, and gender belongings penetrate deeply into the ontology of the individual in ways rendered opaque (it will be claimed) by liberalism's foundational individualism.

But what those seeking to retrieve liberalism would point out is that we need to distinguish different senses of "individualism." The individualism that is foundational to liberalism is a *normative* individualism (as in the Gray quote above), which makes individuals rather than social collectivities the locus of *value*. But that does not require any denial that individuals are shaped in their *character* (the "second nature" famously highlighted by left theory) by oppressive social forces and related group memberships. Once the first two criticisms have been refuted—that liberal individuals cannot be "social," and that the involuntary group memberships central to the social in oppressive societies cannot be accommodated within a liberal framework—then this third criticism collapses also. One can without inconsistency affirm both the value of the individual and the importance of recognizing how the individual is socially molded, especially when the environing social structures are oppressive ones. As already noted, dominant liberalism tends to ignore or marginalize such constraints, assuming as its representative figures individuals not merely morally equal, but *socially recognized* as morally equal, and equi-powerful rather than group-differentiated into the privileged and the subordinated. But this misleading normative and descriptive picture is a function of a political agenda complicit with the status quo, not a necessary implication of liberalism's core assumptions. A revisionist, radical liberalism would make the analysis of group oppression, the denial of equal standing to the majority of the population, and their impact on the individual's ontology, a theoretical priority. Thus Cudd's book, after explicating the ontology of involuntary groups, goes on to detail the various different ways—through violence, economic constraint, discrimination, group harassment, and the internalization of psychological oppression—that the subordinated are shaped by group domination.[13] But nothing in her account is meant to imply either that they thereby cease to be individuals or that their involuntary group memberships preclude a normative liberal condemnation of the injustice of their treatment.

4. Liberal Humanist Individualism Is Naïve about the Subject

A different kind of challenge is mounted by Foucault (though arguably originating in such earlier sources as the "anti-humanism" of Althusserian Marxism).[14] Here, as John Christman points out, in contrast to the "thick" conception of the person advocated by communitarianism, in critique of liberalism, we get the theoretical recommendation that "the notion of a singular unified subject of any sort, however thin the conception, [must be] abandoned."[15] As Foucault writes:

> How, under what conditions, and in what forms can something like a subject appear in the order of discourse? What place can it occupy in each type of discourse, what functions can it assume, and by obeying what rules? In short, it is a matter of depriving the subject (or its substitute) of its role as originator, and of analyzing the subject as a variable and complex function of discourse.[16]

The subject is not merely *molded* by power, but *produced* by power, and, in effect, vanishes.

I agree that liberalism cannot meet such a challenge, but I think the premise of the challenge should be rejected. Here I am in sympathy with Christman, who, reviewing various critiques of the classic liberal humanist conception of the self, argues for a socio-historical conception that concedes the absurdity of the notion of people springing from their own brow ("originators") while nonetheless making a case for "degrees" of self-creation:

> Selves should be seen as to a large extent formed by factors not under the control of those reflective agents themselves. . . . This will help accomplish two things: to provide grounds for the rejection of models of agency and citizenship that assume Herculean abilities to fashion ourselves out of whole cloth; and to force us to focus more carefully on what powers of self-shaping we therefore are left with. . . . The point must be that the role of the self's control of the self (and the attendant social elements of both 'selves') will be circumscribed by the ways in which our lives are shaped *for* us and not *by* us.[17]

A commitment to humanism does not, as pointed out above, require the denial of the obvious fact that human beings—especially the oppressed—are constrained by material structures and social restrictions in what they can accomplish, nor that, as products of particular epochs and group memberships, their consciousness will have been shaped by dominant concepts and norms. Marx emphasized long ago that though people make history, they do not make it under conditions of their own choosing, that agency is constrained by structure and circumstance. But, contra Althusser, this was never intended as a rejection of the claim that it is still people who ultimately assert their personhood in struggle.

And in my opinion, the retort applies to the Foucauldian version of the thesis also. To make the familiar left critiques: such an analysis not only deprives us of a normative basis for indicting structures of oppression, not only deprives the subject of agency, but is flagrantly inconsistent with the actual history of people's resistance to the systems that have supposedly "produced" them as subjects. The anti-colonial struggle, the anti-Fascist and anti-Stalinist struggles, the civil rights struggles of white women, people of color, gays, the recent "Arab spring" all give the lie to such a diagnosis. Radical liberalism is capable of recognizing both the extent of our socialization by the existing oppressive social order and the ways in which, nonetheless, many people resist and struggle against this oppressive social order.

5. Liberalism's Values (Independently of the Ontology Question) Are Themselves Problematic

Even if the ontological challenge can be beaten back, though, another front remains open. It will be argued that liberal humanist values are themselves problematic in nature and incapable of advancing a radical agenda. But the obvious reply is, Which values? And what exactly is the problem supposed to be: (a) that the values are *intrinsically* problematic? (b) that the values involved have historically been extended in an *exclusionary* discriminatory way? (c) that the values have been developed in a fashion that is predicated on the experience of the *privileged*? These are all different claims.

Start with the first. Admittedly, some values associated with the liberal tradition could be judged to be intrinsically problematic, such as the "possessive individualism" C. B. Macpherson famously attributed to Hobbes and Locke.[18] But this is a value specific to right-wing liberalism, not liberalism in general (it does not appear on Gray's list), and would be opposed by left-wing/social democratic liberalism. Such values as "freedom," "equality" (moral egalitarianism), and "fraternity/sorority" classically emblematic of the liberal tradition have not usually been seen as problematic by radicals and have indeed been emblazoned on radical banners. Freedom from oppression, equal rights/equal pay/equal citizenship ("I <u>AM</u> A MAN"), fraternity/sorority with the subordinated ("Am I not a man and a brother? Am I not a woman and a sister?") have all served as values for progressive movements seeking social emancipation.

To be sure, it is a familiar point to radicals, if somewhat less so to the non-radical majority, that the population as a whole has not historically been recognized as deserving the protections of these norms, so that the opponents of emancipation have all too often *themselves* been liberals. Freedom has been construed as justifiably resting on the enslavement of some; equality has been restricted to those deemed worthy of it (i.e., those more equal than others); fraternity has been literal, an all-boys' club. Domenico Losurdo's recently translated *Liberalism: A Counter-History* provides a devastating exposé of "liberal thought [not] in its abstract purity, but liberalism, and hence the liberal movement and liberal society, in their concrete reality." It is an illuminatingly sordid history of the ideology's complicity with racial slavery, white working-class indentureship, colonialism and imperialism ("A 'Master-Race Democracy' on a Planetary Scale," in one chapter's title), and the conceptual connection between the Nazi "final solution" and Europe's earlier extermination programs against indigenous peoples.[19]

Yet it is noteworthy that in his concluding pages, Losurdo still affirms the "merits and strong points of the intellectual tradition under examination." His "counter-history" has been aimed at dispelling the "habitual hagiography" that surrounds liberalism, and the related "myth of the gradual, peaceful transition, on the basis of purely internal motivations and impulses, from liberalism to democracy, or from general enjoyment of negative liberty to an ever wider recognition of political rights."[20] In reality, he emphasizes, "the classics of the liberal tradition" were generally hostile to democracy; the "exclusion clauses" required "violent upheavals" to be overcome; progress was not linear but a matter of advances and retreats; external crisis often played a crucial role; and white working-class and black inclusion in the polity came at the cost of their participation in colonial wars against native peoples.[21] Nonetheless, his final paragraph insists:

> However difficult such an operation might be for those committed to overcoming liberalism's exclusion clauses, to take up the legacy of this intellectual tradition is an absolutely unavoidable task. . . . [L]iberalism's merits are too significant and too evident for it to be necessary to credit it with other, completely imaginary ones. Among the latter is the alleged spontaneous capacity for self-correction often attributed to it. . . . Only in opposition to [such] pervasive repressions and transfigurations is the book now ending presented as a "counter-history": bidding farewell to hagiography is the precondition for landing on the firm ground of history.[22]

So for Losurdo one can accept the indictment of actual historic liberalism, and its failure to live up to its putative universalism, without going on to conclude either that liberalism must therefore be abandoned or that liberalism's own internal dynamic will naturally correct itself. Rather, the appropriate conclusion is that liberalism can be retrieved, but that it will take political struggle to do so.

Finally, even when the "exclusion clauses" are formally overcome, their legacy may well remain in the form of values now *nominally* extended to everybody, but in reality articulated in such a fashion as to continue to reproduce group privilege—for example, a "freedom" that repudiates caste status but does not recognize illicit economic constraint as unfairly limiting liberty, or an "autonomy" that does not acknowledge the role of female caregiving in enabling human development, or a "justice" resolutely forward-looking that blocks issues of rectification of past injustices. But what such tendentious conceptual framings arguably call for is a critique and a rethinking of these values and principles in the light of these exclusions (as with left, feminist, and black liberalism). That does not refute their normative worth; it just underlines the necessity for taking the *whole* population into account in revising them and developing a blueprint of their internal architecture adequately sensitized to the differential social location and social history of such groups, particularly those traditionally oppressed.

6. Liberalism's Enlightenment Origins Commit It to Seeing Moral Suasion and Rational Discourse as the Societal Prime Movers

Liberalism is often associated with a historical progressivism, but a belief in the possibility and desirability of meliorism (see Gray) certainly does not commit one to Whiggish teleologies. One can oppose conservative fatalism and pessimism in its different versions—Christian claims about original sin, Burkean distrust of abstract reason, biological determinism in its ever-changing and ever-renewed incarnations—without thinking that there is any inevitability about the triumph of progress and reason. A liberalism that is "radical" will necessarily need to draw on the left tradition's demystified analysis of the centrality of group domination to the workings of the social order.[23] As earlier noted (sections 2 and 3 above), a revisionist ontology that recognizes as key social players nonvoluntary social groups in structural relations of domination and subordination will perforce have a more realistic view of the (in)efficacy of moral suasion than an ontology of atomic individuals.

Mills : radical Liberalism

Such a revisionist liberalism will acknowledge the role of hegemonic ideologies and vested group interests in the preservation of the status quo, and their refractoriness to appeals to reason and justice. Indeed, it will often be precisely in the names of a "reason" and "justice" shaped by the norms and perspectives of group privilege—of class, gender, and race—that egalitarian social change is resisted. As Losurdo makes clear, no immanent developmentalist moral dynamic drives liberalism's evolution. It is not at all the case that an endorsement of democratized liberal norms implies any corollary belief that the democratic struggle for a more egalitarian social order is guaranteed to be successful. Progress is possible; defeat and rollback are also possible. In general, a radical liberalism should, in some sense, be "materialist," recognizing the extent to which both people and the social dynamic are shaped by material forces and not over-estimating the causal role of rational argumentation and moral suasion on their own. Radical liberalism takes for granted that political and ideological struggle will be necessary to realize liberal values against the opposition of those who all too frequently think of themselves as the real liberals. Radical liberalism can be descriptively realist (realizing the centrality of interest-based politics) without being normatively realist (abandoning morality for *realpolitik*).

7. Liberalism Is Naïve in Assuming the Neutrality of the State and the Juridical System

Again, while such a claim may be true of dominant varieties of liberalism, it need not be true of all. (Note that nowhere in Gray's characterization is any such assumption made.)

The neutrality of the juridico-political system is a liberal *ideal*, a norm to be striven for to reflect citizens' equal moral status before the law and entitlement to equal protection of their legitimate interests. To represent it as a *sociological* generalization of liberal theory about actual political systems, including systems self-designated as liberal, would be to confuse the normative with the descriptive. Liberalism has certainly historically had no trouble in seeing the illicit influence of concentrated group power in the socio-political systems it *opposed* (see section #2). The original critique of "feudal" absolutism, the twentieth-century critique of "totalitarianism," relied in part on the documentation and condemnation of the extent of legally backed state repression in curbing individual freedom. Liberalism's blind spot has been its failure to document and condemn the enormity of the historic denial of equal rights to the majority of the population ruled by self-styled "liberal" states: the "absolutism" and "totalitarianism" directed against white women and white workers, and the nonwhite enslaved and colonized. Patriarchal democracy, bourgeois democracy, *Herrenvolk* democracy have all been represented as "democracy" *simpliciter*, with no analysis of the mechanisms of structural subordination that have characterized such polities, or the ideological sleights-of-hand that have rationalized them. But to claim a necessary conceptual connection between such evasions and liberal assumptions is to confuse the *contingent* necessities of the discourse of hegemonic liberalism—aimed at preserving, whether by justifying or obfuscating, patriarchal, bourgeois, and racial power—with what is taken to be some kind of transworld essence of liberalism. In recent decades, a large body of literature has developed that investigates the impact of class, race, and gender dynamics in the actual functioning of the state and the legal system.[24] Radical liberalism would draw on this body of literature in seeking to put in place the safeguards necessary for guaranteeing equal protection not merely on paper but in reality.

8. Liberalism Is Necessarily Anti-Socialist, So How "Radical" Could It Be?

"Socialism" is used in different senses. Assuming that a romanticized return to pre-industrial communal systems is not in the cards for a globalized world of seven-plus billion people, there are three main alternatives so far (two tried, one theorized about): state-commandist socialism, social democracy, market socialism. State-commandist socialism (a.k.a. "communism") is indeed incompatible with liberalism but would seem to have been refuted as an attractive ideal by the history of the twentieth century.[25] Social democracy is just left-liberalism, whether in Rawls's version or in versions further left, like Brian Barry's, more worried about the inequalities Rawls's two principles of justice leave intact.[26] Market socialism is yet to be implemented on a national level, but many of the hypothetical accounts of how it would work emphasize the importance of respecting liberal norms.[27] In other words, market socialism's putative superiority to capitalism is not defended by invoking distinctively socialist values but by showing how such uncontroversial and traditional liberal values as democracy, freedom, and self-realization are not going to be achievable for the majority under the present system (or through the appeal to more recent values like sustainability, generated by awareness of the impending ecological disaster, which the present order will make achievable for *nobody*!)[28] Other possibilities are not ruled out, but their proponents would have to explain how their models have learned the lessons of the past in both (a) being economically viable and (b) respecting human rights, the common global moral currency of the postwar epoch, which is best developed in the liberal tradition. Criticism of the existing order is not enough; one has to show how one's proposed "socialist" alternative will be superior (and in more than a vague hand-waving kind of way).

9. The Discourse of Liberal Rights Cannot Accommodate Radical Redistribution and Structural Change

Marxism's original critique of liberalism, apart from deriding its (imputed) social ontology, represented liberal rights—for example, in "On the Jewish Question"[29]—as a bourgeois concept. But that was more than a century and a half ago. Lockean rights-of-non-interference centered on private property, "negative" rights, are indeed deficient as an exclusivist characterization of people's normative entitlements, but such a minimalist view has been contested by social democrats (some self-identifying as liberal) for more than a century. A significant literature now exists on "welfare" rights, "positive" rights, "social" rights, whose implementation would indeed require radical structural change. The legitimacy of these rights as "liberal" rights is, of course, denied by the political right. But that's the whole point, with which I began—that liberalism is not a monolith but a set of competing interpretations and theorizations, fighting it out in a common arena.[30] The US hostility to such rights is a manifestation of the historic success of conservatives in framing the normative agenda in this country, not a necessary corollary of liberalism as such. As earlier emphasized, liberalism must not be collapsed into neo-liberalism. Nor is it a refutation to point out that having such rights on paper does not guarantee their implementation, since this is just a variation of the already discussed imputation to liberalism of a necessarily idealist conception of the social dynamic (section #6), in which morality is a prime mover. But such a sociological claim is neither a foundational nor a derivative assumption of liberalism.

Moreover, in the specific case of the redress of racial injustice, one does not even need to appeal to such rights, since the situation of, for example, blacks in the United States is arguably the result of the historic and current violation of traditional *negative* rights (life, liberty, property), which are supposed to be the uncontroversial ones in the liberal tradition, as well as the legacy of such practices as manifest in illicitly accumulated wealth and opportunities. Here again the hegemony of Rawlsian "ideal theory" over the development of the mainstream political philosophy of the last forty years has had pernicious consequences, marginalizing such issues and putting the focus instead on principles of distributive justice for an ideal "well-ordered" society. But an emancipatory liberalism would be reoriented from

too much plurality already

the start toward *non-ideal* theory and would correspondingly make rectificatory justice and the ending of social oppression its priority.[31]

10. American Liberalism in Particular Has Been so Shaped in Its Development by Race that Any Emancipatory Possibilities Have Been Foreclosed

Liberalism in general (both nationally and internationally) has been shaped by race, but that does not preclude reclaiming it.[32] Moreover, it is precisely such shaping that motivates the imperative of recognizing the multiplicity of liberalisms, not merely for cataloging purposes but in order to frame them as *theoretical objects* whose dynamic requires investigation. The conflation of all liberalisms with their racialized versions obstructs seeing these ideologies as historically contingent varieties of liberalism, which could have developed otherwise. A Brechtian "defamiliarization" is necessary, a cognitive distancing that "denaturalizes" what is prone to appear as the essence of liberalism. Jennifer Pitts's *A Turn to Empire*, for example, which is subtitled *The Rise of Imperial Liberalism in Britain and France*, and Sankar Muthu's *Enlightenment against Empire*, both seek to demarcate within liberalism the existence of anti- as well as pro-imperialist strains, thereby demonstrating that liberalism is not a monolith.[33] Admittedly, other scholars have been more ambivalent about some of their supposed exemplars; see, for example, Losurdo, already cited, and John Hobson's recent *The Eurocentric Conception of World Politics*, which develops a detailed and sophisticated taxonomy of varieties of Eurocentrism and imperialism that demonstrates the *compatibility* of racism, Eurocentrism, and anti-imperialism.[34] (For instance, many European liberal theorists were anti-imperialist precisely because of their racism—their fears that the white race would degenerate as a result of miscegenation with inferior races and the deleterious consequences of prolonged residence in the unsuitable tropical climates of colonial outposts.) But the mere fact of such a range of positions illustrates that a liberalism neither Eurocentric nor imperialist is not a contradiction in terms.

In the United States in particular, as Rogers Smith has demonstrated, liberalism and racism have been intricately involved with one another from the nation's inception, a relationship Smith conceptualizes in terms of conflicting "multiple traditions," racism versus liberal universalism, and which I see as a conflict between "racial liberalism" and non-racial liberalism.[35] My belief is that formally identifying "racial liberalism" as a particular evolutionary (and always evolving) ideological phenomenon better enables us to understand the role of race in writing and rewriting the most important political philosophy in the nation's history, from the overtly racist liberalism of the past to the nominally color-blind liberalism of the present. From the eighteenth- to nineteenth-century accommodation to racial slavery and aboriginal expropriation to the twentieth-century tainting of welfare and social democracy on this side of the Atlantic,[36] race has refracted crucial terms, concepts, and values in liberal theory so as to remove any cognitive dissonance between the privileging of whites and the subordination of people of color. Correspondingly, the shaping of white moral psychology by race and the distinctive patterns of uptake of abstract liberal values ("equality," "individualism") in such a psychology then become legitimate objects of investigation for us.[37] One begins from the assumption that these norms will be color-coded in their actual operationalization, so that any efficacious framing of an interracial political project will need to anticipate and correct for this differential understanding rather than being naively surprised by it. But such racialization (as popular interpretation and reception) is going to be a common problem for *any* American ideology with emancipatory pretensions. Liberalism is certainly not unique in that respect, as the history of the white American left and socialist movements illustrates. As Jack London famously put it at a meeting of the Socialist Party in San Francisco "when challenged by various members concerning his emphasis on the yellow peril": "What the devil! I am first of all a white man and only then a Socialist!"[38] *Herrenvolk* socialism existed no less than *Herrenvolk* liberalism.

CHAPTER 3

Racial Liberalism

Liberalism is globally triumphant. The anti-feudal egalitarian ideology of individual rights and freedoms that emerged in the seventeenth and eighteenth centuries to oppose absolutism and ascriptive hierarchy has unquestionably become, whether in right- or left-wing versions, the dominant political outlook of the modern age. Normative justifications of the existing order as well as normative critiques overwhelmingly use a liberal framework. Debate typically centers on the comparative defensibility of "neo-liberal" or free market conceptions versus social democratic or welfarist conceptions of liberalism. But liberalism itself is rarely challenged.

Within liberalism there are rival perspectives on the moral foundations of the state and the ultimate basis of people's rights. For a century and a half from the 1800s onward, the utilitarianism of Jeremy Bentham, James and John Stuart Mill, and Henry Sidgwick was most politically influential. But the World War II experience of the death camps and the global movement for postwar decolonization encouraged a return to a natural rights tradition that seemed to put individual personal protections on a more secure basis. Not social welfare but "natural," pre-social individual entitlements were judged to be the superior and infrangible foundation. Thus it is the language of rights and duties—*independent* of social utility— most strongly associated with the earlier, rival social contract tradition of 1650–1800, particularly in John Locke's and Immanuel Kant's versions, that is now ubiquitous.[1] Unsurprisingly, then, especially with the revival of social contract theory stimulated by John Rawls's 1971 *A Theory of Justice*, contractarian (also called "deontological") liberalism has now become hegemonic.[2]

But in these myriad debates about and within liberalism, a key issue tends to be missed, to remain unacknowledged, even though—or perhaps precisely because—its implications for the rethinking of liberalism, and for the world order that liberalism has largely rationalized, would be so far-ranging. Liberalism, I suggest, has historically been predominantly a *racial* liberalism,[3] in which conceptions of personhood and resulting schedules of rights, duties, and government responsibilities have all been racialized. And the contract, correspondingly, has really been a *racial* one, an agreement among white contractors to subordinate and exploit nonwhite non-contractors for white benefit.[4] Insofar as moral debate in contemporary political theory ignores this history, it will only serve to perpetuate it.

RACE AND THE SOCIAL CONTRACT

Let me begin with some general points about the social contract. The concept is, of course, to be taken not literally but rather as an illuminating metaphor or thought experiment. We are asked to imagine the socio-political order (society, the state) as being self-consciously brought into existence through a "contract" among human beings in a pre-social, pre-political stage of humanity (the "state of nature"). The enduring appeal of the metaphor, despite its patent absurdity as a literal representation of the formation of socio-political systems, inheres in its capturing of two key insights. The first (against theological views of divine creation or secular conceptions of an organicist kind) is that society and the polity are artificial human constructs. The second (against ancient and medieval views of natural social hierarchy) is that human beings are naturally equal and that this equality in the state of nature should somehow translate into egalitarian socio-political institutions.[5]

For the Lockean and Kantian contracts that (in conjunction and in competition) define the mainstream of the liberal tradition—but not for the Hobbesian contract—*moral* equality is foundational.[6] The social ontology is classically individualist, and it demands the creation of a polity that respects the equal personhood of individuals and (whether in stronger or weaker versions) their property rights. Basic moral entitlements for the citizenry are then juridically codified and enforced by an impartial state. Economic transactions are, correspondingly, ideally supposed to be non-exploitative, though there will, of course, be controversy about how this concept should be cashed out. So fairness in a broad sense is the overarching contract norm, as befits an apparatus ostensibly founded on principles antithetical to a non-individual-respecting, welfare-aggregating utilitarianism. The moral equality of people in the state of nature demands an equality of treatment (juridical, political, and economic) in the liberal polity they create. The state is not alien or antagonistic to us but the protector of our rights, whether as the constitutionalist Lockean sovereign or the Kantian

Rechtsstaat. The good polity is the just polity, and the just polity is founded on safeguarding our interests as individuals.

But what if—not merely episodically and randomly, but systematically and structurally—the personhood of some persons was historically disregarded, and their rights disrespected? What if entitlements and justice were, correspondingly, so conceived of that the unequal treatment of these persons, or sub-persons, was *not* seen as unfair, not flagged as an internal inconsistency, but accommodated by suitable discursive shifts and conceptual framings? And what if, after long political struggles, there developed at last a seeming equality that later turned out to be more nominal than substantive, so that justice and equal protection were still effectively denied even while being triumphantly proclaimed? It would mean that we would need to recognize the inadequacy of speaking in the abstract of liberalism and contractarianism. We would need to acknowledge that race had underpinned the liberal framework from the outset, refracting the sense of crucial terms, embedding a particular model of rights-bearers, dictating a certain historical narrative, and providing an overall theoretical orientation for normative discussions. We would need to confront the fact that to understand the actual logic of these normative debates, both what is said and what is not said, we would have to understand not just the ideal, abstract social contract but also its incarnation in the United States (and arguably elsewhere) as a non-ideal racial contract.

Consider the major divisions in the political philosophy of the last few decades. In *Liberalism and the Limits of Justice*, Michael Sandel makes the point that Rawls's *A Theory of Justice* is important because—apart from carrying the Kantianism versus utilitarianism dispute to a higher theoretical level—it was central to not one but two of the major political debates of the 1970s and 1980s, left/social-democratic liberalism versus right/laissez-faire liberalism (John Rawls versus Robert Nozick) and liberalism or contractarianism versus communitarianism (Rawls versus Michael Walzer, Alasdair MacIntyre, Charles Taylor, and Sandel himself).[7] A third major debate, initiated by Rawls's essays of the 1980s and culminating in *Political Liberalism*, could be said to be the debate of the 1990s and 2000s on "comprehensive" versus "political" liberalism.[8] In their domination of the conceptual and theoretical landscape, these overarching frameworks tend to set the political agenda, establishing a hegemonic framing of key assumptions and jointly exhaustive alternatives. One locates oneself as a theorist by choosing one or the other of these primary alternatives and then taking up the corresponding socio-political and normative picture, adopting the defining terms, and making the argumentative moves characteristically associated with it. So though other theoretical and political alternatives are not logically excluded, they tend to be marginalized.

But there is another debate—one that has been going on for hundreds of years, if not always in the academy—which is, in a sense, orthogonal to all three of the foregoing and is arguably more pressing than any of them: the conflict between racial liberalism (generally known just as liberalism) and deracialized liberalism. Racial liberalism, or white liberalism, is the actual liberalism that has been historically dominant since modernity: a liberal theory whose terms originally restricted full personhood to whites (or, more accurately, white men) and relegated nonwhites to an inferior category, so that its schedule of rights and prescriptions for justice were all color-coded. Ascriptive hierarchy is abolished for white men, but not white women and people of color.[9] So racism is not an anomaly in an unqualified liberal universalism but generally symbiotically related to a qualified and particularistic liberalism.[10] Though there have always been white liberals who have been anti-racist and anti-imperialist, whose records should not be ignored,[11] they have been in the minority. Indeed the most striking manifestation of this symbiotic rather than conflictual relation is that the two philosophers earlier demarcated as central to the liberal tradition, Locke and Kant, both limited property rights, self-ownership, and personhood racially. Locke invested in African slavery, justified Native American expropriation, and helped to write the Carolina constitution of 1669, which gave masters absolute power over their slaves.[12] Kant, the most important ethicist of the modern period and the famous theorist of personhood and respect, turns out to be one of the founders of modern scientific racism, and thus a pioneering theorist of sub-personhood and disrespect.[13] So the inferior treatment of people of color is not at all incongruent with racialized liberal norms, since by these norms nonwhites are less than full persons.

If this analysis is correct, such inequality, and its historic ramifications, is arguably more fundamental than all the other issues mentioned above, since in principle at least all parties to the many-sided political debate are supposed to be committed to the non-racial moral equality of all. Thus the rethinking, purging, and deracializing of racial liberalism should be a priority for us—and in fact the struggles of people of color for racial equality over the past few hundred years can to a significant extent be most illuminatingly seen as just such a project. As Michael Dawson writes in his comprehensive study of African American political ideologies:

> The great majority of black theorists challenge liberalism as it has been practiced within the United States, not some abstract ideal version of the ideology. . . . [T]here is no necessary contradiction between the liberal tradition in *theory* and black liberalism. The contradiction exists between black liberalism and how liberalism has come to be understood in practice within the American context.[14]

Yet the need for such a reconstruction has been neither acknowledged nor acted on. Rawls and Nozick may be in conflict over left-wing versus right-wing liberalism, but both offer us idealized views of the polity that ignore the racial subordination rationalized by racial liberalism. Rawls and Sandel may be in conflict over contractarian liberalism versus neo-Hegelian communitarianism, but neither confronts how the whiteness of the actual American contract and its conception of the right and of the actual American community and its conception of the good affects their views of justice and the self. Late Rawls may be in conflict with early Rawls about political versus comprehensive liberalism, but neither addresses the question of the ways in which both versions have been shaped by race, whether through an "overlapping consensus" (among whites) or a "reflective equilibrium" (of whites). From the perspective of people of color, these intramural and intra-white debates all fail to deal with the simple overwhelming reality on which left and right, contractarian and communitarian, comprehensive or political liberal, should theoretically all be able to agree: that the centrality of racial exclusion and racial injustice demands a reconceptualization of the orthodox view of the polity and calls for radical rectification.

THE "WHITENESS" OF POLITICAL PHILOSOPHY, DEMOGRAPHIC AND CONCEPTUAL

Political philosophers need to take race seriously. Unfortunately, for a combination of reasons, both externalist and internalist, they have not generally done so. Demographically, philosophy is one of the very whitest of the humanities; only about 1 percent of American philosophers are African American, with Latinos, Asian Americans, and Native Americans making up another 2 to 3 percent or so.[15] So while the past two decades have generated an impressive body of work on race, largely by philosophers of color though with increasing white contributions, it has tended to be ghettoized and not taken up in the writings of the most prominent figures in the field. Basically, one can choose to do race or choose to do philosophy. Nor do ads in *Jobs for Philosophers*, the profession's official listing of available employment, usually include race as a desired area of specialization in their job descriptions. So though Africana philosophy and critical philosophy of race are formally recognized by the American Philosophical Association as legitimate research areas, which represents progress, they remain marginal in the field, far more so than issues of gender and feminism, a sign of the greater proportion of (white) women in the profession (about 20 percent). Indeed, in the entire country, out of a total population of more than 11,000 professional philosophers, there are only about thirty black women PhDs employed in philosophy departments.

(UPDATE: I would be remiss not to cite some positive developments in the field since the original [2008] *PMLA* appearance of this article. In October 2007, the Collegium of Black Women Philosophers under the leadership of Kathryn Gines was launched as an attempt to remedy the situation of black women in particular and they have been holding regular conferences ever since. More recently, the Society of Young Black Philosophers has been formed to reach out to and encourage black undergrads contemplating a future in philosophy as well as to provide a solidarity network for black graduate students and black junior professors.)

But the problem is not at all just demographic. Philosophers of color are absent not only from the halls of academe but from the texts also. Introductions to political philosophy standardly exclude any discussion of race, except, perhaps, for brief discussions of affirmative action.[16] Historical anthologies of political philosophy will present a lineup of figures extending from ancient Greece to the contemporary world—from Plato to NATO in one wit's formulation—but with no representation of nonwhite theorists. Almost to the point of parody, the Western political canon is limited to the thoughts of white males. Steven Cahn's *Classics of Political and Moral Philosophy*, for example, a widely used Oxford anthology of more than 1,200 pages includes only one nonwhite thinker, Martin Luther King Jr., and not even in the main text but in the appendixes.[17] So it is not merely that the pantheon is closed to nonwhite outsiders but that a particular misleading narrative of Western political philosophy—indeed a particular misleading narrative of the West itself—is being inculcated in generations of students. The central debates in the field as presented—aristocracy versus democracy, absolutism versus liberalism, capitalism versus socialism, social democracy versus libertarianism, contractarianism versus communitarianism—exclude any reference to the modern global history of racism versus anti-racism, of abolitionist, anti-imperialist, anti-colonialist, anti-Jim Crow, anti-apartheid struggles. Quobna Cugoano, Frederick Douglass, W. E. B. Du Bois, Mahatma Gandhi, Aimé Césaire, C. L. R. James, Frantz Fanon, Steve Biko, Edward Said are all missing.[18] The political history of the West is sanitized, reconstructed as if white racial domination and the oppression of people of color had not been central to that history. A white supremacy that was originally planetary, a racial political structure that was transnational, is whitewashed out of existence. One would never guess from reading such works that less than a century ago, "the era of global white supremacy" was inspiring "a global struggle for racial equality."[19] One would never dream that the moral equality supposedly established by modernity was in actuality so racially restricted that at the 1919 post–World War I peace conference in Versailles, the Japanese delegation's proposal to insert a "racial equality" clause in the League of Nations' Covenant was soundly defeated by the "Anglo-Saxon" nations (including, of course, the United States), which refused to accept such a principle.[20]

(UPDATE: Here also I am happy to report that some progress has been made since 2008. Sections on race are included in several recent introductory social and political philosophy anthologies that I am aware of: Andrea Veltman's *Social and Political Philosophy: Classic and Contemporary Readings*, Diane Jeske and Richard Fumerton's *Readings in Political Philosophy: Theory and Applications*, Omid Payrow Shabani and Monique Deveaux's *Introduction to Social and Political Philosophy*, and the second edition of Matt Zwolinski's *Arguing about Political Philosophy*.[21] The 2015 third edition of Cahn's Oxford anthology now has a selection by Kwame Anthony Appiah.[22])

Moreover, it is not just that the political theorists of the struggle against racism and white supremacy are Jim-Crowed but, even more remarkably, that *justice itself* as a subject is Jim-Crowed. Contemporary political philosophy, at least in the Anglo-American tradition, is focused almost exclusively on normative issues. Whereas the original contract theorists used the contract idea to address questions of our political obligation to the state, contemporary contract theorists, following Rawls, only use it to address questions of social justice. So how, one might ask, could white political philosophers possibly exclude race and racial justice as subjects, considering that racial *injustice* has been so central to the making of the modern world and to the creation of the United States in particular? The answer: through the simple expedient of concentrating on what has come to be called "ideal theory."

Ideal theory is not supposed to contrast with non-ideal theory as a moral outlook contrasts with an amoral, *realpolitik* outlook. Both ideal and non-ideal theory are concerned with justice, and so with the appeal to moral ideals. The contrast is that ideal theory asks what justice demands in a perfectly just society while non-ideal theory asks what justice demands in a society with a history of injustice. So non-ideal theory is concerned with corrective measures, with remedial or rectificatory justice.[23] Racial justice is pre-eminently a matter of non-ideal theory, of what corrective measures are called for to rectify a history of discrimination. So by the apparently innocuous methodological decision to focus on ideal theory, white political philosophers are immediately exempted from dealing with the legacy of white supremacy in our actual society. You do not need affirmative action—and you certainly do not need reparations—in a society where no race has been discriminated against in the first place. In fact, if the social constructionist position on race is correct and race is brought into existence through racializing processes linked with projects of exploitation (aboriginal expropriation, slavery, colonial rule), then a perfectly just society would be raceless! By a weird philosophical route, the "color-blindness" already endorsed by the white majority gains a perverse philosophical sanction. In a perfectly just society, race would not exist, so we do not (as white philosophers working in ideal theory) have to concern ourselves with matters of racial justice in our own society, where it does exist—just as the white citizenry increasingly insist that the surest way of bringing about a raceless society is to ignore race, and that those (largely people of color) who still claim to see race are themselves the real racists.

The absurd outcome is the marginalization of race in the work of white political philosophers across the spectrum, most strikingly in the Rawls industry. The person seen as the most important twentieth-century American political philosopher and theorist of social justice, and a fortiori the most important American contract theorist, had nothing to say about the remediation of racial injustice, so central to American society and history. His five major books (excluding the two lecture collections on the history of ethics and political philosophy)—*A Theory of Justice, Political Liberalism, Collected Papers, The Law of Peoples,* and *Justice as Fairness: A Restatement*—together total over 2,000 pages.[24] If one were to add together all their sentences on race and racism, one might get half a dozen pages, if that much. So the focus on ideal theory has had the effect of sidelining what is surely one of the most pressing and urgent of the "pressing and urgent matters" that Rawls conceded at the start of *A Theory of Justice*[25] should be most important for us: the analysis and remedying of racial injustice in the United States. The racial nature of the liberalism of Rawls and his commentators manifests itself not (of course) in racist characterizations of people of color but in a racial avoidance—an artifact of racial privilege—of injustices that do not negatively affect whites.

In sum, the seeming neutrality and universality of the mainstream contract is illusory. As it stands, it is really predicated on the white experience and generates, accordingly, a contractarian liberalism that is racially structured in its apparatus and assumptions. Deracializing this racial liberalism requires rethinking the actual contract and what social justice demands for its voiding. It forces us to move to non-ideal theory and to understand the role of race in the modernity for which the contract metaphor has seemed peculiarly appropriate.

DERACIALIZING RACIAL LIBERALISM

My suggestion is, then, that if we are going to continue to work within contract theory, we need to use a contract model that registers rather than obfuscates the non-ideal history of white oppression and racial exploitation: the domination contract.[26]

Adopting the Domination Contract as a Framework

Even in the liberal tradition, contract theory has long been criticized for its emphasis on agreement. David Hume pointed out long ago that, rather than popular consent, "conquest or usurpation, that is, in plain terms, force" was the origin of most "new governments"; his conclusion was that the metaphor of the contract should simply be abandoned.[27] Rousseau, on the other hand, had the brilliant idea of incorporating the radical critique of the contract into a subversive conception of the contract itself. In his *The Social Contract*, Rousseau maps an ideal polity.[28] But unlike any of the other classic contract theorists, he earlier distinguished, in *Discourse on the Origins of Inequality*, a non-ideal, manifestly unjust polity that also rests on a "contract," but one that "irreversibly destroyed natural freedom, forever fixed the Law of property and inequality, [and] transformed a skillful usurpation into an irrevocable right."[29] So this, for Rousseau, is the actual contract that creates political society and establishes the architecture of the world we live in: a class contract among the rich. Instead of including all persons as equal citizens, guaranteeing their rights and freedoms, this contract privileges the wealthy at the expense of the poor. It is an exclusionary contract, a contract of domination.

Rousseau can be seen as initiating an alternative, radical democratic strain in contract theory, one that seeks to expose the realities of domination behind the façade and ideology of liberal consensuality. He retains the two key insights captured by the contract metaphor, the constructed nature of the polity and the recognition of human moral equality, but he incorporates them into a more realistic narrative that shows how they are perverted. Some human beings come to dominate others, denying them the equality they enjoyed in the state of nature. Carole Pateman's *The Sexual Contract*, which analogously posits an intra-male agreement to subordinate women, can be read as applying Rousseau's innovation to gender relations.[30] Drawing on both Rousseau and Pateman, I in turn sought in my *The Racial Contract* to develop a comparable concept of an intra-white agreement that—through European expansionism, colonialism, white settlement, slavery, apartheid, and Jim Crow—shapes the modern world.[31] Whites "contract" to regard one another as moral equals who are superior to nonwhites and who create, accordingly, governments, legal systems, and economic structures that privilege them at the expense of people of color.

So in all three cases, the "contract" is an exclusionary one among a subset of the population rather than a universal and inclusive one. As such, it acknowledges what we all know to be true, that real-life societies are structured through and through by hierarchies of privilege and power. The concept of a domination contract captures better as a metaphor the patterns of socio-political exclusion characterizing actual modern polities and puts us in a better position for dealing with the important normative questions of social justice. Rather than a fictitious universal inclusion and a mythical moral and political egalitarianism, this revisionist contract expresses the reality of group domination and social hierarchy. So by contrast with an ideal-theory framework, the domination contract is firmly located on the terrain of non-ideal theory. Not only does it point us toward the structures of injustice that need to be eliminated, unlike the evasive ideal mainstream contract, but it also recognizes their link with group privilege and group causality. These structures did not just happen to come into existence; rather, they were brought into being and are maintained by the actions and inactions of those privileged by them.

For the idealization that characterizes mainstream liberalism is descriptive as well as normative, extending to matters of fact as well as varieties of justice. It is not only that the focus is on a perfectly just society but also that the picture of our own society is carefully sanitized. The contract in its contemporary incarnation does not, of course, have the social-scientific pretensions—the contract as ur-sociology or anthropology—of (at least some variants of) the original. Yet I would claim that even in its modern version some of the key factual assumptions of the original contract still remain. It is not—the standard reply—just a necessary disciplinary abstraction, one that goes with the conceptual territory of philosophy, but rather, in the phrase of Onora O'Neill, an *idealizing* abstraction, one that abstracts away from social oppression.[32] And in this case it is a white abstraction.

Consider Rawls. He says we should think of society as a "cooperative venture for mutual advantage" governed by rules "designed to advance the good of those taking part in it."[33] But Rawls is a citizen of the United States, a nation founded on African slavery, aboriginal expropriation, and genocide. How could this possibly be an appropriate way to think of the nation's origins? Only through a massive and willful ignoring of the actual history, an ignoring that is psychologically and cognitively most feasible for the white population.

When I make this criticism, I am standardly accused of confusing the normative with the descriptive. Rawls, I am told, obviously meant that we should think of an *ideal* society as "a cooperative venture for mutual advantage." But Thomas Pogge and Samuel Freeman, both prominent Rawls scholars and former Rawls students, seem to endorse this reading themselves.

Pogge writes: "This [Rawlsian] explication [of society] seems narrow, for there are surely many historical societies (standardly so-called) whose rules fail . . . to be designed for mutual advantage," adding in a footnote "I think Rawls is here defining what a society *is*," not "what a society ought to be."[34] Freeman agrees, stating in his massive *Rawls*, "Basically [Rawls] conceives of society in terms of social cooperation, which he regards as productive and mutually beneficial, and which involves an idea of reciprocity or fair terms," and noting in his later glossary "Rawls regards society as a fair system of social cooperation."[35] Moreover, if Rawls means an ideal society, then how could there be further conceptual room for his later category of a "well-ordered society?" Wouldn't this be *already* subsumed under the ideal? And what could he mean by going on to say on the next page, as he does, "Existing societies are of course seldom well-ordered in this sense"?[36] This is a statement about *actual* societies, not ideal societies (which presumably have no real-life exemplars on the planet). So what Rawls seems to think is that societies in general—or perhaps modern Western societies, given the retreat in scope of his later work—*are* cooperative ventures, even if few are well-ordered—a view with no basis in reality, given the long history of social oppression of various kinds even in Western nations, and a conception particularly inappropriate for the origins of the United States.

Or consider Nozick. He begins his book with chapters reconstructing how, through the voluntary creation of what he calls "protective associations" in the state of nature, a "dominant protective association" would eventually emerge through invisible-hand processes, which becomes the state.[37] He concedes, of course, that things did not actually happen this way but claims that as a "potential explanation," the account is still valuable, even if it is "law-defective" and "fact-defective"(!): "State-of-nature explanations of the political realm *are* fundamental potential explanations of this realm and pack explanatory punch and illumination, even if incorrect. We learn much by seeing how the state could have arisen, even if it didn't arise that way."[38] But what do we learn from such reality-defective hypothetical accounts that could be relevant to determining racial social justice in the United States? How does a reconstruction of how the US state did *not* arise assist us in making normative judgments about how it actually *did* arise, especially when—although Nozick is the justice theorist most famous for advancing "historical" rather than "end-state" principles of social justice—its real-life origins in expropriative white settlement are never discussed?

In the US context, these assumptions and conceptual devices—the state of nature as empty of aboriginal peoples, society as non-exploitative and consensually and cooperatively founded, the political state supposedly illuminatingly conceived of as arising through the actions of an invisible hand—are unavoidably an abstraction from the European and

Euro-American experience of modernity. It is a distinctively white (not colorless) abstraction away from Native American expropriation and African
slavery and from the role of the state in facilitating both. It is in effect—
though at the rarefied and stratospheric level of philosophy—a conceptualization ultimately grounded in and apposite for the experience of white
settlerdom. Making racial socio-political oppression methodologically central would put us on very different theoretical terrain from the start.

The domination contract, here as the racial contract, thus provides a
way of translating into a mainstream liberal apparatus—social contract
theory—the egalitarian agenda and concerns of political progressives. It
offers a competing metaphor that more accurately represents the creation
and maintenance of the socio-political order. The white privilege that is systematically obfuscated in the mainstream contract is here nakedly revealed.
And the biasing of liberal abstractions by the concrete interests of the privileged (here, whites) then becomes transparent. It is immediately made
unmysterious why liberal norms and ideals that seem so attractive in the
abstract—freedom, equality, rights, justice—have proved unsatisfactory,
refractory, in practice and failed to serve the interests of people of color.
But the appropriate reaction is not (or so I would claim anyway) to reject
these liberal ideals but rather to reject the mystified individualist social
ontology that blocks an understanding of the political forces determining
the ideals' restricted and exclusionary application. The group ontology of
the domination contract better maps the underlying metaphysics of the
socio-political order.

So if the actual contract has been a racial one, what are the implications
for liberal theory, specifically for the desirable project of deracializing racial
liberalism? What rethinkings and revisions of seemingly colorless, but actually white, contractarian liberalism would be necessary?

Recovering the Past: Factually, Conceptually, Theoretically

To begin with, it would be necessary to recover the past, not merely factually but conceptually and theoretically, in terms of how we conceive of and
theorize the polity. The idealizing white cognitive patterns of racial liberalism manifest themselves in a whitewashing not merely of the facts but
also of their organizing conceptual and theoretical political frameworks.
The contractarian ideal is classically social transparency, in keeping with a
Kantian tradition of a *Rechtsstaat* that scorns behind-the-scenes *realpolitik*
for ethical transactions that can stand up to the light of day. But the centrality of racial subordination to the creation of the modern world is too

explosive to be subjected to such scrutiny and so has to be retroactively edited out of national (and Western) memory because of its contradiction of the overarching contract myth that the impartial state was consensually created by reciprocally respecting rights-bearing persons.

For the reality is, as David Theo Goldberg argues in his book *The Racial State*, that modern states in general are racialized: "race is integral to the emergence, development, and transformations (conceptually, philosophically, materially) of the modern nation-state."[39] What should have been a *Rechtsstaat* is actually a *Rassenstaat*, and the citizenry are demarcated in civic status by their racial membership. The modern world order, what Paul Keal calls "international society," is created by European expansionism, and the conquest and expropriation of indigenous peoples is central to that process: "non-Europeans were progressively conceptualized in ways that dehumanized them and enabled their dispossession and subordination."[40] So race as a global structure of privilege and subordination, normative entitlement and normative exclusion, is inextricably tied up with the development of the modern societies for which the contract is supposed to be an appropriate metaphor, whether in the colonized world or the colonizing mother countries. A model predicated on the (past or present) universal inclusion of colorless atomic individuals will therefore get things fundamentally wrong from the start. Races in relations of domination and subordination centrally constitute the social ontology. In their failure to admit this historical truth, in their refusal to acknowledge (or even consider) the accuracy of the alternative political characterization of *white supremacy*, mainstream contractarians reject social transparency for a principled social opacity not merely at the perceptual but at the conceptual and theoretical levels.

If this is an obvious general reality that contemporary white Western contract theorists have ignored in their theorizing, it is a truth particularly salient in the United States (and its denial here is, correspondingly, particularly culpable). For, in the historian George Fredrickson's judgment, "more than the other multi-racial societies resulting from the 'expansion of Europe'" the United States (along with apartheid South Africa) can be seen as "a kind of *Herrenvolk* society in which people of color . . . are treated as permanent aliens or outsiders."[41]

The distinctive and peculiar nature of the founding of the American New World in comparison to the origins of the Old World European powers cuts both ways for the contract image. The youth of the United States as a nation, its creation in the modern period, and the formal and extensively documented establishment of the Constitution and the other institutions of the new polity have made the social contract metaphor seem particularly apt here. Indeed, it might seem that it comes close to leaving the metaphoric for the literal, especially given that the terrain of this founding was conceptualized as a "wilderness," "Indian country," a "state of nature" only redeemed by a civilizing and Christianizing European presence. But if the general metaphor of a social contract comes closest to being non-metaphoric here, so does the competing metaphor of a racial contract because of the explicit and formal dichotomy of Anglo racial exclusion, more clear-cut and uncompromising than racial exclusion in, say, the Iberian colonies of the Americas, where *mestizaje* was the norm. The opposition between white and nonwhite has been foundational to the workings of American social and political institutions. (The United States Congress made whiteness a prerequisite for naturalization in 1790, and social and juridical whiteness has been crucial to moral, civic, and political status.) As Matthew Frye Jacobson points out:

> In the colonies the designation "white" appeared in laws governing who could marry whom; who could participate in the militia; who could vote or hold office; and in laws governing contracts, indenture, and enslavement. Although there were some exceptions, most laws of this kind delineated the populace along lines of color, and the word "white" was commonly used in conferring rights, never abridging them.... [W]hat a citizen really was, at bottom, was someone who could help put down a slave rebellion or participate in Indian wars.[42]

Similarly, Judith Shklar writes that citizenship in the United States has depended on "social standing" and that the standing of white males as citizens was defined "very negatively, by distinguishing themselves from their inferiors.... [B]lack chattel slavery stood at the opposite social pole from full citizenship and so defined it."[43]

This historical reality is completely obfuscated in the myth of an all-inclusive contract creating a socio-political order presided over by a neutral state equally responsive to all its colorless citizens. Far from being neutral, the law and the state were part of the racial polity's apparatus of subordination, codifying whiteness and enforcing racial privilege.[44] Native peoples were expropriated through what Lindsay Robertson calls "conquest by law," the "discovery doctrine," as enshrined in the 1823 Supreme Court decision *Johnson v. M'Intosh*: "Discovery converted the indigenous owners of discovered lands into tenants on those lands.... Throughout the United States, the American political descendants of these [European] discovering sovereigns overnight became owners of land that had previously belonged to Native Americans."[45] Blacks were enslaved in the South and racially stigmatized in the North, where they had a lesser schedule of rights—indeed, according to the 1857 *Dred Scott* decision, "no rights which the white man was bound to respect." Despite the passage of the Thirteenth, Fourteenth, and Fifteenth Amendments, post-bellum abolition did not lead to juridical

and moral equalization because the withdrawal of federal troops following the Hayes-Tilden compromise of 1877 restored southern blacks to the
mercies of their former owners, and formal segregation was given federal
sanction through the 1896 *Plessy v. Ferguson* decision, not to be overturned
until 1954 with *Brown v. Board of Education.*[46] Discriminatory legislation
codified the inferior legal status of people of color; the state functioned as
a racial state, enforcing segregation in federal bureaucracies, prisons, and
the army;[47] and national narratives and dominant white moral psychology
took white superiority for granted. As the black trade union leader A. Philip
Randolph put it in 1943, "The Negroes are in the position of having to fight
their own Government."[48] In effect, the United States was "subnationally a
divided polity,"[49] in which blacks were separate and manifestly unequal, a
despised and ostracized race.

Nor has the racial progress of the last six decades eliminated the racial
nature of the polity. The civil rights victories of the 1950s and 1960s—
Brown in 1954, the 1964 Civil Rights Act, the 1965 Voting Rights Act, the
1967 *Loving v. Virginia* decision that finally judged anti-miscegenation law
(still on the books in sixteen states) unconstitutional, the 1968 Fair Housing
Act—raised hopes of a second Reconstruction more successful than the
first one, but have not lived up to their promise because de facto discrimination has survived the repeal of de jure discrimination, as whites have
devised various new strategies for circumventing anti-discrimination law
(where it still exists and is enforced anymore). Thus Eduardo Bonilla-Silva
speaks sardonically of "color-blind racism" and "racism without racists."[50]
The 2014 celebrations of the sixtieth anniversary of the *Brown* decision
were rendered somewhat hollow by the reality that many schools today are
more segregated than they were at the time of the decision.[51] Nearly half a
century after the passage of the Fair Housing Act, residential segregation in
big cities with large black populations is virtually unchanged.[52] The failure
of the 1965 Voting Rights Act to prevent widespread disenfranchisement
of blacks has not merely local but sometimes national repercussions (e.g.,
black exclusion in Florida making the 2000 Republican victory possible),
and the act has yet to produce black political representation in proportion
to African Americans' numbers in the population. Its crucial weakening by
the 2013 Supreme Court *Shelby v. Holder* decision can only exacerbate these
problems. Affirmative action is basically dead, most whites regarding it as
unfair "reverse discrimination." The disproportionately black and Latino
"underclass" has been written off as an insoluble problem. Only 13 percent
of the population nationally, blacks are now 40 percent of those imprisoned.[53] The Sentencing Project's 2013 report to the United Nations says
that "if current trends continue, one of every three black American males
born today can expect to go to prison in his lifetime, as can one of every six

Latino males—compared to one of every seventeen white males."[54] Some authors have argued despairingly that racism should be seen as a permanent feature of the United States,[55] while others have suggested that substantive racial progress in US history has been confined narrowly to three periods, the Revolutionary War, the Civil War, and the Cold War, requiring the triple condition of war mobilization, elite intervention, and an effective mass protest movement, an "unsteady march" always punctuated by periods of backlash and retreat, such as the one we are living in now.[56] So though progress has obviously been made in comparison to the past, the appropriate benchmark should not be the very low bar of emancipation from slavery and the formal repeal of Jim Crow but the simple ideal of racial equality.

Unsurprisingly, then, people of color, and black American intellectuals in particular, have historically had little difficulty in recognizing the centrality of race to the American polity and the racial nature of American liberalism. No material or ideological blinders have prevented blacks and other people of color from seeing that the actual contract is most illuminatingly conceptualized as a racial one that systematically privileges whites at the expense of nonwhites:

> Indeed, with the exception of black conservatism, all black ideologies contest the view that democracy in America, while flawed, is fundamentally good. . . . A central theme within black political thought has been . . . to insist that the question of *racial* injustice is a central problematic in *American* political thought and practice, not a minor problem that can be dismissed in parentheses or footnotes.[57]

But such dismissal is (as earlier documented) precisely what occurs descriptively and prescriptively in the racial liberalism of contemporary white contractarians. If the racial subordination of people of color was matter-of-fact and taken for granted by racial liberalism in its original, overtly racist incarnation, it can no longer be admitted by racial liberalism in its present race-evading and calculatedly amnesiac incarnation. The atrocities of the past now being an embarrassment, they must be denied, minimized, or simply conceptually bypassed. A cultivated forgetfulness, a set of constructed deafnesses and blindnesses, characterizes racial liberalism: subjects one cannot raise, issues one cannot broach, topics one cannot explore. The contractarian ideal of social transparency about present and past would, if implemented, make it impossible to continue as before: one would see and know too much. Instead, the European colonizing powers and the white settler states they created are paradigms of what Stanley Cohen calls "states of denial," where the great crimes of native genocide and African slavery, and their deep imbrication with the everyday life of the polity, are erased from national memory and consciousness: "Whole societies have unmentioned and unmentionable rules about what should not be openly talked about."[58] Rogers Smith's *Civic Ideals* documents the consistency with which theorists of American political culture, including such leading figures as Alexis de Tocqueville, Gunnar Myrdal, and Louis Hartz, have represented it as essentially egalitarian and inclusive, placing racism and racial oppression in the categories of the anomalous and deviant—a perfect correlate at the more empirical level of political science of the evasions of political philosophy.[59]

The repudiation of racial liberalism will thus require more than a confrontation with the actual historical record. It will also require an acknowledgment at the conceptual and theoretical levels that this record shows that the workings of such a polity are not to be grasped with the orthodox categories of raceless liberal democracy. Rather, the conceptual innovation called for is a recognition of white supremacy as itself a political system— a "white republic" (Saxton), a "white-supremacist state" (Fredrickson), "a racial order" (King and Smith), a "racial polity" (Mills)—and of races themselves as political entities and agents.[60] Racial liberalism's facial racelessness is in fact its racedness; deracializing racial liberalism requires us to color in the blanks.

Recognizing the Reality and Centrality of Racial Exploitation

Finally, since contemporary political philosophy is centered on normative issues, we need to look at the implications of deracializing racial liberalism for social justice. The moral appeal of the social contract is supposed to be its fairness, not merely in contrast to pre-modern hierarchies, but, as emphasized at the start, against possible modern utilitarian abuses, the maximizing of well-being for some at the expense of others. As such, the social contract is supposed to prohibit exploitation, since the terms on which people create and enter society impose moral constraints on the realization of personal advantage. That is why the Marxist claim that liberal capitalism is *intrinsically* exploitative (quite apart from questions of low wages and poor working conditions) has always been so deeply threatening to liberal contract pretensions to be establishing a just society and why the labor theory of value (now widely seen as refuted) is so subversive in its implications.

It is noteworthy, then, that in the two texts that originally staked out the boundaries of respectable left- and right-wing liberalism in contemporary American political philosophy, Rawls's *A Theory of Justice* and Nozick's *Anarchy, State, and Utopia*, both authors loudly proclaim their fealty to Kantian prohibitions against an exploitative using of people, against treating others with less than equal Kantian respect.[61] Rawls outlines a left-liberal or social democratic vision of an ideal polity ("justice as fairness") in which educational resources and transfer payments from the state to the worst-off are supposed to ensure as far as possible that opportunities are expanded and class disadvantage minimized for the poorest, so that they are not exploited by those better off. Nozick develops a competing libertarian ideal ("entitlement theory") in which Kantian principles are interpreted through the prism of Lockean self-ownership, and respect for the property rights of others is the overriding principle of justice. In this framework, Rawlsian transfer payments and the idea of a fraternal sharing of natural assets constitute the real exploitation, since the more talented and productive are being sacrificed, used—against Kantian principles—for the benefit of the feckless and irresponsible. Hardworking individuals whose own labor has made them what they are and produced what they have, in fair competition for opportunities open to all, are taken advantage of, exploited, by those who simply do not want to work.

Forty years later the debate continues, but the outcome is clear. Rawls may have won the battle in the left-leaning academy, insofar as *A Theory of Justice* is now canonized as the most important work in twentieth-century political philosophy. But Nozickian-Friedmanist-Hayekian ideas won the war in the larger society, and indeed the world, given the triumph of anti-statism in the West since the Reagan and Thatcher revolutions of the 1980s, the 1989–91 collapse of state-commandist socialism, and the general global shift away from Keynesian state-interventionist policies and toward neo-liberalism.[62] Yet what needs to be emphasized for our purposes is that, though at opposite ends of the liberal spectrum, Rawls and Nozick both take for granted as constraining norms the equal, rights-bearing personhood of the members of the polity and the imperative of respect for them. This is not at all in dispute. So the debate centers not on these (supposedly) uncontroversial liberal shibboleths but rather on how "respect" and "using" are best thought of in a polity of equal contractors. And at the less rarefied level of public policy debates in the United States and elsewhere, the key opposing positions in part recapitulate these traditional left-right differences in liberal theory and the enduring controversies in this framework over the most defensible account of fairness, rights, entitlement, and justice.

But neither Rawls nor Nozick deals with *racial* exploitation, which radically upends this egalitarian, individualist picture, can be formulated independently of the labor theory of value, and in its blatant transgression of norms of equal treatment clearly represents ("clearly," that is, for non-racial liberalism) a massive violation of liberal contractarian ideals in whatever version, left or right.[63] To a large extent, as earlier emphasized, this is because by transplanting without modification onto American soil the European contract apparatus, both theorists in effect take up the perspective of the white settler population. Nozick's self-confessedly counterfactual account of how a state could have arisen from a state of nature and Rawls's hypothetical consensual contract both completely exclude the perspective of indigenous peoples. (Even when, in the last decade of his life, Rawls concedes that race and ethnicity raise "new problems," he only refers to blacks.[64] Native Americans and their possible claims for justice are eliminated as thoroughly from the idealizing contract apparatus as they were eliminated in reality.) Carole Pateman points out that "much contemporary political theory obliterates any discussion of embarrassing origins; argument proceeds from 'an abstract starting point . . . that had nothing to do with the way these societies were founded.'"[65] In effect, Rawls and Nozick assume *terra nullius*, ignoring the genocide and expropriation of native peoples.

Yet as Thomas Borstelmann reminds us, "White appropriation of black labor and red land formed two of the fundamental contours of the new nation's development and its primary sources of wealth."[66] Whites as a group have benefited immensely from the taking of native territory. The unpaid labor of African slavery provided another huge contribution to white welfare, not just to the slave owners themselves but as a surplus diffused within the economy. And as numerous commentators have pointed out in recent years, the cumulative result of the century and a half of discriminatory practices following emancipation has been to give whites vastly better access to education, jobs, bank loans, housing, and transfer payments from the state.

> Jim Crow was a system that institutionalized categorical inequality between blacks and whites at every level in southern society, with exploitation and opportunity hoarding built into virtually every social, economic, and political interaction between the races. . . . [In the North] it was just as effective . . . [but] constructed under private rather than public auspices.[67]

The distribution of resources is heavily racialized, the key differentials increasingly recognized to be manifested more in wealth than income.[68] And as mentioned in the opening interview, the wealth gaps remain huge: sixteen-to-one for the ratio of median white to median black households and thirteen-to-one for median white to median Latino households— a result of racial disparities in homeownership, college graduation rates, and access to the labor market.[69]

In contrast to the Lockean-Nozickian ideal of a polity of self-owning proprietors respecting one another's property rights, then, and in contrast to the Kantian-Rawlsian ideal of a polity of reciprocally respecting persons fraternally linked by their recognition of the moral arbitrariness of their natural assets, the actual polity is one in which the property rights of non-self-owning people of color are systematically violated and rights, liberties, opportunities, income, and wealth are continually being transferred from the nonwhite to the white population without any recognition of the pervasiveness and illegitimacy of these processes. If in Nozick's and Rawls's ideal contractarian polities exploitation is nowhere to be found, in the actual racial-contractarian polity in which Nozick and Rawls wrote their books it is everywhere, central, and ongoing. And, to repeat, this is exploitation in a sense that (non-racial) liberals would have to (or should have to) admit, resting on standard (deracialized) Lockean-Kantian norms about equitable treatment, fair wages, respect for property rights, and prohibitions against using people.[70] Racial exploitation is the background constant against which other debates take place, sometimes mitigated but never eliminated, because racial exploitation is part of the contract itself.

So a racialized moral economy complements a racialized political economy, in which whites do not recognize their privileging *as* privileging, as differential and unfair treatment. To differing extents, both Rawls and Nozick appeal to our moral intuitions about fairness and what people are entitled to. But neither looks at the way race shapes whites' sense of what is just. Yet an understanding of the contours of white moral psychology is an indispensable prerequisite for comprehending the typical framing and trajectory of public policy debates. Their "favored status has meant that whites are commonly accepted as the 'normal' and norm-setting."[71] Rawls's left-liberal ethico-metaphysical notion that we should regard the distribution of our natural assets as pooled found no resonance in the famously individualist United States. But there is a sense, underpinning the "reasonable" expectations of the representative white person, in which whites have traditionally thought of nonwhite assets as a common white resource to be legitimately exploited. Originally, whites saw their systemic advantage as differential but fair, justified by their racial superiority. Now, in a different "color-blind" phase of the contract and of racial liberalism, they do not see it as differential at all, the long history and ongoing reality of exploitative nonwhite-to-white transfer being obfuscated and occluded by individualist categories and by a sense of property rights in which white entitlement is the norm.

In his research on the causes of the deepening racial inequality between whites and blacks, Thomas Shapiro found that "[white] family assets are more than mere money; they also provide a pathway for handing down racial legacies from generation to generation."[72] Since we are in the middle of the greatest intergenerational transfer of wealth in United States history, as first the parents of the baby boomers and then the boomers themselves die and pass on nine *trillion* dollars of assets to their children, these inequalities can only be exacerbated.[73] But in Shapiro's interviews with white families, they consistently deny or downplay this racial head start they get from the legacy of white supremacy:

> Many whites continue to reap advantages from the historical, institutional, structural, and personal dynamics of racial inequality, and they are either unaware of these advantages or deny they exist. . . . [T]heir insistence upon how hard they work and how much they deserve their station in life seems to trump any recognition that unearned successes and benefits come at a price for others.[74]

In Cheryl Harris's famous analysis, whiteness itself becomes "property," underwriting a set of baseline entitlements and "reasonable" expectations that are part of one's legitimate rights as a full citizen.[75] Unsurprisingly, then, few public policy proposals so unite whites in opposition as the idea of reparations: a 2000 public opinion poll showed that no less than 96 percent of whites were hostile to the idea.[76] And by the standards and norms of racial liberalism, they are justified in their scorn of such a proposal, which would represent a contractual violation of the founding principles of the polity.

CONCLUSION

Race and liberalism have been intertwined for hundreds of years, for the same developments of modernity that brought liberalism into existence as a supposedly general set of political norms also brought race into existence as a set of restrictions and entitlements governing the application of those norms. Political theorists, whether in political science or political philosophy, have a potentially valuable role to play in contributing to the dismantling of this pernicious symbiotic normative system. But such a dismantling cannot be achieved through a supposed color-blindness which is really a blindness to the historical and enduring whiteness of liberalism. Racial liberalism, established by the racial contract, must be recognized for what it is before the promise of a non-racial liberalism and a genuinely inclusive social contract can ever be fulfilled.

CHAPTER 4
White Ignorance

White ignorance...
It's a big subject. How much time do you have?
It's not enough.

Ignorance is usually thought of as the passive obverse to knowledge, the darkness retreating before the spread of Enlightenment.
But ...
Imagine an ignorance that resists.
Imagine an ignorance that fights back.
Imagine an ignorance militant, aggressive, not to be intimidated, an ignorance that is active, dynamic, that refuses to go quietly—not at all confined to the illiterate and uneducated but propagated at the highest levels of the land, indeed presenting itself unblushingly as knowledge. ...

Classically individualist, indeed sometimes—self-parodically—to the verge of solipsism, blithely indifferent to the possible cognitive consequences of class, racial, or gender situatedness (or, perhaps more accurately, taking a propertied white male standpoint as given), modern mainstream Anglo-American epistemology was for hundreds of years from its Cartesian origins profoundly inimical terrain for the development of any concept of structural group-based miscognition. The paradigm exemplars of phenomena likely to foster mistaken belief—optical illusions, hallucinations, phantom limbs, dreams—were by their very banality universal to the human condition, and the epistemic remedies prescribed—for example, rejecting all but the indubitable—were correspondingly abstract and general. Nineteenth-century Marxism, with its theoretical insistence on locating the individual agent and the individual cognizer in group (basically class) structures of domination, and its concepts of ideology, fetishism, societal "appearance," and divergent group (basically class) perspectives on the social order, offered a potential corrective to this epistemological individualism. But to the extent that there was a mainstream twentieth-century appropriation of these ideas, in the form of *Wissenssoziologie*, the sociology of knowledge, it drew its genealogy from Karl Mannheim rather than Karl Marx, was frequently (despite terminological hedges such as Mannheim's "relationism") relativistic, and was in any case confined to sociology.[1] So though some figures, such as Max Scheler and Mannheim himself, explicitly argued for the epistemological implications of their work, these claims were not engaged with by philosophers in the analytic tradition. A seemingly straightforward and clear-cut division of conceptual and disciplinary labor was presumed: descriptive issues of recording and explaining what and why people actually believed could be delegated to sociology, but evaluative issues of articulating cognitive norms would be reserved for (individualist) epistemology, which was philosophical territory.

But though mainstream philosophy and analytic epistemology continued to develop in splendid isolation for many decades, W. V. O. Quine's naturalizing of epistemology would initiate a sequence of events with unsuspectedly subversive long-term theoretical repercussions for the field.[2] If articulating the norms for *ideal* cognition required taking into account (in some way) the practices of *actual* cognition, if the prescriptive needed to pay attention (in some way) to the descriptive, then on what principled basis could cognitive realities of a *supra*-individual kind continue to be excluded from the ambit of epistemology? For it then meant that the cognitive agent needed to be located in her specificity—as a member of certain social groups, within a given social milieu, in a society at a particular time period. Whatever Quine's own sympathies (or lack thereof), his work had opened Pandora's box. A naturalized epistemology had, perforce, also to be a socialized epistemology; this was "a straightforward extension of the naturalistic approach."[3] What had originally been a specifically Marxist concept, "standpoint theory," was adopted and developed to its most sophisticated form in the work of feminist theorists,[4] and it became possible for books with titles like *Social Epistemology* and *Socializing Epistemology*, and journals called *Social Epistemology*, to be published and seen as a legitimate part of philosophy.[5] The Marxist challenge thrown down a century before could now finally be taken up.

Obviously, then, for those interested in pursuing such questions this is a far more welcoming environment than that of a few decades ago. Nonetheless, I think it is obvious that the *potential* of these developments for transforming mainstream epistemology is far from being fully realized. And at least one major reason for this failure is that the conceptions of society in the literature too often presuppose a degree of consent and inclusion that does not exist outside the imagination of mainstream scholars—in a sense, a societal population essentially generated by simple iteration of that originally solitary Cartesian cognizer. As Linda Martín Alcoff has ironically observed, the "society" about which these philosophers are writing often seems to be composed exclusively of white males, so that one wonders how it reproduces itself.[6] The Marxist critique is seemingly discredited, the feminist critique is marginalized, and the racial critique does not even exist. The concepts of domination, hegemony, ideology, mystification, exploitation, and so on that are part of the lingua franca of radicals find little or no place here.[7] In particular, the analysis of the implications for social cognition of the legacy of white supremacy has barely been initiated. The sole reference to race that I could find in the Schmitt collection, for example, was a single cautious sentence by Philip Kitcher, which I here reproduce in full: "Membership of a particular ethnic group within a particular society may interfere with one's ability to acquire true beliefs about the distribution of characteristics that are believed to be important to human worth (witness the history of nineteenth-century craniometry)."[8]

What I want to do in this chapter is to sketch out some of the features and the dynamic of what I see as a particularly pervasive—though hardly theorized—form of ignorance, what could be called white ignorance, linked to white supremacy. (So the chapter is an elaboration of one of the key themes of my 1997 book, *The Racial Contract*.[9]) The idea of group-based cognitive handicap is not an alien one to the radical tradition, if not normally couched in terms of "ignorance." Indeed, it is, on the contrary, a straightforward corollary of standpoint theory: if one group is privileged, after all, it must be by comparison with another group that is handicapped. In addition, the term has for me the virtue of signaling my theoretical sympathies with what I know will seem to many a deplorably old-fashioned, "conservative" realist intellectual framework, one in which *truth, falsity, facts, reality*, and so forth are not enclosed with ironic scarequotes. The phrase "white ignorance" implies the possibility of a contrasting "knowledge," a contrast that would be lost if all claims to truth were equally spurious, or just a matter of competing discourses. In the same way that *The Racial Contract* was not meant as a trashing of contractarianism as such but rather the critique of a contractarianism that ignored racial subordination, so similarly, mapping an epistemology of ignorance is for me a preliminary to reformulating an epistemology that will give us genuine knowledge.

The meta-theoretical approach I find most congenial is that outlined by Alvin Goldman in his book *Knowledge in a Social World*.[10] Goldman describes his project as "an essay in social veritistic epistemology," oriented "toward truth determination," as against contemporary post-structuralist or Kuhn/Feyerabend/Bloor/Barnes-inspired approaches that relativize truth.[11] So though the focus is social rather than individual, the traditional concerns and assumptions of mainstream epistemology have been retained:

> Traditional epistemology, especially in the Cartesian tradition, was highly individualistic, focusing on mental operations of cognitive agents in isolation or abstraction from other persons. ... [This] individual epistemology needs a social counterpart: *social epistemology*. ... In what respects is social epistemology social? First, it focuses on social paths or routes to knowledge. That is, considering believers taken one at a time, it looks at the many routes to belief that feature interactions with other agents, as contrasted with private or asocial routes to belief acquisition. ... Second, social epistemology does not restrict itself to believers taken singly. It often focuses on some sort of group entity ... and examines the spread of information or misinformation across that group's membership. Rather than concentrate on a single knower, as did Cartesian epistemology, it addresses the distribution of knowledge or error within the larger social cluster. ... Veritistic epistemology (whether individual or social) is concerned with the production of knowledge, where knowledge is here understood in the "weak" sense of *true belief*. More precisely, it is concerned with both knowledge and its contraries: *error* (false belief) and *ignorance* (the absence of true belief). The main question for veritistic epistemology is: Which practices have a comparatively favorable impact on knowledge as contrasted with error and ignorance? Individual veritistic epistemology asks this question for nonsocial practices; social veritistic epistemology asks it for social practices.[12]

Unlike Goldman, I will use *ignorance* to cover both false belief and the absence of true belief. But with this minor terminological variation, this is basically the project I am trying to undertake: looking at the "spread of misinformation," the "distribution of error" (including the possibility of "massive error")[13] within the "larger social cluster," the "group entity," of whites, and the "social practices" (some "wholly pernicious")[14] that encourage it. Goldman makes glancing reference to some of the feminist and race literature (there is a grand total of a single index entry for *racism*), but in general, the implications of systemic social oppression for his project are not addressed. The picture of "society" he is working with is one that—with perhaps a few unfortunate exceptions—is inclusive and harmonious. Thus his account offers the equivalent in social epistemology of the mainstream theorizing in political science that frames American sexism and racism as "anomalies": US political culture is conceptualized as *essentially* egalitarian and inclusive, with the long actual history of systemic gender and racial subordination being relegated to the status of a minor "deviation" from the norm.[15] Obviously, such a starting point crucially handicaps any realistic social epistemology since in effect it turns things upside-down. Sexism and racism, patriarchy and white supremacy, have not been the *exception* but the *norm.* So though his book is valuable in terms of conceptual clarification and some illuminating discussions of particular topics, the basic framework is flawed insofar as it marginalizes domination and its consequences. A less naïve understanding of how society actually works requires drawing on the radical tradition of social theory, in which various factors he does not consider play a crucial role in obstructing the mission of veritistic epistemology.

FOLK RACIAL STANDPOINT THEORY

Let me turn now to race. As I pointed out in an article more than a quarter-century ago,[16] and as has unfortunately hardly changed since then, there is no academic philosophical literature on racial epistemology that remotely compares in volume to that on gender epistemology. (Race and gender are not, of course, mutually exclusive, but usually in gender theory it is the perspective of white women that is explored.) However, one needs to distinguish academic from lay treatments. I would suggest that "white ignorance" has, whether centrally or secondarily, been a theme of many of the classic fictional and non-fictional works of the African American experience, and also that of other people of color.

In his introduction to a collection of black writers' perspectives on whiteness, David Roediger underlines the fundamental epistemic *asymmetry* between typical white views of blacks and typical black views of whites: these are not cognizers linked by a reciprocal ignorance but rather groups whose respective privilege and subordination tend to produce self-deception, bad faith, evasion, and misrepresentation on the one hand and more veridical perceptions on the other.[17] Thus he cites the early twentieth-century black activist James Weldon Johnson's remark: "colored people of this country know and understand the white people better than the white people know and understand them."[18] Often for their very survival, blacks have been forced to become lay anthropologists studying the strange culture, customs, and mindset of the "white tribe" that has such frightening power over them that in certain time periods whites can even determine their life or death on a whim. (In particular circumstances, then, white ignorance may need to be actively *encouraged*. Hence the black American folk poem: "Got one mind for white folks to see / Another for what I know is me." Or in James Baldwin's brutally candid assessment: "I have spent most of my life, after all, watching white people and outwitting them, so that I might survive."[19]) For what people of color quickly come to see—in a sense the primary epistemic principle of the racialized social epistemology of which they are the object—is that they are not seen at all. Correspondingly, the "central metaphor" of W. E. B. Du Bois's *The Souls of Black Folk* is the image of the "veil,"[20] and the black American cognitive equivalent of the shocking moment of Cartesian realization of the uncertainty of everything one had taken to be knowledge is the moment when for Du Bois, as a child in New England, "it dawned upon me with a certain suddenness that I was different from the others; or like, mayhap, in heart and life and longing, but shut out from their [white] world by a vast veil."[21]

Similarly, Ralph Ellison's classic *Invisible Man*, generally regarded as the most important twentieth-century novel of the black experience, is arguably in key respects—while a multi-dimensional and multi-layered work of great depth and complexity, not to be reduced to a single theme—an *epistemological* novel.[22] For what it recounts is the protagonist's quest to determine what norms of belief are the right ones in a crazy looking-glass world where he is an invisible man "simply because [white] people refuse to see me. . . . When they approach me they see only my surroundings, themselves, or figments of their imagination—indeed, everything and anything except me." And this systematic misperception is not, of course, due to biology, the intrinsic properties of his epidermis, or physical deficiencies in the white eye, but rather to "the construction of their inner eyes, those eyes with which they look through their physical eyes upon reality."[23] The images of light and darkness, sight and blindness, that run through the novel, from the blindfolded black fighters in the grotesque battle royal at the start to the climactic discovery that the Brotherhood's (read: American Communist Party) leader has a glass eye, repeatedly raise, in context after context, the question of how one can demarcate what is genuine from only apparent insight, real from only apparent truth, even in the worldview of those whose historical materialist "science" supposedly gave them "super-vision."

Nor is it only black writers who have explored the theme of white ignorance. One of the consequences of the development of critical white studies has been a renewed appreciation of the pioneering work of Herman Melville, with *Moby-Dick* now being read by some critics as an early, nineteenth-century indictment of the national obsession with whiteness, Ahab's pathological determination to pursue the white whale regardless of its imperilment of his multi-racial crew.[24] But it is in the 1856 short novel *Benito Cereno*—used as the source of one of the two epigraphs to *Invisible Man* by Ellison—that one finds the most focused investigation of the unnerving possibilities of white blindness.[25] Boarding a slave ship—the *San Dominick*, a reference to the Haitian (Saint Domingue) Revolution—which, unknown to the protagonist, Amasa Delano, has been taken over by its human cargo, with the white crew being held hostage, Delano has all around him the evidence for black insurrection, from the terror in the eyes of the nominal white captain, the eponymous Benito Cereno, as his black barber Babo puts the razor to his throat, to the Africans clashing their hatchets ominously in the background. But so unthinkable is the idea that the inferior blacks could have accomplished such a thing that Delano searches for every possible alternative explanation for the seemingly strange behavior of the imprisoned whites, no matter how far-fetched. In Eric Sundquist's summary,

> Melville's account of the "enchantment" of Delano, then, is also a means to examine the mystifications by which slavery was maintained.... Minstrelsy—in effect, the complete show of the tale's action staged for Delano—is a product, as it were, of his mind, of his willingness to accept Babo's Sambo-like performance.... Paradoxically, Delano watches Babo's performance without ever seeing it.... Delano participates in a continued act of suppressed revolt against belief in the appearances presented to him.... [a] self-regulation by racist assumptions and blind "innocence."[26]

The white delusion of racial superiority insulates itself against refutation. Correspondingly, on the positive epistemic side, the route to black knowledge is the self-conscious recognition of white ignorance (including its blackfaced manifestation in black consciousness itself). Du Bois prescribes a critical cognitive distancing from "a world which yields [the Negro] no true self-consciousness, but only lets him see himself through the revelation of the other world," a "sense of always looking at one's self through the eyes of others."[27] The attainment of "second sight" requires an understanding of what it is about whites and the white situation that motivates them to view blacks erroneously. One learns in part to see through identifying white blindness and avoiding the pitfalls of putting on these spectacles for one's own vision.[28]

So this subject is by no means unexplored in white and black texts. But as noted, because of the whiteness of philosophy, very little has been done here.[29] (One exception is Lewis Gordon's work on bad faith, which is obviously relevant to this subject, though not itself set in a formal epistemological framework.)[30] In this chapter, accordingly, I want to gesture toward some useful directions for the mapping of white ignorance and developing, accordingly, epistemic criteria for minimizing it.

DEMARCATING "WHITE IGNORANCE"

What I want to pin down, then, is the idea of an ignorance, a non-knowing, that is not contingent, but in which race—white racism and/or white racial domination and their ramifications—plays a crucial causal role. So let me begin by trying to clarify and demarcate more precisely the phenomenon I am addressing, as well as answering some possible objections.

To begin with, *white ignorance* as a cognitive phenomenon has to be clearly historicized. I am taking for granted the truth of some variant of social constructivism, which denies that race is biological. So the causality in the mechanisms for generating and sustaining white ignorance on the macro-level is social-structural rather than physico-biological, though it will of course operate through the physico-biological. Assuming the growing consensus in critical race theory to be correct—that race in general, and whiteness in particular, is a product of the modern period[31]—then you could not have had white ignorance in this technical, term-of-art sense in, say, the ancient world because whites did not exist then. Certainly people existed who by today's standards would be counted as white, but they would not have been so categorized at the time, either by themselves or others, so there would have been no whiteness to play a causal role in their knowing or non-knowing.[32] Moreover, even in the modern period, whiteness would not have been universally, instantly, and homogeneously instantiated; there would have been (to borrow an image from another field of study) "uneven development" in the processes of racialization in different countries at different times. Indeed, even in the United States, in a sense the paradigm white supremacist state, Matthew Frye Jacobson argues for a periodization of whiteness into different epochs, with some European ethnic groups only becoming fully white at a comparatively late stage.[33]

Second, one would obviously need to distinguish what I am calling white ignorance from general patterns of ignorance prevalent among people who are white but in whose doxastic states race has played no determining role. For example, at all times (such as right now) there will be many facts about the natural and social worlds on which people, including white people, have no opinion, or a mistaken opinion, but race is not directly or indirectly responsible. For instance, the exact temperature in the earth's crust twenty miles down right now, the precise income distribution in the United States, and so forth. But we would not want to call this white ignorance, even when it is shared by whites, because race has not been responsible for these non-knowings; other factors have.

Third (complicating the foregoing), it needs to be realized that once indirect causation and diminishing degrees of influence are admitted, it will sometimes be very difficult to adjudicate when specific kinds of non-knowings are appropriately categorizable as white ignorance or not. Recourse to counterfactuals of greater or lesser distance from the actual situation may be necessary ("what they should and would have known if . . ."), whose evaluation may be too complex to be resolvable. Suppose, for example, that a particular true scientific generalization about human beings, *P*, would be easily discoverable in a society were it not for widespread white racism, and that with additional research in the appropriate areas, P could be shown to have further implications, Q, and beyond that, R. Or suppose that the practical application of P in medicine would have had as a spin-off empirical findings p_1, p_2, p_3. Should these related principles and these factual findings all be included as examples of white ignorance as well? How far onward up the chain? And so forth. So it will be easy to think up all kinds of tricky cases where it will be hard to make the determination. But the existence of such problematic cases at the borders does not undermine the import of more central cases.

Fourth, the racialized causality I am invoking needs to be expansive enough to include both straightforward racist motivation and more impersonal social-structural causation, which may be operative even if the cognizer in question is not racist. It is necessary to distinguish the two not merely as a logical point, because they are analytically separable, but because in empirical reality they may often be found independently of each other. You can have white racism in particular white cognizers, in the sense of the existence of prejudicial beliefs about people of color, without (at that time and place) white domination of those people of color having been established; and you can also have white domination of people of color at a particular time and place without all white cognizers at that time and place being racist. But in both cases, racialized causality can give rise to what I am calling white ignorance, straightforwardly for a racist cognizer but also indirectly for a non-racist cognizer who may form mistaken beliefs (e.g., that after the abolition of slavery in the United States, blacks generally had opportunities equal to whites) because of the social suppression of the pertinent knowledge, though without prejudice himself. So white ignorance need not always be based on bad faith. Obviously from the point of view of a social epistemology, especially after the transition from de jure to de facto white supremacy, it is precisely this kind of white ignorance that is most important.

Fifth, the "white" in "white ignorance" does not mean that it has to be confined to white people. Indeed, as the earlier Du Bois discussion emphasized, it will often be shared by nonwhites to a greater or lesser extent because of the power relations and patterns of ideological hegemony involved. (This is a familiar point from the Marxist and feminist traditions—working-class conservatives, "male-identified" women, endorsing right-wing and sexist ideologies against their interests.) Providing the causal route is appropriate, blacks can manifest white ignorance also.

Sixth, and somewhat different, *white* racial ignorance can produce a doxastic environment in which particular varieties of *black* racial ignorance flourish—so that racial causality is involved, but one would hesitate to subsume them under the category of white ignorance itself, at least without significant qualification. Think, for example, of "oppositional" African

American varieties of biological and theological determinism: whites as melanin-deficient and therefore inherently physiologically and psychologically flawed, or whites as "blue-eyed devils" created by the evil black scientist Yacub (as in early Black Muslim theology).[34] Insofar as these theories invert claims of white racial superiority, though still accepting racial hierarchy, they would seem to be deserving of a separate category, though obviously they have been shaped by key assumptions of "scientific" and theological white racism.

Seventh, though the examples I have given so far have all been factual ones, I want a concept of white ignorance broad enough to include moral ignorance—not merely ignorance of facts *with* moral implications but also moral non-knowings, incorrect judgments about the rights and wrongs of moral situations themselves. For me, the epistemic desideratum is that the naturalizing and socializing of epistemology should have, as a component, the naturalizing and socializing of *moral* epistemology also and the study of pervasive social patterns of mistaken *moral* cognition.[35] Thus the idea is that improvements in our cognitive practice should have a practical payoff in heightened sensitivity to social oppression and the attempt to reduce and ultimately eliminate that oppression.

Eighth, it presumably does not need to be emphasized that white ignorance is not the only kind of privileged-group-based ignorance. Male ignorance could be analyzed similarly, and clearly it has a far more ancient history and arguably a more deep-rooted ancestry in human inter-relations, insofar as it goes back thousands of years.[36] I am focusing on white ignorance because, as mentioned, it has been relatively undertheorized in the white academy compared to the work of feminist theorists on gender.

Ninth, speaking generally about white ignorance does not commit one to the claim that it is uniform across the white population. Whites are not a monolith, and if the analysis of white ignorance is to be part of a social epistemology, then the obvious needs to be remembered—that people have other identities beside racial ones, so that whites will be divisible by class, gender, nationality, religion, and so forth, and these factors will modify, by differential socialization and experience, the bodies of belief and the cognitive patterns of the sub-populations concerned. But this is, of course, true for all sociological generalizations, which has never been a reason for abandoning them, but one for employing them cautiously. White ignorance is not indefeasible (even if it sometimes seems that way!), and some people who are white will, because of their particular histories (and/or the intersection of whiteness with other identities), overcome it and have true beliefs on what their fellow-whites get wrong. So white ignorance is best thought of as a cognitive tendency—an inclination, a doxastic disposition—which is not insuperable. If there is a sociology of knowledge, then there should also be a sociology of ignorance.[37]

Tenth, and finally, the point of trying to understand white ignorance is, of course, *normative* and not merely sociological (hence the emphasis on the continuity with classic epistemology). The goal is to improve our cognitive practices by trying to reduce or eliminate white ignorance. In classic individualist epistemology, one seeks not merely to eliminate false belief but to develop an understanding, wariness, and avoidance of the cognitive processes that typically produce false belief. For a social epistemology, where the focus is on supra-individual processes and the individual's interaction with them, the aim is to understand how certain social structures tend to promote these crucially flawed processes, how to personally extricate oneself from them (insofar as that is possible), and how best to do one's part in undermining them in the broader cognitive sphere. So the idea is that there are typical ways of going wrong that need to be adverted to in the light of social structure and specific group characteristics, and one has a better chance of getting things right through a self-conscious recognition of their existence and corresponding self-distancing from them.

WHITENESS AND SOCIAL COGNITION

Let us turn now to the processes of cognition, individual and social, and the examination of the ways in which racial "whiteness" may affect some of their crucial components. As examples, I will look at perception, conception, memory, testimony, and motivational group interest (in a longer treatment, differential group experience should also be included). Separating out these various components is difficult because they are all constantly in interaction with one another. For example, when the individual cognizing agent is perceiving, he is doing so with eyes and ears that have been socialized. Perception is also in part conception, the viewing of the world through a particular conceptual grid. Inference from perception involves the overt or tacit appeal to memory, which will be not merely individual but also social. As such, it will be founded on testimony and ultimately on the perceptions and conceptions of others. The background knowledge that will guide inference and judgment, eliminating (putatively) absurd alternatives and narrowing down a set of plausible contenders, will also be shaped by testimony, or the lack thereof, and will itself be embedded in various conceptual frameworks and require perception and memory to access. Testimony will have been recorded, requiring again perception, conception, and memory; it will have been integrated into a particular framework and narrative; and from the start it will have involved the selection of certain voices as against others, selection in and selection out (if these others have been allowed to speak in the first place). At all levels, interests may shape cognition, influencing what and how we see, what we and society choose to remember, whose testimony is solicited and whose is not, and which facts and frameworks are sought out and accepted. Thus at any given stage, it is obvious that an interaction of great complexity is involved, in which multiple factors will be affecting one another in intricate feedback loops of various kinds. So an analytic separating-out of elements for purposes of conceptual isolation and clarification will necessarily be artificial, and in a sense each element so extracted leaves a ghostly trail of all the others in its wake.

Start with perception. A central theme of the epistemology of the past few decades has been the discrediting of the idea of a raw perceptual "given," completely unmediated by concepts. Perceptions are in general simultaneously conceptions, if only at a very low level of abstraction. Moreover, the social dimension of epistemology is obviously most salient here, since individuals do not in general make up these categories themselves but inherit them from their cultural milieu. As Kornblith says: "The influence of social factors begins at birth, for language is not reinvented by each individual in social isolation, nor could it be. Because language acquisition is socially mediated, the concepts we acquire are themselves socially mediated from the very beginning."[38] But this means that the conceptual array with which the cognizer approaches the world needs itself to be scrutinized for its adequacy to the world, for how well it maps the reality it claims to be describing. In addition, it is not a matter of monadic predicates, reciprocally isolated from one another, but concepts linked by interlocking assumptions and background belief-sets into certain complexes of ideation that by their very nature tend to put a certain interpretation on the world. So in most cases the concepts will not be neutral but oriented toward a certain understanding, embedded in sub-theories and larger theories about how things work.

In the orthodox left tradition, this set of issues is handled through the category of "ideology"; in more recent radical theory, through Foucault's "discourses." But whatever one's larger meta-theoretical sympathies, whatever approach one thinks best for investigating these ideational matters, such concerns obviously need to be part of a social epistemology. For if the society is one structured by relations of domination and subordination (as of course all societies in human history past the hunting-and-gathering stage have been), then in certain areas this conceptual apparatus is likely going to be negatively shaped and inflected in various ways by the biases of the ruling group(s). So crucial concepts may well be misleading in their inner makeup and their external relation to a larger doxastic architecture. Moreover, what cognitive psychology has revealed is that rather than continually challenging conceptual adequacy by the test of disconfirming empirical data, we tend to do the opposite—to interpret the data through the grid of the concepts in such a way that seemingly disconfirming, or at least problematic, perceptions are filtered out or marginalized. In other words, one will tend to find the confirmation in the world whether it is there or not.

Now apply this to race: consider the epistemic principle of what has come to be called "white normativity," the centering of the Euro- and later Euro-American reference group as constitutive norm. Ethnocentrism is, of course, a negative cognitive tendency common to all peoples, not just Europeans. But with Europe's gradual rise to global domination, the European variant becomes entrenched as an overarching, virtually unassailable framework, a conviction of exceptionalism and superiority that seems vindicated by the facts, and thenceforth, circularly, shaping perception of the facts. We rule the world because we are superior; we are superior because we rule the world. In the first essay of a posthumous book collection of his pioneering 1940s–1960s essays against Eurocentrism, world historian Marshall G. S. Hodgson invokes the "New Yorker's map of the United States," which—like Saul Steinberg's later and more famous March 29, 1976, *New Yorker* cover cartoon depiction of the "View of the World from 9th Avenue"—offers us the bizarrely foreshortened perspective on the country afforded from its self-nominated cultural center.[39] Hodgson argues that the standard geographical representations of Europe by Europeans, as in the Mercator projection world map, are not really that radically different:

> It would be a significant story in itself to trace how modern Westerners have managed to preserve some of the most characteristic features of their ethnocentric medieval image of the world. Recast in modern scientific and scholarly language, the image is still with us. . . . The point of any ethnocentric world image is to divide the world into moieties, ourselves and the others, ourselves forming the more important of the two. . . . We divide the world into what we call "continents.". . . Why is Europe one of the continents but not India?. . . . Europe is still ranked as one of the "continents" because our cultural ancestors lived there. By making it a "continent," we give it a rank disproportionate to its natural size, as a subordinate part of no larger unit, but in itself one of the major component parts of the world. . . . (I call such a world map the "Jim Crow projection" because it shows Europe as larger than Africa.). . . . [Mercator] confirms our predispositions.[40]

And this geographical misrepresentation and regional inflation have gone in tandem with a corresponding historical misrepresentation and inflation. Criticizing the standard historical categories of Western historians, Hodgson suggests that "the very terms we allow ourselves to use foster distortion." The "convenient result" is that Europe, an originally peripheral region of what Hodgson calls the "Afro-Eurasian historical complex," is lifted out of its context and elevated into a self-creating entity unto itself, "an independent division of the whole world, with a history that need not be integrated with that of the rest of mankind save on the terms posed by European history itself."[41]

From this fatally skewed optic, of course, stem all those theories of innate European superiority to the rest of the world that are still with us today but in modified and subtler versions. Whiteness is originally coextensive with full humanity so that the nonwhite Other is grasped through a historic array of concepts whose common denominator is their subjects' location on a lower ontological and moral rung.

Consider, for example, the category of the "savage" and its conceptual role in the justification of imperialism. As Francis Jennings points out, the word was "created for the purposes of conquest rather than the purposes of knowledge." "Savagery" and "civilization" were "reciprocals," "both independent of any necessary correlation with empirical reality." The conceptual outcome was a "conjoined myth" that "greatly distorted [white] Americans' perceptions of reality," necessarily involving "the suppression of facts."[42] In effect,

> the Englishman devised the savage's form to fit his function. The word *savage* thus underwent considerable alteration of meaning as different colonists pursued their varied ends. One aspect of the term remained constant, however: the savage was always inferior to civilized men. . . . The constant of Indian inferiority implied the rejection of his humanity and determined the limits permitted for his participation in the mixing of cultures. The savage was prey, cattle, pet, or vermin—he was never citizen. Upholders of the myth denied that either savage tyranny or savage anarchy could rightfully be called government, and therefore there could be no justification for Indian resistance to European invasion.[43]

When Thomas Jefferson excoriates the "merciless Indian Savages" in the Declaration of Independence, then, neither he nor his readers will experience any cognitive dissonance with the earlier claims about the equality of all "men," since savages are not "men" in the full sense of the word. Locked in a different temporality, incapable of self-regulation by morality and law, they are humanoid but not human. To speak of the "equality" of the savage would then be oxymoronic, since one's very location in these categories is an indication of one's inequality. Even a cognizer with no personal antipathy or prejudice toward Native Americans will be cognitively disabled in trying to establish truths about them insofar as such a category and its associated presuppositions will tend to force his conclusions in a certain direction, will limit what he can objectively see. One will experience a strain, a cognitive tension between possible egalitarian findings and overarching category, insofar as "savage" already has embedded in it a narrative, a set of assumptions about innate inferiority, which will preclude certain possibilities. "Savages" tend to do certain things and to be unable to do others; these go with the conceptual territory.

Thus the term itself encourages if not quite logically determines particular conclusions. Concepts orient us toward the world, and it is a rare individual who can resist this inherited orientation. Once established in the social mindset, their influence is difficult to escape since it is not a matter of seeing the phenomenon with the concept discretely attached but rather of seeing things *through* the concept itself. In the classic period of European expansionism, it then becomes possible to speak with no sense of absurdity of "empty" lands that are actually teeming with millions of people, of "discovering" countries whose inhabitants already exist, because the nonwhite Other is so located in the guiding conceptual array that different rules apply. Even seemingly straightforward empirical perception will be affected—the myth of a nation of hunters in contradiction to widespread Native American agriculture that saved the English colonists' lives, the myth of stateless savages in contradiction to forms of government from which the white Founders arguably learned, the myth of a pristine wilderness in contradiction to a humanized landscape transformed by thousands of years of labor.[44] In all these cases, *the concept is driving the perception, with whites aprioristically intent on denying what is before them.* So if Kant famously said that perceptions without concepts are blind, then here it is the blindness of the concept itself that is blocking vision.

Originally, then, foundational concepts of racialized difference, and their ramifications in all socio-political spheres, preclude a veridical perception of nonwhites and serve as a categorical barrier against their equitable moral treatment. The transition away from old-fashioned racism of this kind has not, however, put an end to white normativity but subtly transformed its character. If previously whites were color-demarcated as biologically and/or culturally unequal and superior, now through a strategic "color-blindness" they are assimilated as putative equals to the status and situation of nonwhites on terms that negate the need for measures to repair the inequities of the past. So white normativity manifests itself in a white refusal to recognize the long history of structural discrimination that has left whites with the differential resources they have today and all its consequent advantages in negotiating opportunity structures. If originally whiteness was race, then now it is racelessness, an equal status and a common history in which all have shared, with white privilege being conceptually erased. Woody Doane suggests that

"color-blind" ideology plays an important role in the maintenance of white hegemony.... Because whites tend not to see themselves in racial terms and not to recognize the existence of the advantages that whites enjoy in American society, this promotes a worldview that emphasizes *individualistic* explanations for social and economic achievement, as if the individualism of white privilege was a universal attribute. Whites also exhibit a general inability to perceive the persistence of discrimination and the effects of more subtle forms of institutional discrimination. In the context of color-blind racial ideology, whites are more likely to see the opportunity structure as open and institutions as impartial or objective in their functioning. . . . this combination supports an interpretative framework in which whites' explanations for inequality focus upon the cultural characteristics (e.g., motivation, values) of subordinate groups. . . . Politically, this blaming of subordinate groups for their lower economic position serves to neutralize demands for antidiscrimination initiatives or for a redistribution of resources.[45]

Indeed, the real racists are the *blacks* who continue to insist on the importance of race. In both cases, white normativity underpins white privilege, in the first case by justifying differential treatment by race and in the second case by justifying formally equal treatment by race that—in its denial of the cumulative effects of past differential treatment—is tantamount to continuing it.

What makes such denial possible, of course, is the management of memory. (Thus, as earlier emphasized, it is important to appreciate the *interconnectedness* of all these components of knowing or non-knowing: this concept is viable in the white mind because of the denial of crucial facts.) Memory is not a subject one usually finds in epistemology texts, but for social epistemology it is obviously pivotal. French sociologist Maurice Halbwachs was one of the pioneers of the concept of a collective, social memory, which provided the framework for individual memories.[46] But if we need to understand collective memory, we also need to understand collective amnesia. Indeed, they go together insofar as memory is necessarily selective—out of the infinite sequence of events, some trivial, some momentous, we extract what we see as the crucial ones and organize them into an overall narrative. Social memory is then inscribed in textbooks, generated and regenerated in ceremonies and official holidays, concretized in statues, parks, monuments. John Locke famously suggested memory as the crucial criterion for personal identity, and social memory plays a parallel role in social identity. Historian John Gillis argues that "the notion of identity depends on the idea of memory, and vice versa. . . . [But] memories and identities are not fixed things, but representations or constructions of reality. . . . '[M]emory work' is . . . embedded in complex class, gender and power relations that determine what is remembered (or forgotten), by whom, and for what end. If memory has its politics, so too does identity."[47] As the individual represses unhappy or embarrassing memories that may also reveal a great deal about his identity, about who he is, so in all societies, especially those structured by domination, the socially recollecting "we" will be divided, and the selection will be guided by different identities, with one group suppressing precisely what another wishes to commemorate.

Thus there will be both official and counter-memory, with conflicting judgments about what is important in the past and what is unimportant, what happened and does matter, what happened and does not matter, and what did not happen at all. So applying this to race, we will find an intimate relationship between white identity, white memory, and white amnesia, especially about nonwhite victims.

Hitler is supposed to have reassured his generals, apprehensive about the launching of World War II, by asking them: "Who now remembers the Armenians?" Because the Third Reich lost, the genocide of the Jews (though far less the Romani) is remembered. But who now remembers the Hereros, the Nama, the Beothuks, the Tasmanians, the Pequots? (For that matter, who does remember the Armenians, except the Armenians themselves?) Who remembers the Congolese? In Adam Hochschild's chilling book on King Leopold II's regime of rubber and extermination, which resulted in the deaths of ten million people in the Belgian Congo, the final chapter is titled "The Great Forgetting."[48] Through the systematic destruction of state archives in Brussels—"the furnaces burned for eight days"—and the deliberate non-commemoration of the African victims—"in none of the [Brussels Royal Museum of Central Africa]'s twenty large exhibition galleries is there the slightest hint that millions of Congolese met unnatural deaths"—a "deliberate forgetting" as an "active deed" was achieved, a purging of official memory so thorough and efficient that a Belgian ambassador to West Africa in the 1970s was astonished by the "slander" on his country in a Liberian newspaper's passing reference to the genocide: "I learned that there had been this huge campaign, in the international press, from 1900 to 1910; millions of people had died, but we Belgians knew absolutely nothing about it."[49]

Similarly, and closer to home, James Loewen's critical study of the silences and misrepresentations of standard American history textbooks points out that "the Indian-white wars that dominated our history from 1622 to 1815 and were of considerable importance until 1890 have disappeared from our national memory," encouraging a "feel-good history for whites": "By downplaying Indian wars, textbooks help us forget that we wrested the continent from Native Americans."[50] In the case of blacks, the "forgetting" takes the form of whitewashing the atrocities of slavery—the "magnolia myth" of paternalistic white aristocrats and happy, singing darkies that dominated American textbooks as late as the 1950s—and minimizing the extent to which "the peculiar institution" was not a sectional problem but shaped the national economy, polity, and psychology.[51] Du Bois refers to "the deliberately educated ignorance of white schools"[52] and devotes the climactic chapter of his massive revisionist 1935 *Black Reconstruction in America* to the documentation of the sanitization by white southern historians of the history of slavery, the Civil War, and Reconstruction.[53]

Moreover, the misrepresentations of national textbooks have their counterpart in monuments and statuary: social memory made marble and concrete, national mnemonics of the landscape itself. In his study of Civil War monuments, Kirk Savage argues, "Monuments served to anchor collective remembering," fostering "a shared and standardized program of memory," so that "local memory earned credibility by its assimilation to a visible national memory." The post-bellum decision to rehabilitate Robert E. Lee, commander in chief of the Confederate Army, thereby "eras[ing] his status as traitor," signified a national white reconciliation that required the repudiation of an alternative black memory:

> The commemoration of Lee rested on a suppression of black memory, black truth.... [US statesman Charles Francis] Adams could not justify a monument to Lee without denying the postwar reality of racial injustice and its congruence with the Confederate cause. "Sectional reconciliation" of this kind was founded on the nonconciliation of African-Americans, and on their exclusion from the legitimate arenas of cultural representation. Black Americans did not have their own monuments, despite the critical role they had played in swinging the balance of power—both moral and military—to the North.... The commemoration of the Civil War in physical memorials is ultimately a story of systematic cultural repression.... Public monuments ... impose a permanent memory on the very landscape within which we order our lives. Inasmuch as the monuments make credible particular collectivities, they must erase others.[54]

At the level of symbolism and national self-representation, then, the denial of the extent of Native American and black victimization underwrites the whitewashed narrative of discovery, settlement, and building of a shining city on the hill. But the editing of white memory has more material and practical consequences also: as earlier emphasized it enables a self-representation in which differential white privilege and the need to correct for it does not exist. In other words, the mystification of the past underwrites a mystification of the present. The erasure of the history of Jim Crow makes it possible to represent the playing field as historically level so that current black poverty just proves blacks' unwillingness to work. As individual memory is assisted through a larger social memory, so individual amnesia is then ratified by a larger collective amnesia. In his research on the continuing, indeed deepening, gap between white and black Americans, Thomas Shapiro remarks on how often white interviewees seemed to "forget" what they had just told him about the extensive parental assistance they received, claiming instead that they had worked for it:

> [X's] memory seems accurate as she catalogues all sorts of parental wealthfare with matching dollar figures. . . . However, as soon as the conversation turns to how she and her husband acquired assets like their home, cars, and savings account, her attitude changes dramatically. . . . The [Xs] describe themselves as self-made, conveniently forgetting that they inherited much of what they own.[55]

Thus the "taken-for-granted sense of [white] entitlement" erases the fact that *"transformative assets,"* "inherited wealth lifting a family beyond their own achievements," have been crucial to their white success, and that blacks do not in general have such advantages because of the history of discrimination against them.[56] Thomas McCarthy points out the importance of a politics of memory for closing the "peculiar gap between academic historical scholarship and public historical consciousness that marks our own situation," and he emphasizes that the eventual achievement of racial justice can only be accomplished through a systematic national re-education on the historic extent of black racial subordination in the United States, and how it continues to shape our racial fates differentially today.[57]

But forgetting, whether individual or social, will not even be necessary if there is nothing to remember in the first place. C. A. J. Coady's now classic book on testimony has made it irrefutably clear how dependent we are on others for so much of what we know; testimony as a concept is thus crucial to the elaboration of a social epistemology.[58] Yet if one group, or specific groups, of potential witnesses are discredited in advance as being epistemically suspect, then testimony from them will tend to be dismissed or never solicited to begin with. Kant's infamous line about a "Negro carpenter"'s views has often been quoted, but never stales: "And it might be, that there were something in this which perhaps deserved to be considered; but in short, this fellow was *quite black* from head to foot, a clear proof that what he said was stupid."[59] Nonwhite inferiority necessarily has cognitive ramifications, undermining nonwhite claims to knowledge that are not backed up by European epistemic authority. In an 1840 letter, Daniel Butrick, a missionary to the Cherokees, gives a long list of the reasons "how whites try and fail to find out what Indians know because they refuse to recognize the humanity or intelligence of Native peoples," the result being "that such persons may spend all their days among the Indians and yet die as ignorant of their true character almost as if they had never been born."[60] During slavery, blacks were generally denied the right to testify against whites because they were not seen as credible witnesses, so when the only (willing) witnesses to white crimes were black, these crimes would not be brought to light. At one point in German South West Africa, white settlers demanded "that in court only the testimony of seven African witnesses could outweigh evidence presented by a single white person."[61] Similarly, slave narratives often had to have white authenticators—for example, white abolitionists— with the racially based epistemic authority to write a preface or appear on stage with the author so as to confirm that what this worthy Negro said was indeed true.

Moreover, in many cases, even if witnesses would have been given some kind of grudging hearing, they were terrorized into silence by the fear of white retaliation. A black woman recalls the world of Jim Crow and the dangers of describing it for what it was: "My problems started when I began to comment on what I saw. . . . I insisted on being accurate. But the world I was born into didn't want that. Indeed, its very survival depended on not knowing, not seeing—and certainly, not saying anything at all about what it was really like."[62] If black testimony could be aprioristically rejected because it was likely to be false, it could also be aprioristically rejected because it was likely to be true. Testimony about white atrocities—lynchings, police killings, race riots—would often have to be passed down through segregated informational channels, black to black, too explosive to be allowed exposure to white cognition. The memory of the 1921 Tulsa race riot, the worst American race riot of the twentieth century, with a possible death toll of 300 people, was kept alive for decades in the black community long after whites had erased it from the official record. Ed Wheeler, a white researcher trying in 1970 to locate documentation on the riot, found that the official Tulsa records had mysteriously vanished, and he was only able with great difficulty to persuade black survivors to come forward with their photographs of the event: "The blacks allowed Wheeler to take the pictures only if he promised not to reveal their names, and they all spoke only on the condition of anonymity. Though fifty years had passed, they still feared retribution if they spoke out."[63]

And even when such fears are not a factor and blacks do feel free to speak, the epistemic presumption against their credibility remains in a way that it does not for white witnesses. Black counter-testimony against white mythology has always existed but would originally have been handicapped by the lack of material and cultural capital investment available for its production—oral testimony from illiterate slaves, ephemeral pamphlets with small print runs, self-published works like those by the autodidact J. A. Rogers laboriously documenting the achievements of men and women of color to contest the white lie of black inferiority.[64] But even when propagated in more respectable venues—for example, the Negro scholarly journals founded in the late nineteenth and early twentieth centuries—they were epistemically ghettoized by the Jim Crow intellectual practices of the white academy. As Stephen Steinberg points out, the United States and its white social sciences have generally "played ostrich" on the issues of race and racial division.[65] The result has been—as in Du Bois's famous image of blacks in a cave trying desperately to communicate to white passersby before gradually realizing that they are silenced behind the updated version of the veil, "some thick sheet of invisible but horribly tangible plate glass"[66]—that "[black critics] of whatever political stripe . . . were simply met with a deaf ear."[67] The testimony of Negro scholars saying the wrong thing (almost an analytic statement!) would not be registered. "The marginalization of black voices in academia was facilitated by an 'invisible but horribly tangible' color line that relegated all but a few black scholars to teach in black colleges far removed from the academic mainstream."[68] Consider, for example, an anthropology founded on the "obvious" truth of racial hierarchy. Or a sociology failing to confront the central social fact of structural white domination.[69] Or a history sanitizing the record of aboriginal conquest and black exploitation. Or a political science representing racism as an anomaly to a basically inclusive and egalitarian polity. Or, finally—in my own discipline—a political philosophy thriving for forty-plus years and supposedly dedicated to the elucidation of justice that makes next to no mention of the centrality of racial *injustice* to the "basic structure" of the United States and assumes instead that it will be more theoretically appropriate to start from the "ideal theory" assumption that society is the product of a mutually agreed upon, non-exploitative enterprise to divide benefits and burdens in an equitable way—and that this is somehow going to illuminate the distinctive problems of a society based on exploitative white settlement. In whatever discipline that is affected by race, the "testimony" of the black perspective and its distinctive conceptual and theoretical insights will tend to be whited out. Whites will cite other whites in a closed circuit of epistemic authority that reproduces white delusions.

Finally, the dynamic role of *white group interests* needs to be recognized and acknowledged as a central causal factor in generating and sustaining white ignorance. Cognitive psychologists standardly distinguish between "cold" and "hot" mechanisms of cognitive distortion, those attributable to intrinsic processing difficulties and those involving motivational factors, and in analytic philosophy of mind and philosophical psychology there is a large and well-established body of work on self-deception and motivated irrationality, though located within an individualistic framework.[70] So claiming a link between interest and cognition is not at all unheard of in this field. But because of its framing individualism, and of course the aprioristic exclusion in any case of the realities of *white* group domination, the generalization to racial interests has not been carried out.

What needs to be done, I suggest, is to extrapolate some of this literature to a social context—one informed by the realities of race. Because
of its marginalization of social oppression, the existing social epistemology literature tends to ignore or downplay such factors. By contrast, in the
left tradition this was precisely the classic thesis: (class) domination and
exploitation were the foundation of the social order, and as such they produced not merely material differentials of wealth in the economic sphere
but deleterious cognitive consequences in the ideational sphere. Marxism's
particular analysis of exploitation, resting as it does on the labor theory
of value, has proven to be fatally vulnerable. But obviously this does not
negate the value of the concept itself, suitably refurbished,[71] nor undercut
the prima facie plausibility of the claim that if exploitative socio-economic
relations are indeed foundational to the social order, then this is likely to
have a fundamental shaping effect on social ideation. In other words, one
can detach from a class framework a "materialist" claim about the interaction between exploitation, group interest, and social cognition and apply it
with what should be far less controversy within a race framework. I argue
in chapter 7 that *racial exploitation* (as determined by conventional liberal
standards) has usually been quite clear and unequivocal (think of Native
American expropriation, African slavery, Jim Crow), requiring—unlike
exploitation in the technical Marxist sense—no elaborate theoretical apparatus to discern, and that it can easily be shown to have been central to
US history. So vested white group interest in the racial status quo—"the
income-bearing value of race prejudice,"[72] in the words of Du Bois—needs
to be recognized as a major factor in encouraging white cognitive distortions of various kinds.[73]

Nor is such "motivated irrationality" confined to the period of overt racism and de jure segregation. Donald Kinder and Lynn Sanders's attitudinal
research on public policy matters linked to race reveals "a deep and perhaps widening racial divide [that] makes the discovery of commonality and
agreement between the races a dim prospect," and central to the shaping of
white opinion, it turns out, is their perception of their group interests: "the
threats blacks appear to pose to whites' collective well-being, not their personal welfare."[74] Race is the primary social division in the United States,
these two political scientists conclude, and whites generally see black
interests as opposed to their own. Inevitably, then, this will affect white
social cognition—the concepts favored (e.g., today's "color-blindness"),
the refusal to perceive systemic discrimination, the convenient amnesia
about the past and its legacy in the present, and the hostility to black testimony on continuing white privilege and the need to eliminate it so as to
achieve racial justice. As emphasized at the start, then, these analytically
distinguishable cognitive components are in reality all interlocked with and

reciprocally determining one another, jointly contributing to the blindness of the white eye.

In his wonderfully titled *States of Denial*, Stanley Cohen argues that "whole societies may slip into collective modes of denial":

> Besides collective denials of the past (such as brutalities against indigenous peoples), people may be encouraged to act as if they don't know about the present. Whole societies are based on forms of cruelty, discrimination, repression or exclusion which are "known" about but never openly acknowledged.... Indeed, distortions and self-delusions are most often synchronized.... Whole societies have mentioned and unmentionable rules about what should not be openly talked about. You are subject to a rule about obeying these rules, but bound also by a meta-rule which dictates that you deny your knowledge of the original rule.[75]

White ignorance has been able to flourish all these years because a white epistemology of ignorance has safeguarded it against the dangers of an illuminating blackness or redness, protecting those who for "racial" reasons have needed not to know. Only by starting to break these rules and meta-rules can we begin the long process that will lead to the eventual overcoming of this white darkness and the achievement of an enlightenment that is genuinely multiracial.

CHAPTER 5

"Ideal Theory" as Ideology

We turn now from general white ignorance to a subject narrower in epistemic scope ("ignorance" as manifested in occlusions in the technical normative apparatus of "ideal theory") but broader in the populations considered (the gender- and class-privileged as well as the racially privileged).

As noted in the previous chapter, feminist theory provides a far more developed critical starting point for the discussion of these matters than critical philosophy of race. Three surveys of feminist ethics from a decade and a half ago emphasize that the exclusive and unitary focus on "care" with which it is still sometimes identified has long been misleading. While paying tribute to the historic significance and continuing influence of Carol Gilligan's and Nel Noddings's pathbreaking work,[1] commentators such as Samantha Brennan, Marilyn Friedman, and Alison Jaggar point to "the increasing connections between feminist ethics and mainstream moral theory,"[2] the "number of diverse methodological strategies" adopted,[3] and the "controversy and diversity" rather than "unity" within feminism, marking "the shift from asserting the radical otherness of feminist ethics to seeing feminist philosophers as making a diverse range of contributions to an ongoing [larger] tradition of ethical discussion."[4] Indeed, Samantha Brennan's 1999 *Ethics* survey article suggests that there is no "one" feminist ethic, and that the distinctive features of a feminist approach are simply the perception of the wrongness of women's oppression, and the resulting construction and orientation of theory—based on women's moral experiences—to the goal of understanding and ending that oppression.[5] Obviously, then, this minimalist definition will permit a very broad spectrum of perspectives. In this respect, feminist ethics has interestingly come to converge with feminist political philosophy, which, at least from the "second wave" onward, also encompassed a wide variety of approaches whose common denominator was simply the goal of ending female subordination.[6]

In this chapter, I want to focus on an ethical strategy best and most self-consciously developed in feminist theory in the writings of Onora O'Neill.[7] However, it can arguably be traced back, at least in implicit and schematic form, to Marxism and classical left theory and would certainly be congenial to many people working on race. I refer to the distinction between idealizing and non-idealizing approaches to ethical theory and the endorsement of the latter. I will argue that this normative strategy has the virtue of being potentially universalist in its application—able to address many of the concerns not only of women but also of men subordinated by class, race, and the underdevelopment of the global "South"—and reflecting the distinctive experience of the oppressed while avoiding particularism and relativism. Moreover, in certain respects it engages with mainstream ethics on what are nominally its own terms, thereby (at least in theory) making it somewhat harder to ignore and marginalize. Correspondingly, I will argue that the so-called ideal theory more dominant in mainstream ethics is in crucial respects obfuscatory and can indeed be thought of as in part *ideological*, in the pejorative sense of a set of group ideas that reflect and contribute to perpetuating illicit group privilege. As O'Neill argues, and as I agree, the best way of realizing the ideal is through the recognition of the importance of theorizing the *non*-ideal.

THE VICES OF IDEAL THEORY

Let us begin by differentiating various sense of *ideal*, since the ambiguities and multiple interpretations of the term partially contribute, in my opinion, to whatever superficial plausibility "ideal theory" may have as an approach. To start with, of course, in a trivial sense "ideal theory" applies to moral theory as a whole (at least to normative ethics as against meta-ethics). Since ethics deals by definition with normative/prescriptive/evaluative issues, as against factual/descriptive issues, and so involves the appeal to values and ideals, it is obviously ideal theory in that generic sense, regardless of any divergence in approaches taken. Call this uncontroversial background normative sense of the ideal, with which we will not be concerned, ideal-as-normative.

Central to our focus, by contrast, is a different sense of *ideal*, ideal as *model*. Call this ideal-as-model. Obviously, this sense is not at all peculiar to ethics but can be found in other branches of philosophy, and it is indeed shared more generally (if not usually in quite the same way) with both natural and social science. Imagine some phenomenon of the natural or social world, *P*. Then an ideal in this sense is a representation of *P*. One kind of representation purports to be descriptive of *P*'s crucial aspects (its essential nature) and how it actually works (its basic dynamic). Call this descriptive modeling sense ideal-as-descriptive-model. Since a model is not coincident with what it is modeling, of course, an ideal-as-descriptive-model necessarily has to abstract away from certain features of *P*. So one will make simplifying assumptions, based on what one takes the most important features of *P* to be, and include certain features while omitting others: this will produce a schematized picture of the actual workings and actual nature of *P*. But for certain *P* (not all), it will also be possible to produce an idealized model, an exemplar, of what an ideal *P* should be like. Call this idealized model ideal-as-idealized-model. Unless the *P* in question is itself an ideal *P*, then obviously a gap will exist between it and the ideal, and correspondingly between ideal-as-descriptive-model (an ideal—in the sense of accurate—model of how *P* actually works) and ideal-as-idealized-model (an ideal—in the sense of an exemplar—model of how *P* should work). And obviously the "should" here will in general not necessarily be a moral "should" but may involve norms of a technical functionalist kind (an ideal vacuum cleaner, an ideal concentration camp, an ideal digestive system, and so on) or just limiting assumptions convenient for the purposes of mathematization and calculation (an ideal gas, a perfect vacuum, a frictionless plane, a resistance-free conductor).

Now in trying to understand the workings of an actual *P*, how useful will it be to start from an ideal-as-idealized-model of *P*? Obviously, this question cannot be answered a priori: it's going to depend on how closely the actual *P* in question approximates the behavior of an ideal *P*. A very smooth, Teflon-coated plane suspended in a vacuum may come close enough that one can regard its behavior as approaching that of an ideal frictionless plane: ideal-as-descriptive-model here will approximate, if falling a bit short of, ideal-as-idealized-model. So one can think of ideal-as-idealized-model as an extrapolation, in the limit, of the behavior of *P* (here the plane), or, from the other direction, regard ideal-as-descriptive-model as just being slightly deviant from this ideal. But if the plane is covered not with Teflon but Velcro, or is pitted, cracked, and abraded in various ways, then obviously this would be absurd. Ideal-as-descriptive-model, the model of the actual workings of the plane, will be quite different from ideal-as-idealized-model, and one will need to start with an actual investigation of the plane's properties; one cannot just conceptualize them in terms of a minor deviation from the ideal, ideal-as-idealized-model. And if one wants to change the actual *P* so it conforms more closely in its behavior to the ideal *P*, one will need to work and theorize not merely with the ideal, ideal-as-idealized-model, but with the non-ideal, ideal-as-descriptive-model, so as to identify and understand the peculiar features that explain P's dynamic and prevent it from attaining ideality.

Let us now turn (doubtless to the relief of readers) from these mechanical comparisons to what we're really interested in: the application of these distinctions to human interaction and moral theory. Since we're dealing with moral agents and not gases, planes, or vacuum cleaners, the ideal in the ideal-as-idealized-model sense has here, of course, a crucial moral dimension along with the factual one. Factually, idealization involves the attribution to the agents (as conceived of in the theory) of human capacities significantly deviant from the norm (for example, their degrees of rationality, self-knowledge, ability to make interpersonal cardinal utility comparisons, and so forth).[8] Morally, idealization involves the modeling of what people should be like (character), how they should treat each other (right and good actions), and how society should be structured in its basic institutions (justice). Different theorists will, of course, diverge on what these ideals are and, correspondingly, on their views of what ideal character, the relation between the right and the good, and the nature of a just society consist in. But they will have in common *an* ideal of some sort.

Now what distinguishes ideal theory is not merely the *use* of ideals, since obviously non-ideal theory can and will use ideals also (certainly it will appeal to the *moral* ideals, if it may be more dubious about the value of invoking idealized human capacities). What distinguishes ideal theory is the reliance on idealization to the exclusion, or at least marginalization, of the actual. As O'Neill emphasizes, this is *not* a necessary corollary of the operation of abstraction itself, since one can have abstractions of the ideal-as-descriptive-model type that abstract without idealizing. But ideal theory either tacitly represents the actual as a simple deviation from the ideal, not worth theorizing in its own right, or claims that starting from the ideal is at least the best way of realizing it. Ideal theory as an approach will then utilize as its basic apparatus some or all of the following concepts and assumptions (there is necessarily a certain overlap in the list, since they all intersect with one another):

- An idealized social ontology. Moral theory deals with the normative, but it cannot avoid *some* characterization of the human beings who make up the society and whose interactions with one another are its subject. So some overt or tacit social ontology has to be presupposed. An idealized social ontology of the modern type (as against, say, a Platonic or Aristotelian type) will typically assume the abstract and undifferentiated equal atomic individuals of classical liberalism. Thus it will abstract *away* from relations of structural domination, exploitation, coercion, and oppression, which in reality, of course, will profoundly shape the ontology of those same individuals, locating them in superior and inferior positions in social hierarchies of various kinds.

- Idealized capacities. The human agents as visualized in the theory will also often have completely unrealistic capacities attributed to them—unrealistic even for the privileged minority, let alone those subordinated in different ways, who would not have had an equal opportunity for their natural capacities to develop, and who will in fact typically be disabled in crucial respects.

- Silence on oppression. Almost by definition, it follows from the focus of ideal theory that little or nothing will be said about actual historic oppression and its legacy in the present or current ongoing oppression, though these may be gestured at in a vague or promissory way (as something to be dealt with later). Correspondingly, the ways in which systematic oppression is likely to shape the basic social institutions (as well as the humans in those institutions) will not be part of the theory's concern, and this will manifest itself in the absence of ideal-as-descriptive-model concepts that would provide the necessary macro- and micro-mapping of that oppression and that are requisite for understanding its reproductive dynamic.

- Ideal social institutions. Fundamental social institutions such as the family, the economic structure, the legal system, will therefore be conceptualized in ideal-as-idealized-model terms, with little or no sense of how their actual workings may systematically disadvantage women, the poor, and racial minorities.

- An idealized cognitive sphere. Separate from, and in addition to, the idealization of human capacities, what could be termed an idealized cognitive sphere will also be presupposed. In other words, as a corollary of the general ignoring of oppression, the consequences *of* oppression for the social cognition of these agents, both the advantaged and the disadvantaged, will typically not be recognized, let alone theorized. A general social transparency will be presumed, with cognitive obstacles minimized by being limited to biases of self-interest or the intrinsic difficulties of understanding the world, while little or no attention is paid to the distinctive role of hegemonic ideologies and group-specific experience in distorting our perceptions and conceptions of the social order.

- Strict compliance. Finally, some theorists, such as, famously, John Rawls in *A Theory of Justice*, also endorse "ideal theory" in the sense of "strict compliance as opposed to partial compliance theory": the examination of "the principles of justice that would regulate a well-ordered society. Everyone is presumed to act justly and to do his part in upholding just institutions." Rawls concedes that "the problems of partial compliance theory are the pressing and urgent matters. These are the things that we are faced with in everyday life." But, he argues, "The reason for beginning with ideal theory is that it provides, I believe, the only basis for the systematic grasp of these more pressing problems."[9] Since Rawls's text is widely credited with reviving postwar Anglo-American normative political theory and of being the most important book of the twentieth century in that tradition, this methodological decision can plausibly be argued to have been a significant factor in influencing the whole subsequent direction of the field, though I would also claim that his decision and its general endorsement also reflect deeper structural biases in the profession.

Now look at this list and try to see it with the eyes of somebody coming to formal academic ethical theory and political philosophy for the first time. Forget, in other words, all the articles and monographs and introductory texts you have read over the years that may have socialized you into thinking that this is how normative theory should be done. Perform an operation of Brechtian defamiliarization, estrangement, on your cognition. Wouldn't your spontaneous reaction be, *How in God's name could anybody think that this is the appropriate way to do ethics?*

I suggest that this spontaneous reaction, far from being philosophically naïve or jejune, is in fact the correct one. If we start from what is presumably the uncontroversial premise that the ultimate point of ethics is to guide our actions and make ourselves better people and the world a better place, then the framework above will not only be unhelpful for, but will in certain respects be deeply *antithetical* to, the proper goal of theoretical ethics as an enterprise. In modeling humans, human capacities, human interaction, human institutions, and human society on ideal-as-idealized-models, in never exploring how profoundly different these are from ideal-as-descriptive-models, we are abstracting away from realities that are crucial to our comprehension of the actual workings of injustice in human interactions and social institutions, and we are thereby guaranteeing that the ideal-as-idealized-model will never be achieved.

It is no accident that historically subordinated groups have always been deeply skeptical of ideal theory, generally see its glittering ideals as remote and unhelpful, and are attracted to non-ideal theory—or what significantly overlaps it, "naturalized" theory. In the same essay cited above, Jaggar identifies a "unity of feminist ethics in at least one dimension," a naturalism "characteristic, though not definitive, of it."[10] Marxism no longer has the appeal it once did as a theory of oppression, but it was famous for emphasizing, as in *The German Ideology*, the importance of descending from the idealizing abstractions of the Young Hegelians to a focus on "real, active men," not "men as narrated, thought of, imagined, conceived," but "as they *actually* are," in (class) relations of domination.[11] And certainly black Americans and others of the racially oppressed have always operated on the assumption that the natural and most illuminating starting point is the *actual* conditions of nonwhites and the discrepancy between that and the vaunted American ideals. Thus Frederick Douglass's classic 1852 speech, "What to the Slave Is the Fourth July?" points out the obvious, that the inspiring principles of freedom and independence associated with the celebration are not equally extended to black slaves: "I am not included within the pale of this glorious anniversary! Your high independence only reveals the immeasurable distance between us. . . . The rich inheritance of justice, liberty, prosperity and independence, bequeathed by your fathers, is shared by you, not by me. . . . This Fourth July is *yours*, not *mine*. *You* may rejoice, *I* must mourn."[12] So given this convergence in gender, class, and race theory on the need to make theoretically central the existence and functioning of the actual *non*-ideal structures that obstruct the realization of the ideal, what defensible arguments for abstracting *away* from these realities could there be?

As a preliminary, we need to quickly clear away some of the ambiguities and verbal confusions that might mistakenly lead one to support ideal theory. All moral theory is ideal in the ideal-as-normative sense, but of course that's not the sense at stake here, so that can't be why we need ideal theory. Nor is ideal theory just a model, which every theory requires, since we have already distinguished models in the ideal-as-descriptive-model and models in the ideal-as-idealized-model sense. Nor can it be claimed that, whatever its faults, ideal theory is the only way to do ethics, or the only theory-supported/generalist way to do ethics (as against unsatisfactory particularist alternatives), since there *is* an alternative that is also generalist, in the form of non-ideal theory. Nor does the simple appeal *to* an ideal (say, the picture of an ideally just society) necessarily make the theory ideal theory, since non-ideal theory can and does appeal to an ideal also.

So these are either obviously bad arguments or simple confusions. What are the real defenses of ideal theory? A first possible argument might be the simple denial that moral theory should have *any* concern with making realistic assumptions about human beings, their capacities, and their behavior. Ethics is concerned with the ideal, so it doesn't have to worry about the actual. But even for mainstream ethics, this wouldn't work, since, of course, *ought* is supposed to imply *can*: the ideal has to be achievable by humans. Nor could it seriously be claimed that moral theory is concerned only with mapping beautiful ideals, not their actual implementation. If any ethicist actually said this, it would be an astonishing abdication of the classic goal of ethics and its link with practical reason. The normative here would then be weirdly detached from the prescriptive: this is the good and the right—but we are not concerned with their actual realization. Even for Plato, a classic example in at least one sense of an ideal theorist, this was not the case: the Form of the Good was supposed to motivate us and help philosophers transform society. Nor could anyone seriously say that ideal theory is a good way to approach ethics because as a matter of *fact* (not as a conceptual necessity following from what "model" or "ideal" means), the normative here *has* come close to converging with the descriptive: ideal-as-descriptive-model *has* approximated to ideal-as-idealized-model. Obviously, the dreadful and dismaying course of human history has not *remotely* been a record of close-to-ideal behavior but rather of behavior that has usually been quite the polar opposite of the ideal, with oppression and inequitable treatment of the majority of humanity (whether on grounds of gender, or nationality, or class, or religion, or race) being the norm.

So the argument cannot be that as a matter of definitional truth, or factual irrelevance, or factual convergence, ideal theory is required. The argument has to be, as in the quote from Rawls above, that this is the *best* way of doing normative theory, better than all the other contenders. But why on earth should anyone think this? Why should anyone think that abstaining from theorizing about oppression and its consequences is the best way to bring about an end to oppression? Isn't this, on the face of it, just completely implausible?

I suggest that since in fact there are no good reasons for making this assumption and many good reasons against it, we have to look elsewhere to understand the dominance within philosophy of ideal theory. Ideal theory, I would contend, is really an *ideology*, a distortional complex of ideas, values, norms, and beliefs that reflects the non-representative interests and experiences of a small minority of the national population—middle- to upper-class white males—who are hugely *over-represented* in the professional philosophical population.[13] Once this is understood, it becomes transparent why such a patently deficient, clearly counterfactual and counterproductive approach to issues of right and wrong, justice and injustice, has been so dominant. As theorists of ideology emphasize, this should not be thought of in terms of conscious conspiratorial manipulation but rather in terms of social privilege and resulting differential experience, a non-representative phenomenological life-world (mis)taken for *the* world, reinforcement (in this case) by professional norms of what counts as respectable and high-prestige philosophy, and—if not to be inflated into the sole variable, certainly never to be neglected in the sociology of belief—the absence of any countervailing group interest that would motivate dissatisfaction with dominant paradigms and a resulting search for better alternatives. Can it possibly serve the interests of *women*, white and nonwhite, to ignore female subordination, represent the family as ideal, and pretend that women have been treated as equal persons? Obviously not. Can it possibly serve the interests of *people of color* to ignore the centuries of white supremacy and to pretend that a discourse originally structured around white normativity now substantively, as against just terminologically, includes them? Obviously not. Can it possibly serve the interests of the *poor and the working class* to ignore the ways in which an increasingly inequitable class society imposes economic constraints that limit their nominal freedoms and undermine their formal equality before the law? Obviously not.[14] If we ask the simple, classic question of *cui bono?* then it is obvious that ideal theory can only serve the interests of the privileged,[15] who in addition—precisely because of that privilege (as bourgeois white males)— have an experience that comes closest to that ideal, and so experience the least cognitive dissonance between it and reality, ideal-as-idealized-model and ideal-as-descriptive-model. So, as generally emphasized in the analysis of hegemonic ideologies, it is not merely the orientation by this group's interests that serves to buttress ideal theory but also their (doubly) peculiar experience of reality.

THE VIRTUES OF NON-IDEAL THEORY

Let me now go through some of the many ways in which I claim that non-ideal theory is clearly superior to ideal theory. As indicated, I will try to make the case that its applicability extends, and in fact that it has historically been applied (even if not always consciously under that banner), to issues of class and race also.

Generalism versus Particularism

First, consider a kind of framing meta-issue, which is related to, though not coincident with, these matters. For at least two decades, one of the most important debates in ethical theory has been that between generalists and particularists.[16] A quick summary of their respective positions is difficult, because definitions tend to be contested by those in the same camp as well as those in the other camp. But roughly, generalists think that there are non-trivial general moral principles while particularists deny this. Within mainstream ethics, the particularism in question is usually located at the individual level, so the debate in this form does not map neatly on to feminist debates. But one way of conceptualizing the challenge from those feminists and people of color hostile to "malestream"/"white" principles is as an affirmation of a *group-based* particularism. (Think of the famous T-shirt slogan worn by some African Americans: "It's a black thang—you wouldn't understand.") The distinctive experience of women, or of nonwhites, it will be argued, requires the rejection of the bogus generality, the spurious universalism, of hegemonic principles that have proven so clearly inadequate for addressing the situation of the subordinated. And since ideal theory classically lays claims to objectivity, it may be felt that rejection requires the abandonment of pretensions (likewise seen as bogus) to objectivity also.

But though particularism (in this group-based form) responds to a real problem, its solution arguably results from a faulty diagnosis. Dominant abstractions may indeed be remote, dominant principles may indeed be unhelpful, dominant categories may indeed be alienating; but this lack of fit between generality and one's experience (the maleness and whiteness of the supposedly general, genderless, and colorless view from nowhere) arguably arises not from abstraction and generality per se, but from an abstraction and generality that *abstract away* from gender and race. The problem is that they are *deficient* abstractions of the ideal-as-idealized-model kind, not that they are abstractions *tout court*. What one wants are abstractions of the ideal-as-descriptive-model kind that capture the essentials of the situation of women and nonwhites, not abstract away from them. Global concepts like *patriarchy* and *white supremacy* arguably fulfill this role, as Marxism's *class society/capitalism* did (however inadequately for non-class oppressions) for earlier generations. These terms are abstractions that *do* reflect the specificities of group experience, thereby potentially generating categories and principles that illuminate rather than obfuscate the reality of different kinds of subordination.

Moreover, particularism holds many dangers, whether individual or group-based. Theory necessarily requires abstraction, and to concede this realm to the adversary is an odd way of challenging him. Rejecting abstraction and generalism deprives one of the apparatus necessary for making general theoretical statements of one's own, and indeed of critiquing those same hegemonic misleading abstractions. One is ghettoizing oneself in a self-circumscribed intellectual space rather than challenging the broader mapping of that space. One also risks the dangers of relativism, which makes it difficult to affirm that, objectively, white women and people of color are indeed oppressed—not merely that they believe they're oppressed. In addition, the mainstream apparatus (for example, of justice and rights) then becomes a necessarily alien tool in the oppressor's arsenal rather than a weapon to be used and turned against him. One can no longer demand gender or racial justice. Finally, another obvious problem with particularism is that since there is more than one oppressed group, it will sometimes be necessary to adjudicate rival justice claims among those subordinated by different systems—for example, race and gender, or gender and North/South domination. The obvious example here is the situation of women of the Global South and the claim that their subordination is not subordination at all but a cultural tradition whose condemnation by the Global North is imperialist and racist.[17] In the absence of some universalist, intertranslatable, non-incommensurable measure of rights or well-being, how can such clashes be resolved?

Non-Idealized Descriptive Mapping Concepts

Moral cognition is no more just a matter of naïve direct perception than is empirical cognition. Unless, as did moral intuitionists in the early twentieth century, one believes in a distinct "moral sense" separate from the more familiar non-moral five senses, then it must be conceded that concepts are necessary to apprehend things, both in the empirical and moral realm. After all, it was Kant, not some anti-Establishment figure, who said that perceptions without concepts are blind. But once one recognizes (unlike Kant) the huge range of possible conceptual systems, then—unless one is a relativist (and I have already suggested that objectivism should be the ideal)—concern about conceptual adequacy becomes crucial. This will be true even for mainstream theory, where the primary sources of possible distortion will be attributed to simple human failings in our cognitive apparatus. But for the radical oppositional theory of class, race, and gender, of course, the case for such alertness goes through a fortiori. Instead of the idealized cognitive sphere that ideal theory tends to presuppose, Marxists, feminists, and critical race theorists all have as part of their theoretical analysis elaborate *meta*-theories (theories about theories) mapping how systems of domination negatively affect the ideational. (This is a direct consequence, of course, of non-ideal theory's recognition of the centrality of oppression, and its insight that in understanding the social dynamic, a theorization of the ideal-as-descriptive-model type is required—it is not just a minor "deviation" from ideal-as-idealized-model that is involved.)

The crucial common claim—whether couched in terms of class ideology, or androcentrism, or white normativity—is that all theorizing, both moral and non-moral, takes place in an intellectual realm dominated by concepts, assumptions, norms, values, and framing perspectives that reflect the experience and group interests of the privileged group (whether the bourgeoisie, or men, or whites). So a simple empiricism will not work as a cognitive strategy; one has to be self-conscious about the concepts that "spontaneously" occur to one, since many of these concepts will not arise naturally but as the result of social structures and hegemonic ideational patterns. In particular, it will often be the case that dominant concepts will obscure certain crucial realities, blocking them from sight or naturalizing them, while, on the other hand, concepts necessary for accurately mapping these realities will be absent. Whether in terms of concepts of the self, or of humans in general, or in the cartography of the social, it will be necessary to scrutinize the dominant conceptual tools and the way the boundaries are drawn.

This is, of course, the burden of standpoint theory—that certain realities tend to be more visible from the perspective of the subordinated than the privileged.[18] The thesis can be put in a strong and implausible form, but weaker versions do have considerable plausibility, as illustrated by the simple fact that for the most part the crucial conceptual innovation necessary to map non-ideal realities has *not* come from the dominant group. In its ignoring of oppression, ideal theory also ignores the consequences of oppression. If societies are not oppressive, or if in modeling them we can abstract away from oppression and assume moral cognizers of roughly equal skill, then the paradigmatic moral agent can be featureless. No theory is required about the particular group-based obstacles that may block the vision of a particular group. By contrast, non-ideal theory recognizes that people *will* typically be cognitively affected by their social location, so that on both the macro and the more local level, the descriptive concepts arrived at may be misleading.

Think of the original challenge Marxist models of *capitalism* posed to liberalism's social ontology: the claim that to focus on relations of apparently equal exchange, free and fair, among equal individuals was illusory, since at the level of the relations of production, the real ontology of workers and capitalists manifested a deep structure of constraint that limited proletarian freedom. Think of the innovation of using *patriarchy* to force people to recognize male domination of women and condemn it as political and oppressive rather than natural, apolitical, and unproblematic. Think of the recent resurrection of the concept of *white supremacy* to map the reality of a white domination that has continued in more subtle forms past the ending of de jure segregation. These are all global, high-level concepts, undeniable abstractions. But they map accurately (at least arguably) crucial realities that differentiate the statuses of the human beings within the systems they describe; so while they *abstract*, they do not *idealize*.

Or consider conceptual innovation at the more local level: the challenge to the traditional way the public/private distinction was drawn, the concept of sexual harassment. In the first case, a seemingly neutral and innocuous conceptual divide turned out, once it was viewed from the perspective of gender subordination, to be contributing to the reproduction of the gender system by its relegation of "women's issues" to a seemingly apolitical and naturalized space. In the case of sexual harassment, a familiar reality—a staple of cartoons in men's magazines for years (bosses chasing secretaries around the desk and so on)—was reconceptualized as negative (not something funny, but something morally wrong) and a contributor to making the workplace hostile for women. These realizations, these recognitions, did not spontaneously crystallize out of nowhere; they required conceptual labor, a different map of social reality, a valorization of the distinctive experience of women. As a result of having these concepts, we can now see better: our perceptions are no longer blinded to realities to which we were previously obtuse. In some sense, ideal observers should have been able to recognize them—yet they did not, as shown by the non-appearance of these realities in male-dominated philosophical literature.

Normative Concepts

Ideal theory might at least seem to be unproblematic in the realm of the ideals themselves: normative concepts. Here if nowhere else, it might be felt, idealization is completely legitimate. But even here the adequacy of ideal theory can be challenged on at least three dimensions: the legitimacy of the normative concept in the first place; the particular way that the normative concept is applied, or operationalized; and the absence of other normative concepts.

Consider *purity* as an ideal. In abstraction, it sounds innocent enough—surely purity is good, as against impurity. Who could object to that? But consider its historic use in connection with race. For many decades in the United States and elsewhere, *racial purity* was an ideal, and part of the point of anti-miscegenation law was to preserve the "purity" of the white race. Since blackness was defined by the "one-drop rule"—any black ancestry makes you black[19]—the idea of black purity would have been a contradiction in terms. So there was a fundamental asymmetry in the way "purity" was applied, and in practice both the law and social custom were primarily on the alert for black male/white female "miscegenation," not white male/black female "miscegenation," which was widely winked at. Apart from what we now, in a more enlightened age, would see as its fundamental incoherence—that since races have no biological existence, they are not the kinds of entities that can be either pure or impure—the ideal of purity served to buttress white supremacy. So here a normative concept once accepted by millions was actually totally illegitimate.[20] (Similarly, think of the historic role of "purity" as an invidious norm for evaluating female sexuality, and the corresponding entrenchment of the double standard.)

Or consider a (today) far more respectable ideal, that of *autonomy*. This notion has been central to ethical theory for hundreds of years, and is, of course, famously most developed in Kant's writings. But recent work in feminist theory has raised questions as to whether it is an attractive ideal at all or just a reflection of male privilege. Human beings are dependent upon others for a long time before they can become self-sufficient, and if they live to old age, are likely to be dependent upon others for many of their later years. But traditionally, this work has been done by women, and so it has been invisible or taken for granted, and not theorized. Some feminist ethicists have argued for the simple abandonment of autonomy as an attractive value, but others have suggested that it can be redeemed once it is reconceptualized to take account of this necessarily inter-relational aspect.[21] So the point is that idealization here obfuscates the reality of care-giving that makes any achievement of autonomy possible in the first place, and only through non-ideal theory are we sensitized to the need to balance this value against other values and rethink it. Somewhat similarly, think of the traditional left critique of a liberal concept of freedom that focuses simply on the absence of juridical barriers and ignores the many ways in which economic constraints can make working-class liberties largely nominal rather than substantive.

Finally, it may be that the non-ideal perspective of the socially subordinated is necessary to generate certain critical evaluative concepts in the first place, since the experience of social reality of the privileged provides no phenomenological basis for them: Marxist concepts of class alienation and labor exploitation; feminist concepts of sexual alienation and affective exploitation; critical race theory concepts of whiteness as oppressive and "color-blindness" as actually whiteness in disguise. Insofar as concepts crystallize in part from experience rather than being a priori, and insofar as capturing the perspective of subordination requires advertence to its existence, an ideal theory that ignores these realities will necessarily be handicapped in principle.

Non-Ideal Theory as Already Contained in Ideal Theory?

Finally, consider the following objection. Suppose it is claimed that the foregoing accusations are unfair because, in the end, non-ideal theory and its various prescriptions are somehow already "contained" within ideal theory. So there is no need for a separate enterprise of this kind—or if there is, it is just a matter of *applying* principles, not of *theory* (it is applied ethics rather than ethical theory)—since the appropriate recommendations can, with the suitable assumptions, all be derived from ideal theory. After all, if the ideal liberal individual, the "person," is supposed to be entitled to certain basic rights and freedoms, then why can't this abstract individual subsume the workers, white women, and nonwhites who are also persons—even if, admittedly, they were not historically recognized as such?

I think the problem here is a failure to appreciate the nature and magnitude of the obstacles to the cognitive rethinking required, and the mistaken move—especially easy for analytic philosophers, used to the effortless manipulation of variables, the shifting about of p's and q's, in the frictionless plane (redux!) of symbolic logic—from the ease of logical implication to the actual inferential patterns of human cognizers who have been socialized by these systems of domination. (This failure is itself, reflexively, a manifestation of the idealism of ideal theory.) To begin with the obvious empirical objection, if it were as easy as all that, just a matter of *modus ponens* or some other simple logical rule, then why was it so hard to do? If it were obvious that women were equal moral persons, meant to be fully included in the variable "men," then why was it not obvious to virtually every male political philosopher and ethicist up to a few decades ago? Why has liberalism, supposedly committed to normative equality and a foundational opposition to ascriptive hierarchy, found it so easy to exclude white women and nonwhites from its egalitarian promise? The actual working of human cognitive processes, as manifested in the sexism and sometimes racism of such leading figures in the canon as Plato, Aristotle, Aquinas, Hobbes, Hume, Locke, Rousseau, Kant, Hegel, and the rest, itself constitutes the simplest illustration of the mistakenness of such an analysis.

Moreover, it is another familiar criticism from feminism that the inclusion of women cannot be a merely terminological gender-neutrality, just adding and stirring, but requires a rethinking of what, say, equal rights and freedoms will require in the context of female subordination. Susan Moller Okin argued decades ago that once one examines the real-life family, it becomes obvious that women's exit options from marriage are far more restricted than men's because of the handicaps resulting from sacrificing one's career to childrearing.[22] So a commitment to fairness, equal rights, and justice in the family arguably requires special measures to compensate for these burdens and to reform social structures accordingly. But such measures cannot be spun out, a priori, from the concept of equality as such (and certainly they cannot be generated on the basis of assuming the *ideal* family, as Rawls did in A Theory of Justice).[23] Rather, they require empirical input and an awareness of how the real-life, *non*-ideal family actually works. But insofar as such input is crucial and guides theory (which is why it is incorrect to see this as just "applied" ethics), *the theory ceases to be ideal.* So either ideal theory includes the previously excluded in a purely nominal way, which would be a purely formal rather than substantive inclusion, or—to the extent that it does make the dynamic of oppression central and theory-guiding—it is doing non-ideal theory without calling it such. (Compare the conservative appeal to a superficially fair "color-blindness" in the treatment of people of color, whose practical effect is to guarantee a blindness to the distinctive measures required to redress and overcome the legacy of white supremacy.)

Similarly, it cannot be claimed that the *possibility* of the extension of ideal theory to previously excluded populations shows that the ideal theory is *really* not exclusionary. The extension (at least in a society where these populations are subordinated, so that hegemonic concepts and argumentative patterns have accommodated to their subordination) is precisely what requires the work and marks the transition *out of* the realm of the ideal. If Kant says all persons should be treated with respect but arguably defines his terms so that being male is a prerequisite for full personhood,[24] it is not a minor change to remove this restriction. A Kantian polity where women can only be passive citizens and a polity where this stipulation is removed are not the same: the latter is not "contained" in the former as a potential waiting to be realized. When Okin uses the original position, a Rawlsian construct, to take the non-ideal family into account from behind the veil, the result is not (somehow) Rawls's "real" view—certainly not the Rawls who originally did not even mention sex as something you do not know behind the veil! What is doing the work are the *real* "general facts about human society"—the *non*-ideal facts about gender subordination that Rawls apparently did not know.

Nor, as I observed in previous chapters, did either he or his followers apparently know the non-ideal facts about imperialism, slavery, Jim Crow, segregation, and so forth that have shaped the United States and the modern world so profoundly and that constitute an ongoing and central injustice yet to be tackled by Rawlsians. How is this possible? Haven't they noticed that they're living in one of the most race-conscious societies in the world, with a history of hundreds of years of white supremacy? Again, how can one resist the obvious conclusion that it is the fact- and reality-avoidance of ideal theory that underwrites such ignorance? In *A Theory of Justice*, as earlier cited, Rawls argues for ideal theory on the grounds that while the injustices of partial compliance are the "pressing and urgent matters," we need to begin with ideal theory" as "the only basis for the systematic grasp of these more pressing problems."[25] But then why in the thirty years up to his death was he still at the beginning? Why was this promised shift of theoretical attention endlessly deferred, not just in his own writings but among the vast majority of his followers? What does this say about the evasions of ideal theory? Is it that the United States has long since achieved racial justice so there is no need to theorize it?

Or consider another example, where the opening for a discussion of race is actually explicitly part of the text rather than perennially postponed to the tomorrow that never comes. In another classic book on justice from four decades ago, Robert Nozick's *Anarchy, State, and Utopia*, Nozick defended the libertarian position that justice consisted simply in the respect for life, liberty, and property rights, and those rights that can be derived from them: justice in original acquisition, justice in transfer, and rectificatory justice.[26] Forty years later *Anarchy, State, and Utopia* remains the most theoretically sophisticated libertarian text, a bible to the far right. Philosophers of color, in keeping with their social origins, are generally left-liberal to radical, social-democratic to Marxist, and find such views anathema. Yet as was pointed out even at the time, the potential implications of Nozick's view were at least in some respects actually not conservative at all but very radical, indeed revolutionary. There could hardly be a greater and more clear-cut violation of property rights in US history than Native American expropriation and African slavery. And Nozick says explicitly (though hedging that he knows of no sophisticated treatment of the question) that populations to whom an injustice has been done are entitled to rectificatory justice that "will make use of its best estimate of subjunctive information about what would have occurred . . . if the injustice had not taken place."[27] So here the principle of rectification is *explicitly* demarcated as one of the three basic principles of justice. But in the large literature on Nozick—not as large as Rawls but substantive nonetheless—the matter of reparations for Native Americans and blacks has hardly ever been discussed. Whence this silence, considering that not even the mental effort of doing a Rawlsian race-behind-the-veil job is required? Doesn't discussion of this issue "logically" follow from Nozick's own premises? And the answer is, of course, that logic radically under-determines what actually gets thought about, researched, and written up in philosophy journals and books. White philosophers are not the population (negatively) affected by these issues, so for the most part white philosophers have not been concerned about them. "Ideally" one would have expected that the pages of libertarian and mainstream journals would have been ringing with debates on this matter. But of course they are not.[28] Only recently, as a result of black activism, has the issue of reparations become less than completely marginal nationally. And apart from white racial disinterest as a factor (or more pointedly phrased, active white racial *interest* in not raising these questions), another contributory factor must surely be Nozick's utterly fanciful opening chapters, which utilize the concept of a "process-defective potential explanation" (an explanation relying on a process that one knows did *not* actually explain the phenomenon in question [!]) to account for how the state arose. Ideal theory with a vengeance! So an entitlement theory of "justice in holdings" that prides itself on being "historical," by contrast with the "current time-slice principles" of utilitarianism, egalitarianism, Rawlsianism, and so on, falls conveniently silent when it comes to the obviously crucial question of the *actual* origins and *actual* history of the United States government. Think how differently constructed the book would have had to be if this flagrantly *non*-ideal history of racial injustice had had to be confronted instead of being marginalized to an endnote.[29]

So the abstractions of ideal theory are not innocent. Nor, as is sometimes pretended, have they simply descended from a celestial Platonic conceptual realm. Apart from their general link with the historic evasions of liberalism, they can be seen in the US context in particular as exacerbated philosophical versions of apologist concepts long hegemonic in the self-image of the nation. In *Civic Ideals*, Rogers Smith argues that the dominant tradition in studies of American political culture has been to represent it as an egalitarian liberal democracy free of the hierarchical and exclusionary social structures of Europe.[30] Taking the writings of Alexis de Tocqueville, Gunnar Myrdal, and Louis Hartz as exemplary, Smith shows that all three writers, even when they admit the existence of racism and sexism in national practices, public policy, legal rules, and central ideologies, still fall back on the conceptualization of an essentially inclusive "liberal democracy." So racism and sexism are framed as "anomalies" to a political culture conceived of as—despite everything—basically egalitarian. Despite the long history of racial subordination of nonwhites (Native American expropriation, black slavery and Jim Crow, Mexican annexation, Chinese exclusion, Japanese internment), despite the long history of legal and civic restrictions on women, the polity is still thought of as essentially liberal-democratic. The result is that mainstream political theory has not until very recently thought about and taken seriously what would be necessary to achieve genuine racial and gender equality.

I suggest that this is a perfect complement, in the more empirical realm of political science, to the abstractions in the more rarefied realm of ethics and political philosophy. In both cases, an idealized model is being represented as capturing the actual reality, and in both cases this misrepresentation has been disastrous for an adequate understanding of the real structures of oppression and exclusion that characterize the social and political order. The opting for "ideal" theory has served to rationalize the status quo.

Finally, I would propose that a non-ideal approach is also superior to an ideal approach in being better able to *realize* the ideals, by virtue of realistically recognizing the obstacles to their acceptance and implementation. In this respect, the debate between ideal and non-ideal theory can be seen as part of a larger and older historic philosophical dispute between idealism and materialism. (I am using "materialism" here as a term of art, not in the sense it is often meant—as a repudiation of ethics in the name of amorality and *realpolitik*—but to signify the commitment to locating moral theory in society and the interactions of human beings as actually shaped by social structures, by "material" social privilege and disadvantage.) Recognizing how people's social location may both blind them to important realities and give them a vested interest in maintaining things as they are is a crucial first step toward changing the social order. Ideal theory, by contrast, too often simply disregards such problems altogether or, ignoring the power relations involved, assumes it is just a matter of coming up with better arguments. Summing it all up, then, one could say epigrammatically that the best way to bring about the ideal is by recognizing the non-ideal, and that by assuming the ideal or the near-ideal, one is only guaranteeing the perpetuation of the non-ideal.[31]

CHAPTER 6
Kant's *Untermenschen*

nd that brings us to personhood, and a title deliberately chosen to be
provocative. In bringing together the moral theorist of the modern
period most famous for his putatively uncompromising commitment to the
infrangibility of our duty to respect *persons*, and the term, *sub-persons*, infa-
mously associated with the Nazi movement, I am seeking to demonstrate
the racialization of this foundational concept of liberalism and thus to challenge how we think about modern Western moral and political philosophy.
Kant's pivotal place in the Enlightenment project and the significance of
his work for ethics, political philosophy, metaphysics, epistemology, and
aesthetics locates him strategically. If Kant is central as an emblematic figure, and if racist ideas were in turn central to his views, then this obviously
implies a radical rethinking of our conventional narratives of the history
and content of Western philosophy. And such a rethinking, as emphasized
from the start, is precisely what I am arguing for.

I will divide my discussion into three sections: (1) some general background points about modernity and personhood, (2) Kant's racial views
and their implications, and (3) objections and replies.

BACKGROUND: MODERNITY AND PERSONHOOD

What are *persons*, and why does the concept become particularly important in the modern period? "Persons" is the non-sexist way of referring to
humans instead of calling them "men." (With science fiction having opened
up our horizons, it would also be appropriately used, as in Kant, to catego-
rize intelligent aliens.) Persons are entities who, because of their characteristics (for example, their threshold level of intelligence, their capacity for

autonomy), morally deserve to be protected by certain rights and freedoms, and who are on a normatively level playing field with respect to one other. And the link with the modern period is that whereas in previous ages (the slave states of ancient Greece and Rome, the feudal hierarchies of medieval Europe) moral *inequality* was the norm, modernity is supposed to usher in the epoch when all humans are seen as, and treated as, equal rights-bearing persons. In the Athenian *polis*, slaves were certainly not equal to citizens, nor could the humble serf of the feudal manor dare to put himself on the same level as the lords and ladies who ruled over him. But these distinctions of (class) rank and status are supposed to vanish in the modern period, so that *liberty* and *equality* become the central slogans of the liberalism of both the American and French revolutions. People may vary tremendously in wealth and social standing, but everybody is supposed to be morally equal and as such to be entitled to equality before the law and equality of political citizenship.

Now as an *ideal*, this is, of course, a very attractive picture. But the problem with mainstream ethics and political philosophy is that—at least until comparatively recently—this moral egalitarianism has been presented not merely as an ideal but as an accomplished *reality*. In other words, the mainstream narratives of the transition to the modern period represent liberalism as the anti-feudal political philosophy for which moral equality is the achieved default mode, the accepted normative standard from which sexism and racism are unfortunate but non-representative deviations. And I want to challenge this picture and argue, as feminist philosophers have done over the past four decades with respect to gender, that racial exclusions generally limit this supposed universal equality to Europeans. *Class* distinctions of rank and status are eliminated by the revolutions of the modern period, but pre-existing distinctions of gender are not, and distinctions of a new kind—of race—are established by modernity itself. If the supposedly equal "men" are really male, they are also generally white.

What I am suggesting, then, is that racism should be seen as a normative system in its own right that makes whiteness a prerequisite for full personhood and generally (the need for this qualification will be explained later) limits nonwhites to "sub-person" status. So whereas mainstream narratives tend to assume that adult humanness was usually sufficient, or at least strongly presumptively sufficient, for one's equal moral personhood to be recognized, I am claiming that in reality there were necessary racial pre-conditions also. In this racist conceptual and normative framework, "person" is really a technical term, a term of art, and non-Europeans are generally seen not as persons but as "savages" and "barbarians." Far from being in contradiction to modernist universalism and egalitarianism, then, racism is simply part of it—since the egalitarian theory's terms were never meant to be extended generally outside the European population. What seem to be racist inconsistencies and anomalies in the writings of the classic political philosophers of the modern period would, if I am right, now turn out to be simple and straightforward implications of racially restricted personhood.

Here is a simple way of thinking about the two rival interpretations under consideration, the mainstream view of modernity (that I am challenging) and my revisionist view. Let T be the (egalitarian) moral/political theory of the modern white Western philosopher in question, p stand for person, and sp for sub-person. Then the mainstream view is claiming that for philosopher P,

> T asserts egalitarianism for all p, where p is race-neutral.
> Racist statements are then an exception, and not part of T.

And what I am recommending as an alternative and superior interpretive framework is that, for philosopher P,

> T asserts egalitarianism for all p, where whiteness is generally a necessary condition for being p.
> T asserts non-egalitarianism for sp, where nonwhiteness is generally a sufficient condition for being sp.[1]
> Racist statements are then part of T, not an exception.

Now if this recommendation were accepted, it would, of course, dramatically alter our conception of liberalism and modern Western moral and political theory. Far from being egalitarian and universalist, in supposed sharp contrast to the hierarchical ideologies of the ancient and medieval world, liberalism too would be revealed to be a multiply tiered ideology. Persons (those humans meeting the gender and racial prerequisites) would have one standing; sub-persons (those humans failing to meet the gender and racial prerequisites) would have a different and inferior standing. So liberalism too would turn out to be a hierarchical political philosophy, though the distinctions are of gender and race rather than of class.

The great virtue of this conceptualization, apart from (I claim, anyway) its correspondence to the actual historical facts, is that it would immediately create a conceptual space for locating the distinctive character of the political struggles of people of color in the modern period in relation to mainstream political philosophy. If liberal universalism already accommodates everybody, if *person* is already race-neutral, then struggles around race and against racial subordination are puzzling. (What are they fighting for?) But once we recognize that personhood has been

racially normed, they become transparent. Mainstream political philosophy textbooks sanitize and mystify the actual record of the past few
hundred years by constructing the West as if white racial domination had
not been central to the history of the West. We go from Plato to Rawls
without a word being uttered about the racist views of the leading modern Western political theorists and the role of these views in justifying
Western political domination over the rest of the world. Acknowledging
the racial exclusions in these thinkers' ideologies provides a far more hon-
est and illuminating political framework, since it unites the anti-feudal
(white) politics of the standard narrative of modernity with the "other"
(nonwhite) politics of the alternative narrative of modernity: the anti-
colonial, anti-slavery, anti-imperialist, and anti-segregationist struggles
of people of color against racialized liberalism and for the recognition of
equal nonwhite personhood. They can then be discussed together rather
than in separate Jim-Crowed conceptual spaces.

KANT'S RACIAL VIEWS AND THEIR IMPLICATIONS

Let us now turn specifically to Kant. Kant is, of course, the famous theorist of personhood whose deontological (duty-based/rights-respecting)
version of liberalism now dominates moral and political discourse, having
triumphed over the previously dominant consequentialist (welfare-based/
utilitarian) version of liberalism originally associated with Jeremy Bentham
and the two Mills, James and John Stuart. Utilitarian liberalism was the
orthodoxy for about a century and a half, but by the mid-twentieth century
it was increasingly perceived to have deep problems of both an operational
and, more important, moral kind. John Rawls's classic *A Theory of Justice*
was one of the most powerful weapons in the attack on utilitarian theory,
and Rawls explicitly drew on Kant for his famous judgment, "Utilitarianism
does not take seriously the distinction between persons."[2] The weakness
of utilitarianism is that it seems, prima facie (utilitarians, of course, have
their comeback counterarguments), to permit infringements on the rights
of some, say an unpopular minority, if social welfare for the majority could
thereby be increased. As a consequentialist theory, it defines the right in
terms of good consequences and as such, it could generate a "right" action
or social policy that clearly seems *wrong*. By contrast, Kantianism defines
the right separately from the good, in terms of the categorical imperative to
respect other persons. So human rights seem to be set on a far firmer and
more trustworthy normative foundation. All persons are morally equal and
may not have their basic rights violated.

In this spirit, Allen Wood speaks of what he sees as Kant's "unqualified egalitarianism":

> People tend to judge themselves to be better than others on various grounds, such as birth, wealth, honor, power. . . . But [for Kant] these judgments are always mere opinions, without truth, and all social inequalities are therefore founded on falsehood and deception. . . . The reason that Kant's egalitarianism is unqualified is that the worth of every human being is a "dignity"—that is, an absolute and incomparable value.[3]

An inspiring picture—but the problem with it is that, as philosophical work by Emmanuel Eze and Robert Bernasconi reminds us (I say "remind" because both writers emphasize that this is old news in other disciplines, if breaking news to contemporary philosophers), Kant is also seen as one of the central figures in the birth of modern "scientific" racism.[4] Whereas other contributors to early racial thought like Carolus Linnaeus and Johann Friedrich Blumenbach had offered only "empirical" (scare-quotes necessary!) observation, Kant produced a full-blown *theory* of race. His lectures and writings on anthropology and physical geography are usually ignored by philosophers, but the question is whether this bracketing is theoretically legitimate considering that they map a human hierarchy of racialized superiors and inferiors: white Europeans, yellow Asians, black Africans, red Amerindians.

Consider the following passages (all cited from Eze or Bernasconi):
· The Racial Hierarchy:

> In the hot countries the human being matures earlier in all ways but does not reach the perfection of the temperate zones. Humanity exists in its greatest perfection in the white race. The yellow Indians have a smaller amount of Talent. The Negroes are lower and the lowest are a part of the American peoples.[5]

Whites:

> The white race possesses *all* motivating forces and talents *in itself.*[6]

> [Whites] contain all the impulses of nature in affects and passions, all talents, all dispositions to culture and civilization and can as readily obey as govern. They are the only ones who always advance to perfection.[7]

Asians:

> [The Hindus] do have motivating forces but they have a strong degree of passivity and all look like philosophers. Nevertheless they incline greatly towards anger and love. They thus can be educated to the highest degree but only in the arts and not in the sciences.

They can never achieve the level of abstract concepts. A great hindustani man is one who has gone far in the art of deception and has much money. The Hindus always stay the way they are, they can never advance, although they began their education much earlier.[8]

Blacks:

The race of the Negroes, one could say, is completely the opposite of the Americans; they are full of affect and passion, very lively, talkative and vain. They can be educated but only as servants (slaves), that is they allow themselves to be trained. They have many motivating forces, are also sensitive, are afraid of blows and do much out of a sense of honor.[9]

Mr [David] Hume challenges anyone to cite a simple example in which a Negro has shown talents, and asserts that among the hundreds of thousands of blacks who are transported elsewhere from their countries, although many of them have been set free, still not a single one was ever found who presented anything great in art or science or any other praiseworthy quality; even among the whites some continually rise aloft from the lowest rabble, and through superior gifts earn respect in the world. So fundamental is the difference between the two races of man, and it appears to be as great in regard to mental capacities as in color.[10]

The Negro can be disciplined and cultivated, but is never genuinely civilized. He falls of his own accord into savagery.[11]

Native Americans:

The race of the American cannot be educated. It has no motivating force, for it lacks affect and passion. They are not in love, thus they are also not afraid. They hardly speak, do not caress each other, care about nothing and are lazy.[12]

That their [Native Americans'] natural disposition has not yet reached a complete fitness for any climate provides a test that can hardly offer another explanation why this race, too weak for hard labor, too phlegmatic for diligence, and unfit for any culture, still stands—despite the proximity of example and ample encouragement—far below the Negro, who undoubtedly holds the lowest of all remaining levels by which we designate the different races.[13]

Americans and Blacks cannot govern themselves. They thus serve only for slaves.[14]

"Miscegenation"

Should one propose that the races be fused or not? They do not fuse and it is also not desirable that they should. The Whites would be degraded. For not every race adopts the morals and customs of the Europeans.[15]

> Instead of assimilation, which was intended by the melting together of the various races, Nature has here made a law of just the opposite.[16]

The Future of the Planet

> All races will be extinguished . . . only not that of the Whites.[17]

Now if the only Kant one knows is the Kant sanitized for public consumption, these views will obviously come as a great shock. Kant believed in a natural racial hierarchy, with whites at the top, and blacks and Native Americans ("savages") at the bottom. He saw the last two races as natural slaves incapable of cultural achievement, and accordingly (like an old-time southern segregationist) he opposed intermarriage as leading to the degradation of whites. Ultimately, he thought, the planet would become all white.

So what are the philosophical implications of these views? Doing an open-minded inquiry into this question requires us, to a certain extent, to bracket what we *think* we know Kant's philosophy is and not substitute hagiography for theoretical investigation. Accordingly, various authors have been grappling with this question in the English-language secondary literature and a range of positions has emerged. Pertinent work would include Allen Wood's *Kant's Ethical Thought*; Robert Louden's *Kant's Impure Ethics*; Eze's *Achieving Our Humanity*, building on his Kant article and other related critiques; Tsenay Serequeberhan's "The Critique of Eurocentrism and the Practice of African Philosophy"; Robert Bernasconi's two articles, cited above; and pieces by Mark Larrimore, and (jointly) Thomas Hill and Bernard Boxill.[18] Representative positions from the German literature would include work by Rudolf Malter and Reinhard Brandt.[19] These authors variously offer condemnations and defenses of Kant, qualified in different ways, so that a set of characteristic moves is now recognizable.

The position that Kant's defenders have taken is not to deny Kant's racial views but to deny that they have the philosophical implications claimed by Eze, Bernasconi, and others (such as myself). So either Kant's racial views do not affect his philosophy *at all* (the extreme position), or they do not affect it in its *key/central/essential/basic* claims (the more moderate position). The assumption, obviously, is that we have a principled, non-question-begging way to demarcate what is central from what is peripheral to his philosophy, and a similarly principled way of showing how the racial views (and, of course, their implications) fail to penetrate to this inner circle. And the case critics must make is that such a penetration does in fact take place, so that what has been represented as Kant's philosophy in innumerable journal articles, monographs, and textbooks over the years is, insofar as it is racially neutral, quite misleading.

Let us focus on the obvious candidate: the ethics and political philosophy. Kant's claims about the imperative to respect *persons*, his views about
the moral state (the *Rechtsstaat*) and its obligations to its citizens, his
vision of a future cosmopolitan order where all peoples on the planet will
be guided by universal law, are all familiar to us. Now suppose it turns out
that not all adult humans are *persons* for him, either (depending on how we
want to draw the conceptual geography) because they constitute a separate
category of their own, or because within the category of personhood, internal differentiations can be made. In other words, what is supposed to be
the starkly polarized moral geography of his theory, with everything being
categorizable either as a *person*, with full moral status, or as a *non-person*, a
thing, with zero moral status, would have to be redrawn to accommodate
the fuzzier category of entities with some *intermediate* status. And what
we think we know his various moral, political, and teleological claims to
be would all then have to be rethought in the light of this category's existence, so that what holds for the full-blooded, 100 percent, 24-karat persons would not always necessarily hold in the same way for those in this
inferior group. If this analysis is correct, it is obviously a radically different
picture of the Kant we all thought we knew. The distinction between "Treat
all persons with respect," where "person" is assumed to be racially inclusive,
and "Treat only whites with respect" (at least here on Earth) is obviously
not minor and trivial at all. It would mean that his vaunted universalism and
egalitarianism are restricted to the white population.

How would the case be made? I think the evidential supports fall into
three main possible categories: (a) attempts to demonstrate how Kant's general theoretical claims can be shown to have these implications; (b) citations
of specific remarks and passages from Kant seemingly consistent with these
implications; (c) the evidence of textual silence. The last is obviously a tricky
category, since silence can speak in more than one way. But if a convincing
background theoretical context has been sketched, the failure to address certain topics, or failure to make certain points that would naturally be expected
when certain topics are raised, can—in conjunction, of course, with other
considerations—at least count as supporting evidence for an interpretation, if not as a definitive proof. Correspondingly, what Kant's defenders
have to do is to argue that no such general theoretical ramifications can be
established, that seemingly damning passages can be reinterpreted, or quarantined, and/or countered with passages pointing the other way, and that
textual silence either has no significance or can be heard differently.

Let us start with (a). Eze takes Kant, inspired by Rousseau's account of
how we develop our humanity, to be working with a general theory by which
humans transform themselves into moral beings. Hence the significance of
Kant's anthropology. Because of his views of natural and immutable racial

hierarchy, Eze argues, Kant thought that nonwhites—especially blacks and Native Americans—were not so constituted as to be able to go through this process of self-development and moral maturation. (I focus on blacks and Native Americans as the clear-cut case. As seen above, Asians are just one rung below whites, and though they "can never achieve the level of abstract concepts," Kant does at least describe them as "look[ing] like philosophers." So perhaps, though still inferior, they can parlay this phenomenal appearance into a noumenal payoff.) In other words, there is a certain minimal threshold of intelligence, capacity for autonomy, and so on required to be a full person, and blacks and Native Americans do not reach this threshold. As such, they are all (in my terminology rather than Eze's) sub-persons. And Eze argues that for Kant this claim is "transcendentally" grounded, so that as a theorist of scientific racism, Kant has advanced beyond the more empiricist Linnaeus:

> Beyond Buffon and Linnaeus, then, Kant practiced a transcendental philosophy of race. . . . In the *Observations* . . . Kant deployed the transcendentalism of the *Critique of Pure Reason* in order to establish ways in which moral feelings apply to humans *generally*, how the feeling differs between men and women, and among the races. . . . The themes Kant presented in these books . . . give synthesis to the principles and practices he philosophically defined as immanent to humans, but only to white human nature. . . . The inferiority of the Negro, as proposed by Hume, is now in Kant successfully grounded in transcendental philosophy.[20]

If this analysis is correct, the implications for the categorical imperative (CI) could be simply expressed as follows:

> CI: All persons should be treated with respect. GLOSS: "Person" is a technical term, a term of art, signifying beings of a certain level of intelligence and capacity for moral maturity, and on this planet, whiteness is a necessary prerequisite for being a person in the full sense.
>
> (Whiteness is not sufficient, because of the parallel feminist case with respect to gender.)

Now this, to say the least, would obviously be a radically different way of thinking of the categorical imperative, and insofar as the categorical imperative is central to Kant's moral and political philosophy, Kant's views on race would indeed have major and central philosophical implications. The case could then be buttressed by (b), specific negative passages on blacks and Native Americans such as those cited above—for example, that they are savages and natural slaves, that Native Americans are completely incapable of moral education, while blacks need to be educated through flogging (and with a specially constructed split bamboo cane),[21] that race mixing leads to the degradation of whites and is contrary to nature, that only the white race is destined to survive, and so forth. It would be contended that these passages constitute obvious prima facie evidence that Kant did not envisage blacks and Native Americans as fully included in his kingdom of ends, "active citizens" of the polity, and equal beneficiaries of the cosmopolitan order toward which the planet is evolving.

Finally, on (c), textual silence, Robert Bernasconi makes the valuable point that, so far as he knows, nowhere in Kant's writings (and remember these comprise numerous volumes) does Kant offer an unequivocal condemnation of African slavery.[22] (Note that one can condemn the *cruelties* of slavery, as some reformers did, while still being anti-abolitionist. Obviously, the ethical desideratum is the principled condemnation of the institution as such.) Yet a more flagrant violation of the prohibition against using one's fellow-persons as mere means to an end could hardly be imagined, and it was not as if the Atlantic slave trade was in its infancy at the time he wrote. Whence this puzzling silence, even when the subject of slavery came up in his writings? Obviously, one simple solution to the mystery would be that Kant did not see blacks as fellow-persons, even if they were fellow-humans.

However, we must now turn to the case for the defense. Above, I distinguished extreme and moderate positions among Kant's defenders. The work of Malter, Wood, and Louden seems to me to fall toward the more extreme end of the spectrum, insofar as they deny that Kant's racial views have any implications for his philosophy at all.

Let us begin with Malter, the most extreme of all, for whom, remarkably, Kant emerges as a committed *anti*-racist: "The *equality* of all individuals of the human race is for Kant knowable by pure reason. . . . The Kantian theory of race not only does not pave the way for racism, (but) it is the most serious, energetic objection to this—the very worst—madness."[23] Morality for Kant is a priori, not empirical, based on pure reason. So the full personhood of nonwhites is guaranteed as a synthetic a priori truth. But this seems to me to rest on an elision of "human" and "person" of precisely the kind I earlier warned against. What is a priori is that all rational beings are deserving of our respect; it is *not* a priori that all humans are rational beings (in the requisite full sense).

By contrast, Allen Wood concedes Kant's racism but argues that it is overridden by his philosophical commitments. Kant, according to Wood, "conspicuously declines to infer from [his] racialist beliefs . . . that there is any difference in the *human rights* possessed by different peoples," and "the most influential philosophical articulation of these values is Kant's theory of moral autonomy, grounded in the dignity of humanity as an end in itself."[24] Similarly, Robert Louden's *Kant's Impure Ethics* draws a contrast between Kant's *theory* and Kant's *prejudices*, denying that the latter should be taken to modify (what we think of as) the former:

> Kant's writings do exhibit many private prejudices and contradictory tendencies. . . . But Kant's theory is fortunately stronger than his prejudices, and it is the theory on which philosophers should focus. We should not hide or suppress the prejudices, but neither should we overvalue them or try to inflate them into something they are not. . . . The prejudices are not centrally connected to the defining features of his theory of human moral development.[25]

Both writers, then, are offering us a conceptual partitioning of Kant's discourse, on the one hand, the philosophical theory (morally egalitarian), and on the other hand views assigned to some lower epistemic category, not rising to the level of the theoretical: unthinking prejudice, bigotry, and so on. So though the prejudices are offensive, the theory itself is untouched, quarantined behind a conceptual cordon sanitaire.

This is obviously a better argument than Malter's,[26] but I would claim it is still problematic. The question is why we should accept this partitioning. I think there are three possible ways of defending this move: one can claim that Kant's egalitarian theory (henceforth T) is not affected by his racist views because they are in a different conceptual space; one can claim that T represents the essence of Kant's position; and one can claim that T can be reconstructed as a sanitized version of Kant's position. But each of these moves faces problems of its own.

The first is assuming that the racism is sub-theoretical and so should be judged to be overridden by T (understood as egalitarian and non-racial). But I began by arguing that racism should be seen as a normative theory in its own right, so this overriding cannot simply be asserted but must be demonstrated. Nor can it casually be inferred from T's apparent race-neutrality, as revealed in its vocabulary of "men," "persons," or "humans," for the very question is whether people of color are being conceived of as full persons, fully human.

The second differentiates Kant's essential from his non-essential views and represents the egalitarian T as the essence of his position. But "essential" is ambiguous: does it mean "essential" for *our* purposes (we later philosophers seeking a usable version of Kant) or "essential" for Kant's view of his own theory? The first shades over into option three, below; the second needs to prove by non-question-begging criteria that Kant himself did not see the racist claims as crucial to his theory, T.

Finally, the problem with the third is that it is a separate question. While it is, of course, always possible to reconstruct a theory in which personhood has no racial or gender restrictions, the question at issue is what Kant thought. And if Kant himself did not think of nonwhites and women as full persons, then this cannot really be said to be *Kant's* theory. Most of the theoretical terms will be the same (respect, the kingdom of ends, the categorical imperative), but at least one crucial theoretical term, "person," will not have the same denotation. So while such an enterprise is justifiable from the perspective of developing a moral theory acceptable for our purposes, it cannot be claimed, except in some scare-quotes sense, that this is still "Kant's" theory.

Consider now the moderate position. This position does not deny that Kant's racial views affect his philosophical claims, but it denies that they affect the *central* ones. I take Hill and Boxill's joint paper to be a good statement of this line of argument:

> Our position, then, is that, while it is important to notice and block the influence of aspects of Kant's writings that reflect or might encourage racism, the charges of racism do not reach Kant's deep theory. . . . [T]he texts do not in fact support the extreme form of racist beliefs that Eze attributes to Kant, e.g. that some races are not human. . . . Eze succeeds in showing that Kant saw his racial theory as a serious philosophical project, that it was not an offhand, unreflective set of conjectures, and that it deserves philosophical attention. . . . But these concessions do not imply that Kant's central philosophical principles are tainted with racism.[27]

So the presumption is that we have at hand a principled, non-question-begging criterion for distinguishing the deep and central from the shallow and peripheral, and that by this criterion it can be shown that Kant's key theses emerge untouched. A different kind of conceptual partitioning is proposed, which concedes philosophical status to Kant's racial views (they are not just "prejudices"), but relegates them to a subordinate status in his thought, and maintains the unaffectedness of what are taken to be the key principles.

Now one way of defending this partitioning is to emphasize the differential epistemic status of Kant's moral claims. As just mentioned, Kant famously thought that there were synthetic a priori truths, substantive claims (as against definitional truths like "bachelors are unmarried males") discoverable by pure reason, and that the categorical imperative was one of them. So the reformulation above could be stated thus:

> CI: All persons should be treated with respect. Status: (supposedly) synthetic a priori truth.➔ CENTRAL

> Auxiliary claim: Whiteness is a prerequisite for personhood. Status: empirical a posteriori claim. ➔ PERIPHERAL

On this basis, then, you could concede that Kant's racial views affect his philosophy, while denying that they affect it *centrally* (deeply, basically, in its key tenets). For you now have a principled demarcation, a conceptual wall, to separate the central from the peripheral.

Opponents of this line of argument have (at least) two moves that could be made in reply. One would be to claim that race also is a transcendental. Whether or not his motivation was to establish centrality by this criterion, this, as we have seen, is Eze's move. But Hill and Boxill argue against this claim, and to my mind make some good points: the inferiority of nonwhites seems (to us, obviously, but more to the point, to Kant) more a matter of an empirical a posteriori claim than something that could be determined by pure reason, or as a condition of experience.[28] And Robert Louden, both in his book and in his paper on Eze's book on a 2002 American Philosophical Association Author-meets-Critics panel, is similarly skeptical.[29]

Perhaps Eze has a reply that will vindicate his position. But whether he has or not, I wonder whether he is not setting himself an unnecessarily onerous task in trying to defend his crucial claim, which I take it is the assertion of the centrality of racial views (in Kant and others) to modern Western philosophy. For the alternative move is to *deny* that being a synthetic a priori truth is a prerequisite for being central/basic/deep for Kant, and to make a case by other, arguably non-question-begging and uncontroversial, criteria of "centrality." Certainly for moral and political theory in general the auxiliary claim *is* absolutely crucial, since it demarcates who/what is included in and who/what is excluded from full membership in the moral/political community.

Consider our moral duties toward non-human animals and the environment. As we all know, non-human animals, trees, plants, and so on have no moral standing for Kant; his is a classic statement of an anthropocentric moral theory (though *anthropos* here is broader than human, including intelligent aliens). But recently some environmental ethicists have argued for an expansion and modification of the Kantian notion of "respect" to accommodate respect for the earth and other living things. Now wouldn't it seem very peculiar to say that this was *not* a major modification of Kant's theory? This expansion of the scope of beings to which respect is supposed to be extended would have major repercussions for how the theory is applied and how we think of it—if it even counts as the "same" theory any more. Kant's own Kantianism and this non-anthropocentric "Kantianism" are worlds apart in their implications for what is obligatory, prohibited, and permissible for us to do as moral agents.

But it could be replied that even if this is true, this is not a legitimate comparison, since extending "respect" to non-human animals obviously requires us to dispense with rationality and the capacity for autonomy as the bearers of moral status, so that Kant's basic principle is altered. In the case of race, however, even if it were true that nonwhites count as sub-persons for Kant by virtue of their inferior rationality and diminished capacity for autonomy, deracializing the theory just requires getting rid of a false factual claim, not modifying the basic moral principle.

I would have to concede that there is something to this objection. However, it seems to me that the claim of centrality can still be made. Consider the following example. A well-known twentieth-century figure, whose views (unlike those of the vast majority of philosophers) actually did touch the lives of millions, had a moral philosophy whose terms could be reconstructed (admittedly in a somewhat idealized way) as follows: group G should flourish, are owed respect, should be protected by the state, have their rights respected, and so forth. I am sure everybody will agree that this all sounds very good and commendable. Now suppose I reveal that the thinker I have in mind is Adolf Hitler, and group G are the Aryan race. "Oh, that's quite different!" you will exclaim in horror. But wait, I say, the *central principles, the essential claims,* of his ethical theory are very attractive. It is just—a minor point, this—that because of his empirical beliefs, he wanted to apply them only to a restricted set of the human population. However, surely we can lightly pass over this minor empirical mistake and argue that his basic views remain untouched, since the ideals of flourishing, the respect for rights and so forth are the really important thing, even if in his own formulation, not everybody was included. So could we not say that Hitler's moral theory is, at its core, at the deep level, a non-racial one . . .?

Now I am not comparing Kant to Hitler. But the point I am trying to bring home is that there is something very strange about dismissing the issue of who gets counted in the moral community as merely a matter of incidental detail. We rightly think that the whole burden of Hitler's moral theory, if it deserves the name, is that it is racially exclusionary, and that once you extend it beyond "Aryans," then obviously it is not the same theory. Even if Hitler had never come to power, even if the Holocaust had never occurred, we would still see this fact of racial restriction as deeply pernicious and as profoundly shaping the theory. How then can it be denied that—whatever their epistemological foundation—these claims about the scope of the populations to which the principles are supposed to extend are indeed philosophically "central" (in theory, and unquestionably in practice)?

So this would be my friendly amendment to Eze's project: that even if the "transcendental" claims cannot be sustained, the thesis of philosophical "centrality" can still be defended on other grounds. And the argument is made all the stronger, of course, by the fact that in the case of Kant at least we are not really talking about a mere "empirical" belief but a sophisticated and elaborated *theoretical* position. Both Eze and Bernasconi see Kant as one of the founders of modern "scientific" racism. So if this is right, then what is involved, while weaker than transcendental necessity, is stronger than empirical fortuitousness: it is a nomological, causal necessity, according to which humanoids of a certain color cannot achieve the basement-level intelligence to be fully moral beings. The color of the skin is a surface indicator of the presence of deeper physico-biological causal mechanisms. If we think of the "ontological" as covering what an entity *is*, then the physical makeup of a dog will have ontological implications (its capacity for rationality, agency, autonomy, and so on), and so similarly will the makeup of these inferior humans: race does not have to be transcendental to be (in a familiar sense) metaphysical.

The other friendly amendment I would offer—in response to Hill and Boxill's other criticism of Eze, that it is false that Kant regarded nonwhites as non-human—is, as discussed earlier, that the case for diminished moral status can be defended (through the "sub-person" category) without making such a strong assumption. One does not have to claim that for Kant nonwhites are non-humans; one just has to assert that for him (and others) humans come in different sub-categories, and that not all humans make it to the (full) "person" level.

This, then, with variants in (a) (Eze's version is not the only possibility) would be the case for the prosecution: when Kant urged on us the overwhelming importance of respecting *persons*, he was really talking (on this planet) about whites (more precisely, a subset of whites).

OBJECTIONS AND REPLIES

Let us now consider some of the objections that could be made to this case from the defense.

The writings in anthropology and physical geography are separate from, and irrelevant to, the writings in ethics and political philosophy.

This just begs the question. Since the case for the prosecution rests crucially on the claim that Kant made internal differentiations in the category of human beings, and since it in these very writings that we find the evidence for the differentiations, they cannot be rejected in advance. This would be to assume that we *know* that when he was speaking of "persons," he fully included nonwhites within the category. But we don't "know" this— we are just assuming it, in keeping with the orthodox view, which is precisely what is being challenged. Eze also makes the useful point that in the course of his academic career Kant gave far more courses on these subjects (seventy-two) than on the moral philosophy (twenty-eight), which would seem to constitute prima facie evidence that he considered them important. Moreover, these subjects were new at the time, and Kant was himself the person who introduced both of them to German universities, drawing on his own research.[30]

Kant's moral community is famously clear-cut in its geography, being starkly divided between persons (with full moral status) and non-persons or things (with zero moral status). So there is simply no conceptual room for your "sub-person" category.

The "sub-person" category is, admittedly, a reconstruction of the normative logic of racial and gender subordination in his thought, a reconstruction that is certainly not openly proclaimed in the articulation of his conceptual apparatus, and may seem, prima facie, to be excluded by it. (In a personal communication, Robert Louden points out as an objection to my reading that nowhere does Kant himself use the term *Untermenschen*.) Nonetheless, I would claim that it is the best way of making sense of the *actual* (as against officially represented) logic of his writings, taken as a whole, and accommodates the sexist and racist declarations in a way less strained than the orthodox reading. In other words, there is an ironic sense in which the principle of interpretive charity—that we should try to reconstruct an author's writings so as to maximize their degree of internal consistency—points toward such a concept's being implicit in his thought, since in this way the degree of contradictoriness among his various claims is reduced.

Consider gender. Work by feminist theorists such as Pauline Kleingeld and Hannelore Schröder emphasizes the stark disparity between Kant's supposed commitment to unqualified personhood and what he actually says about women. Kleingeld points out that while Kant supposedly "asserts both the equality and autonomy of all human beings," he simultaneously "regards men as naturally superior to women, and women as unfit for the public, political and economic domain," implies that women, being guided by "inclination," are incapable of autonomy, asserts that women "have to be legally represented by men," "are under permanent male guardianship," "have no legal competence, cannot go to court," and "lack the right to citizenship," being merely "passive citizens" who do not have the attributes of lawful freedom, civil equality, and civil independence.[31] So Kleingeld does not at all want to downplay Kant's sexism. But she thinks the correct approach is to highlight (what she sees as) the tension between his universalism and his gender-differentiated views, and in her comments on my presentation of this paper she argued that we should conceptualize his racism in the same way, as being inconsistent with his stated position elsewhere.[32] By contrast, I would claim that it is, ironically, more charitable to Kant to see him as tacitly operating with a concept of personhood that is gender- and race-restricted. This reduces the degree of cognitive dissonance involved in his writings: the *flagrant* contradiction contained in the assertions that women are (full) persons but can be only passive citizens, or that blacks and Native Americans are (full) persons who are simultaneously natural slaves, becomes the less dissonant position that personhood comes in degrees.

On the other hand, if defenders of the orthodox interpretation reply that though women and nonwhites are "persons" in a somewhat different way for Kant, they are nonetheless still *persons* and not "sub-persons," then it seems to me that they face the following simple dilemma. Either (a) they are conceding the point in all but terminology, so the difference between us becomes merely verbal and not substantive (though I would claim that my vocabulary, formally divided, signals the real differentiations in reference, and so is superior to theirs, which obfuscates these differentiations), or (b) they are so weakening the concept of a "person," so evacuating it of significant normative content, that it loses most of the moral force supposedly associated with it.

The German scholar Reinhard Brandt, for example, argues that for Kant "women and people of color cannot act in accordance with principles of their own, but can only imitate morality. . . . [T]herefore from the moral perspective they constitute intermediate creatures (*Zwischenwesen*) in between the human and animal kingdoms." This might seem to be an endorsement of something very like my "sub-person" reading. But despite appearances, it is not, for in the very next paragraph Brandt goes on to conclude: "People of color and women are for Kant legal persons and enjoy the protection of universal moral and legal principles. . . . Respect for the moral law as such knows no bounds of sex and race."[33]

Brandt does not explain how enjoying "the protection of universal moral and legal principles" and savoring one's entitlement to gender- and race-neutral respect are compatible with persons' being restricted to passive citizenship or being viewed as natural slaves who have to be whipped to further their moral education. If a sub-category exists within "persons" of somewhat-differently-constituted-persons, *Zwischenwesen*, and if this difference in constitution is (as it is) one of *inferiority*, precluding the full array of rights, entitlements, and freedoms of full persons, then what is this but to concede in all but *name* the category of sub-personhood? On the other hand, if it is still possible to be a person in some sense, and yet (as with women) to be denied the basic rights of political participation, or (as with blacks and Native Americans) to be judged to be natural slaves, then what is this "personhood" worth? Would you raise the flag of liberty, man the barricades, prepare to sacrifice your lives for it? Obviously not. Such a concept would be a radically etiolated version of the one that is supposed to be the normative soul of the modern epoch. So if personhood in the standard sense is supposed to be a robust notion linked with moral egalitarianism and an associated bundle of moral rights and freedoms that translates into juridical and political equality, then this concept clearly is not it.

Kant was an orthodox Christian, and as such a believer in monogenesis; so he could not possibly have accepted such a radical differentiation in the human race.

See the last five hundred years of global history. Who do you think has been responsible for the origination and implementation of the most important variants of racism over the past half-millennium, from anti-Semitism to colonial white domination, if *not* orthodox Christians? The opening chapter of George Fredrickson's book, *Racism: A Short History*, is in fact explicitly titled "Religion and the Invention of Racism"—and he is not talking about Buddhism.[34] The two most unqualifiedly racist governments of the twentieth century, Nazi Germany and apartheid South Africa, were both located in Christian countries, as was, of course, the American Old South. In general, Christianity's ostensible universalism has never constituted more than a weak, easily overcome barrier against racism. And as recently as the late nineteenth century and early twentieth centuries, Social Darwinists had no problem in reconciling monogenesis with the view that some races, though of the same origin as Europeans, and thus human, were "lower," less evolved, and destined for permanent inferiority and/or extinction.

The simple refutation of your thesis is that Kant explicitly condemned European colonialism and urged that Europeans make contracts with Native Americans.

If, as I claim, people of color, especially blacks and Native Americans, were sub-persons for Kant, then how could he have condemned their colonization and demanded that treaties be made with the latter?[35] This is probably the strongest argument in the arsenal of Kant's defenders (it is emphasized by both Wood and Louden).[36] Here is a set of possible moves.

First, one needs to distinguish condemnations in principle of colonialism from condemnations of specific aspects of it. At least some of the passages in his writings seem to be focused on specific colonial atrocities, and insofar as, given my analysis, nonwhites (unlike animals) *do* have a non-zero moral status, it is not inconsistent with my reading that there should be moral constraints on how people of color are treated. Over the history of European imperialism, there were, after all, many European reformers who deplored its cruelties while still endorsing it in principle, and who proselytized for a reformed, enlightened colonialism. So Kant could be one of those theorists.

Second, Robert Bernasconi has argued that even where Kant does seem to condemn colonialism in principle, he is really denying the validity of *one kind* of justification of colonialism, leaving open the possibility that other kinds of justification could be developed.[37]

Finally, there is the fallback position that such passages are simply inconsistent with the theoretical implications (i.e., on the sub-person reading) of his work, and that rather than concluding it is the theory which must give way, we should take the opposite tack and conclude that it is these passages that must give way. In other words, rather than claiming that there is complete unity and consistency in all his writings, we would contend that some are inconsistent with others, so the decision has to be made as to which are better supported by the overall logic of his thought. Insofar as we should privilege a theoretically based claim over one that seems lacking in such support, the theory should dominate. This is Eze's own solution in the opening pages of the Kant chapter of his book, where he argues that Kant is *not* entitled, given the assumptions of his own theory, to such condemnation.[38] Obviously, however, there is the danger of circularity here, since defenders of Kant will claim that no such theory has in fact been established, so that where the condemnation is uncontroversial and the putative theory is contested, greater adjudicative weight has to be placed on the specific passages than on question-begging theoretical claims. (Pauline Kleingeld argues that a virtue of her interpretation in contrast to mine is that such passages do not pose a problem for her, since she is claiming that Kant's views do lead to contradictions.)[39]

With respect to Native Americans in particular, though, Maureen Konkle's *Writing Indian Nations* has provided me with some illuminating insights, from real-life history, on the possibilities for reconciling equality and inferiority.[40] Naïve and simple-minded philosophers, bewitched by seemingly obvious syllogisms (treaties are only made with those seen as equals; treaties were made with Native Americans; therefore, Native Americans were seen as equals), would have been lost in dealing with the far subtler minds of colonial jurisprudence, for whom the affirmation of p & $\sim p$ was a routine matter. Konkle begins by pointing out that "no other instance of European colonization produced as many or as significant treaties" as in US relations with Native Americans. But this by no means implied unequivocal recognition of their equality. Citing the 1831 and 1832 *Cherokee Nation* cases ("which remain the key cases of Indian law"), Konkle emphasizes that the problem was "to assert colonial authority—tyrannical, imperial authority, of the kind the United States had thrown off in the Revolution—while appearing not to." So while Native peoples were conceded to form sovereign nations, these were also, in Chief Justice John Marshall's formulation, "domestic dependent nations," thus reconciling nationhood with "the necessity of colonial control":

> Indians formed *nations*, he posits, but because they were *Indian* nations and because Indians could be characterized by their essential difference from and inferiority to Europeans, they are in a permanent state of "pupilage" to the United States.... [In his concurring opinion, Justice William Johnson] exposes the high political stakes in the concept of Indians' inherent difference: it is the only available means of displacing and denying Native legal claims while retaining the notion of their consent to give up their land, which is still necessary to legitimate EuroAmerican control of territory.[41]

The fact that American justices saw Native Americans as inferior while making treaties with them does not, of course, prove that Kant had a similar view. But I think the actual historical record here demonstrates the mistakenness of the smooth and unproblematic inference from treaty-making to the commitment to moral egalitarianism and should alert us that colonial and racial discourse has the ability (as with gender ideology) to take away with one hand what it gives with the other (European givers?).

Your attempted critique runs aground on the following simple dilemma: either, (a), you are arguing, absurdly, that we must now throw out Kant's moral theory, or, (b), you are forced, more reasonably, to wind up conceding (somewhat anti-climactically) that we should keep it, in which case your whole critique has been much ado about nothing.

If my analysis is correct, then we certainly should throw out Kant's moral theory, since Kant's moral theory makes whiteness and maleness prerequisites for full personhood!

But of course when people make this rejoinder, they do not mean that. What they mean is "Kant's moral theory" in the racially inclusive and gender-inclusive sense, which (if I am right) is not Kant's moral theory at all but a bowdlerized, idealized, and sanitized reconstruction that draws on crucial Kantian concepts but, in its inclusivity, violates Kantian principles. Nonetheless, it will be insisted, that is just a quibble. So this could be thought of as the "So what?" challenge, raised not merely against this analysis of Kant but against parallel analyses of other canonical philosophers. The claim will be made—the claim *is* made—that from a philosophical point of view, Kant's, or P's, racial views are irrelevant (even if conceded), either because they do not affect his philosophy at all, or because even if they do, even if (it may be grudgingly admitted) my argument goes through, it is in ways that can easily be purged from the theory. So even if P's pronouncements about "men" or "people" were actually only about males and whites, the extension to all humans can readily be made. According to the "So what?" challenge, this kind of project is just sensationalism, "tabloid phi-losophy,"[42] muckraking, and muckraking without much or any theoretical payoff either.

I think this view is fairly widespread in philosophy, and as I have argued elsewhere, I think it is mistaken. I want to conclude by listing at least three reasons why I think it is wrong.

To begin with, if it is indeed the case that Kant, or more generally P, was just describing whites, or was morally and politically prescribing just for whites in his (egalitarian) theory, then surely this is an important fact about his thought that needs to be known and made explicit. Even if P's thought can be easily sanitized, to talk as if P were putting forward race-neutral theories when he is really putting forward racially differentiated theories is still a fundamental misrepresentation. As argued above, there is something deeply troubling and profoundly misleading about racially san-itizing Kant's views and then representing them as if they *were* the views of the pre-sanitized Kant.[43] Who and what makes the cut in a moral theory is central to what kind of theory it is. Obviously the principle of respect for persons can be extended in a racially indifferent way to include all races. But if this is an extension, it is not a minor technicality that is somehow "already" (essentially, really) implicit in the theory. At the basic level of doing an accurate history of Western philosophy, then, the official narra-tives need to be rethought and rewritten. So there are meta-theoretical implications for how we think of the development of philosophy. As the discipline standardly presents itself, matters of race are unimportant to its development; Western philosophy is supposed to be universal and inclu-sive. Now it would turn out that matters of race were indeed important to its evolution, at least in the modern period. The colonial dimensions of the thought of, and in some cases actual colonial roles of Hobbes, Hume, Locke, Kant, Hegel, Mill, and so on would become a legitimate part of the history of modern philosophy.

Second, it could well be that these exclusions do in fact affect the think-er's thought in other ways whose ramifications need to be worked out. In the case of gender, the connection is easier to make, in part because femi-nists have been laboring on these questions longer than critical race theo-rists. If you have been generalizing about humanity on the basis of one-half of it, then there will obviously be vast areas of history and experience that need to be brought in to correct for these omissions. Political theorists such as Susan Moller Okin have argued against a merely "terminological" gender neutrality, which contents itself with a self-conscious alternation of "he" and "she" without considering how the originally sexist theory's basic concep-tual apparatus, assumptions, and pronouncements may have been shaped by these gender exclusions.[44] Do crucial concepts such as "autonomy" need to be given a different emphasis, if a case can be made that a tacitly masculine experience has grounded their formation? Is the disdain for "inclination" linked with its identification with the body and the feminine? It could be argued similarly that genuine race neutrality requires a careful rethinking of white philosophy's content in the light of racial domination. If nonwhite "savagery" is the negative antipode against which civilized (white) humanity is going to define itself, then obviously the interlocking conceptual relationships are likely to shape how these concepts of "civilization," and what it is to rise above nature, develop. Both in the descriptive realm, where full humanity is conceptualized in Eurocentric and culturally loaded terms, and in the prescriptive realm, the implications could be far-reaching.

Finally, ignoring the racial exclusions in Kant's (and other modern Western philosophers') moral and political theory obfuscates the distinctive moral topography opened up by recognizing the experience of those persons systematically treated as less than persons. Instead of seeing these exclusions as merely an embarrassment, we should be taking them as a philosophical challenge. Instead of pretending that Kant was arguing for equal respect to be extended to everybody, we should be asking how Kant's theory needs to be rethought in the light not merely of his own racism but of a modern world with a normative architecture based on racist Kant-like principles. How is "respect" to be cashed out, for example, for a population that has historically been seen as less than persons? Should it be reconceptualized with a supplementary group dimension, given that white supremacy has stigmatized entire races as less than worthy of respect, as appropriately to be "dissed?" What corrective measures would be required of the *Rechtsstaat* to redress racial subordination? How is cosmopolitanism to be realized on a globe shaped by hundreds of years of European expansionism? Even if we still want to call the theory "Kantianism," it would be a Kantianism radically transformed by the challenge of addressing the moral demands of the sub-person population.[45]

In short, the moral and political agenda of those persons not originally seen as full persons will be significantly different from the agenda of those whose personhood has traditionally been uncontested, and we need concepts, narratives, and theories that register this crucial difference. So that's what.[46]

CHAPTER 7

Racial Exploitation

What philosophical framework should we use to theorize racial injustice? Clearly, given the discussions of the last two chapters, it should be located within non-ideal theory, rejecting Rawlsian conceptions of society as "a cooperative venture for mutual advantage" among reciprocally respecting "persons."[1] Rather, the history of the racial subordination and exploitation of those seen as sub-persons must be central to the normative framing of the issue. Reparations for African Americans, for example, would be an obvious example of such a racial justice corrective policy, which would presumably fall under what Rawls calls "compensatory justice."[2] And for a brief period a decade and a half ago, stimulated by the 2000 publication of Randall Robinson's *The Debt*,[3] this issue became sufficiently provocative for city councils across the country to take a position on the question, and for "white" universities to debate the matter.[4]

Philosophy, however, was not a central player. Very little of the credit for this development could go to the discipline, despite the fact that philosophers are by their calling supposed to be the group professionally concerned about justice as a concept and an ideal. Yet there is certainly enough blame to go around—one would not want to pick just on one's own profession. The indictment for (relative) historic silence on the question of racial justice can be extended to American social and political theory in general, not merely social and political philosophy, but mainstream "white" American sociology and political science. (Depending on how one defines "mainstream"—and from the racial margins, pretty well everything else looks mainstream—this judgment also holds true for a lot of orthodox left theory in these fields, not just liberalism, since Marxists have tended to dissolve the specificities of these racial problems into the general oppression of capital, with socialism then being plugged as the universal panacea.)

How do we correct this situation? In this chapter, I want to make some suggestions toward the development of a possible long-term theoretical strategy for remedying this deficiency. My recommendation is that we (a) retrieve and elaborate, as an alternative, more accurate global socio-political paradigm, the concept of *white supremacy*; (b) develop an analysis of a specifically *racial* form of exploitation, in its manifold dimensions; (c) uncover and follow the trail of what W. E. B. Du Bois called the "payoff" of whiteness;[5] and then (d) locate normative demands for racial justice within this superior descriptive conceptual framework.[6]

"WHITE SUPREMACY" AS AN ALTERNATIVE PARADIGM

Major political battles are in part ideological battles, struggles over rival understandings of the socio-political order and conflicting framings of the crucial issues. Normative debates about right and wrong, justice and injustice, typically involve not merely value disputes but competing narratives of what has happened in the past and what is happening right now, alternative descriptive frameworks and interpretations. The ignoring of race as a global issue in American socio-political theory—I distinguish "global" from, say, "local" discussions of race in sub-sections of a field such as the sociology of race relations, urban politics, or affirmative action debates in applied ethics—is made possible by a certain conception of the American polity and social order. With appropriate disciplinary adjustments for the particular subject in question (whether sociology or political science or political philosophy), this picture provides the common overarching framework of debate in the field. The United States is conceptualized as basically an egalitarian (if a bit flawed) liberal democracy free of the hierarchical social structures of the Old World.

This profoundly misleading picture is Eurocentric in at least two interesting ways: (a) it focuses on the Euro-American population, those we call "whites," and takes their experience as representative, as the raw material from which to construct theoretical generalizations; (b) it draws on a set of theoretical paradigms drawn *from* European socio-political theory— the classic writings of the great figures in European sociology and modern political thought, centered on class as the primary social division, and either not recognizing race as an emergent structure in its own right or biologizing it. The New World is being intellectually grasped with the tools of the Old World and with reference to the Old World's transplanted population. So the possibility that the experience of expropriated reds, enslaved blacks, annexed browns, and excluded yellows may be sufficiently different as to warrant the development of a new tool kit and, accordingly, a new paradigm is doubly ruled out. To the extent that race is not ignored altogether, it is naturalized or marginalized.

The results can be seen in the typical silences and evasions of these disciplines. In an article giving a historical overview of American sociology, for example, Stanford Lyman argues that from the very start the discipline has had a "resistance to a civil rights orientation":

> Race relations has been conceived of as a social problem within the domain of sociology ever since that discipline gained prominence in the United States; however, the self-proclaimed science of society did not focus its attention on the problem of how the civil rights of racial minorities might be recognized, legitimated, and enforced. . . . Indeed, tracing the history of the race problem in sociology is tantamount to tracing the history and the central problem of the discipline itself—namely, its avoidance of the issue of the significance of civil rights for a democratic society. . . . Sociology, in this respect, has been part of the problem and not part of the solution.[7]

In political science, similarly, Rogers Smith's important and prizewinning book, *Civic Ideals*, outlines the various ways in which the most important theorists of American political culture, Alexis de Tocqueville, Gunnar Myrdal, and Louis Hartz, managed to represent racism as an "anomaly" within a polity conceived of as basically egalitarian:

> When restrictions on voting rights, naturalization, and immigration are taken into account, it turns out that for over 80 percent of U.S. history, American laws declared most people in the world legally ineligible to become full U.S. citizens solely because of their race, original nationality, or gender. For at least two-thirds of American history, the majority of the domestic adult population was also ineligible for full citizenship for the same reasons. . . . Although such facts are hardly unknown, they have been ignored, minimized, or dismissed in several major interpretations of American civic identity that have massively influenced modern scholarship. . . . All these Tocquevillian accounts falter because they center on relationships among a minority of Americans—white men, largely of northern European ancestry—analyzed in terms of categories derived from the hierarchy of political and economic status such men held in Europe. . . . [Writers in the Tocquevillian tradition] believe . . . that the cause of human equality is best served by reading egalitarian principles as America's true principles, while treating the massive inequalities in American life as products of prejudice, not rival principles.[8]

Finally in philosophy, it is notorious—at least among black philosophers—that racial justice has been a major theme or sub-theme of hardly *a single one* of the numerous books on justice by white political philosophers written in the four decades-plus since the revival of political philosophy following

John Rawls's work. (UPDATE: Since the original version of this chapter appeared in 2003, Elizabeth Anderson's major work, *The Imperative of Integration*, has been published, constituting a welcome exception to this pattern.[9] However, it is noteworthy that Anderson begins her book with an explicit repudiation of the usefulness of Rawlsian ideal theory for her project.)[10]

How are such evasions possible in a country built on Native American expropriation and hundreds of years of African slavery, followed by 150 years of first de jure, and now de facto, segregation? An interesting essay, or even a whole book, in the sociology of knowledge (or here, more accurately, the sociology of ignorance) could certainly be written on this question. But briefly, one would need to highlight the role of historical amnesia (the suppression, or the downplaying of the significance, of certain facts), the group interests and non-representative experience of the privileged race (what cognitive psychologists would identify respectively as hot and cold factors of cognitive distortion), and, crucially, a conceptual apparatus inherited, as I said, from European socio-political theory, for which race is marginal. So the problem is by no means confined to philosophy but is much broader, though in philosophy it is worst of all, because of the much greater possibilities for abstracting away from reality provided by the non-empirical nature of the subject.

Thus there has been a debilitating "whiteness" to mainstream political philosophy in terms of the crucial assumptions, the issues typically taken up, and the mapping of what is deemed to be the appropriate and important subject matter. And my claim is that the trans-disciplinary framing of the United States as an if-not-quite-ideal-then-pretty-damn-close-to-it liberal democracy, particularly in the exacerbatedly idealistic and abstract form typical of philosophy, has facilitated and underwritten these massive evasions on the issue of racial injustice. Accordingly, I have suggested in my own work that to counter this framing we need to revive "white supremacy" (which is already being used by many people in critical race theory and critical white studies) as a descriptive concept.[11] Normative questions, as pointed out above, hinge not merely on clashes of values but also on rival factual claims, both with respect to specific incidents and events and with respect to determining and constraining social structures. And particularly when challenges are coming from the perspective of *radical* political theory (for example, Marxism, feminism, critical race theory), it may well be the case that most or all of the work in claims about injustice is being done by the divergent factual picture put forward rather than different values. So the point is that one can utilize mainstream values to advance quite radical demands: the key strategy is to contest the factual assumptions with which mainstream theorists are operating. With the feminist concept of *patriarchy* and the Marxist concept of *class society*, women and the left have been better able to intervene in mainstream discussions of justice because they have also contested the factual picture that has framed these discussions.

My proposal is, then, that African American philosophers and others working on race, and critical race theorists more generally, should make a comparable theoretical move: challenge the mainstream liberal "anomaly" framing of race by developing the concept of white supremacy. Doing so would have several advantages.

To begin with, just on the conceptual level, this *is* the term that was traditionally used to denote white domination, so one would be drawing on a vocabulary already established and familiar.[12] Feminists had to appropriate a term ("patriarchy") with a somewhat different sense and shift its meaning; Marx had to provide an analysis of class society not merely in terms of rich and poor but, more rigorously, in terms of ownership/non-ownership of the means of production. So both are being employed as terms of art. But in the case of race in the United States, "white supremacy" was the term standardly used. What would now be necessary, of course, would be to give it a more detailed theoretical specification than it has hitherto had, map in detail its various dimensions, and try to work out its typical dynamic.

Second, and more important, the term carries with it the connotation of systematicity. Unlike the current, more fashionable "white privilege," "white supremacy" implies the existence of a system that does not just privilege whites but is also run by whites for white benefit. As such it is a global conception, including not just the socio-economic but also the juridical, political, cultural, and ideational realms. Thus it contests—paradigm versus paradigm—the liberal individualist framework of analysis that has played, and continues to play, such an important and pernicious role in obfuscating the real centrality of race and racial subordination to the polity's history.

Finally, by shifting the focus from the individual and attitudinal (the discourse of "racism") to the realm of structures and power, the concept of white supremacy facilitates the highlighting of the most important thing from the perspective of justice, which is how the white population benefits illicitly from their social location. Current debates about "racism" are hampered by the fact that the term is now used in such a confusingly diverse range of ways that it is difficult to find a stable semantic core. Moreover, the dominant interpretation of white racism in the white population is probably individual beliefs about innate nonwhite biological inferiority and individual hostility toward people of color. Given this conception, most whites think of themselves as non-racist—one positive thing about the present period is that nobody wants to be called a racist, though this has also motivated a shift in how the term is defined—while still continuing to endorse racial, particularly anti-black stereotypes. But in any case, with the decline in overt racism in the white population, the real issue for a long time has not been individual racism but, far more important, the reproduction of wrongful white advantage and unjust nonwhite (particularly black and Latino) disadvantage through the workings of racialized social structures. Insofar as, since Rawls, our attention as philosophers concerned about justice is supposed to be on the "basic structure" of society and its functioning, the concept of white supremacy then forces us to confront the possibility that the basic structure is itself systemically racialized and thus unjust. Corrective measures to end racial injustice would therefore need to begin here.

However, the term also has one major and perhaps insuperable disadvantage. Apart from sounding "extremist" to white and some black audiences, it will just seem flagrantly inaccurate, a description that (if this much is conceded) may once have been true but is no longer so. White supremacy for most people will be identified with slavery, the Ku Klux Klan, "White" and "Colored" signs, legal segregation and discrimination, police dogs attacking black demonstrators, and so on. So considerable spadework will have to be done to argue that the key referent of the term is white domination and unfair white advantage, which can persist in the absence of overt nonwhite subordination, white terrorism, and legal persecution (indeed, even in the presence of a black president!). But there is a sense in which such spadework would have to be done regardless of the term chosen, inasmuch as individualist analyses of the socio-political order are hegemonic in the American popular mind, denying the existence of structures of domination not just for race but in general. So this would be an ideological obstacle to be overcome no matter what language is used. And in the case of race, by contrast with class and gender, one should in theory at least face a somewhat easier task in convincing people since it cannot be denied that people of color were long legally suppressed. Even if whites are reluctant to concede the *continuing* existence of white supremacy, the concession that it *once* existed provides at least some theoretical foothold, since one can then make an argument that it would of necessity have left some legacy.

RACIAL EXPLOITATION

I now want to turn specifically to the idea of racial exploitation and draw a comparison between racial and class exploitation since it will be illuminating for us to consider both their similarities and their differences. Exploitation is, of course, central to Marxist theory since what distinguishes his analysis of capitalism from the analysis of liberal theorists is that he sees it as an exploitative system. Exploitation is not a matter of low wages or poor working conditions, though these certainly make it worse. Rather, exploitation has to do with the transfer of surplus value from the workers to the capitalists. To the extent that there is a normative critique in Marxism, it has often been taken to rely crucially on the claim that this relation is an exploitative one. Moreover, it is not just capitalism but class society in general that is exploitative, which is why we need to move toward a class-less society. Finally, the exploitative nature of the system does not reside in class prejudice, in hostile views of the workers, but rather in their structural disadvantaging by this transfer of surplus value through the wage relation. If Marx is right, class exploitation is *normal*; it does not require extraordinary measures but flows out of the routine functioning of the system.

But Marx was also hopeful that exploitation would stimulate proletarian resistance. It was in part precisely because of their exploitation that the workers were supposed to develop class consciousness, form trade unions, question the existing order, and ultimately participate in a revolutionary movement to overthrow capitalism. So exploitation provides both an explanation for the logic of domination and a potential basis for its political overcoming. What is supposed to make the socio-political wheels go round are class interests of a material kind, tied to perceptions of economic advantage, actual and possible (i.e., in an alternative society). But the problem is that the claim that capitalism is necessarily exploitative historically rested on the labor theory of value, and with the discrediting of this theory it has now become harder to defend.[13]

Liberal and Marxist Views

The case I want to make is that racial exploitation can provide a parallel, perhaps in some respects superior, illumination of the inner workings of modern society, and that it is greatly advantaged over the Marxist concept by not being tied to a dubious economic theory. Comparatively little work has been done on the concept of racial exploitation. I think this is because it has fallen between both theoretical and political stools in an interesting way. In his book on "mutually advantageous and consensual exploitation," Alan Wertheimer points out that though the term is routinely bandied about, mainstream liberal theorists have had surprisingly little to say about it: "Exploitation has not been a central concern for contemporary political and moral philosophy." He suggests that there are at least three reasons for this silence: the concept's guilt-by-association with Marxism; the aforementioned post-Rawlsian focus on ideal theory, the normative theory appropriate for a perfectly just society (in which, by definition, exploitation would not occur); and the fact that whereas exploitation is typically a "micro-level

wrong" characterizing individual transactions, "much of the best contemporary political philosophy tends to focus on macro-level questions, such
as the just distribution of resources and basic liberties and rights."[14] (The
presumptive contrast in this last point arguably vindicates my earlier claim
about the racially sanitized picture of the United States dominant in mainstream normative political theory. Don't *macro*-level questions about the
unjust "distribution of resources and basic liberties and rights" arise from
the long history of American racism, a history of indigenous expropriation,
African slavery, and de jure or de facto segregation?)

On the other hand, where Marxists have looked at race, as Gary Dymski
points out in a left-wing anthology on exploitation, they have typically
reduced it to a variant of class exploitation: "Race has been virtually ignored
in Marxian theorizing about exploitation. Race is assumed to enter in only
at a level of abstraction lower than exploitation; and anyway, since minorities are disproportionately workers, racial inequality is simply a special case
readily accounted for by a racially neutral exploitation theory."[15] And this of
course is part of a larger problematic pattern of Marxist theory: its failure
to recognize race as a system of domination in itself.[16] Racial domination is
subsumed under capitalist domination, and no separate theorization of its
distinctive features is seen to be necessary. Even when race is cashed out in
terms of super-exploitation, the process is still assimilated to class exploitation in that the "race" in question is thought of as a differentially subordinated section of the working class and the exploitative relation involves
getting extra value for the bourgeoisie, not for whites as a group.

So neither in mainstream (white) liberal theory nor in oppositional
(white) Marxist theory has racial exploitation been properly recognized
and theorized. In keeping with the shift in the radical academy in the 1980s
from Marxism to post-structuralism, much of the 1990s' and later literature
on "whiteness" focuses on the discursive, the cultural, and the personal tes-
timonial, as Ashley Doane and Margaret Andersen complain in their introductory essays in *White Out: The Continuing Significance of Racism*.[17] This
is not to deny that whiteness has numerous aspects and that the orthodox
left of the past was deficient (following Marx's own footsteps) in its handling of what were dismissed as "superstructural" issues. But it is arguably
the material payoff from whiteness, the *political economy* of race, that is crucial, and the discussion needs to be brought back to these fundamentals.
A growing body of work in the last two decades on such themes as "whiteness as property," on the differentials in "black wealth/white wealth," on the
"possessive investment in whiteness," on the "legacies of white skin privilege," on an unacknowledged history of "affirmative action for whites," on a
self-reproducing "white racial cartel," on an ongoing discriminatory "black
tax," and various other mechanisms of racialized dis/advantage and wealth

extraction has brought a newfound analytic and academic respectability to a concept that would once have been associated only with controversial black radical figures.[18]

Objections and Replies

Before getting into the analysis, though, we have to deal with some preliminary objections.

To begin with, one objection might be that racial exploitation cannot exist because races do not exist. If, as the growing scholarly consensus in anthropology and genetics agrees, races have no biological existence, then how can they be involved in relations of exploitation or for that matter any other relations? And here, of course, the standard answer from critical race theorists is that races can have a reality that, though social rather than biological, is nonetheless causally efficacious within our racialized world. From the fact that race is socially constructed, it does not follow that it is unreal.[19]

Second, however, it might be claimed that insofar as race *is* socially constructed, then it is to the constructing agent that causality and agency really have to be attributed. In historical materialist versions of this claim, for example, it might be insisted that class forces, and ultimately the ruling class, the bourgeoisie, are the real actors. (So we could think of these as two Marxist reasons—though they come in other theoretical varieties also—to deny racial exploitation: races do not exist in the first place, or if their social reality is grudgingly conceded, then, as a fallback position, this reality is reduced to an underlying class reality.) But even if Y is created by X, so that there is generating causation, it does not follow that Y continues to be moved, either wholly or at all, by X, so that there may not be sustaining and ongoing causation. In other words, even if we concede (and an argument would be necessary to prove this) that race is originally created by a class dynamic, this does not mean that race cannot attain what used to be called, in Marxist theory, at least a "relative autonomy" (if not more), an intrinsic dynamic, of its own.

Finally, it might be objected that "whites" come in all classes, different genders, and divergent ethnicities, that there are power relations and great power differences among them, and that many or most whites are exploited also. But the claim that racial exploitation exists does not commit one to the claim that its benefits are all necessarily distributed *equally*, so if some whites get more than others, this is still consistent with the thesis. Nor does it require that all whites be equally active in the processes of racial exploitation—some may be both actors and beneficiaries while others are just beneficiaries. And as should be obvious, claiming that racial exploitation exists does not imply that it is the *only* form of exploitation. All of us will have different hats, and so it will not merely be possibly but *routinely* the case that people are simultaneously the beneficiaries of one system of exploitation while being the victims of another, as with white women, for example. Society can be thought of as a complex of interlocking and overlapping systems of domination and exploitation, and I am by no means asserting that race is the only one. My contention rather is that it is an under-theorized one and that it has repercussions for holding the overall system together that are not generally recognized.

Racial Exploitation versus Class Exploitation

Let us contrast then racial and class exploitation. To begin with, assuming that the dominant position on the origins of race is correct, race is a product of the modern period,[20] so that racial exploitation is limited to the last few hundred years and is much younger than class exploitation—and even more so by comparison with gender exploitation. Moreover, it is a historically very contingent form of exploitation. While it is almost impossible to imagine the development of human society as having taken place without class and gender hierarchy and exploitation, the fact that race might never even have come into existence to begin with implies that racial exploitation might likewise never have happened.

Suppose we use the terms R1 and R2 for the races involved, respectively dominant and subordinate. (Obviously, it is possible to have more than two races, but we will make this simplifying assumption.) Now, to begin with, it needs to be pointed out that the mere fact that two races are involved in relations of exploitation does not mean it is a relationship of *racial* exploitation. Racial exploitation is, as emphasized, just one variety of exploitation, and if it is a necessary condition that races be involved in the transaction, it is not a sufficient one. For it could be that the relations between R1 and R2 are simply standard capitalist relations. Imagine, say, that a group of capitalists from one racial group hires a group of workers from another racial group, but race plays no role in the establishment or particular character or reproduction of the relations of exploitation. What is also required is that the relations of race play a role in the nature and degree of the exploitation itself. What makes racial exploitation *racial* exploitation, then, is not merely that the parties to the transaction are racialized persons, but that race determines, or significantly modifies, the nature of the relation between them. (Note also that it is not necessary for racial exploitation that the parties in every transaction be of *different* races, for it could be that the overall structure of R2 subordination allows for a few R2s to participate in the exploitation of their fellow R2s, for example, the small number of black slaveholders in the pre-bellum South.)

In what does this determination or modification consist? We are a bit handicapped here by the fact that the transaction has to be described in suitably general terms, encompassing (as I will soon argue) such a wide range of possibilities. But I suggest that the paradigm case of racial exploitation is one in which the moral/ontological/civic status of the subordinate race makes possible the transaction in the first place (that is, the transaction would have been morally or legally prohibited had the R2s been R1s) or makes the terms significantly worse than they would have been (the R2s get a much poorer deal than if they had been R1s). And the term "transactions" is being used broadly to encompass not merely cases in which R2s are directly involved but also (and this is another significant difference from classic class exploitation) cases in which they are *excluded*. In Marx's vision of class exploitation, surplus value is extracted through the expenditure of the labor power of the working class, so obviously the workers have to be actually working for this transfer to take place. But I want to include scenarios in which R2s are kept out of the transaction but are nonetheless exploited, because R1s benefit from their exclusion (for example, in the case of racial restrictions on hiring). For me, then, racial exploitation is being conceptualized so as to accommodate both differential and inferior treatment of R2s in employment (for example, lower wages) and their exclusion where they should legitimately have been included (for example, the denial of the opportunity to get the job in the first place).

It needs to be noted that the role of R2 normative inequality is in sharp contrast to Marx's vision of class exploitation under capitalism. In the class systems of antiquity and the Middle Ages, the subordinate classes did indeed have a lower normative status. But capitalism, as the class system of modernity, is distinguished by the fact that these distinctions of ascriptive hierarchy are leveled. So in Marx's discussion of capitalism, the whole point of his analysis—what made capitalism different from slave and feudal modes of production—was that the workers nominally had *equal* moral status. Hence his sarcasm in *Capital* about the freedom and equality supposedly obtaining on the level of the relations of exchange, which are undercut at the level of the relations of production.[21] But at least juridically, that freedom and equality are real. So it is not that the subordinated are overtly forced to labor for the dominant class (as with the slave or the serf), since such coercion would be inconsistent with liberal capitalism. Rather, it is the economic structure that (according to Marx anyway) coerces them, reduces their options, and forces them to sell their labor power.

But in what I suggest is the paradigm case of racial exploitation, the R2s do *not* have equal status, which implies that liberal democratic norms either do not apply to them at all or do not apply fully. In both liberal and many Marxist theories of racism, this has usually been represented as a return to the *pre-modern*. But as various theorists, including myself, have argued, it is better thought of in terms *of* the modern, but within the framework of a revised narrative and conceptual framework that denies that egalitarianism is in fact the universal norm of modernity. In other words, to represent racism as a throwback to previous class systems accepts the mystificatory representation of the modern as the epoch when equality becomes the globally hegemonic norm, when in fact we need to reject this characterization and see the modern as bringing about white (male) equality while establishing nonwhite inequality as an accompanying norm. What justifies African slavery and colonial forced labor, for example, is the lesser moral status of the people involved—they are not seen as fully equal humans in the first place. If in the colonies blacks and browns are coerced by the colonial state to work, while in the metropole, according to Marxist theory, white workers are compelled by the market to work, this is not a minor but a major and qualitative difference.

Now, one of the straightforward implications of this distinction is that in comparison with class exploitation, racial exploitation in its paradigm form is straightforwardly unjust by deracialized liberal democratic standards, a source of "unjust enrichment." By contrast, in the Marxist tradition, as is well known, there has been a general leeriness about appealing to morality and a specific leeriness about appealing to justice, because of the dominant meta-ethical interpretation of Marx as a theorist disdainful of ethical norms in general and hostile to justice in particular as a transhistorical value.[22] So some Marxists have repudiated moral argument in principle as a return to a supposedly discredited "ethical" (as against "scientific") socialism. But if one does want to make a moral case for socialism, some theorists have argued, one has to appeal to freedom rather than justice, or to social welfare, or to Aristotelian self-realization. A discourse of rights is not amenable to advancing the proletarian cause insofar as proletarian rights *are* being respected under capitalism. (One can, of course, appeal to positive "welfare" rights, but these are far more controversial in the liberal tradition.) And such an argument would have to rely on factual and conceptual claims that were obviously highly controversial even then—and far more so now in a post-Marxist world—about capitalist economic constraint undermining substantive freedoms, or people as a whole doing better under socialism.

By contrast, the striking feature of demands for racial justice in the paradigm cases of racial injustice is that they can be straightforwardly made in terms of the dominant discourse, since the whole point of racial exploitation is that (at least in its paradigm form) it trades on the differential status of the R2s to legitimate its relations. For example, contrast the (white) working-class struggle in the United States with the black struggle. The banner under which the latter has been organized has typically been the banner of equal rights: for civil rights—indeed for human rights—and for first-class rather than second-class citizenship. But it would be far more difficult to represent the struggle for socialism as a struggle for equal rights, since it would, of course, be denied that capitalist wage relations *are* a violation of workers' rights.

So in the first instance (in the period of overt white supremacy), what justifies racial exploitation is that the R2s are seen as having less human worth, or zero worth. They have fewer rights, or no rights. A certain normative characterization of the R2s is central to racial exploitation in a way that it is not to class exploitation in the modern period.

But apart from this paradigm form, there is also a secondary derivative form, which becomes more important over time (so there is a periodization of varieties of racial exploitation, with the salience of different kinds shifting temporally) and which arises from the legacy of the first form. Here the inequity does not arise from the R2s' being still stigmatized as of inferior status, or at least such stigmatization is not essential to the process. White supremacy is no longer overt, and the statuses of R1s and R2s have been formally equalized (for example, through legislative change). Of course the perception of R2s as inferior, as not quite of equal standing, may continue to play a role in tacitly underwriting their differential treatment. But it is no longer essential to it. Rather, what obtains here is that the R2s inherit a disadvantaged material position that handicaps them—by comparison with what, counterfactually, would have been the case if they had been R1s—in the bargaining process or the competition in question. At this stage, then, it *is* possible for them to be treated "fairly," by the same norms that apply to the R1 population. Nonetheless, it is still appropriate to speak of racial exploitation because they bring to the table a thinner package of assets than they otherwise would have had, and so they will be in a weaker bargaining position than they otherwise would have been. Whites are differentially and wrongfully benefited by this history insofar as they have a competitive advantage that is not the result of superior innate ability and/or effort, but the inheritance of the legacy of the past. So unfairness here is manifested in the failure to redress this legacy, which makes the perpetuation of racial domination the most likely outcome.

I would also contend (and will elaborate in the next section) that another crucial difference between class and racial exploitation is that the latter takes place much more broadly than at the point of production. For insofar as racial exploitation in its paradigm form requires only that the R2s receive differential and inferior treatment, this can be manifested in a much wider variety of transactions than proletarian wage-labor. Society is characterized by economic transactions of all kinds, and if race becomes a normative dividing line running through all or most of these transactions, then racial exploitation can pervade the whole economic order. Moreover, it is not only the market that is involved; the state has an active role also—in writing the laws and fostering the moral economy that makes racial exploitation normatively and juridically acceptable, and also in creating opportunities for the R1s not extended to the R2s and making transfer payments on a racially differentiated basis.

Finally, whereas Marx's famous claim is that capitalism needs to be abolished to achieve the end of class exploitation (since a capitalism that did not extract surplus value would liquidate itself), racial exploitation is at least in theory eliminable within a capitalist framework. That is, it is possible to have a non-racial capitalism, either because races do not exist as social entities within the system or because, though they do exist, there is no additional racial exploitation on top of class exploitation. Since we live in a post-Marxist world in which Marx's vision seems increasingly unrealizable, with no attractive "communist" models to point at, this conclusion is welcome because it implies that the struggle for racial justice need not be anti-capitalist. One simple formulation of the political project would thus be the demand for a non-racial or non-white-supremacist capitalism. (Representing white supremacy as a system in its own right, with its distinctive modes of exploitation, has the virtue of clarifying what the real target is.)

However, I qualified the term "eliminable" with "in theory." The counterargument that needs to be borne in mind is that while a non-racial capitalism could certainly have developed in another world, the fact that the capitalism in *our* world has been so thoroughly racialized from its inception means that racial inequality has long been crucial to its reproduction *as* a particular kind of capitalist formation. Logical distinctions in theory between US capitalism and white supremacy are all very well, but their fusion in reality into the composite entity of white-supremacist capitalism makes any political project of attempting to separate the two a non-starter, in part because of the reciprocal imbrication of class and race, class being racialized and race being classed. I will not say anything more about this counterargument, but it should be noted as an important objection to the whole project.

To summarize, by comparison with class exploitation, racial exploitation (a) benefits R1s generally, not just the capitalist class of the R1s; (b) disadvantages R2s generally, not just the working class of the R2s; (c) involves the causality and agency (albeit to different extents) of R1s besides the capitalist class; (d) is in its paradigmatic form straightforwardly wrong by (deracialized) liberal norms; (e) includes economic transactions other than labor; (f) typically involves the intervention and/ or collusion of the state; and (g) could in theory be eliminated within a capitalist framework.

THE PAYOFF OF WHITENESS

The discussion so far has been very abstract. Let us now move to the level of the concrete.

Specific Examples of Racial Exploitation

In the United States, the members of the privileged race, the R1s, are, of course, whites. There will be a core whiteness that is relatively clear-cut and a penumbral whiteness that is fuzzier. A significant part of the burden of the whiteness literature over the past two decades has, of course, been the emphasis on the historically variant character of whiteness, and various books—most famously Noel Ignatiev's *How the Irish Became White* but also Karen Brodkin's *How Jews Became White Folks*, Matthew Frye Jacobson's *Whiteness of a Different Color*, and, more recently, Nell Irvin Painter's *The History of White People*—have tracked the shifting boundaries of the (fully) white population.[23] And part of the motivation for aspiring to and becoming white is precisely so that one can benefit from this exploitation, as manifest not just in the wages of whiteness but whiteness as property, whiteness as a joint-stock company, the interest on whiteness, the rent on whiteness, the profit on whiteness, the residuals on whiteness, the returns on whiteness, and so on. The point is that racial exploitation is manifest in many more economic relations than just that of wage labor.

Let us now go through some concrete examples to put some flesh on these abstractions.

- Native Americans are cheated out of their land. They are not given a fair price in the first place, or the original deal is reneged upon, or their understanding of what they were signing away was mistaken because of deliberate deceit, or the land is simply expropriated, and so on.
- Africans are enslaved at a time when slavery is dead or dying out in the West. (Obviously, if Africans were enslaved in the ancient and medieval world, as they were, there was nothing *racial* about this, since race played no role in their enslavement—indeed, at the time they did not even have a race.)[24]

- Blacks freed from slavery are conscripted into "debt servitude" as sharecroppers, from which they can never get free, since the plantation owner forces them to buy goods he provides, at higher prices, and weighs the cotton they produce himself at the end of the season, cheating them, so that at the end of each year they owe more than before.
- Blacks are not permitted, or only permitted to a far lesser extent, to stake their claim on lands opened up by the settling of the West. (This illustrates the complexities of racial exploitation, since had they been allowed to do so, they would, of course, have been participating in the exploitation of Native Americans.)
- Male Chinese immigrants are forced to pay a head-tax for admission into the United States at a time when no such tax is imposed on white immigrants.
- Black children are given an inferior education by state governments, with most of the resources going to white children.
- Blacks are given higher sentences than whites for comparable crimes, so that they can supply a population of convict lease labor in the South.
- Black enterprises are not permitted access to white markets.
- Black enterprises are burned down or otherwise illicitly driven out of business by white competitors.
- Blacks pay higher rent in the ghettos for housing.
- Blacks pay more for inferior goods in the ghettos.
- White workers refuse to admit blacks into their unions.
- Blacks, Mexican Americans, and Asian immigrants hired in jobs are paid less than white workers would be.
- Blacks, Mexican Americans, and Asian immigrants hired in jobs are not promoted or are promoted at slower rates and to lower levels than whites with comparable credentials.
- Black candidates with superior credentials are turned down in favor of white candidates.
- Black candidates with inferior credentials are turned down in favor of white candidates, when the reason blacks' credentials are inferior is that they have had poorer schooling and poorer opportunities at every step of the way than they would have had if they were white.
- Black performers are forced to sign contracts on worse terms than white performers because they have no alternative non-racist company to give them a better deal.
- Black performers sign contracts with worse terms because they are not sufficiently educated to know better, and a history of racism explains their lack of the relevant knowledge.

- Blacks and Latinos do not get a chance to hear about and compete for certain jobs in the first place because racially exclusionary word-of-mouth networks restrict notice of these jobs to white candidates.
- Federal money earmarked for Native Americans ends up in white hands instead.
- Transfer payments from the state (for example, unemployment benefits, welfare, the GI Bill) are not extended equally to the black population, either through overt racial exclusion or because the terms are carefully designed to exclude certain jobs in which blacks are differentially concentrated. The Federal Housing Agency (FHA), established under the New Deal, discriminates against would-be black homeowners, thereby denying them access to the main route to wealth accumulation by the middle class. The Wagner Act and the Social Security Act "excluded farm workers and domestics from coverage, effectively denying those disproportionately minority sectors of the work force protections and benefits routinely afforded to whites."[25]

The Diversity, Multidimensionality, and Cumulative Consequences of Racial Exploitation

There are several things about this (very short) list that should be striking.

One is the diversity of examples of racial exploitation. Far from being a theoretical appendage or minor codicil to Marxist class exploitation, racial exploitation is *much broader* and should long ago have received the theoretical attention it deserves. Marx's focus was on just one relation because he was working within a framework in which it was assumed (since he was really talking about the white population) that normative status differentials had been eliminated, so that exploitation had to take place in a framework of the transaction of (formal) equals. Once we reject this crucial assumption, we should immediately recognize that the relation can manifest itself in *any* economic transaction, or any transaction with economic effects, and is thus ubiquitous. And this is one of the very important ways in which Marxism is Eurocentric: in its failure to conceptualize how broadly exploitation as a concept can be shown to apply once one takes the focus off the white population.

Second, notice the cumulative and negatively synergistic effect of these transactions. It is not merely that blacks (for example) are exploited serially in different transactions but that the different forms of exploitation interact with one another, exacerbating the situation. For example, blacks receive inferior education, thereby losing an equal opportunity to build human capital, thereby losing out in competition with white candidates, thereby having to take inferior jobs, thereby having less money, thereby being disadvantaged in dealings with banks that are already following patterns of mortgage discrimination, thereby being forced to live in inferior neighborhoods, thereby having homes of lesser value, thereby providing a lower tax base for schooling, thereby being unable to pass on to their children advantages comparable to whites, and so on. It is not a matter of a single transaction, or even a series, but a *multiply interacting* set, with the repercussions continually compounding and feeding back in a destructive way.

But what has been negative for blacks has been very beneficial for whites. Utilizing the political-economy category of "exploitation," as against just talking with a liberal vocabulary about the "unfairness" of discrimination against nonwhites, brings home the importance, as emphasized at the start, of shifting the discussion from the personal to the social-structural, so that we can start seeing white supremacy as itself a *system* for which this payoff is the motivation. Melvin Oliver and Thomas Shapiro's prizewinning *Black Wealth/White Wealth*, judged by many to be one of the most important books on race of the last two decades, argues that to understand racial inequality, its origins, and its reproduction, wealth is a far better investigative tool than income. As they point out:

> Whites in general, but well-off whites in particular, were able to amass assets and use their secure economic status to pass their wealth from generation to generation. What is often not acknowledged is that the accumulation of wealth for some whites is intimately tied to the poverty of wealth for most blacks. Just as blacks have had "cumulative disadvantages," whites have had "cumulative advantages." Practically, every circumstance of bias and discrimination against blacks has produced a circumstance and opportunity of positive gain for whites. When black workers were paid less than white workers, white workers gained a benefit; when black businesses were confined to the segregated black market, white businesses received the benefit of diminished competition; when FHA policies denied loans to blacks, whites were the beneficiaries of the spectacular growth of good housing and housing equity in the suburbs. The cumulative effect of such a process has been to sediment blacks at the bottom of the social hierarchy and to artificially raise the relative position of some whites in society.[26]

And if one were to go back to slavery and Native American expropriation, and track the financial consequences of these institutions and processes for the respectively racialized populations, the size and ubiquity of the white payoff would be even greater. Whites will sometimes receive the payoff directly, by themselves participating in these transactions, but far more often they receive it indirectly—from their parents, from the state and federal governments, from the general advantage of being the privileged race in a system of racial subordination. The transparency of the connection between race and social advantage or disadvantage also has implications for social consciousness. Marx famously claimed that capitalism was differentiated from slave and feudal modes of production by the seemingly egalitarian nature of the transactions involved: the "fair exchange" between worker and capitalist requires conceptual labor to be revealed as (allegedly) inequitable. As a result, the subordinated workers often do not recognize their subordination—capitalism is the classless class society. By contrast, the transparency of racial exploitation, certainly in its paradigmatic form, means that the R2s will usually have little difficulty in seeing the unfairness of their situation. If Marxist "class consciousness" has been more often dreamed of by the left than found in actual workers, "racial consciousness" in the racially subordinated has been far more evident historically.

RACIAL JUSTICE
Illicit White Benefit and the Racialized "Basic Structure"

I claim that the articulation of such a framework would greatly facilitate discussions about racial justice. Instead of focusing exclusively on "racism," our attention would shift to *wrongful white benefit*. The ideal for racial justice would, quite simply, be the end to current racial exploitation and the equitable redistribution of the benefits of past racial exploitation. Obviously, working out the details would be hugely complicated and in fine points impossible, but at least on the level of an ideal to be simply stated, and by which present-day society could be measured, it would give us something to shoot at. In dialoguing with the white majority, the imperative task has usually been to convince them that independently of whether they are "racist" (however that term is to be understood), they are the beneficiaries of a system of racial domination and that *this* is the real issue, not whether they have goodwill toward people of color or whether they ever owned any slaves. The concept of racial exploitation is designed to bring out this central reality. Relying not on controversial claims about surplus value, it derives its legitimacy from the simple appeal to the very normative values (albeit in their inclusive, race-neutral incarnation) to which the white majority already nominally subscribes. And because it encompasses a derivative as well as a primary form (exploitation inhering not in the assumption of unequal normative status but in the continuing intergenerational impact of the unfair distribution of assets resulting from that original normative inequality), it can handle transactions seemingly just but actually inequitable because of the legacy of the past.

That is not to say that it will not be very controversial; obviously it *will* be very controversial and will be militantly and furiously opposed. But such hostility goes with the territory and will greet *all* attempts to advance the struggle for racial justice, no matter what conceptual banner is chosen to fly over it. At least the advantage of selecting this framework is that it appeals to norms central to the American tradition (if not historically extended to nonwhites) and a factual picture for which massive documentation, at least in broad outline, can be provided.

In addition, the macro, big-picture, social-systemic analysis—the emphasis on the structural dynamic—locates it in the same conceptual space as the famous "basic structure" that, since Rawls, has been the central focus of discussions of social justice. Thus, we would be better positioned, as I emphasized at the start, to pose the simple and crucial challenge to mainstream white liberals: what if the basic structure is itself unjust because it is predicated on racial exploitation?

Obstacles to, and Possible Solutions for, Achieving Racial Justice

Moreover, another signal virtue of approaching things this way is that it would provide a more realistic sense of the *obstacles* to achieving racial justice. It is a standard criticism of normative political philosophy, especially from non-philosophers, that the authors of these inspiring works give us no indication at all as to how these admirable ideals are to be *realized*, of how we are to get from A to Z. By contrast, in the left tradition—at least the non-amoralist strain of it—the claim has always been that the strength of a materialist approach is that it not only articulates ideals but also shows how they can be made real, that it unites description and prescription by identifying both the barriers to a more just social order and the possible vehicles for overcoming those barriers. If race and racism are thought of in the standard individualistic terms of irrational prejudice, lack of education, and so on, then their endurance over so many years becomes puzzling. Once one understands that they are tied to benefit, on the other hand, the mystery evaporates: racial discrimination is, in one uncontroversial sense of the word, "rational," linked to interest. Studies have shown that the major determinant of both white and black attitudes on issues related to race is their respective perceptions of their *collective group interests*—of how, in other words, their group will be affected by whatever public policy matter is up for debate.[27] (To repeat an earlier point of comparison with class, the role of group interests in determining consciousness, which was Marx's hoped-for engine of proletarian revolution, is *far more* convincingly borne out, at least in the United States, for race than it is for class.) Rational white perception of their vested group interest in the established racial status quo can then be understood as the primary reason for their resistance to change.

But, as with orthodox left theory, a materialist or at least realist privileging of group interests as the engine of the social dynamic also opens up the possibility of progressive social change. The natural constituency is, of course, the population of color, who would be the obvious beneficiaries of the end or considerable diminution of white supremacy. But given their minority status both in straightforward quantitative terms, and, more important, the qualitative dimension of access to social sources of power, they will clearly not be able to do it on their own. I suggest there are two main political strategies for recruiting a larger or smaller section of the white population to the struggle.

The centrist strategy would try to appeal to the white population as a whole, the argument being that in a sense racism hurts everybody, given the costs of racial exclusion (the expenses of incarcerating the huge, disproportionately nonwhite prison population; the untapped resources of marginalized racial groups), and that from an efficiency point of view, the overall GDP would be greater in a non-racist United States.

The left strategy comes in a classic Marxist version as well as a milder, left-liberal/social-democratic version. The plan here would be to disaggregate the white population and target in particular those whites who benefit less from white supremacy: the working class, the poor, the unemployed. One would try to persuade them that they—or perhaps they and their children (the appeal might be more convincing in terms of long-term outcomes)—would be better off in an alternative non-racial social order that combined "class" justice with "racial" justice. For classic Marxism, this would have been socialism/communism; for left-liberals, it would be a social-democratic redistributivist capitalism ("socialism" as "democratic socialism") that centrally incorporated measures of corrective racial justice.[28] So the idea would be to appeal to group interests as well as justice, since justice, alas, has historically proven itself to be not that efficacious as a social prime mover. White workers, for example, would be asked to compare their present situation not to blacks in this actual racist system but to what their situation (and that of their descendants) would be in a counterfactual non-racial system, the presumption being that a convincing case can be made that though they do gain in this present order, they lose by comparison to an alternative one. Given the tremendous transfer of wealth to the upper echelons of society in recent years, which has provoked even conservative commentators to use the term "plutocracy," it might be that there has not in decades been a more favorable environment for such a political appeal than today.[29]

Of course, some might feel, understandably enough, that there is something ignoble, perhaps even demeaning, about such arguments and that the case for racial justice should be made on moral grounds alone. I am in sympathy with such a feeling, but I want to differentiate two ways of presenting these arguments: (a) the demand for racial justice cannot be justified on purely moral grounds, and (b) the motivation for the white majority to join in the struggle for racial justice cannot be activated on purely moral grounds. Endorsing the second does not commit one to endorsing the first. The struggle for racial justice is indeed a noble struggle, and on moral grounds alone its advancement is indeed justifiable. But unfortunately—whether as a general truth about human beings or a more contingent truth about human beings socialized by racial privilege—I do not think the historical evidence supports the view that many whites will be effectively motivated purely by such considerations. Derrick Bell's "realist" "interest-convergence" thesis seems a more accurate diagnosis and prognosis, that is, that most whites support such movements only when they perceive them as being in their own interests.[30]

I want to conclude by pointing out a possible obstacle to interest-based theoretical optimism about the possibilities for the realization of a non-racial social order—that is, an obstacle apart from the obvious ones of transition costs as a factor in one's calculations, the temptations of free-riding, and the simple preference for the comfortable familiar rather than the dangerous unknown. The multi-dimensionality of the payoff from whiteness means that it is possible for the benefits to come apart and be in opposition to one another in a way not found in straightforward working-class computations of gain under socialism. Material benefit does not necessarily include any relational aspect to others, but benefits of a political or status or cultural or "ontological" kind do. (They are what are termed "positional" goods.) In other words, if it has become important to whites that they be politically dominant, have higher racial social status, enjoy the hegemonic culture, and be positioned "ontologically" as the superior race, then the threatened loss of these perks of whiteness may well outweigh for them the gains they will be able to make in straight financial terms in a deracialized system. One can only be white in relation to nonwhites. So some or many whites may calculate, consciously or unconsciously, that by this particular metric of value they gain more by retaining the present system than by trying to alter it, even if by conventional measures they would be better off in the alternative one. It may well be, then, that apart from all the other problems to be overcome, this simple fact alone is powerful enough to derail the whole project.

Nonetheless, the important thing is obviously to get the debate going, so that discussion of these issues in an increasingly nonwhite United States can move from the margins to the mainstream. Facing up to the historically white-supremacist character of the society and the polity will be an important conceptual move in facilitating this debate, and philosophy, committed by its disciplinary pretensions to both Truth (getting it right) and Justice (making it right), can and should play an important role in bringing about this paradigm shift, even if—or rather especially since—it has been culpably absent so far.

PART II

Racial Liberalism

Rawls and Rawlsianism

CHAPTER 8

Rawls on Race/Race in Rawls

Let us now turn to the work of John Rawls, which has been mentioned repeatedly and critically throughout the book but has not yet been engaged with in detail. As pointed out earlier, Rawls's *A Theory of Justice* is widely credited with having revived post–World War II Anglo-American political philosophy, and, with his other four books, is routinely judged to constitute the most important body of work in that field.[1] Indeed, with the collapse of Second World and Third World socialist ideologico-political alternatives, liberalism in one form or another has become globally hegemonic, so that for many commentators, the qualifiers "postwar" and "Anglo-American" should just be dropped. Thus the blurb on the jacket of *The Cambridge Companion to Rawls* simply asserts without qualification: "John Rawls is the most significant and influential political and moral philosopher of the 20th century."[2]

Yet for those interested in issues of racial justice, philosophers of color in particular, Rawls's work and the secondary literature it has generated has long been deeply frustrating, producing a weird feeling of incongruity and dissonance.[3] Here is a huge body of work focused on questions of social justice—seemingly the natural place to look for guidance on normative issues related to race—which has nothing to say about racial injustice, the distinctive injustice of the modern world.[4]

What explains this systematic omission? Any elementary sociology of belief would tell us that the demography of the profession (overwhelmingly white) will itself be an obvious major causal factor, group membership in the privileged race tendentially producing certain distinctive interests (uninterests), priorities (marginalities), and concerns (indifferences). But apart from this major extra-ideational factor, I suggest, as indicated in previous chapters, that there is a key internal conceptual factor as well: Rawls's methodological decision to focus in *A Theory of Justice* on "ideal theory"—the reconstruction of what a perfectly just society would look like. If this might have seemed reasonable enough when first propounded—after all, what's wrong with striving for the asymptotic realization of perfect justice?—it is, I propose, because of a crucial ambiguity: "ideally just" as meaning a society without *any* previous history of injustice and "ideally just" as meaning a society with an unjust history that has now been *completely corrected for*. Rawls really means the former, not the latter. But the difference between the two will obviously make a significant difference to the recommendations respectively appropriate in the two sets of cases. *Preemptive* precautions to prevent injustices entering the "basic structure" of a society are not the same as *rectificatory* measures aimed at correcting them once they have already entered. Prevention generally differs from cure. Insofar as Rawls's focus is on the former, his prophylactic recommendations will be of limited if any use when it comes to remediation. Thus by a simple conceptual stipulation, the theoretical problems raised of how to adjudicate the redressing of past injustices are immediately shunted aside. In particular, the manifestly *non*-ideal record of our country on race can now be ignored, since such matters fall into an area of dikailogical territory not covered by the mandate of the program. As Thomas Nagel observes in two of the few sentences referring to race (and elliptically and non-specifically at that) in the *Cambridge Companion*:

> Affirmative action . . . is probably best understood in Rawlsian terms as an attempt at corrective justice—an attempt to rectify the residual consequences of a particularly gross violation in the past of the first principle of equal rights and liberties. Affirmative action therefore does not form a part of what Rawls would call "strict compliance theory" or ideal theory, which is what the two principles of justice are supposed to describe.[5]

In contrast, my 1997 book, *The Racial Contract*, was explicitly and self-describedly a work in non-ideal theory.[6] I sought to show there that—insofar as the contractarian tradition has descriptive pretensions ("contract" as a way of thinking about the creation of society)—the modern "contract" is better thought of as an exclusionary agreement among whites to create racial polities rather than as a modeling of the origin of colorless, egalitarian, and inclusive socio-political systems. Since Rawls's updating of the contract is purely normative and hypothetical, however, a thought-experiment for generating judgments about justice rather than a historical account, it might seem that my challenge, even if successful, is irrelevant, doubly missing the mark. The contract for Rawls is not meant to be descriptive in the first place, and in the second place, as just emphasized, his normative project is confined to the realm of ideal theory. But my claim would be that this twofold displacement in fact constitutes a double *evasion* and that the ghost of the ostensibly repudiated *factual* dimension of contractarianism continues to haunt the *normative* account, as manifested precisely in this silence on racial justice.[7] A mystified and idealized story of the creation of the modern world, which denies the centrality of racial subordination to its genesis, makes the achievement of corrective racial justice a less pressing matter, if it is seen as necessary at all, for contemporary white ethicists and political philosophers.

In this chapter, I will both document what (little) Rawls does say about race ("Rawls on Race"), and attempt, from a critical philosophy of race perspective ("Race in Rawls"), to bring out what I see as the larger significance of these silences. For me, in other words, they are not contingent but are structurally related to the architecture of what I characterized at the start of the book as "racial liberalism." Even now, in a putatively post-racist epoch, a conceptual apparatus inherited from a period of de jure white racial domination continues in numerous ways—in conjunction with white racial privilege—to shape and orient (occident?) the work of white liberals.

RAWLS ON RACE: THE TEXTUAL RECORD

For this exercise, I will look at Rawls's five major books: *A Theory of Justice* (1971/1999), *Political Liberalism* (1993/1996), the *Collected Papers* (1999), *The Law of Peoples* (1999), and *Justice as Fairness: A Restatement* (2001). (For ease of reference, I will cite page numbers here in the main text rather than in the endnotes.) The two edited volumes of Rawls's lectures—*Lectures on the History of Moral Philosophy* (2000) and *Lectures on the History of Political Philosophy* (2007)—provide expositions of the thought of central figures in Western moral and political theory rather than discussions of justice, so they are less appropriate sources for us.[8] But it makes no difference since in any case they manifest the same pattern of silence. Nowhere in either of these books does Rawls discuss the racial views of, for example, Locke, Hume, Kant, Hegel, Mill, or their relation to European colonialism.

A Theory of Justice

Race is not initially listed (see, e.g., Rawls 1999, 11, 118) as one of the features you do not know about yourself behind the veil of ignorance (nor is sex, as Susan Moller Okin has famously pointed out).[9] However, Rawls does explicitly condemn racism. He declares "we are confident that religious intolerance and racial discrimination are unjust" (17), and that no one behind the veil of ignorance would "put forward the principle that basic rights should depend on the color of one's skin or the texture of one's hair" (129). Similarly, he says: "From the standpoint of persons similarly situated in an initial situation which is fair, the principles of explicit racist doctrines are not only unjust. They are irrational. For this reason we could say that they are not moral conceptions at all, but simply means of suppression" (129–30).

Rawls seems to regard race as natural. Thus at one point he refers to "fixed natural characteristics" that "cannot be changed," and asserts: "Distinctions based on sex are of this type, and so are those depending upon race and culture" (84–85). He considers the possibility of a society whose basic structure allocates "unequal basic rights" according to these "starting places in the basic structure" (84–85). However, he says such "racial and ethnic inequalities" "are seldom, if ever, to the advantage of the less favored," and so would be ruled out by the difference principle (99). Later he states: "There is no race or recognized group of human beings that lacks this attribute [the capacity for moral personality]" (443).

These are the only overt references I can find to race in the 538 pages of *A Theory of Justice*. He does talk about slavery at various places (e.g., 135, 137, 218, 286), but the first two references just raise the abstract possibility of "slavery and serfdom" as a traditional objection to utilitarianism, while the second two are explicitly to the non-racial slavery of antiquity rather than American racial slavery. Chapter 53, "The Duty to Comply with an Unjust Law," does talk about "permanent minorities that have suffered from injustice for many years" (312), while chapter 57, "The Justification of Civil Disobedience," refers to "subjected minorities" (330) and to situations when "certain minorities are denied the right to vote or to hold office, or to own property and to move from place to place" (327). But race is not explicitly mentioned. Finally, it should be noted that neither "race" nor "racism" appears in the index, though there are brief textual mentions, as cited above, while such topics as "segregation," "Jim Crow," and "white supremacy" appear neither in the index nor anywhere in the text.

Political Liberalism

Rawls's second book, two decades later, shows a self-conscious defensiveness about *Theory*'s silences that suggests that these points of criticism had in fact been raised to him. In his original introduction to the cloth edition (Rawls 1993), he concedes that the first book does not deal with race: "Among our most basic problems are those of race, ethnicity, and gender. These may seem of an altogether different character calling for different principles of justice, which *Theory* does not discuss" (xxviii). Similarly, in his introduction to the later paperback edition (Rawls 1996), he admits the need for changes over time in the content of "public reason," since "Social changes over generations also give rise to new groups with different political problems. Views raising new questions related to ethnicity, gender, and race are obvious examples, and the political conceptions that result from these views will debate the current conceptions" (liii). Race is also cited on a list of factors that give rise to conflict among citizens ("[conflicts deriving] from their different status, class position, and occupation, or from their ethnicity, gender, and race" [lx]). In addition, "race and ethnic group" are now explicitly mentioned as something you do not know behind the veil (25) and are included as an illustration of illegitimate restrictions in advertisements of jobs and positions, which Rawls's principles would prohibit, that is, those that "exclude applicants of certain designated ethnic and racial groups" (363). Whereas *Theory* only referred to ancient slavery, Rawls now expressly refers to American slavery and its legacy: "similarly, slavery, which caused our Civil War, is rejected as inherently unjust, and however much the aftermath of slavery may persist in social policies and unavowed attitudes, no one is willing to defend it" (8; also 234, 238, 254, 398). He also mentions the work of the abolitionists (lii, 249–51), the Abraham Lincoln-Alexander Stephens correspondence (45), Lincoln's Second Inaugural condemnation of "the sin of slavery" (254), and the *Dred Scott* decision (232n15, 233n18). Blacks are described at one point as "a subjugated race" (during slavery: 238). He also refers several times, in discussions of "public reason," to Martin Luther King Jr.'s doctrines (lii, 247n36, 250), and mentions the *Brown v. Board of Education* decision and segregation (250). The Jewish Holocaust is also cited as illustrating "manic evil" (lxii). So the second book obviously represents—admittedly by a very low benchmark—some progress in at least conceding the special problem posed by race. It should be noted though that, as before, "race," "racism," "segregation," and "white supremacy" appear nowhere in the index, and "white supremacy" appears nowhere in the text.

Collected Papers

In 1999, Samuel Freeman edited a collection of twenty-six of Rawls's published papers, spanning almost half a century (1951 to 1997) and including a 1998 interview of Rawls with the magazine *Commonweal*. According to Freeman's preface (ix–x), the collection is almost comprehensive, the excluded essays being variously earlier versions of more polished articles, minor occasional pieces, or essays later incorporated into the paperback edition of *Political Liberalism.*

Rawls's first published paper, in 1951, characterizes "ideologies" negatively as claiming "a monopoly of the knowledge of truth and justice for some particular race, or social class, or institutional group, and competence is defined in terms of racial and/or sociological characteristics" (5). Appearing only a few years after the end of World War II, with the defeat of the Third Reich still a powerfully overshadowing memory in the West, this comment is pretty clearly a reference to National Socialism. A 1969 essay, "The Justification of Civil Disobedience," discusses civil disobedience in the context of oppressed "minorities," though race is not mentioned. Apart from the implicit and brief 1951 Nazi reference, then, race does not appear in any of the essays leading up to the 1971 publication of *Theory.* Subsequent to its publication there are a few appearances of the topic, or at least the term. A 1975 essay lists "sex and race" among the data about themselves to which parties behind the veil should not have access (268) and cites as examples of unjust conceptions of the good those "that require the repression or degradation of certain groups on, say, racial or ethnic . . . grounds" (280). A 1988 essay says it is permissible for "a constitutional regime" to discourage "various kinds of religious and racial discrimination (in ways consistent with liberty of conscience and freedom of speech)" (461) and repeats that any conceptions of the good requiring racial repression, "for example, slavery in ancient Athens or in the antebellum South," are ruled out (462). There is a footnote in a 1989 essay to another author's discussion of the *Dred Scott* and *Brown* decisions (496n51). Finally, the last essay (1997), "The Idea of Public Reason Revisited," which also appears in *The Law of Peoples,* has some brief discussion in connection with "public reason" of the abolitionists, Martin Luther King Jr., and the civil rights movement (593, 610), as well as the Lincoln-Douglas debates (609–10). As before, race is cited on a list of the factors giving rise to "three main kinds of conflicts" (612). That is all that I can find in the collection's 600+ pages.

The Law of Peoples

In this book, Rawls is focused on international relations. He discusses anti-Semitism and Nazism (19–23, 99–101), characterizes the Jewish Holocaust as unique (19), and refers to "The fact of the Holocaust and our *now* [my emphasis] knowing that human society admits this demonic possibility" (21). There is a footnote on the South and slavery ("This was as severe a violation of human rights as any, and it extended to nearly half the population": 38n45). Rawls condemns the World War II firebombing of Japanese cities and the use of nuclear weapons on Hiroshima and Nagasaki (99–105), but he does not, unlike some other authors, link these military decisions to anti-Japanese racism.[10] He refers briefly to the "empire building" of European nations (53–54) but makes no reference to the genocide of non-European peoples as part of this process. Though he later talks about the "outlaw states of modern Europe in the early modern period" (105–6), this judgment of "outlawry" is clearly inspired by their intra- rather than extra-European policies, as his listing and subsequent gloss make evident: "Spain, France, and the Hapsburgs—or, more recently, Germany, all tried at one time to subject much of Europe to their will" (106). The final chapter, "The Idea of Public Reason Revisited," has the same references cited above to abolitionists, the civil rights movement, Martin Luther King Jr., the Lincoln-Douglas debates, and race as a factor causing conflicts (154, 174, 177). The concept of imperialism appears nowhere in the text (the above brief references aside), nor colonialism, nor the Atlantic slave trade, nor any mention of their legacy in the Third World.

Justice as Fairness: A Restatement

Finally, this 2001 book—edited by Erin Kelly, and unfinished because of Rawls's ill health before his 2002 death—originated in Rawls's lectures updating and restating his final position on "justice as fairness."

As before, Rawls now lists "race and ethnic group" as information prohibited to the parties in the original position (15), says that "we view a democratic society as a political society that excludes . . . a caste, slave, or a racist one" (21), and emphasizes that "fixed status ascribed by birth, or by gender or race, is particularly odious" (131). He refers to Lincoln's condemnation of slavery (29) and repeats the point that conceptions of the good "requiring the repression or degradation of certain persons on, say, racial, or ethnic, or perfectionist grounds—for example, slavery in ancient Athens or in the antebellum South"—would be ruled out (154). In a discussion of the application of the difference principle, he emphasizes that the "least advantaged are never identifiable as men or women, say, or as whites or blacks, or Indians or British," since the term is "not a rigid designator" picking out the same individuals across all possible worlds (59n26; see also 69–71). A footnote on public reason says of Political Liberalism's position that "the inclusive view [of public reason] allowed comprehensive doctrines to be introduced only in nonideal circumstances, as illustrated by slavery in the antebellum South and the civil rights movement in the 1960s and later" (90n12).

However, the most detailed and illuminating passage on race (not merely in this book, but in his entire body of work) is the following:

> We have seen that the two principles of justice apply to citizens as identified by their indexes of primary goods. It is natural to ask: Why are distinctions of race and gender not explicitly included among the three contingencies noted earlier (§16)? [In this earlier section, Rawls had listed "three kinds of contingencies" that affect "inequalities in citizens' life-prospects": social class, native endowments and opportunities to develop them, good or ill fortune.] How can one ignore such historical facts as slavery (in the antebellum South) . . . ? The answer is that we are mainly concerned with ideal theory: the account of the well-ordered society of justice as fairness. (64–65)

So it is his focus on ideal theory that justifies the exclusion of race, since racial justice is a matter of non-ideal theory. However, Rawls continues:

> Nevertheless, sometimes other positions must be taken into account. Suppose, for example, that certain fixed natural characteristics are used as grounds for assigning unequal basic rights, or allowing some persons only lesser opportunities; then such inequalities will single out relevant positions. Those characteristics cannot be changed, and so the positions they specify are points of view from which the basic structure must be judged. Distinctions based on gender and race are of this kind. Thus if men, say, have greater basic rights or greater opportunities than women, these inequalities can be justified only if they are to the advantage of women and acceptable from their point of view. Similarly for unequal basic rights and opportunities founded on race (*Theory*, §16: 85). It appears that historically these inequalities have arisen from inequalities in political power and control of economic resources. They are not now, and it would seem never have been, to the advantage of women or less favored races. (65–66)

Finally, he summarizes:

> To conclude: when used in a certain way, distinctions of gender and race give rise to further relevant positions to which a special form of the difference principle applies (*Theory*, §16: 85). We hope that in a well-ordered society under favorable conditions, with the equal basic liberties and fair equality of opportunity secured, gender and race would not specify relevant points of view. *Theory* takes up only two questions of partial compliance (or nonideal) theory. . . . *The serious problems arising from existing discrimination and distinctions based on gender and race are not on its agenda* [my emphasis], which is to present certain principles of justice and then to check them against only a few of the classical problems of political justice as these would be settled within ideal theory. This is indeed an omission in *Theory*; but an omission is not as such a fault, either in that work's agenda or in its conception of justice. Whether fault there be depends on how well that conception articulates the political values necessary to deal with these questions. Justice

as fairness, and other liberal conceptions like it, would certainly be seriously defective should they lack the resources to articulate the political values essential to justify the legal and social institutions needed to secure the equality of women and minorities. (66)

In the end, then—a few years before his death—Rawls does concede that *A Theory of Justice*'s silence on race is an omission. But he insists that the principles he articulated there can be adapted and utilized to address racial injustice, even if he himself did not so use them.

RACE IN RAWLS: A CRITICAL OVERVIEW

With the actual textual record established, I now want to turn to its evaluation. As emphasized at the start, I am seeking to make a point deeper than the fact of simple omission. My claim is that the ignoring of race in Rawls's work is structural and symptomatic of white political philosophy in general.

Rawls's Silences

To begin with the obvious: one would get the impression just from a superficial skimming of the texts that Rawls does not have much to say about race, and this is amply confirmed, an impression that is not at all misleading but—as finally conceded by Rawls himself—quite accurate. The five books canvassed above total about 2,000 pages; if all the sentences that mentioned race were to be collected together, I doubt that they would add up to half a dozen pages. Moreover, there is a significant degree of duplication, not just because of chapter overlap between texts but because Rawls is repeating the same points. Eliminating repetition would make the page count even lower. In some cases, the points being made are really general, as when race is coupled with gender; in some cases they are relegated to footnotes; in no case are they ever central to his discourse. Race, racism, and racial oppression are marginal to Rawls's thought. Merely consulting the indexes of these five books would be enough to establish this truth. Indeed, if a single textual (non-)reference could be chosen to summarize and epitomize Rawls's lack of concern about race it is the following startling fact: nowhere in these 2,000 pages on justice penned over five decades by the American philosopher most celebrated for his work on social justice is the most important American postwar measure of corrective racial justice—affirmative action—even mentioned. It is not merely that the concept is not discussed—even the *term* itself never appears![11] Such is the whiteness of Rawls's dikailogical world.

And this prescriptive albinism is, as earlier emphasized, complemented by a similarly bleached-out factual picture and corresponding descriptive/explanatory conceptual framework. It is not just a matter of what Rawls does *not* say—the omissions—but of how what he *does* say is conceptualized—the tendentious conceptual commissions. Rawls condemns racism and racial discrimination, of course, and (eventually) lists race as something you do not know about yourself behind the veil. But even (by now) respectable concepts like *institutional racism* never appear in his work, let alone *white supremacy* as a global concept. The marginalization of race in both his explicit normative theory and his (usually more tacit) underlying descriptive theory sanitizes the actual history of the modern world and obfuscates the centrality of white racial domination to its making. No one reading this work by an American would be able to guess, in historian George Fredrickson's judgment of thirty-five years ago, that "the phrase 'white supremacy' applies with particular force to the historical experience of two nations—South Africa and the United States," since

> more than the other multi-racial societies resulting from the "expansion of Europe"
> that took place between the sixteenth century and the twentieth, South Africa and the
> United States . . . have manifested over long periods of time a tendency to push the prin-
> ciple of differentiation by race to its logical outcome—a kind of *Herrenvolk* society in
> which people of color . . . are treated as permanent aliens or outsiders.[12]

So the historic reality is that race—white racial privilege and nonwhite racial subordination—has been foundational to the actual "basic structure" of the United States. How theoretically useful is it then going to be in the philosophical investigation of social justice to start from a raceless ideal so remote from this reality?

Moreover, his broader global perspective—pertinent both for his discussion of international issues in *The Law of Peoples* and for what becomes his key reference group of "modern democratic societies"—is similarly idealized. As pointed out above, there is no sense in his discussion of global matters (the natural place for it) of imperialism as a central reality shaping the history of the modern world, leaving a legacy of racial genocide and subordination. The Jewish Holocaust is represented, in keeping with conventional Western wisdom and amnesia, as unique, a "demonic" event[13] of "manic evil,"[14] linked to the history of Christian anti-Semitism,[15] but with no apparent continuity with the West's own racist history in the nonwhite world. Thus he speaks of our "now knowing" (but apparently not knowing before) "that human society admits this demonic possibility," and in reviewing comparable evils can apparently only think of the Inquisition and the 1572 Catholic massacre of the

Huguenots as examples. A book like David Stannard's *American Holocaust*, on the Spanish genocide of Native Americans, is beyond the horizon of Rawls's comprehension.[16] Indeed, it is surely significant, as I pointed out in chapter 3, that although the black civil rights struggle is (eventually) mentioned, Native Americans are completely absent from every page of these five books. American slavery is, in the later work, condemned as an evil and its legacy episodically cited, but the killing and expropriation of indigenous peoples is never referred to. And in a sense, how could it be? Facing up to the origins of the United States (and not just the United States) as a white settler state established through invasion and conquest[17] would explode the foundations of a conceptual framework predicated on treating society as "a cooperative venture for mutual advantage." But—if this is too embarrassingly close to home, too thoroughly disintegrative of the entire framework of assumptions, to be mentioned—there is also no reference to any of the other epochal crimes of the Western colonial powers, such as the holocaust in the Belgian Congo at the start of the twentieth century which, as Adam Hochschild suggests, may well have been responsible for the deaths of ten million people.[18] The European "outlaw states" apparently do not include England, since its global empire—the successful (not merely attempted) "subjection of much of the world to its will"—was not being established on European soil.[19] Nor does the Atlantic slave trade as an international institution, with its death toll in the millions, appear anywhere in these five books, though most of the Western European powers were involved in it.[20]

The fact is—unthinkable as it may be within Rawls's framework of assumptions—that in a sense *all* the Western European nations (and their offshoots, such as the United States) were "outlaw states" jointly involved in a criminal enterprise on a planetary scale. The cosmopolitan "Society of Peoples" Rawls seeks will have to be established in a world fundamentally shaped by what was, in effect, the Western conquest of the "peoples" of the rest of the globe. As Paul Keal points out in his *European Conquest and the Rights of Indigenous Peoples*, "international society was itself a society of empires," and "the expansion of the European society of states to an international society global in scope entailed the progressive dispossession and subordination of non-European peoples" who were "progressively conceptualized in ways that dehumanized them," so that "'the West' bears a collective responsibility for historic injustices" of "the loss of life, land, culture and rights":[21]

> The expansion of international society cannot be separated from dispossession, genocide and the destruction of cultural identity. . . . To the extent that [these states] were founded on genocide and dispossession they are morally flawed states and the moral

foundations of the international society that is constituted by them is also called into question.[22]

Or as Mark Cocker writes more bluntly:

Europe's encounter with and treatment of the world's tribal peoples is . . . in essence . . . the story of how a handful of small . . . nation-states at the western extremity of Eurasia embarked on a mission of territorial conquest. And how in little more than 400 years they had brought within their political orbit most of the diverse peoples across five continents. It is . . . a tragedy of staggering proportions, involving the deaths of many millions of victims and the complete extinction of numerous distinct peoples. In fact, when viewed as a single process the European consumption of tribal society could be said to represent the greatest, most persistent act of human destructiveness ever recorded.[23]

Rawls's failure to cite any of these facts and his corresponding deployment of obfuscatory and apologist categories—all too typical of white political theorists even today, let alone of his generation—are thus an abdication of both moral and theoretical responsibility, producing a grotesquely sanitized and Eurocentric picture of the history of the last few hundred years, one from which race, racial conquest, and racial atrocity have been whitewashed out.

Rawls's Eurocentrism

Let me now turn specifically to Eurocentrism. That his political philosophy is Eurocentric may seem so trivially and obviously true as to be not even worth mentioning; after all, we are dealing with Western political philosophy, and social contract theory is itself a Western invention. But my point is a deeper one—that even granted these origins, there were conceptual and theoretical moves open to him to extend the scope of the traditional apparatus to address the issues cited above that he refused to make. The Eurocentrism is not the (relatively) innocent one of genealogy (which does not necessarily foreclose subversive creative development) but a systematic ignoring of the experience of the nonwhite political subject, ubiquitously manifest in the "whiteness" of Rawls's perspectives on time and space, his tacit conceptions of the populations he is speaking about and to, and his assumptions about how best to frame their narrative. Rawls's conception is *multiply* Eurocentric. It is not merely that he focuses on Europe, but that he also focuses on Europeans and the problems and issues that affect the white population, and not—in his native United States—the problems of blacks and Native Americans. (The former, as we have seen, eventually make a belated appearance, but the latter remain invisible in his writing till his death.) Moreover, he does so within a (sanitized) European conceptual apparatus, ethnically cleansed of its actual discursive history of ethnic cleansing. (And this, to repeat, is why though Rawls's contract is hypothetical and normative rather than descriptive, the factual critique *is* still relevant, since the factual picture presupposed shapes the orientation of the normative inquiry and the concepts deemed appropriate for it.)

For Rawls, the pivotal political periodization is determined by the origin of political liberalism in "the Reformation and its aftermath, with the long controversies over religious toleration in the sixteenth and seventeenth centuries."[24] Internationally, the crucial date for him is the 1648 Peace of Westphalia that supposedly established the beginnings of the international system. It does not occur to him that 1492 might have more resonance for the non-European world, the date eventually leading to the joint European domination of the planet—the international *racial* system, or global white supremacy—and the complementary development of a *racialized* liberalism with one set of rules for whites and another for nonwhites.[25] Within the United States itself, of course, it is the European population that is his focus, albeit in the displaced, abstract, and (ostensibly) general form typical of philosophy in general and social contract theory in particular. One need only ask for whom the contractarian founding as a consensual event is supposed to be an illuminating normative starting point to see that the audience Rawls is tacitly presupposing for his work is really white settlerdom and their descendants. Only for this population could it not be ludicrously inapposite to represent society as actually (not merely ideally) being "a cooperative venture for mutual advantage," as Rawls suggests we do in *Theory*. Native Americans did not "agree" to be killed and to end up losing 98 percent of their land through "conquest by law"[26] any more than captured Africans "agreed" to be enslaved. Domination and coercion of the nonwhite population are the founding moments for the American (and not just the American) polity, not democratic inclusion and consent.

To ignore this basic, framework-establishing, political agenda-setting reality means that from the very beginning, whether overtly acknowledged or not, one is really addressing oneself to the white population. Nor, as I have tried to demonstrate, is it an adequate reply to say that we are dealing with normative matters and with ideal theory, so that these admitted (though they are *not* usually admitted) and unhappy truths, deplorable as they may be, need not detain us. Insofar as the overarching metaphor of the contract paradigmatically models consent (rather than coercion), insofar as the normative agenda is the mapping of an ideal ideal (rather than how ideally to rectify the non-ideal), it means that we are *already* located on the conceptual terrain (with its accompanying normative priorities) of the racially privileged population rather than that of their victims.

Indeed, the Eurocentrism is manifest not merely in the evasive idealizations but even in the main domestic and international "non-ideal" issues with which Rawls chooses to deal. Domestically, his famous "difference principle," which puts him on the left of the liberal spectrum, is supposed to address the problems of the worst-off in a constrained market society, or "property-owning democracy," as he would later put it. But it does not offer guidance on dealing with the specific demands of the *racially* oppressed (Native peoples' land claims, affirmative action). Rather, it is inspired by the long tradition of European social democracy and really focused on the white working class. But in taking class as the main axis of social disadvantage, Rawls is importing a European socio-political framework that is applicable without modification in the United States only through ignoring the nonwhite population and their distinctive experience of systemic racial subordination. He is treating a white settler state as if it were merely a transplant on different soil of a European society. In this respect, he is very much part of a long-standing American political tradition that, as Rogers Smith has pointed out, follows Alexis de Tocqueville, Gunnar Myrdal, and Louis Hartz in conceptualizing the United States as a liberal democracy free of the caste hierarchies of the Old World, a triumph of intellectual evasion achieved by utilizing orthodox class categories imported across the Atlantic and ignoring the emergence in the New World of a *new kind* of ascriptive social hierarchy: race.[27]

As various political theorists, including myself, have argued, the distinctive feature of New World polities is precisely the *centrality* of race to their makeup, because, of course, they were founded as white settler states and racial slave states. So to marginalize race in your apparatus means that from the very start your intellectual framework is going to be inadequate for comprehending their workings and prescribing justice for them. Rawls came of intellectual age in the pre-decolonization 1940s, with white Western domination of the world taken for granted; he is transparently a product of this political mindset, as revealed by his characterization in the 1996 *Political Liberalism* introduction of "race and ethnicity" as "new" political questions.[28] Don't white and black abolitionism and native peoples' struggles against white encroachment go back centuries? Aren't they appropriately to be thought of as "political?" But not, of course, from the perspective of a political theory that takes the European and Euro-American experience as normative, as demarcating the proper boundaries of the field.

As for the global arena, in *The Law of Peoples*, unlike *A Theory of Justice*, Rawls has an entire part of the book dedicated to non-ideal theory (Part III). But the focus is on what Rawls calls—from the perspective of the modern Western democratic nations that are his main reference class—"outlaw states" who "refuse to comply with a reasonable Law of Peoples" and "burdened societies" whose "historical, social, and economic circumstances make their achieving a well-ordered regime ... difficult if not impossible."[29] Again, then, the implicit or explicit perspective is that of the privileged West, the former colonial powers. That these nations could themselves be thought of as "outlaw states" whose record of enslavement, expropriation, and genocide constitutes a massive violation of the "Law of Peoples," that Third World societies could pre-eminently be "burdened" by the legacy of underdevelopment of an exploitative world economic system established by these very same nations is, as earlier emphasized, excluded by the framework of Rawls's assumptions.[30] Thus there is a Eurocentric idealization both domestically and internationally, and not merely in the officially "ideal" but even where the "non-ideal" is treated in Rawls's theory. It is a systemic white idealization away from the ugly empirical non-ideal realities affecting the nonwhite population.

Rawls's Argument for Not Dealing with Race, I: The Classical Tradition

Let us now turn to Rawls's explanation (cited above) in *Justice as Fairness* for why he does not deal with race. He actually mentions two factors: his self-location within the "classical" (Western) political tradition and his focus on ideal theory. I see this explanation, which is very terse, as unsatisfactory, and I want to disentangle various possible components to it so as to demonstrate this.

To begin with, as Rodney Roberts has emphasized,[31] it should be noted that on occasion, if admittedly not often and in any detail, the classical tradition *has* dealt with non-ideal theory—for example, Aristotle on rectificatory justice and Locke on reparations for violations of natural law. So it is not that there is no classical precedent for treating these matters. Moreover—though this is not usually admitted in history of philosophy texts—race is indeed part of the classical tradition in the sense that, at least for the modern period and possibly even earlier, most of the "classical" modern Western philosophers, such as Hume, Locke, Kant, Mill, Hegel, and others, had racial views that arguably shaped how they intended their principles to be applied to the nonwhite population.[32] So if Rawls's tacit assumption is that race is a new and alien incursion into the classical Western tradition, this is quite wrong. Precisely because race has been *central* to that tradition in the modern period, even if not currently acknowledged as such, recognizing and correcting for its legacy rather than abstracting away from it and pretending it does not exist is extremely important. In effect, his Eurocentrism is compounded, reflexively exacerbated: he uses the Western tradition as his reference point to begin with, and then he conceives of that tradition in an ethnically cleansed and sanitized way only possible if you restrict your attention to the norms governing the treatment of Europeans.

But even if the classic European thinkers had themselves all been blamelessly non-racist, the second and arguably more significant point is how these principles of the Western tradition were *applied* in the world made by the West, in the Americas, in Asia, in Australasia, in Africa. *A Theory of Justice* was originally interpreted by most commentators as being in the normative spirit of the classic contract, providing an ideal of justice for all societies at all times (except perhaps at low levels of technological development). In this "classical" conception, the contract then provides an Archimedean conceptual and theoretical vantage point from which to adjudicate issues of social justice in a transhistorical and transnational way. But from his essays of the 1980s onward, Rawls began a long and elaborate retreat from such an interpretation. Justice was "political," not "metaphysical," the epistemological touchstone was the "overlapping consensus" in our Western tradition rather than eternal truths, and his theory of justice was the theory for *us* (the West), not the world as a whole. But once this shift to the local has been made, race declares itself even more imperatively as a subject that needs to be addressed, since, of course, modern Western societies and the world they made were deeply racist. Racial justice is not a transhistorical issue because racial injustice is limited to the modern period. So if you're taking the long view, *sub specie aeternitatis*, then a case can be made for abstracting away from racial justice. But if your rationale for developing a revisionist contractarianism appropriate to a "political liberalism" is that concern is now explicitly supposed to be focused on the local and contingent rather than the global and transhistorical, then the investigation and adjudication of matters of racial justice has to be *central* for you. So by his own criterion, if Rawls is restricting his ambit of concern to the specific features of the modern Western tradition he should not be simultaneously ignoring one of the most salient features of that tradition.

Finally, Rawls's argument is also problematic because of the tendentious way it defines the "Western" tradition (again, his Eurocentrism at work). Rawls forgets—or perhaps, more likely, never knew—that there is a long intellectual countertradition of those subordinated by the West contesting its racial oppression. In some cases, for example, in the anticolonial theory of Asia and Africa, one can try to partition it from the West. But, to cite only the most obvious example, this cannot be done for African Americans, ineluctably "Western," and the long history of

African American political thought, whether in terms of black nationalism and Pan-Africanism, or black liberalism and black Marxism, needs
to be seen as an oppositional element *within* this tradition, both shaped
by and reacting against it.[33] In the work of David Walker, Martin Delany,
Frederick Douglass, Ida B. Wells, W. E. B. Du Bois, Martin Luther King
Jr., Malcolm X, and many others, we have a political tradition for which
race and the battle for racial justice have been crucial, whether in terms
of abolitionism, anti-Jim Crow, anti-imperialism, or anti-segregation. But
apart from some ritualistic genuflection at King's name, Rawls ignores all
of this work. In effect, Rawls defines the West so that the West is white
and the political problems of the West are limited to the political problems of its white members.

Rawls's Argument for Not Dealing with Race, II: The Focus on Ideal Theory

So one cannot just appeal to the intrinsic nature of the "classical" tradition
to explain one's omission of race. The burden of the argument really has to
rest heavily on the "ideal theory" component. Accordingly, let us now turn
to that aspect.

First, a simple reminder. Ideal theory is not supposed to be an end
in itself but is instrumental to the goal of more adequately dealing with
injustice. Recall that Rawls himself said that the point of starting with
ideal theory was to provide a foundation for the more "urgent" matters
of non-ideal theory. "The problems of [non-ideal] partial compliance
theory are the pressing and urgent matters. These are the things that we
are faced with in everyday life." But ideal theory "provides, I believe, the
only basis for the systematic grasp of these more pressing problems."[34]
Yet thirty years after *Theory*, he had still not moved on to race—surely
one of the most pressing, if not *the* most pressing, issues of justice in the
American polity. What was keeping him? It could not be a principled
refusal (and what would such a principle be anyway?) to deal with non-
ideal theory, given both his own earlier contrary declaration and the fact
that in *The Law of Peoples* he does broach such matters to a limited extent.
So if he could shift to the non-ideal for international issues, over which
the American polity has limited influence, why could he not do the same
for domestic issues of race? These *are* in our power to affect and they raise
with acute urgency those questions of the "especially deep inequalities"
in "men's initial chances in life"[35] about which a theory of justice is supposed to be particularly concerned. Why at the end of his life had he still
not even begun to tackle this non-ideal issue?

It might be urged in reply that criticizing an author for articles and books he did *not* write is a tricky and perhaps even a completely misguided enterprise. Authors know best, it might be insisted, on what they should focus their energies, and they should not be second-guessed. And yet . . . and yet I cannot resist pointing out the following. Rawls was for decades at the most prestigious academic institution in the country, at one of the most prestigious philosophy departments in the country, and, post-*Theory*, as the book's fame spread, he was the best-known and most celebrated political philosopher in the country. If any philosopher ever had an academic bully pulpit from which to influence public policy and intellectual debate—not merely in philosophy, but in numerous other fields, given the book's crossover interdisciplinary success—it was John Rawls. Moreover, Rawls grew up in a United States segregated by the 1896 *Plessy v. Ferguson* decision, fought in World War II in a Jim Crow army, went to university at a time when blacks were still largely barred from "white" institutions. The start of his academic career coincided with the birth of the modern (postwar) civil rights movement, the demonstrations and marches organized by Martin Luther King Jr., and the Southern Christian Leadership Conference in the 1950s, and the later more radical movements and ghetto uprisings of the 1960s. Certainly nobody in the United States of the period could have been unaware of segregation, racial subordination, and the struggle against them as problems daily making national headlines. In addition, Rawls knew not merely how white the academy in general was but how white philosophy in particular was. He knew that if (white) women were under-represented in his discipline, people of color were virtually completely absent. So why—in the three decades up to his death, enjoying the success of *Theory*—could he not find the time to write even *one essay* on racial justice? Just *one essay* on how his theory would need to be developed to take race into account? What does this say about his priorities? And, symptomatically, what does it say about white political philosophy in general?

But there is a deeper criticism, which hinges on the distinction I drew at the start between an ideally just society in the sense of a society with no past history of injustice and an ideally just society in the sense of a society whose past unjust history has been corrected for. Let us demarcate these as the ideal ideal (ideal theory in ideally just circumstances) and the rectificatory ideal (what is ideally required to remedy past injustices). I suggest that if we think of ideal theory as being able to play an adjudicative role in determining which public policy option is morally superior, it is because we really have the second in mind. In other words, the rectificatory ideal is a goal to be approached, if only asymptotically, and used as a criterion in determining whether option A or option B comes closer to it. Thus Rawls writes, in seeming support of this interpretation,

> [Nonideal] theory presupposes that ideal theory is already on hand. For until the ideal is identified, at least in outline . . . nonideal theory lacks an objective, an aim, by reference to which its queries can be answered.[36]

But as earlier emphasized, this claim of his is problematic since by his own earlier avowal, he is talking about the *ideal* ideal. And the problem, I would claim, is that the ideal ideal cannot in general play this role because it represents a goal located in a different metaphysical space, on an alternate-worlds timeline to which we have no access. We would have to abandon our present social order and build a new "basic structure" from scratch, from the ground up.

We can see this simply by considering how the ideal ideal would play itself out in the context of trying to correct for racial injustice. The Rawlsian ideal, starting from ground zero, is a society with no history of racial (or any other kind of) injustice. So all we need is appropriate anti-discrimination legislation to make sure that this injustice does not enter the basic structure. But not only would this produce a racism-free polity; it would produce a *race-free* polity. As the huge and ever-growing body of literature over the last three decades in critical race theory and critical white studies demonstrates, race is socially constructed, and without systemic discrimination race would not even have come into existence in the first place. So it is not merely that we would have a basic structure without systemic racism; we would have a basic structure without races existing as social entities at all. It is not merely that there would be no need for rectificatory public policy measures like affirmative action and, more radically, reparations, but that there would be no identifiable groups to whom these policies could even be targeted. (By contrast, Rawls's ignorance and naivety about race are manifested in the fact that in both *Theory* and *Justice as Fairness* he represents race—and even culture!—as "fixed" and "natural." Admittedly, when he wrote *Theory* he did not, as we do, have the benefit of the aforementioned huge body of literature in the left academy on the construction of race. But even so, Ashley Montagu's well-known *Man's Most Dangerous Myth: The Fallacy of Race* had been around since 1942 and has gone through numerous editions ever since.[37] It would have been available to Rawls, making clear to him that race is not natural at all but social.)

Now how can this ideal ideal—a society not merely without a past history of racism, but without races themselves—serve to adjudicate the merits of competing policies aimed at correcting for a long history of white supremacy manifest in Native American expropriation, African slavery, residential and educational segregation, large differentials in income and huge differentials in wealth, nonwhite under-representation in high-prestige occupations and over-representation in the prison system, contested national narratives and cultural representations, widespread white evasion and bad faith on issues of their racial privilege, and a corresponding hostile white backlash against (what remains of) those mild corrective measures already implemented? Obviously, it cannot. Ideal theory represents an unattainable target that would require us to turn back the clock and start over. So in a sense it is an ideal with little or no practical worth. What is required is the non-ideal (rectificatory) ideal that starts from the reality of these injustices and then seeks some fair means of correcting for them ("compensatory justice"),[38] recognizing that in most cases the original pre-discrimination situation (even if it can be intelligibly characterized and stipulated) cannot be restored. Trying to rectify systemic black disadvantage through affirmative action is not the equivalent of not discriminating against blacks, especially when there are no blacks to be discriminated against. Far from being indispensable to the elaboration of non-ideal theory, ideal theory would have been revealed to be largely useless for it.

But the situation is worse than that. As the example just given illustrates, it is not merely a matter of an ideal with problems of operationalization and relevance, but of an ideal likely to lend itself more readily to retrograde political agendas. If the ideal ideal rather than the rectificatory ideal is to guide us, then a world without races and any kind of distinction-drawing by race may seem to be an attractive goal. One takes the ideal to be "colorblind" non-discrimination, as appropriate for a society beginning from the state of nature, and then—completely ignoring the non-ideal history that has given whites a systemic illicit advantage over people of color—one conflates together as "discrimination" all attempts to draw racial distinctions for public policy goals, no matter what their motivation, on the grounds that this perpetuates race and invidious differential treatment by race. In the magisterial judgment of Chief Justice John Roberts in the June 2007 Supreme Court decision on the Seattle and Louisville cases where schools were using race as a factor to maintain diversity, "The way to stop discrimination on the basis of race is to stop discriminating on the basis of race,"[39] a statement achieving the remarkable feat of depicting not merely as true, but as *tautologically* true, the equating of Jim Crow segregation and the attempt to remedy Jim Crow segregation! What is ideally called for under ideal circumstances is not, or at least is not necessarily, what is ideally called for under non-ideal circumstances. Claiming that all we need to do is to cease (what is here characterized as) discrimination ignores the differential advantages and privileges that have accumulated in the white population because of the past history of discrimination.

So the defense in terms of ideal theory is doubly problematic. In the first place, ideal theory was never supposed to be an end in itself but a means to improving our handling of non-ideal matters, and the fact that Rawls and his disciples and commentators have for the most part stayed in the realm of the ideal represents an evasion of the imperative of dealing with what were supposed to be the really pressing issues. And in the second place, it is questionable in any case how useful the ideal ideal in the Rawlsian sense is or ever would have been in assisting this task. So it is not merely that ideal theory has not come to the aid of those dealing with non-ideal injustice but that it was unlikely to have been of much help when and if it ever did arrive.

RETRIEVING CONTRACTARIANISM

Does this mean, then, that contractarianism is a completely useless apparatus for the exploration of these matters of racial justice? My claim would be that it is not, that it can indeed be retrieved, but that a fundamental modification of some of its crucial assumptions is necessary.[40] As argued throughout, the problem is the methodological focus on ideal theory. So what we need to do is to modify the apparatus to deal with non-ideal theory. The way to do this is to reject the key assumption of a founding moment that is consensual and inclusive, which—whether taken literally or metaphorically—is obviously hopelessly inappropriate as a characterization of the actual origins of modern polities, whether in the West or elsewhere. Rousseau's demystificatory "domination contract" of *Discourse on the Origins of Inequality* should be the model for us instead since it directs our theoretical attention from the start to domination and exploitation as central to the socio-political order.[41] We can then see Rousseau's "class contract" and its conceptual descendants, Pateman's "sexual contract" and my "racial contract," as all falling within an alternative undeveloped strain of contract theory, one that retains the key "contract" ideas of human moral equality and the human creation of the socio-political order, but drops the misleading additional ideas with which they are standardly conflated of *socially recognized* moral equality and *equal consensual* input into this creation.[42] Correspondingly, the moral framework would then be centered on the imperative of eliminating the structures of socio-political domination—whether of class, gender, or race—that preclude the realization of genuine equality for the majority of the population.

From the cognitive vantage point of this alternative contractarianism, we would be able to see more clearly what has always been at least dimly visible: that the orthodox contract apparatus, far from being methodologically neutral, in fact embeds within its framework a *substantive* and deeply wrong vision of the polity as *consensual* and *non-oppressive*. Making oppression central would mean that from the start we would be locating ourselves unequivocally on the terrain of non-ideal theory. The normative project would then no longer be the adjudication of competing versions of an ideally just social order, but, rather, the adjudication of competing policies for redressing social injustice. The evasions in the Rawls literature would no longer be possible—and that, obviously, would be a very different variety of contractarianism.[43]

CHAPTER 9

Retrieving Rawls
for Racial Justice?

How then—given the problems outlined in the previous chapter—should political philosophers in the liberal tradition interested in the issue of racial justice relate to Rawls's work?[1] Some, such as Elizabeth Anderson, have rejected a Rawlsian approach altogether, a repudiation all the more stinging considering that Anderson is herself a former Rawls student, and (to add to the irony) was the John Rawls Collegiate Professor of Philosophy and Women's Studies at the University of Michigan.[2] Others such as myself have argued that an approach in some sense Rawlsian can be fruitfully employed to tackle racial injustice, but that a radical revision of Rawls's apparatus will be required.[3] Still others, such as Tommie Shelby, have contended that no such radical revisions are necessary, and that a Rawlsian apparatus, more or less unchanged, can indeed—contra Anderson and myself—be successfully turned to this task.[4] Thus we get an interesting spectrum of rival theoretical positions, from the simple abandonment of a Rawlsian approach through more or less radical attempts to modify it.

In this chapter, I critique Shelby's position,[5] thereby strengthening by elimination the case I have made elsewhere for a more radical approach.[6] If in the previous chapter I documented the "whiteness" of Rawls's own writings, here I begin by documenting (in greater detail than before) the "whiteness" of the Rawlsian secondary literature.[7] I will then turn to a close analysis of Shelby's appropriation of Rawls and show why I think it does not work.

RAWLSIANISM AND RACE

The intellectual chasm between the worlds of the black American freedom struggle for justice and the white American academic philosophical community's discussions of justice is nowhere more clearly illustrated than in the centrality of racial justice as a theme to the former and its virtually complete absence from the latter. *A Theory of Justice* is generally credited with the revival of Anglo-American political philosophy, taking it from its postwar mid-twentieth-century deathbed to its present standing as one of the healthiest and most vibrant branches of the discipline.[8] Translated (as of 2007) into more than thirty languages,[9] *Theory* shifted the traditional focus of political philosophy from the question of our obligation to obey the state to the question of the justice of a society's "basic structure." A vast literature has been generated around Rawls's work, his importance being recognized even by those who sharply disagree with the design of his apparatus and its prescriptions. For Samuel Freeman, Rawls is "a world-historical thinker," "the preeminent theorist of justice in the modern era," "the foremost political philosopher of the twentieth century, and . . . one of the great political philosophers of all time," who "wrote more on the subject of justice than any other major philosopher."[10]

But as I pointed out in the previous chapter, this body of work, extensive and world historical as it may be, does not extend to the subject of racial justice, despite the fact that Rawls was a citizen of the Western democracy most *centrally* structured by racial injustice, a white-supremacist state founded on Amerindian expropriation and genocide, and African slavery and subsequent Jim Crow.[11] Nor has there been much attempt in the secondary literature to develop a "Rawlsian" perspective on racial justice comparable to what feminist political theorists have been doing for the past quarter-century for gender justice.[12] (I should clarify that by *racial justice* I mean primarily not pre-emptive measures to prevent racial injustice but corrective measures to rectify injustices *that have already occurred*. That is the important question: how could such policies as affirmative action, preferential treatment, and, more radically, reparations, be articulated and justified—if they can—within Rawls's apparatus, had he chosen to make this a central concern of his?) Inevitably one is handicapped in making such generalizations by the huge size of this literature, which is moreover multilingual. But anthologies, guidebooks, and companions can provide the necessary evidence, since surveys of the literature are part of their mandate. So here are my findings from ten of these works, drawn from a time span of nearly forty years.

Norman Daniels's well-known pioneering anthology, *Reading Rawls* (1975), has nothing on race.[13] However, H. Gene Blocker and Elizabeth H. Smith's collection from five years later, *John Rawls's Theory of Social Justice: An Introduction* (1980), does have a chapter with a general discussion of discrimination (sex, race, religion) and of whether Rawls's theory would permit "compensatory treatment" and "reverse discrimination."[14]

A five-volume 1999 collection of eighty-eight articles on Rawls covering more than a quarter-century has exactly one essay on race, by the African American ethicist Laurence Thomas.[15] Samuel Freeman's edited *Cambridge Companion to Rawls* (2003) has fourteen chapter overviews of different themes in the literature on Rawls, not one of which is on race, or even contains any sub-section on race.[16] Freeman's own massive 500-plus-page *Rawls* (2007), cited above, has only sporadic one- or two-sentence references to racial discrimination and a brief paragraph on affirmative action.[17] Jon Mandle's *Rawls's* A Theory of Justice: *An Introduction* (2009) has no index entries for race, racism, or affirmative action, nor do Percy B. Lehning's *John Rawls: An Introduction* (2009) or Paul Voice's *Rawls Explained* (2011).[18] Sebastiano Maffettone's *Rawls: An Introduction* (2010) has three index entries for "racial discrimination," the first two of which are brief discussions of what the principle of fair equality of opportunity might allow and the third of which is just a quote from Rawls.[19] Finally, Jon Mandle and David Reidy's recent, nearly 600-page edited *Companion to Rawls* (2014) has a grand total of one-and-a-half pages on race and a single one-sentence endnote on affirmative action.[20]

If we look at essay-length overviews, we find the same pattern. In 2006, *Perspectives on Politics*, one of the American Political Science Association's official journals, published a sixty-page symposium on Rawls's legacy, with essays by several authors, that has exactly two paragraphs on racial justice.[21] Leif Wenar's entry on Rawls in the online *Stanford Encyclopedia of Philosophy* lists race only as one of the things you do not know about yourself behind the veil.[22] Henry Richardson's entry in the *Internet Encyclopedia of Philosophy* has nothing at all.[23] In sum, as I said, racial justice is a theme virtually non-existent in the secondary literature.

The natural question then is: what attempts have been made by black normative philosophers over the years to break this white silence? The efforts that I know about—again, one has to be cautious in making definitive pronouncements, given the size of the literature—are few and far between. Moreover, for the most part they do not actually try to mobilize the apparatus itself to tackle racial justice as a theme but rather select particular concepts in Rawls for more limited and local purposes. For example, the Thomas essay cited above looks at Rawlsian self-respect and the black consciousness movement, though it critiques Rawls for confusing self-esteem with self-respect.[24] An essay by Michele Moody-Adams (herself a former Rawls student) examines race, class, and the social construction of self-respect.[25] However, neither of these philosophers has made race a central concern of their writing, nor do they regard the "African American philosopher" identity as particularly significant for their own work.[26] More

pertinent for our purposes; then, are the two prominent black analytic normative philosophers who do, and who have worked on race throughout
their careers, Bernard Boxill and Howard McGary. Their similarly titled
books are *Blacks and Social Justice* and *Race and Social Justice*.[27] Boxill's most
extensive discussion of Rawls centers on Rawls's claims about the efficacy
of civil disobedience, though Boxill is also critical of Rawls's treatment of
international justice.[28] So he is not adopting Rawls's apparatus himself in
his prescriptions for racial justice. McGary has brief scattered discussions of
Rawlsian ideas and their relevance to racial injustice throughout his book—
for example on the relation between injustice and self-respect, on the black
underclass, on African American exclusion from social institutions, and in
a comparison of Cornel West's and Rawls's strategies for arriving at principles of social justice.[29] The discussion most important for us concludes, in
a chapter on reparations, that "Rawls does not go far enough in his deontological thinking," and that (what McGary sees as) Rawls's unacknowledged
teleologism would rule out certain kinds of programs for rectificatory justice, thereby being an inadequate basis for remedying racial social oppression.[30] So neither author judges a Rawlsian framework to be helpful.

SHELBY ON RETRIEVING RAWLS

I believe that it is in the writings of Tommie Shelby that we find one of the
most sustained attempts by any philosopher—and certainly by any black
philosopher—to use Rawls's apparatus for pursuing the project of racial
justice. Hence the significance of Shelby's work, underscored by his location at Harvard, Rawls's institutional base for more than thirty years. My
focus will be on Shelby's 2004 article in the *Fordham Law Review*'s special
issue on Rawls.[31]

But first a brief summary of the Rawls essentials.[32] Rawls revived social
contract theory in the form of a hypothetical thought-experiment, in which
you choose principles of justice not on moral but prudential grounds, with
crucial aspects of your identity and the society you will be entering being
hidden from you by a "veil of ignorance." So this choice in the "original position," through the combination of self-interest and stipulated ignorance, is
supposed to produce an equivalent to a moral choice, as you may turn out,
once the veil lifts, to be a member of one of the sub-populations negatively
affected by unjust principles. Rawls emphasizes that we are choosing principles for a "well-ordered," that is, perfectly just, society, since in his view
ideal normative theory (dealing with perfect justice) is the only adequate
theoretical foundation for properly doing non-ideal normative theory

(addressing injustice). He argues that we would choose two principles, a guarantee of basic liberties (BL), lexically prior to a second principle in which fair equality of opportunity (FEO), the correction for being born into a disadvantaged social group by the "social lottery," is itself lexically prior to the difference principle (DP), that permits social inequalities only if they better the condition of the worst-off social group, who are handicapped by a thin bundle of talents inherited in the "natural lottery." In sum, BL → (FEO → DP). In his later work, post-*Theory*, he argued that given a plurality of "reasonable" views in modern democratic societies, liberalism cannot be imposed as a "comprehensive," self-contained, and self-sufficient ethico-metaphysical doctrine, so that a more minimal, freestanding "political" liberalism that does not rely on such foundations is all that can be required of citizens.

Let us now turn to Shelby's article "Race and Social Justice: Rawlsian Considerations."[33] Appearing in a section on race and ethnicity of a *Fordham Law Review* special issue on Rawls, it is part of the most extensive discussion I know in the secondary literature about the non-discussion of race in the secondary literature. Shelby was one of four contributors, the others being Seana Shiffrin, Anita Allen, and Sheila Foster. Part of Shelby's concern in this article is to defend Rawls against Shiffrin's charge that anti-racial-discrimination provisions should have been incorporated directly into the principles of justice.[34] I am sympathetic to Shiffrin's critique but will not get into this matter here, since our primary concern is corrective racial justice, which is the really interesting issue, rather than preventive anti-racist measures.

Shelby's strategy for addressing these matters, as detailed in part V of his article, is to use FEO (fair equality of opportunity) as the crucial Rawlsian principle.

> In most modern democratic societies . . . many, though by no means all, of the socio-economic disadvantages that racial minorities currently suffer are caused by racial injustice perpetrated in the past—e.g., chattel slavery, genocide, land expropriation, colonization, disenfranchisement, denial of basic liberties, relentless terrorism and intimidation, and forced segregation. The racially disparate distribution of income, wealth, and opportunities that currently obtains in the United States, for example, can be partly explained by the cumulative impact of this history of racial violence and domination. Past racism has led to the development of a class structure in which the members of certain racial minorities (e.g., Native Americans and African Americans) are disproportionately located in its lowest ranks. Given that ideal theory does not directly address matters of compensatory justice, how, if at all, can Rawls's theory be useful for addressing this injustice?[35]

And the answer, for Shelby, is an expanded use of FEO:

> Here it is helpful to appreciate the richness of Rawls's fair equality of opportunity principle. This principle, were it to be institutionally realized in a well-ordered society in which the basic liberties were secure and their fair value guaranteed, would mitigate, if not correct, these race-based disadvantages by insuring that the life prospects of racial minorities are not negatively affected by the economic legacy of racial oppression. Rawls glosses the principle of fair equality of opportunity this way:
>
> > [T]hose who are at the same level of [natural] talent and ability, and have the same willingness to use them, should have the same prospects of success regardless of their initial place in the social system. In all sectors of society there should be roughly equal prospects of culture and achievement for everyone similarly motivated and endowed. The expectations of those with the same abilities and aspirations should not be affected by their social class.[36]

Shelby continues:

> While I am not sure what set of institutional reforms would be required to realize the principle of fair equality of opportunity in the United States, it seems clear that it would require, at a minimum, considerable redistribution of wealth, the expansion of educational and employment opportunities and aggressive measures to address discrimination in employment, housing, and lending. My main point here, though, is that a basic structure that provided fair equality of opportunity for all citizens regardless of race would remove many of the socioeconomic burdens that racial minorities presently shoulder because of the history of racial injustice. . . . In this way, the fair equality of opportunity principle addresses one of the most urgent concerns of members of the least favored races, namely, to insure that their life prospects are not unfairly diminished by the economic inequalities that have been created by a history of racism. Were this principle institutionally realized and widely recognized, it might also have the effect of sharply reducing the resentment for past racial injustice that some members of disadvantaged racial groups harbor, maybe even leading them to reconsider their insistence on claims to reparations.[37]

In sum, structural criticisms of the Rawlsian apparatus are unjustified, since though it is true that Rawls had little to say about racial justice—even less than he had to say about gender justice—the apparatus can be turned to this end without any problems.

So it is in this way that a Rawlsian path to racial justice can be mapped. But I disagree, and I now want to raise five objections to this line of argument.

FIVE POINTS AGAINST SHELBY
Rawls's Non-Endorsement

To begin with the most obvious objection to Shelby's proposed reconstruction of a Rawlsian reply: the most glaring problem is that *Rawls himself did not make use of it in contexts where it would have been natural for him to do so*. We are not dealing here with an obscure issue that understandably never surfaced within Rawls's discursive universe in the thirty years between the publication of *A Theory of Justice* and Rawls's death, or did so only as a minor, low-priority matter. As mentioned earlier, racial injustice and the white-supremacist constitution of the actual "basic structure" has been more salient in the United States than in any other of the Western democracies. Moreover, race and racism were on Rawls's radar from the start in *Theory* in a way that gender and sexism were not. Though neither racial nor gender identity are included as things you do not know about yourself behind the veil in this first formulation of his theory,[38] Rawls does explicitly condemn racism. Thus he states "we are confident that religious intolerance and racial discrimination are unjust," says that no one behind the veil would "put forward the principle that basic rights should depend on the color of one's skin or the texture of one's hair," and asserts

> from the standpoint of persons similarly situated in an initial situation which is fair, the principles of explicit racist doctrines are not only unjust. They are irrational. For this reason we could say that they are not moral conceptions at all, but simply means of suppression.[39]

So the point is that Rawls is aware from the beginning that racism is an important issue. In addition, in his introduction to the cloth edition of *Political Liberalism*, more than twenty years later, he admits that *Theory* does not deal with race, writing: "Among our most basic problems are those of race, ethnicity, and gender. These may seem of an altogether different character calling for different principles of justice, which *Theory* does not discuss."[40] So his first book condemns racism and his second book concedes that, despite his condemnation, the remedying of racism was not discussed in it.

The obvious question then is, how are we supposed to read this passage? I suggest that there are three main possibilities. Rawls believed that (a) despite appearances, the principles of justice formulated in *Theory* can indeed be used to deal directly with race; or (b) the "seeming" is correct, and "altogether" different principles of justice are required to deal with race;

or (c) although different principles of justice are required to deal with race, they are not "altogether" different, since they can (somehow) be derived from ideal-theory principles. Shelby's use of FEO commits him to endorsing (a),[41] whereas I think Rawls (rightly or wrongly) actually believed (c). But if the first interpretation were correct, surely the natural thing for Rawls to have done at this point would have been to continue (as I just said in [a]), "However, this appearance is misleading, because . . ." He does *not* do this, despite the fact that he is reporting a response to the book that obviously troubles him. If Shelby is right, and all that is needed is the extrapolation of FEO to take race into account, why does Rawls himself not just say so? It is hardly plausible to hypothesize that this obvious move, were it implicit in his theory, did not occur to him. The far more plausible interpretation is that for him, FEO could *not* be applied in this way.

Further evidence for this reading can be found in Rawls's concession, in his introduction to the 1996 paperback edition of *Political Liberalism* that changes over time in the content of "public reason" are necessary:

Social changes over generations also give rise to new groups with *different* political problems. Views raising *new* questions related to ethnicity, gender, and race are obvious examples, and the *political conceptions that result from these views* will debate the current conceptions [my emphases].[42]

Again, the natural reading is that race and ethnicity do indeed raise new and different political and normative questions, which is why they are to be contrasted to and seen as in contestation with the "current conceptions." If Shelby were right, this would have been the obvious place for Rawls to say that in fact the principles he outlined a quarter-century earlier could readily be extrapolated to handle these questions, so that the "newness" was only a matter of the particular groups now being included in the scope of the principles, not the content of the conceptions themselves. But he does not say this; he leaves the issue hanging and moves on.

Finally, the clincher, I would claim, is that in *Justice as Fairness*,[43] his last book, where Rawls is trying to produce the definitive summary of the essentials of his view, he returns again to the issue of race and gender.

We have seen that the two principles of justice apply to citizens as identified by their indexes of primary goods. It is natural to ask: Why are distinctions of race and gender not explicitly included among the three contingencies noted earlier (§16)? [In this earlier section, Rawls had listed "three kinds of contingencies" that affect "inequalities in citizens' life-prospects": social class, native endowments and opportunities to develop them, good or ill fortune.] . . . The answer is that we are mainly concerned with ideal theory: the account of the well-ordered society of justice as fairness.[44]

Note what he does *not* say. He does not say that although race and gender are not "explicitly included" among these "contingencies," it would be easy enough to add them, and then work out how the "two principles of justice" (including FEO) would "apply" to citizens disadvantaged by race and/or gender. Instead he asserts explicitly that this exclusion is a *principled* (not merely contingent) one, arising out of the fact that the two principles are principles of ideal theory for a well-ordered society, while race and gender problems fall under the different category of non-ideal theory. He does *not* say it is just a matter of applying FEO, as Shelby thinks. Instead, he suggests tentatively that what would be required is "a special form of the difference principle."[45] *So this is in direct contradiction of Shelby's claim.*

In sum, insofar as Shelby is supposed to be giving us a sympathetic recon-struction of how Rawls would extrapolate his principles to deal with racial injustice, he would obviously have to explain (a) why his reconstruction runs directly opposite to what Rawls himself says, to the limited extent that he does make positive recommendations (that is, he endorses a modified DP rather than FEO), and (b) why Rawls himself is so tentative and hesi-tant in the more frequent textual locations where he raises the problem but gives *no* positive recommendation, when according to Shelby it would just be a simple and straightforward matter of extending FEO to include race.[46]

The Importance of the Ideal Theory/Non-Ideal Theory Distinction

So what explains Rawls's tentativeness, and why does Shelby not appreci-ate its significance? My suggestion is that though Shelby does mention the ideal theory/non-ideal theory distinction, he does not really attribute that much weight to it. He believes either that non-ideal theory just involves populating the terms of ideal theory with different variables, or that you can pre-empt the need for non-ideal theory altogether by appropriately extrap-olating ideal theory. In my opinion, both of these judgments are wrong and Shelby—to use old-fashioned Rylean language—is guilty of a category mistake.[47] As Thomas Nagel points out, affirmative action, that policy of racial justice actually implemented in the United States, "is probably best understood in Rawlsian terms as an attempt at corrective justice," rectifying violations of the basic liberties, and thus not part of ideal theory.[48] Similarly, Samuel Freeman judges that "so-called 'affirmative action,' or giving prefer-ential treatment for socially disadvantaged minorities, is not part of FEO for Rawls, and is perhaps incompatible with it."[49]

The distinction between ideal and non-ideal theory is related to the dis-tinction between distributive and rectificatory justice, a distinction which goes all the way back to Aristotle's *Nicomachean Ethics*.[50] Distributive justice deals with norms and principles for the distribution of goods, rectificatory justice with norms and principles for the correction of wrongful distributions. So rectificatory justice is supposed to correct past wrongdoing. In Rawls's framework, rectificatory justice (what Rawls calls "compensatory justice")[51] falls under non-ideal theory. It is not coextensive with non-ideal theory, because non-ideal theory also includes such domestic issues as civil disobedience and conscientious refusal (dealt with in *Theory of Justice*) and such international issues as "burdened societies" and "outlaw states" (dealt with in *The Law of Peoples*).[52] Over the course of Rawls's lifetime, his work was focused almost exclusively on ideal theory (principles of distributive justice under ideal circumstances), and his brief forays into non-ideal theory were centered on problems other than rectification. *There is no discussion of rectificatory justice in Rawls's work.*

Now though one could choose to subsume anti-racial-discrimination measures under the category of racial justice (as pre-empting racial *injustice*),[53] racial justice, as I earlier emphasized, is pre-eminently a matter of rectificatory justice, the correction of the legacy of the past. In a well-ordered society, one that is regulated by Rawls's two principles, structural racial subordination will not exist, nor will the legacy of such subordination. That is uncontroversial. But the question is how do we get to there from here? This is the transition problem: what route to take and by which principles to be guided. And the problem is that Rawls does not tell us how to travel. His principles of justice are supposed to be principles of distributive justice for the regulation of an ideal well-ordered society, not principles of transitional justice to transform an ill-ordered society *into* a well-ordered society. In this enterprise, as Rawls himself seems to concede, the applicability or extensibility of the principles of ideal theory is limited:

> The principles define then a perfectly just scheme; they belong to ideal theory and set up an aim to guide the course of social reform. But even granting the soundness of these principles for this purpose, we must still ask how well they apply to institutions under less than favorable conditions, and whether they provide any guidance for instances of injustice. The principles and their lexical order were not acknowledged with these situations in mind and so it is possible that they no longer hold. I shall not attempt to give a systematic answer to these questions. . . . The intuitive idea is to split the theory of justice into two parts. The first or ideal part assumes strict compliance. . . . My main concern is with this part of the theory. Nonideal theory, the second part, is worked out after an ideal conception of justice has been chosen; only then do the parties ask which principles to adopt under less happy conditions. This division of the theory has, as I have indicated, two rather different subparts. One consists of the principles for governing

adjustments to natural limitations and historical contingencies, and the other of principles for meeting injustice.[54]

Note the hedged and cautious language of this passage. Rawls is basically conceding that he has not worked out what principles of justice would apply under the "less happy conditions" of non-ideal circumstances. As Thomas Nagel admits in a brief article on affirmative action for the *Journal of Blacks in Higher Education*, ideal theory "does not tell you what to do if, as is almost always the case, you find yourself in an unjust society, and want to correct that injustice."[55] Moreover, to the extent that Rawls explains how his ideal-theory principles are (somehow) supposed to "guide the course of social reform," it is (in his later discussion of civil disobedience and conscientious refusal) limited to the severely restricted "context . . . of a state of near justice, that is, one in which the basic structure of society is nearly just."[56] But obviously a society with a history of white supremacy like the United States is quite remote from being a well-ordered society; it is not slightly but *radically* deviant from perfect justice. So the already problematic issue of how Rawls's ideal principles are supposed to be developed into principles for "meeting injustice" is even further exacerbated under these circumstances, and the challenge to the applicability of FEO is even more forcefully raised.

It needs to be recalled that at the time of the original publication of Shelby's article (2004), the challenge to Rawlsian ideal theory was only in its infancy. But since then a growing body of work has begun to demonstrate how problematic and untheorized the relation between ideal and non-ideal theory is in Rawls's writings, and to raise the question of whether ideal theory, far from being a necessary foundation for constructing non-ideal theory, as Rawls thought, might actually be a hindrance to it.[57] Shelby's argument is not sufficiently informed by an awareness of these complexities. Nothing Rawls says would unambiguously authorize Shelby's use of FEO as a principle of transitional justice, and there are things he says that would seem to directly prohibit it. Thus in *Justice as Fairness* he emphasizes, "Justice as fairness is a political conception of justice for the special case of the basic structure of a modern democratic society," and a few pages later says that "we view a democratic society as a political society that excludes a confessional or an aristocratic state, not to mention a caste, slave, *or a racist one*" [my emphasis].[58] As with Rawls's judgment that a modified form of the difference principle will be required to deal with racial injustice, this seems centrally to contradict Shelby's project. Rawls is telling us unambiguously that his two principles of justice, including FEO, cannot be applied directly to racist societies as Shelby is doing.

Suppose, however, that someone were to object at this point that to insist on a difference between distributive and rectificatory justice is pedantic, not worth making a fuss over. After all, if some entity (money/ opportunities/tax breaks/free education) has been distributed or redis- tributed, what does it matter what we call it? (Re)Distribution is (re) distribution. But it is a general truth about all actions, including moral actions, that they must be carried out under the appropriate description, with the appropriate belief and motivational set on the part of the relevant agents, for them to merit a certain characterization. As we watch, A takes a twenty-dollar bill out of his pocket and gives it to B. Can we tell, given only this information, what has just happened? No, we cannot. We could have witnessed a loan, the repayment of a loan, a gift, a down-payment, an investment, a blackmail payoff, a purchase, and so forth. When the trans- action is over B will have twenty dollars more and A will have twenty dol- lars less, but that tells us little about what the nature of the transaction was, about *what action took place*. Insofar as rectification targets and seeks to correct ("repair") a wrong, it is not achieved by merely, say, giving the black population money. The question is under what auspices and under what characterization this transfer occurs. Advocates of reparations, for example—the variety of rectificatory justice for black Americans most dis- cussed over the past fifteen years—would contend that justice *has not been done* unless the circumstances make a particular description appropriate. (As an illustration: some conservative critics of the reparations move- ment have argued that the expansion of the welfare state under Lyndon Johnson's "Great Society" could be thought of as reparations. In other words, guys, *you've already got them!*)

Moreover, even apart from the material transfer, whatever form it might take, many theorists have argued that other measures, including symbolic ones, are crucial also. Truth and reconciliation commissions, acknowledg- ments of wrongdoing, apologies, genuine repentance, community repair, restoration of civic trust, have all been put forward as necessary elements for outstanding wrongs to be corrected.[59] Thomas McCarthy has sug- gested that a crucial component in the United States needs to be a national debate about slavery and Jim Crow to reconstitute public memory.[60] None of these issues is addressed by FEO redistribution, which is unsurprising, since it is not a principle motivated by and constructed for dealing with this kind of problem in the first place. I would suggest that Rawls's reluc- tance to follow the path Shelby reconstructs for him arises precisely out of his recognition of this non-identity. If FEO, a principle of ideal theory, could be turned into a principle of non-ideal theory simply by substituting race and gender as the pertinent variables in place of the ones Rawls him- self acknowledged, then Rawls would not have justified his non-treatment of race and gender by the fact of their falling under non-ideal theory in the first place.

FEO as Lexically Subordinate and Deontologically Constrained

Let me now raise some further problems for Shelby's assumption that despite these moves of his, he is still within the parameters of Rawlsianism as standardly understood. (For the sake of the argument, I will now assume what I have just contended is false, viz., that FEO can be applied under non-ideal circumstances.) Rawls's principles of justice for a well-ordered society are not conjunctively linked in any arbitrary order (P1.P2.P3 or P2.P3.P1) but lexically ordered: BL → (FEO → DP). One cannot extract one element as if it were a discrete module and apply it to a situation and still claim to be performing a Rawlsian exercise; the relationship of the three is crucial. So we need to know how Shelby's proposed use of FEO is related to the other principles, especially since Shelby is not just extending FEO to educational opportunity but to wealth also ("considerable redistribution of wealth").

In standard interpretations of Rawls, the point of FEO is to guarantee as far as possible in a well-ordered society (*modulo* the inevitable privileging by the nuclear family of children of the better-off) equal chances for the equally talented, and not have smart working-class kids lose out in market competition because their class background deprives them, for example, of "equal opportunities of education. . . . [T]he school system, whether public or private, should be designed to even out class barriers."[61] But in the actual ill-ordered society that is the United States, such equalization—desirable as it would be—would not be sufficient to equalize life chances across the racial divide, because even if poor black kids got the chance to go to better schools, they would still be hugely handicapped by the fact of intra-class wealth disparities between white and black households in corresponding racial quintiles (e.g., the bottom white 20 percent vis-à-vis the bottom black 20 percent). Ever since the 1995 publication of Melvin Oliver and Thomas Shapiro's *Black Wealth/White Wealth*,[62] differences in wealth have been recognized as central to the perpetuation of racial inequality, which is precisely why reparations advocates have made the need to correct or at least somewhat mitigate these disparities central to their arguments.

Now Shelby is well aware of these issues (and indeed cites Oliver and Shapiro himself), which is why he argues for a massive redistribution of wealth. In other words, he is using FEO *as if* it were a principle of rectificatory justice authorizing wealth transfer. But so far as I can see, he is not entitled to do this, because such an extrapolation goes far beyond what Rawls himself intended. An article by Robert Taylor, "Rawlsian Affirmative Action," concludes that even under non-ideal circumstances, FEO would not sanction aggressive affirmative action (bonus points for women and racial minorities in the applicant pool, targets for admissions and hiring) because of deontological constraints "imported" across the border from ideal theory.[63] For Taylor (following Christine Korsgaard), the three constraints under which non-ideal theory must operate are (a) consistency with the "general" conception of justice (equal distribution of social values, unless unequal distribution advantages everyone, thus permitting trade-offs); (b) the "reflect[ion of] the priority relations of ideal theory" in the attempt to bring about ideal conditions (seeking first the conditions required for the priority of BL, then for the priority of FEO, etc.); and (c) "consisten[cy] with the [deontological] spirit of the ideal theory," thereby ruling out consequentialist policies such as a moratorium on the hiring of white males "until racial and gender parity has been achieved."[64] The first would not be an obstacle to strong affirmative action, while for the second, Taylor suggests, we can just stipulate that "the conditions for the priority of [BL] have already been attained."[65] I will follow him in this stipulation for now but will soon argue that in actuality, the attainment of such conditions involves complicated considerations that would require far more extensive discussion than he provides.

For Taylor it is really the third constraint that poses the difficulty. Taylor contends that strong affirmative action violates Rawls's pure proceduralism, since we do not have the knowledge of "what the counterfactual results of a 'clean' competition would look like unless we run one," and "we would need precisely this knowledge to carry out the requisite outcome compensations."[66] But such objections would apply even more strongly to the attempt to invoke the counterfactual *wealth* distributions that would have resulted from an alternate non-discriminatory timeline, one not so profoundly marked as our own by decades of exclusion from good jobs, promotions, bank loans, federally underwritten mortgages, home ownership in decent neighborhoods, transfer payments from the state, and so forth. If Taylor is correct that FEO would not even permit strong affirmative action, it certainly would not permit the more radical redistributivist program—the transfer of wealth—that Shelby seeks to extract from it. For the counterfactuals here are even more indeterminate and speculative.

Yet I would claim that there is a problem more basic still, one that raises questions about both Taylor's and Shelby's diagnoses and prescriptions. Taylor says we can stipulate that "the conditions for the priority of [BL] have already been attained" and Shelby speaks of applying FEO for redistributive purposes in "a well-ordered society in which the basic liberties [are] secure and their fair value guaranteed." But (a question for Shelby) how could the society be well ordered in the first place given this history of structural white domination and its likely legacy? And (a question for both Taylor and Shelby), insofar as the basic liberties include the right to private property, how could the "attainment," the "securing," of these liberties for the black population have been achieved *without* addressing the correction of the huge property differences between the white and black populations?

For reparations advocates, existing property distributions are illegitimate because they rest on a history of racial discrimination and its cumulative intergenerational result over decades, or centuries if you go back to slavery, which violated the BL rights of blacks. Neither Taylor nor Shelby wish to move fully on to the terrain of non-ideal rectificatory theory, preferring instead to adapt FEO (a principle of ideal theory) to non-ideal conditions.[67] But trying to make such an argument within the existing Rawlsian framework causes considerable strain to it, not merely because of the unresolved issue of whether the norm of pure proceduralism was really intended by Rawls to apply to the determination of non-ideal justice but because the correction of BL violations would seem—by the very lexical priority relations both authors emphasize—to need to be dealt with first, even *before* we get to the question of the applicability of FEO. So how can this be achieved by employing a different and lexically subordinate principle?

Moreover, such transfers will be quite different in kind from the equalization of opportunity under ideal conditions putatively already agreed to behind the veil. Whether wealth is going to be transferred out of white hands directly, by expropriation, or indirectly, by taxation, whites are going to object that such transfer would violate *their* property rights. So apart from the issue of fuzzy counterfactuals, a debate within "public reason" between whites and blacks will need to take place that is not going to be the same as the debate over the acceptance of progressive taxation for the purposes of "keep[ing] property and wealth evenly enough shared over time" in what is a "property-owning democracy."[68] Rather, it will be a matter of convincing whites that they have benefited from "unjust enrichment," that their current holdings are unjust, and that corrective redistribution is therefore justified on those grounds. But that would require precisely the debate that Taylor and Shelby, through their refusal of an explicitly rectificatory framework, are trying to sidestep. Instead, they both rely on FEO, Taylor with negative, Shelby with positive, conclusions, but both outcomes problematically related to the lexical priority of BL that both authors claim to be acknowledging. In the final section I will point out another crucial implication of this lexical relationship.

Non-Controversiality as a Screening Factor for "Public Reason"

The marshaling of the evidence necessary to make Shelby's case also runs into difficulties. We want these measures of racial justice, radical as they may seem, to be endorsed by whites and not forced on them by black threats. So appeal to the kind of considerations acceptable to Rawlsian "public reason" becomes crucial: factual claims and social-scientific analy-ses about the history of white domination in the United States and the various ways in which its legacy continues to manifest itself in the pres-ent. In the original choice of Rawls's two principles of justice, the choosers behind the veil were limited to "general facts about human society."[69] Now, in the legislative stage of what Rawls calls "the four-stage sequence," they are permitted knowledge of "general facts about their society" that inform the enactment of "just laws and policies,"[70] and it is here (on this reading of Rawls) that the case for aggressive use of FEO would be made. But such factual claims and social-scientific theoretical analyses are going to be sub-ject to the Rawlsian stipulation that they fall under the category of "the presently accepted facts of social theory," "the methods and conclusions of science when not controversial."[71] And if we know anything about the history of race in the United States we know that such matters are going to be *hugely* controversial.

At every step of the way, from post-bellum Reconstruction in the 1860s–1870s to the 1950s–1960s period of civil rights legislation dubbed by some the "Second Reconstruction," whites have opposed measures of racial progress and racial justice, a consistent zigzag pattern of advances against "massive resistance" followed by later retreat.[72] As early as the period immediately after emancipation, arguments were already being made that the freedmen needed to stand on their own feet and not be cod-dled by the state. And today, of course, "color-blindness" is the hegemonic view among the white majority, who believe that the legacy of racism has long since been largely overcome—and that, if anything, it is *whites* who are more likely to be the victims of discrimination.[73] Divisions on race-related matters, whether specific events or public policy, have produced some of the largest public opinion gaps in recent decades, from the O. J. Simpson acquittal to the Katrina "social" disaster. As Donald Kinder and Lynn Sanders concluded years ago, in their classic *Divided by Color*, race creates "divisions more notable than any other in American life": "Political differences such as these are simply without peer: differences by class or gender or religion or any other social characteristic are diminutive by comparison."[74]

The point is, then, that were Shelby to accede to the Rawlsian stipulation to leave controversy at the door, *he would immediately be depriving himself of the weapons he needs to win his case.* The data about the white/black wealth gap, great differentials in incarceration rates, continuing employment dis-crimination, and so on, can all—even when not challenged outright—be given alternative explanations than the ones Shelby (and I) would favor.

These dramatic divisions obtain not merely at the layperson level but at the level of academic theory. As Thomas McCarthy writes:

> [Conservative] theorists treat "underclass" values, attitudes, behavior, and the like as independent variables and make them the causes of the social, economic, and political inequities afflicting its members. Extreme residential segregation, failed schools, dire poverty, chronic unemployment, and the breakdown of the black family are thereby regarded as effects of irresponsible behavior rather than its causes or as both its causes and effects. Accordingly, the remedy proposed is self-improvement rather than institutional change or than some combination of both. Institutional racism, on this view, is a thing of the past.[75]

If Shelby is claiming to be relying on an unmodified Rawls, he cannot use left-wing social-scientific materials, since they violate Rawlsian norms. Even armed with such theoretical analyses, of course, the left have already lost the battle with the right, as shown by the neo-liberal shift of recent decades.[76] But without them, they would be helpless even to put up a fight. Note by contrast that because I believe more radical changes are necessary, the reliance on such social science claims is not problematic for me, since I believe Rawls's methodology *does* have to be modified to deal adequately with racial injustice and other non-ideal realities.[77] I take for granted that under non-ideal circumstances, where social oppression is the norm, the group interests of the privileged and their differential group experience will generate rationalizations of the existing order so that contesting social privilege to realize social justice will necessarily mean encountering and combating such ideologies.[78] Controversiality for me goes with the theoretical territory, the territory of the systematically non-ideal. But this revision is not open for Shelby.

Racial Injustice versus Class Injustice

Finally, I want to elaborate on another way in which Shelby's attempted use of FEO to address racial injustice represents a category mistake. It is not merely that two different species of justice, distributive and corrective, are being conflated, but that two different kinds of wrongs are being jumbled together.

In trying to turn a principle meant to remedy class disadvantage into a principle for addressing the legacy of racial discrimination, Shelby is blurring the difference between wrongs that involve the violation of (left-liberal) norms of opportunity and wrongs that involve the violation of personhood. The difference between left-liberalism (such as Rawls's) and right-liberalism (such as Robert Nozick's)[79] hinges on what kind of rights are recognized and what kind of equality can licitly be promoted as a norm. Left-liberals want "positive" rights, "social" rights, "welfare" rights as well as the traditional ones (which will need to be suitably qualified to make possible general Hohfeldian rights-consistency across this expanded schedule). Right-liberals will only admit "negative" rights of non-interference with life, liberty, and property and will see the additional rights argued for by the left as not truly liberal but as alien incursions from the socialist tradition. Correspondingly, we can distinguish a "strong" or "substantive" egalitarianism that judges material equality, whether in full or as a default mode (a presumptive if defeasible starting point), to be a moral desideratum, from a "weak" or "formal" egalitarianism that recognizes only moral, legal, and political equality as legitimate norms.

Now racial discrimination is a violation of negative rights and weak egalitarianism, in that the "inferior" race in a racist society, the R2s, will have a moral status lowered beneath the level of the equal socially recognized personhood of the R1s, that as a result typically deprives the R2s of equal legal protection of their interests, political standing, and access to economic opportunities. As such, racial discrimination can be condemned *across* the liberal spectrum since it breaches the norm of equal personhood and respect upon which liberalism qua liberalism is supposed to rest— the "equal rights" of all "men" trumpeted by the American and French Revolutions against the pre-modern world, the ancien régime of ascriptive hierarchy and differentiated status. Robert Nozick no less than John Rawls would, and in fact does, condemn racial discrimination—indeed formally making the remedy of such violations part of his theory in a way that Rawls does not.[80] Racial injustice is, most fundamentally, a refusal to respect equal personhood, whether in the original rights-violations or in the legacy of such violations. *Racial injustice is anti-liberal.*[81]

Contrast that with class disadvantage arising out of market workings. In a modern class society, as against a pre-modern caste society, the white (male) working class is not being kept down by anti-liberal laws and discriminatory social practices. Rather, people compete on the market, some do worse than others, and the children of the latter grow up in homes and neighborhoods where family resources are thinner and the schools are worse. Presuming the competition was fair by capitalist norms, children will be disadvantaged in escaping their parents' status, but not barred. But a racist society where through discrimination, segregation, and other barriers poor black kids do not get an equal chance *does* violate capitalist market norms. To be on a lower rung of the social ladder because of bad luck in the social lottery is different from being on a lower rung because of social oppression that denies equal personhood. *Class injustice is anti-left-liberal.*

So, in a kind of metaphysical—rather than the more familiar sociological—class reductionism, a crucial conceptual distinction is being erased by Shelby, in that a moral wrong uncontroversially exemplifying the violation of equal personhood is being assimilated to what is a moral wrong only by the standards of a particular variant of liberalism. As Robert Taylor points out:

Even classical-liberal supporters of what Rawls calls the "system of natural liberty" [libertarianism] would regard the disadvantages wrought by past and present discriminatory behavior as great injustices because they are the result of violations of formal [equality of opportunity], a principle that (unlike substantive [equality of opportunity/ FEO]) classical liberals themselves accept.[82]

In fact, one way of bringing out the oddness of Shelby's position (and, for that matter, Taylor's) is by seeing what it does to the identities of Rawls's two principles: BL → (FEO → DP). The lexical priority of BL represents the moral priority of personhood, whether in the original full-blooded Kantian sense of "comprehensive liberalism" or the somewhat more anemic version of "political liberalism." Racism is a violation of BL. As such, we want a principle of rectificatory justice that acknowledges the moral primacy of BL, the rights and freedoms of persons, the heart of liberalism. To try to transform FEO, a norm of justice lexically *subordinate* to BL, into a principle putatively correcting for *violations* of BL is to force it into a role it was never meant to play.[83] The goal of FEO is to make opportunities fair by the standards of left-liberalism; the goal of BL is to safeguard basic liberties. Corrections for violations of BL should reflect its lexical priority and the morally more fundamental nature of violations of personhood. By making corrective racial justice depend on left-liberal assumptions, Shelby mislocates the basic wrongness of racial injustice, which violates principles shared by all (decent) liberals.

Moreover, on a closing note, the desideratum for such policies should be to make assumptions as "weak" (uncontroversial) as possible, and to seek to attract as broad a basis of political support as possible. The traditionally center-right United States is not going to get on board with a program that rests on moral claims accepted only by left-liberals. An approach such as mine, which derives racially rectificatory principles directly from violations of rights of non-interference, is, I would suggest, both morally superior (in targeting the actual wrong involved rather than hoping to reach an extensionally equivalent victim population through indirect means) and politically more attractive (in not excluding in advance a large proportion of potential supporters, who would endorse racial justice but reject social democracy).[84]

I hope I have shown why Shelby's strategy is problematic in a way that does not at all reflect on his own exposition of the position but rather makes clear the inherent problems in the approach itself. Nonetheless, critics may still reply that even if I have raised questions about Shelby's particular version, other variants are possible.[85] The key point for me, however, is the difference between distributive and rectificatory justice, and the shaping of Rawls's work and virtually the entire secondary literature by the imperatives of the former. That more than forty years after the publication of *A Theory of Justice* there has not been more debate on the flagrant absence of racial justice as a theme in this literature, and the questions this absence raises about its possible intrinsic "whiteness," is a sad manifestation both of the continuing demographic and conceptual whiteness of philosophy and its resistance to seeing itself as such.

CHAPTER 10

The Whiteness
of Political Philosophy

I got my PhD from the University of Toronto in 1985, which (to my alarm) puts me in the category of really senior African American philosophers in the profession working on Africana philosophy, junior only to such pioneering figures in the field as Leonard Harris, Howard McGary, Al Mosley, and Lucius Outlaw, all 1970s graduates, and a few early 1980s graduates like Robert Gooding-Williams, Tommy Lott, and Cornel West. As I have recounted in greater detail elsewhere, I originally went to graduate school in philosophy in the hopes of exploring the issues of race and imperialism then being hotly debated in my native Jamaica.[1] Not finding any appropriate philosophical frameworks in a white field in an all-white department in a white Canadian university without even a black studies program to assist me, I decided to do a dissertation on Marxism instead. So in a sense, my 1990s turn to race in my work was a *return*, a coming back to what I had originally wanted to do. Since by many conventional measures—publications, recognition, visibility—I have succeeded, it might be illuminating to reflect on what this "success" is worth, and the changes I have seen, as well as the changes I have not seen, in academic philosophy over this period and what they say about the profession. My conclusions are, unfortunately, somewhat pessimistic. I now believe that what has been self-satirizingly described as the "long march" through the academy for campus radicals wanting to transform their disciplines will be much longer and harder for blacks seeking to establish Africana philosophy than for theorists elsewhere. Whiteness has become—in effect, if not de jure—more structurally central to the very self-conception of the field than in other subjects, so that by pursuing this agenda one is, in a sense, challenging philosophy itself in a way that black scholars in other areas like, say, literature, history, sociology, are not challenging theirs.

PHILOSOPHY THEN AND NOW

Let me begin with the positives, looking at such representative indices as publications, conference visibility, and the placement of people in the academy. In 1985, there was only one really good anthology in African American philosophy, Leonard Harris's pathbreaking *Philosophy Born of Struggle*, which came out in 1983.[2] (A second edition, so radically revised it might as well have been a different book, appeared in 2000.)[3] *The Philosophical Forum* had dedicated a special double issue to philosophy and the black experience in 1977–78, guest edited by Jesse McDade and Carl Lesnor, but it was never brought out in book form, although a subsequent triple issue of the journal on a similar theme in 1992–93, edited by John Pittman, was later published by Routledge.[4] Harris has recounted his experience of shopping the *Philosophy Born of Struggle* manuscript around to all the publishers at the American Philosophical Association (APA) book exhibit and being turned down by all of them, the consensus being that only black philosophy students and black philosophers would be interested in such a book, and clearly there were not enough of either, or both put together, to make it a viable proposition. It was eventually published by Kendall/Hunt, a well-known publishing house in other areas but with no reputation in philosophy, and certainly *not* one to be found at the book exhibit. Around the same time period, two other pathbreaking texts would appear: Cornel West's first book, *Prophesy Deliverance!* (1982), which would launch the career of the person who would go on to become the best-known black philosopher in the country, and Bernard Boxill's *Blacks and Social Justice* (1984), which remained for many years the only text in analytic black normative political philosophy.[5]

But the point is that these were isolated works, each one by its very existence being a noteworthy event. Samuel Johnson is a man of many quotable lines, but one of my favorites, sexist and speciesist though it may be, is his comment about a woman preacher and a dog walking on its hind legs: "It is not done well; but you are surprised to find it done at all." To many white eyes of the time, black philosophy had that same kind of quasi-oxymoronic character: its very existence (never mind its definition—an endless debate of the period) was remarkable. A bookshelf of contemporaneous monographs and anthologies on African American philosophy (as against classic writings by Douglass, Du Bois, et al.) would not have needed to be more than a few inches wide. Today, books on race and Africana philosophy are being published by the most prestigious presses in the business—see such entries of the last decade as Lewis Gordon's *An Introduction to Africana Philosophy* and Derrick Darby's *Rights, Race, and Recognition* with Cambridge, Christopher Lebron's *The Color of Our Shame* with Oxford, Tommie Shelby's *We Who Are Dark* and Robert Gooding-Williams's *In the Shadow of Du Bois* with Harvard, Leonard Harris and Charles Molesworth's *Alain J. Locke: The Biography of a Philosopher* with Chicago.[6] The total over the past twenty years for single-author monographs and article collections, and edited general and thematic anthologies, is now (depending on how and what you count) approaching 100; articles on race can appear in places like the *Journal of Philosophy*; and Africana philosophy is formally recognized as a category and a legitimate area of specialization by the APA. In this environment, it would be difficult for contemporary graduate students to realize how radically different things were a mere three decades ago.

For it was not merely the absence of books in the area that marked this earlier period. The marginalization of race and Africana philosophy in the profession was, of course, also manifest in the content of APA meetings. As a graduate student in Canada, I was not in the United States in the 1970s and most of the 1980s. But people like Lucius Outlaw have given accounts of what it was like during that time.[7] To find the panel on race or African American philosophy one consulted the marginalized and stigmatized "group program," descended to the hotel basement for the special midnight session, followed the cockroaches to a cobwebbed door, whispered "Lucius sent me," and was then admitted to a broom closet—but nothing more than a closet would have been needed for an audience that was, if one was lucky, the same size as the panel, or, more frequently, *was* the panel. (OK, I exaggerate slightly, but not much.) Now, when panels on race are not only routinely on the main program but sometimes competing with one another, with dozens of people (mostly white) in attendance, so that it is not possible to go to them all, the existence of this epoch may seem unbelievable.

What changed things was the determined activism of a handful of black philosophers: caucuses within the APA, such as the Committee on the Status of Black Philosophers, or outside, such as the New York Society for the Study of Black (now Africana) Philosophy. These groups were usually assisted by committed black scholars without formal philosophical training, working sometimes with the aid of white sympathizers in organizations like the Radical Philosophy Association (RPA), continually lobbying for more room and representation in APA programs while simultaneously organizing meetings and conferences in other venues—for example, at historically black institutions such as Tuskegee and Morgan State, and at white institutions with friendly faculty.[8] Though it was long before my time there, the first ever black philosophy conference at a "white" university was held in 1970 at the institution I would later join in 1990, the University of Illinois at Chicago (UIC, then "Chicago Circle"), with the late Irving Thalberg being a key facilitator. In 2001, while I was still at UIC, I organized the second black philosophy conference there, including some participants like Bernard Boxill, Howard McGary, Al Mosley, Leonard Harris, and Lucius Outlaw, who were present at the first one and were able to give some historical perspective on the event.

Today, there is an annual Philosophy Born of Struggle conference, going steadily since 1994, inspired by Leonard Harris's anthology, under the guidance of Harris and J. Everet Green; the more recently (2004) inaugurated California Roundtable on Philosophy and Race, which holds annual workshops; and the "South"-oriented Caribbean Philosophical Association, seeking to "shift the geography of reason" and meeting annually in Caribbean and Caribbean diasporic locations (so far: Barbados, Puerto Rico, Montreal, Jamaica, Guadeloupe, Miami, Colombia, New Brunswick, Trinidad & Tobago, Puerto Rico [again], St. Louis, Mexico). Also there have been numerous special occasion events at different campuses on African American philosophy in general, or "whiteness," or on particular classic texts, or in honor of key past or contemporary figures in black philosophy, or other themes.

Moreover, progress has also been manifest in the greater visibility and prominence of black philosophers both within and outside the profession. In 1995, the irrepressible Leonard Harris published an infamous letter in the *APA Proceedings and Addresses* (for which, he reports in the second edition of *Philosophy Born of Struggle*, he received death threats)[9] in which he suggested that American Philosophy was so white that it was clearly a creation of the Klan:

> The Ku Klux Klan secretly created a profession: American Philosophy. . . . The most noted Black philosophers are relegated to the status of kitchen help on the plantation: Cornel West, at Harvard, holds a joint appointment in African American Studies and the Harvard Divinity School. Anthony Appiah, also at Harvard, holds a full time faculty line in African American Studies. Neither costs philosophy any money.[10]

Harris pointed out that blacks constituted only 1 percent of American philosophers (only nine of whom were black women) and that apart from the question of numbers, black philosophers and black philosophy were generally not shown any respect.

Consider, by contrast, the situation today, twenty years later. The Eastern Division has had its first black president, in the person of that same (former "kitchen helper") Anthony Appiah (2007–08), who left Harvard for Princeton and has more recently taken up the position of

Professor of Philosophy and Law at New York University. Appiah is also nationally—indeed internationally—visible and multiply honored, with numerous books (including many translations) and public appearances, honorary degrees, elected memberships to the American Academy of Arts and Sciences, the American Philosophical Society, and the American Academy of Arts and Letters, past chairmanship of the Executive Board of the APA and the Board of the American Council of Learned Societies, and the Modern Language Association.[11] Who among us thirty years ago would have dreamed that a black philosopher could attain such status and honors, or that a book on black nationalism written by a black philosopher in Harvard's African and African American Studies department would be published by Harvard University Press and reviewed by the *New York Times*, as Tommie Shelby's *We Who Are Dark*[12] was, gaining him tenure at Harvard and membership in the philosophy department, or that the most visible black intellectual in the country, veteran of thousands of conferences and campus appearances, a fixture on the talk show circuit, would be a philosopher, Cornel West? Harris had complained that there were no blacks in philosophy at any of the eight Ivy League universities (Brown, Columbia, Cornell, Dartmouth, Harvard, Penn, Princeton, Yale). Today, by my count, there are eight. Harris had said that only two blacks had endowed chairs/distinguished professorships in philosophy departments. Today, by my count (including emeritus professors), there are at least ten. Harris had listed only fourteen blacks empowered to sit on philosophy doctoral committees. Today, by my count, there are two to three times that number.

So given all this obvious progress, what could the grounds of my pessimism be?

YES, BUT ...

Well, let's take them in reverse order: people and placement, APA presence, publications. To begin with, it has to be pointed out that the overall numbers have not changed, proportionally. Twenty years ago, as Harris said, only 1 percent of US philosophers were black; today, twenty years later, only 1 percent of US philosophers are black.[13] (And "black" here is being used to include not just African Americans but Afro-Caribbean and African immigrants to the United States. Restricting the count just to native black Americans would make it significantly smaller.) Enough graduates are being produced that this percentage is being maintained; it is certainly in no danger of doubling, or tripling, or anything like that.[14] And only about thirty of these black philosophers are women, doubly disadvantaged in the profession by the intersection of race and gender.

Moreover, it is instructive to look at the number of blacks in top-ranked institutions who are actually working *on* race and Africana philosophy. By no means do I want to prescribe that all black philosophers choose this specialization. Creating and expanding a black presence in the profession means encouraging people to go into a number of areas, especially since the reality is that blacks who succeed in "white" fields ("real" philosophy) will be taken more seriously than those working in Africana and race, and there might be an eventual halo effect by which their success validates the latter's research focus simply by demonstrating that, *mirabile dictu*, blacks are indeed capable of philosophizing. (Although it might instead work the other way: those who continue to focus on race instead of following their wiser peers' example prove thereby that they are the subset of blacks *not* so capable.) But from the perspective of trying to diagnose the future of Africana philosophy, this is obviously the crucial question. So the issue of the representation of more black philosophers needs to be conceptually separated from the issue of the wider representation of black philosophy, even if there is considerable overlap. (In other words, I am rejecting the definition that says that anything black philosophers do is black philosophy.) Barriers to the former have come down considerably, but the question is what this means for barriers to the latter. Even if Africana *philosophers* (African American, Afro-Caribbean, African) are increasingly and more prominently represented in professional philosophy, to what extent will Africana *philosophy* be flourishing comparably?

Consider, in this light, the numbers of black philosophers in top institutions and what their areas of specialization are. I have used as my source the Philosophical Gourmet Report (2009 for the original chapter, 2014–15 for this updated version). This ranking is, of course, very controversial and has been criticized for its analytic bias (and indeed for its very existence). Nonetheless, it does give us information of some kind, even if it is only about perceived realities.

From the 2009 ranking of the top twenty-five schools, I came up with a count of fourteen black philosophers: Rutgers: Howard McGary; Princeton: Kwame Anthony Appiah and Delia Graff Fara; Harvard: Tommie Shelby; Stanford: Kenneth Taylor; University of North Carolina at Chapel Hill: Bernard Boxill and Ryan Preston-Roedder; Columbia: Macalester Bell, Michele Moody-Adams, and Elliot Paul;[15] Arizona: Joseph Tolliver; CUNY Graduate Center: Frank Kirkland (at Hunter College); UC San Diego: Michael Hardimon; University of Chicago: Anton Ford. Of these fourteen, only *five* people—McGary, Shelby, Boxill (all in ethics, political philosophy, and African American philosophy), Kirkland (Hegel, Husserl, African American philosophy), and Hardimon (nineteenth-century German philosophy, ethics and social and political philosophy, race)[16]—were really working centrally and currently on race and/or Africana philosophy.

Fast forward now to the 2014–15 ranking of the schools in the top twenty-five positions (thirty departments in total). In the intervening five years, some people have moved around and retired, and there have been some new hirings. But the count is still (despite the larger number of departments included) only fourteen black philosophers: New York University: Kwame Anthony Appiah; Princeton: Delia Graff Fara; Rutgers: Howard McGary; Michigan: Derrick Darby; Yale: Christopher Lebron (primary appointment in African American Studies); Harvard: Tommie Shelby; Stanford: Kenneth Taylor; Columbia: Robert Gooding-Williams (joint position with African American Studies), Michele Moody-Adams, and Elliot Paul; CUNY Graduate Center: Frank Kirkland and Charles Mills; Chicago: Anton Ford; UC San Diego: Michael Hardimon. The number of people who work on race and/or African American philosophy is now eight: McGary, Shelby, Kirkland, and Hardimon, as listed above, but now in addition Darby (social and political philosophy, race, philosophy of law), Lebron (ethics, political philosophy, race), Gooding-Williams (social and political philosophy, African American, nineteenth-century European, aesthetics), and Mills (social and political philosophy, African American, Marxism, race). (Appiah, the highest placed black philosopher in the country [indeed the world] is, of course, well known for his work on race. But from the beginning his project has been the discrediting of race as a category, and his work in recent years has shifted to issues of cosmopolitanism and liberal theory, though admittedly he did recently publish a set of lectures on Du Bois and identity.)[17]

So the total number of black philosophers is the same, while the number working on race and Africana has increased by just three. And it should be noted that of these eight philosophers in the top thirty departments, one of them, McGary, as a 1970s graduate, will presumably be retiring in another few years, possibly followed by Kirkland. So unless there are some new hirings, this is still only a handful, if a slightly larger one. That is not to say, of course, that there are not many very good black philosophers making contributions at other institutions. But insofar as in any discipline the top departments tend to establish the norms for what is considered important and cutting-edge philosophy, one can easily see that Africana philosophy is going to be marginalized for a long time to come simply by virtue of these numbers.[18] Lucius Outlaw, one of the pioneers in establishing the field in the first place, is now at Vanderbilt, but he taught for most of his career at an undergraduate institution, Haverford College, and he too is likely to be retiring soon. Lewis Gordon, one of the most active and prolific Africana philosophers—by some estimates, the central figure in the field today—as well as a tireless institution- and network-builder, was for many years at Brown before moving to Temple (he has recently left Temple for the University of Connecticut), but in Africana Studies, with no relationship (or a poisoned relationship) with the Brown philosophy department. And in addition, of course, both men are Continental philosophers and are thus—quite apart from Africana research focus—disadvantaged for that reason alone by the prevailing North American analytic hegemony. Since the top schools tend to hire from one another, PhDs in Africana philosophy produced by such lower-ranked departments are unlikely to be hired "upstream."

So the figures are not encouraging. Partly the problem is just statistical, an artifact of the interrelation of large and small numbers. If one starts with a marginal subject area that only attracts a small fraction of the applicant pool to begin with, and then multiplies that fraction by the similarly small fraction of applicants likely to be able to *get into* the best schools, and that fraction by the fraction of top schools with qualified supervisors in the area, then what one ends up with is a number quite tiny. Low numbers tend to perpetuate themselves as low. And a background factor increasingly affecting all potential recruits to the field, of course, is the national underfunding of the humanities and the diminishing percentage of tenure-track positions in the academy as against limited sessional appointments—the fate of "permanent temping." In times of such uncertainty even for white males about the viability of an academic career, black students would have to be very strongly motivated to take such a risk. Unfortunately, the quest to increase a black presence in philosophy, the ivory tower's ivory tower so to speak, is being undertaken at precisely the time that jobs are drying up for everybody.

THE SUCCESS AND FAILURE OF *THE RACIAL CONTRACT*

That brings us to the issues of conference presence and publications. The concept of tokenization may be useful here. Personal tokenization is of course a familiar problem since the affirmative action debates of the 1970s onward: the black figure, sometimes prominent, whose hiring is supposed to prove the institutional commitment to non-discrimination, but whose presence does nothing to change the reproductive dynamic of the underlying exclusionary structures. So we are all now sophisticated enough to be able to see through this kind of stratagem. I want to suggest (if no one else has already done so) the idea of *conceptual* tokenization, where a black perspective is included but in a ghettoized way that makes no difference to the overall discursive logic of the discipline, or subsection of the discipline, in question: the framing assumptions, dominant narratives, prototypical scenarios. My fear is that the dramatically increased presence of black bodies and black panels in APA programs, and even black texts in philosophy, may in the end amount to no more than conceptual tokenization.

It is natural to use one's own work as illustrative because one knows it and its fate best. So let me now do so. Including the current manuscript, I have written six books (the fourth, *Contract and Domination*, being co-authored with Carole Pateman).[19] But what is and probably will always be my best-known book is my first one, *The Racial Contract*, which came out in 1997.[20]

The book was written out of my frustrations with mainstream political philosophy. I still recall my first encounter with Rawls, in a graduate seminar in the 1970s at the University of Toronto taught by none other than David Gauthier before his move to Pittsburgh. Looking back all these years later, what I remember is the utter disconnection I felt between Rawls's work and my interests. I had gone to graduate school hoping to explore philosophically issues of race and imperialism; I was working in social and political philosophy; I planned to do a dissertation that would address problems of social injustice. But at no stage in reading Rawls did it *remotely* occur to me that this was a book that could in any way be relevant to my project, even though its title was *A Theory of Justice*.[21] Admittedly, at the time I was not sufficiently sophisticated philosophically to appreciate how absolutely crucial to the architecture of the text was the distinction between the ideal theory on which Rawls focuses and the non-ideal theory he virtually ignores, and would largely continue to ignore for the rest of his career. This was a revelation that would only come a long time later. But what did seem overwhelmingly obvious was that—whatever this book was about—it was not about anything that was going to be of any help to me. So to repeat, it is not that I was looking for guidance and was disappointed, but that I simply did not see Rawls's work as having anything to do with what I was concerned about. It seemed to exist in a different conceptual world altogether. And there is a sense in which—although my book with Pateman does self-consciously try to engage with Rawls—that simple episode sums up everything about the field. With only apparent paradox, I will put it this way. Since its revival by Rawls, mainstream Anglo-American political philosophy's primary focus has been normative theory and social justice. However, *racial justice is not a species of justice but belongs in a different genus altogether*. And, as a corollary: *you can do political philosophy or race, but not both*.

Now I am sure that to an outsider, these claims will seem quite bizarre, just as, in a different but related way, non-philosophers I have met at political science or sociology or interdisciplinary conferences have found it unbelievable that I did not have to deal with a flood of job offers from higher-ranked philosophy departments after *The Racial Contract* came out (in fact, I did not receive even one), or that in the ten-year period after it appeared, I did not have a single student doing his dissertation on race. (Later, at Northwestern, I did supervise and graduate one for the first time, Chike Jeffers, who in 2010 started as an assistant professor at Dalhousie in Canada and is now tenured there.) But for black philosophers within the field, more knowing about our peculiar profession, I doubt that they are particularly controversial or surprising. That's the way the discipline works, and one needs to understand that.

Back to *The Racial Contract*, however. Far from expecting the book to have the success it has had, I had been unsure whether I would even be able to get it accepted by any reputable press in the first place. But my Cornell University Press editor Alison Shonkwiler's faith in the manuscript's potential turned out to be completely justified. It was reviewed very widely at the time, not just in philosophy journals, but in sociology, political science, and gender studies, and not just in the academy but in the popular press also, gaining positive evaluations from journals/newspapers as far apart politically as *In These Times* and *The Nation*, on the one hand, and the *Jerusalem Post*, on the other. As of December 31, 2015, the last date for which I received sales figures, it had sold over 36,000 copies, making it an academic bestseller, with widespread and continuing course adoption across numerous disciplines and in scores of universities, at both the undergraduate and the graduate levels. Excerpts from the book have been reprinted in several anthologies, most recently in the second edition of Matt Zwolinski's edited *Arguing about Political Philosophy* anthology, a collection of classic and contemporary readings in the field.[22] The online *Stanford Encyclopedia of Philosophy*'s entry "Contractarianism" has a paragraph on Carole Pateman (author of *The Sexual Contract*)[23] and myself, under the sub-heading "Subversive Contractarianism." The online *Internet Encyclopedia of Philosophy*'s entry "Social Contract Theory" has several paragraphs on the book, under the sub-heading "Contemporary Critiques of Social Contract Theory."[24] Students can buy essays on the book at the appropriate websites, a sure sign, if a morally dubious one, of routine course adoption. Before it came out, I was averaging three to four presentations a year (conferences, campus invitations). After its publication, my figures jumped for a while to nearly twenty a year—not remotely in the league of a Cornel West, of course (this would be a slow month for Cornel), but certainly very busy by my standards. In total, I have now (fall 2016) given over 380 presentations. And all this for a book dealing with race, imperialism, white supremacy, and genocide—the very kinds of topics that mainstream white philosophy is reluctant to talk about.

What on earth could I be complaining about then, given this degree of success?

The problem is this. It seems to me that the simple and crucial test to be imposed is, what impact has the book actually had—a book that has now, to repeat, been out for nearly twenty years—on mainstream political philosophy in general and social contract theory in particular? This is the kind of criterion one would routinely use in other disciplines about work widely perceived to be successful and innovative. And I think the objective answer that has to be faced is: close to zero. I don't think I can truly say that the course of mainstream ("white") political philosophy has in any way been affected by the book's publication. So, consider a philosophy text on race that has sold over 36,000 copies—almost certainly more than any other such academic philosophy book on the topic over the period (I am excluding, obviously, popular works like Cornel West's *Race Matters*),[25] a philosophy text that has been and is widely adopted in courses across the country, a philosophy text that tries to engage (albeit somewhat polemically) with the liberal tradition and a framework central to that tradition rather than simply arguing for the dismissal of liberalism as such—if such a text cannot affect the direction of white political philosophy, what can?

But what (you ask) about the online encyclopedia entries I cited? Well, it is noteworthy that both of them are by anti-racist white feminists (Ann Cudd, Celeste Friend), allies in the struggle for a more inclusive vision of philosophy (not to mention personal acquaintances), but they are hardly representative of the white male-dominated field as a whole. What could be regarded as the mainstream white-male *Stanford Encyclopedia* contract entry, by contrast—"Contemporary Approaches to the Social Contract," by Fred D'Agostino, Gerald Gaus, and John Thrasher—has no mention of gender or racial subordination, and, accordingly, no reference to Carole Pateman or Charles Mills.[26] What about all the book sales? Well, the book is sufficiently short and accessible that it can be used in introductory courses, which may have 100 to 150 students in them, so that a few such adoptions lead to huge sales. Moreover, because of its accessibility, where these course adoptions are at top universities, it is usually (apart from one's few sympathetic black philosophy colleagues in top programs) in disciplines *outside* of philosophy, for example in political science, sociology, African American, ethnic studies, education, anthropology, literature, American Studies.

In other words, for many (non-philosophy) people of color and white progressives in the academy, *The Racial Contract* has now become a standard text to assign as a self-contained crash course on imperialism, critical race theory, and white supremacy that exposes the hypocrisies of liberalism and the Western humanist tradition, and puts US racism in a global and historical context. But the contract framework itself is quite dispensable for them except as it provides another useful target to be trashed. It is not the case that most of these academics—certainly not those outside philosophy—are interested in the exercise of seeing how Rawlsian contract theory can be *revised* and *reconstructed* to deal with these issues.

But as emphasized, the clearest indicator of failure is the lack of engagement in the mainstream political philosophy literature. Consider what I say in the introductory opening pages of *The Racial Contract*. I indict the whiteness of the "conceptual array and . . . standard repertoire of concerns" of mainstream political philosophy and call on African American philosophers to follow the (white) feminist example and "aggressively engage the broader debate":

> What is needed is a global theoretical framework for situating discussions of race and white racism, and thereby challenging the assumptions of white political philosophy, which would correspond to feminist theorists' articulation of the centrality of gender, patriarchy, and sexism to traditional moral and political theory. What is needed, in other words, is a recognition that racism (or, as I will argue, global white supremacy) is *itself* a political system. . . . The "Racial Contract" . . . is intended as a conceptual bridge between two areas now largely segregated from each other: on the one hand, the world of mainstream (i.e., white) ethics and political philosophy, preoccupied with discussion of justice and rights in the abstract, on the other hand, the world of Native American, African American, and Third and Fourth World political thought, historically focused on issues of conquest, imperialism, colonialism, white settlement, land rights, race and racism, slavery, jim crow, reparations, apartheid, cultural authenticity, national identity, *indigenismo*, Afrocentrism, etc.[27]

So what I was trying to accomplish, through using while radically revising the device of a contract, was a desegregation, an integration, of these two conceptual and theoretical worlds because in reality, of course, they are just *one* world in which one pole deludes itself about its relation to the other pole. I hoped that my book would be part of a dialogue on rethinking the canon and making it harder, if not impossible, to go on as before, with traffic going both ways, to and fro, on this "conceptual bridge."

But such discussions as have taken place have basically been organized and carried out by those on just one side of the bridge. On Lewis Gordon's initiative, the APA Committee on Blacks in Philosophy and the RPA arranged a very successful panel (in terms of turnout and participation) on my work at the 1998 Eastern APA meetings.[28] A related symposium on *The Racial Contract* was put together by the RPA and eventually published (the original arrangement for the RPA newsletter having fallen through) some years later in a collection of pieces based on a panel at a

1999 Michigan State interdisciplinary conference on race.[29] Another symposium appeared in *Small Axe*, the Caribbean post-colonial theory journal edited by David Scott.[30] And a retrospective symposium—"Revisiting the 'Racial Contract'"—organized at the 2013 American Political Science Association (APSA) annual meeting by Anna Marie Smith has just been published (two of the original panelists and two other contributors, with my reply) in the new political science journal *Politics, Groups, and Identities*.[31]

Thus none of the symposia was organized by a mainstream philosophy organization or journal, or even appeared in a philosophy venue. (UPDATE: At the time of writing, a mini-symposium on my work based on a 2014 SPEP [Society for Phenomenology and Existential Philosophy] Scholar Panel is scheduled to appear in *Critical Philosophy of Race*. But SPEP is sharply segregated from the analytic mainstream, and *Critical Philosophy of Race* is, of course, a specialty journal.) The most detailed (published) critique is by Jorge Garcia, a black/Latino philosopher, again hardly a representative figure, and published in the Africana philosophy journal, *Philosophia Africana*.[32] At least one philosophy dissertation has been done on it, but as a "Marxist-Leninist" critique by another black philosopher, Stephen Ferguson (so both red and black), it is doubly minoritarian.[33]

If we look instead at the response of the white political philosophy establishment, what do we find? Basically, nothing. Samuel Freeman's 2003 edited *Cambridge Companion to Rawls* has, unsurprisingly, no chapter on race (that would require there to have been a significant secondary literature on Rawls and race at the time), but—with far less excuse—nor does Jon Mandle and David A. Reidy's 2014 edited Blackwell *Companion to Rawls*, published more than a decade later.[34] Nor is *The Racial Contract* even listed in the extensive bibliographies of either book. Brooke Ackerley does at least mention it in a footnote to her introduction to a sixty-page symposium on Rawls's legacy in *Perspectives on Politics*, but none of the other contributors cite it, or indeed talk about race and racial justice at any length.[35] So the book is there as a standing challenge to mainstream contractarianism and liberalism—a challenge I have sought to develop further in my chapters in the follow-up book with Carole Pateman, *Contract and Domination*, but so far it is not a challenge that shows any sign of being taken up, or even noticed.[36] (Of course, an ironist might point out that given my claims in the book, such an ignoring is precisely what I should have *expected*, and that any other outcome, however academically satisfying, should actually be dreaded by me as a disconfirmation of my thesis! In other words, the failure of *The Racial Contract* to change anything is precisely a sign of the success of the Racial Contract.)

THE WHITENESS OF POLITICAL PHILOSOPHY

So what is the source of the problem? Let me conclude with an attempt to tease out the peculiar whiteness of philosophy in general,[37] and political philosophy in particular, and illustrate it with a recent standard reference work.

The exclusion of racial minorities from the academy is, of course, a complex phenomenon that is a function of numerous factors, including, historically, straightforwardly racist views of people's worth and competence, discriminatory practices, and limitations on opportunities both material and juridical. But in philosophy, as various people have pointed out, there is an additional factor that is more structurally related to the very nature of the subject. Contrast philosophy with, say, literature, sociology, history. If you think people of color are incapable of writing poetry or fiction or plays worth reading by anyone, then such work, having no aesthetic value, will naturally be excluded from the canon. But it is not part of the definition of literature that it be restricted, either formally or de facto, to whites. Insofar as literature is canonized as white, this rests on additional contingent claims. Moreover, there is nothing at all self-contradictory about the idea of different national literatures, or different ethnic literatures within one nation, that may provide us with different insights into the multi-faceted human experience. In this sense, the flourishing of African American literature does not threaten *literature*. Or consider sociology. Sociology is, in Auguste Comte's famous formulation, the scientific study of society. Now one may, of course, have a sanitized picture of the centrality of racial subordination to modern society's origins and workings that black work on race may contest, as in the 1970s debates stimulated by Joyce Ladner's *The Death of White Sociology*[38] (reports of this demise were greatly exaggerated, as it turned out). So there will be both vested intellectual and material interests at stake in such disciplinary battles. But again, there is obviously nothing in the definition of the field itself which precludes taking objective account of the role of race, especially because one would expect that different societies in different time periods will have different social groups and social dynamics. Or take history. History is supposed to be the account of what happened. If you think people of color are incapable of making history, whether as "great men (and women)" or en masse, then they will play no part in your historical narratives. But once more, this is because of racist beliefs about nonwhite capabilities, not part of the definition of history itself. So in each case, a set of false empirical claims unrelated to the conception of the discipline is doing most of the exclusionary work.

What makes philosophy distinctive is that not merely have there been racist views in the tradition of the intellectual capacities of people of color, but that the conception of the discipline itself is inimical to the recognition of race. Philosophy is supposed to be abstracting away from the contingent, the corporeal, the temporal, the material to get at necessary, spiritual, eternal, ideal truths. Because race as a topic is manifestly not one of those eternal truths, even by the claims of those insistent on its contemporary importance, it is necessarily handicapped from the start. (The simple fact that philosophy's past is so present is, in my opinion, another major factor. In philosophy, we are still reading texts from thousands of years ago, which make no reference to race, since, of course, it didn't exist then. So the sheer weight of tradition itself militates against the inclusion of race as a legitimate philosophical subject.) Philosophy aspires to the universal, while race is necessarily local, so that the unraced (whites) become the norm.

But political philosophy, it may be objected, is, even for its mainstream practitioners, necessarily more time-bound and local than, say, metaphysics and epistemology because it formally recognizes a periodization (ancient, medieval, modern) that mandates sensitivity to different kinds of political systems. Yet insofar as contemporary political philosophy is largely focused on normative issues, justice for equal persons, these temporal and geographical contingencies tend to drop away. The ideal (as normative) character of the enterprise lifts it above mere sociology and political science, even if such disciplines are supposed to provide an empirical input, while the ideal (as perfectly just) hegemonic Rawlsian orientation limits that input to generalities that abstract away from social oppression. Moreover, location in the modern period is supposed to legitimate a framework predicated not merely on human moral equality but on *socially recognized* human moral equality. We are no longer in ancient Greece and Rome, or feudal Europe, but in the world of the American and French Revolutions. The quest for the good society, the just polis, can thus be framed in a way that emphasizes the trans-historical continuities and commonalities in the Western socio-normative project, ignoring the reality that—*in this very same modern period*—race emerges as a new social category that radically and ineluctably differentiates the moral status and corresponding experience of whites and people of color.

Take one of the primary political debates of the last few decades, communitarianism versus contractarianism. Communitarians and contractarians may be in dispute over whether it is more illuminating to consider individuals as socially embedded Aristotelian *zoa politika* or the pre-social and pre-political atoms of Thomas Hobbes. However, they are both in agreement on the moral equality of these individuals,[39] their requisite equal status before the law, and the protection of their interests by the state, not merely as a desirable ideal but (with a few anomalies) as an accomplished reality. But of course the existence of people of color necessarily transgresses and disrupts the key assumptions of *both* of these political framings. Expropriated Native

Americans and enslaved Africans are clearly not part of the European and, later, Euro-implanted/Euro-imposed "community" in question. But neither can they be conceptualized as pre-social and pre-political atoms considering that their very existence *as* people of color arises from a particular socio-political history. In other words, this category would not even exist absent the history of European expansionism, colonialism, imperialism that transforms people from different Native American and African nations into "Indians" and "Negroes," reds and blacks.

So the seeming colorlessness of these competing political visions is revealed as white. They share common taken-for-granted assumptions even in their contestation with each other. Assimilating the experience of non-whites to either of these political frameworks necessarily distorts it because the political starting point is so different. Your moral equality and person-hood are certainly *not* recognized; you are *not* equal before the law; and the state is *not* seeking to protect but to encroach upon your interests in the interests of the white population. This is not at all the anomaly but rather the norm. So your whole political orientation as a person of color in modernity is oppositional in a way that the white political orientation is not, and this has obvious implications for your normative priorities. Making sense of your distinctive politics, understanding your particular perspective on justice requires—even for seemingly abstract philosophy—contextualizing it within this history, taking account of the input of other pertinent disciplines, and developing, accordingly, a set of categories sensitized to these differences. Any bracketing of this history and this input will in effect mean—even if it is not advertised as such (and these days, of course, it will *not* be advertised as such)—that it is the white experience of modernity, the experience of Europeans and Euro-Americans, that is tacitly shaping the narrative. Whether conceived of as a community or as a "contracting" population, both visions of the polity presume its whiteness.

Consider, from this perspective, the second (2007) edition of the Blackwell *Companion to Contemporary Political Philosophy*,[40] an important reference work in Blackwell's invaluable "Companions" series that is particularly apropos here, in part because I commented on the first (1993) edition in an essay, "The Racial Polity," which appeared in 1998.[41] So since the second edition appeared nearly fifteen years after the first, this will provide a useful benchmark of the progress (or not) in the sub-field.

I wrote at the time, comparing gender with race:

There has been such a burgeoning of feminist scholarship in philosophy—articles, books, special journal issues, anthologies, series—that it now merits its own category, whereas race (as against routine condemnations of racism) has yet to arrive. Thus, to cite one reference work, Robert Goodin and Philip Pettit's nearly 700-page Blackwell

Companion to Contemporary Political Philosophy (1993) has feminism as one of the six entries in the "major ideologies" section (along with anarchism, conservatism, liberalism, Marxism, socialism), but no entry on, say, black nationalism or Pan-Africanism. Nor does either appear, or the related subjects of race, racism, and white supremacy, in the subsequent list of twenty-eight "special topics," though this list extends all the way to such nontraditional political topics as environmentalism and sociobiology. Frantz Fanon and W. E. B. Du Bois do not even make the index. . . . [A] political philosophy necessarily involves factual (descriptive and theoretical) assumptions as well as normative claims about the polity. . . . The Blackwell editors' inclusion of entries on economics, history, law, political science, and sociology shows that they recognize this descriptive dimension of their subject. But as one would expect, these entries are no more neutral and politically disengaged than the listing of major ideologies. The economics and history of imperialism, colonialism, slavery—the law, politics, and sociology of imperial rule, white settler states, Jim Crow, apartheid, racial polities—make no appearance here either. The "whiteness" of the text, of this vision of what political philosophy is and is not, inheres . . . in the political whiteness and Eurocentrism of the *outlook*, one that takes for granted the truth of a certain account of world history and the centrality and representativeness to that history of the European experience. The pattern of exclusion is thereby epistemically complete, the theoretical circle closed.[42]

So that was then and this is now. What has changed in the nearly fifteen years between editions? Thomas Pogge, well-known left-Rawlsian, has been added to the lineup of editors, and the book has now been expanded to two volumes, so that the total pagination is now nearly 900 pages (in a small font). The listing of "major ideologies" has been increased from six to eight, with the addition of cosmopolitanism and fundamentalisms. The listing of "special topics" has been expanded from twenty-eight to thirty-eight, with the addition of such topics as criminal justice, historical justice, international distributive justice, personhood, and such *recherché* issues as intellectual property, and trust and social capital. But there is still no recognition of the black nationalist or Pan-Africanist traditions as ideologies worthy of examination, or, more generally, any change in what I originally characterized as the "political whiteness and Eurocentrism of the outlook."

As an appropriate stage-setter, look at Philip Pettit's opening essay (in the "disciplinary contributions" section) on analytical philosophy. From the late nineteenth century to the 1950s, he tells us, "political philosophy ceased to be an area of active exploration. . . . [T]here was little or nothing of significance published in political philosophy."[43] The anti-colonial and anti-racist tradition of people of color is, of course, simply erased by this judgment.[44] But apparently there was no need for such a tradition, because we later learn that over this same time period, "the majority of analytical philosophers lived in a world where such values as liberty and equality and democracy held unchallenged sway."[45] But didn't these philosophers live in a world ruled by European colonialism, where hundreds of millions of people were denied liberty, seen as unequal, and excluded from the democratic process? Didn't these philosophers live in a world where, even in independent nations like the United States and Australia and the Latin American countries, people of color were systematically racially subordinated, treated as second-class or non-citizens? Obviously, the "world" that Pettit is talking about extends only as far as the boundaries of white skin, the population of the racially privileged. This is further confirmed when he later goes on to cite Ronald Dworkin's suggestion that "all plausible, modern political theories have in mind the same ultimate value, equality. . . . [E]very theory claims to treat all individuals as equals."[46] But this is a completely anachronistic and sanitized reading of modern political theories, which, until very recently, generally took the racial inferiority of people of color for granted. It is an account of modernity from the white (really, white male) point of view. If the right of each individual to be treated as an equal to others, independent of race, was such an uncontroversial normative principle of the modern period, embraced by all plausible political theories, then why, at the 1919 post–World War I Versailles Conference, did the "Anglo-Saxon nations" (where these same analytical philosophers mostly lived) veto the Japanese proposal to include a "racial equality" clause in the League of Nations' Covenant?[47] And why is this not-insignificant historical fact mentioned nowhere in the 900 pages of these two volumes?

So there is a mystification of the political, which is then further complemented and compounded by the evasions in the "disciplinary contributions" of history, sociology, economics, international political economy, political science, international relations, legal studies, and the silences (or complete absences) in the "special topics" listing. Over the last quarter-century, a large body of work has emerged across numerous disciplines that looks at issues of race and racism; colonialism, anti-colonialism, and neo-colonialism; and the role of Western ideology and Western legal systems in facilitating white domination, both globally and nationally. And the point is that virtually *none* of this work is taken into account by the editors and the authors they have chosen.[48] The chapter on the history of political thought makes no reference to such works as Anthony Pagden's *Lords of All the World*, or James Tully's *Strange Multiplicity*, or Barbara Arneil's *John Locke and America*, or Uday Singh Mehta's *Liberalism and Empire*, or Jennifer Pitts's *A Turn to Empire*; there is no mention of any of the philosophy anthologies on race, such as Emmanuel Eze's *Race and the Enlightenment* and Andrew Valls's *Race and Racism in Modern Philosophy*, or any of the other numerous recent books and essays exposing the interconnections between the development of modern European political theory, empire, and white racism.

The chapter on sociology does not draw on such historical/sociological accounts as George Fredrickson's *White Supremacy*, or Matthew Frye Jacobson's *Whiteness of a Different Color*, or Howard Winant's *The World Is a Ghetto*, or any of the huge literature on contemporary racism, like Douglas Massey and Nancy Denton's *American Apartheid*, or Stephen Steinberg's *Turning Back*, or Joe Feagin's *Racist America*, or Eduardo Bonilla-Silva's *White Supremacy and Racism in the Post-Civil Rights Era*, or Michael Brown et al.'s *Whitewashing Race: The Myth of a Color-Blind Society*, nor does this chapter mention any of the other numerous recent books and essays examining the centrality of white racial domination to recent global history and US social structure. The chapter on economics takes no account of work like Melvin Oliver and Thomas Shapiro's *Black Wealth/White Wealth*, or Dalton Conley's *Being Black, Living in the Red*, or Thomas Shapiro's *The Hidden Cost of Being African American*, or Ira Katznelson's *When Affirmative Action Was White*, or Deborah Ward's *The White Welfare State*, or any of the other numerous recent books and essays showing how white political privilege makes possible the systemic white economic exploitation of blacks. The chapter on political science shows no awareness of Desmond King's *Separate and Unequal*, or Donald Kinder and Lynn Sanders's *Divided by Color*, or Michael Goldfield's *The Color of Politics*, or Rogers Smith's *Civic Ideals*, or Anthony Marx's *Making Race and Nation*, or Michael Dawson's *Black Visions*, or Anthony Bogues's *Black Heretics, Black Prophets*, or Linda Faye Williams's *The Constraint of Race*; it fails to acknowledge any of the other numerous recent books and essays demonstrating the racial nature of the US state, its historic roots in the birth of the nation as a white settler state, and the concomitant systemic advantaging of whites in the polity, necessitating a black politics of resistance. The chapter on legal studies does have a paragraph on critical race theory (a few sentences out of an entire article), but it is ghettoized, with no exploration of the centrality of law in expediting European conquest, as documented in Paul Keal's *European Conquest and the Rights of Indigenous Peoples*, Lindsay Robertson's *Conquest by Law: How the Discovery of America Dispossessed Indigenous Peoples of Their Lands*, and Antony Anghie's *Imperialism, Sovereignty and the Making of International Law*; there is no examination of the role of the legal system in establishing whiteness as a privileged juridical category, as shown in Ian F. Haney López's *White by Law*, or the subordination of blacks, as exhaustively detailed in A. Leon Higginbotham's two-volume *Race and the American Legal Process*. Nor is there any exploration of the ways in which the legacy of this racist legal history is perpetuated by seemingly color-blind legislation that in effect functions to reproduce white privilege, as illustrated in the essays in Kimberlé Crenshaw et al.'s classic *Critical Race Theory* anthology. The chapters on international political economy and international relations make no reference to the Atlantic slave trade (indeed I don't think it is mentioned anywhere in these 900 pages), an institution lasting hundreds of years that was central to the shaping of the modern world, its currently racialized distributions of wealth and poverty, and its planetary stigmatization of blackness, nor is there any reference to imperialism and genocide, as in King Leopold II's Belgian Congo.

In other words, the political history of the West has been so reconstructed that race and racial domination and the emancipatory struggles against them have been eliminated from the record in an intellectual purge, a feat of documentary falsification, as thorough and impressive as anything Stalin's history rewriters could have engineered. In 1967, historian Geoffrey Barraclough wrote: "When the history of the first half of the twentieth century . . . comes to be written in a longer perspective, there is little doubt that no single theme will prove to be of greater importance than the revolt against the West."[49] But not, evidently, for white political philosophers. The anti-imperialist and anti-colonial political struggle that involved tens of millions of people finds no place in this text, any more than the racial legacy of the world created by the West. Instead, these configurations of power and subordination are presented as neutral and raceless, with no genealogical connection to their past history; they are approached through philosophical abstractions that carefully elide the racial dimensions of virtually every major topic mentioned. And no, Fanon and Du Bois can still not be found in the index.

The pretensions of philosophy are to illuminate the world, factually and normatively, to show us what it is like and how it should be improved. But the abstraction that is structurally central to the discipline has, as a result of its overwhelming demographic whiteness, mutated into a lethal cognitive pattern of collective white self-deception and group evasion that inhibit the necessary rethinking long under way in other subjects. Far from being the queen of the sciences, far from being in the vanguard of Truth and Justice, philosophy lags pathetically in the rear of the forces of intellectual inquiry in comparison to the progress being made elsewhere. Without a new disciplinary willingness to face how seemingly colorless abstraction is really generalization from the white experience, the discipline's exclusions, both demographic and theoretical, can only perpetuate themselves.

It's going to be a long haul.

Epilogue (as Prologue):
Toward a Black Radical Liberalism

Finally, some closing words. In keeping with my subtitle—*The Critique of Racial Liberalism*—this book has been largely critical, focusing on what I see as the problems of a racialized liberalism but not offering much in the way of a positive alternative. That—large—task will have to await another time and another book. But I did want to add this epilogue as at least a brief indicator of the line of argument I will be taking in my attempt to produce a self-consciously anti-racist liberalism.[1] So I end here with an outline of what I am calling "black radical liberalism."

Two key clarifications are necessary. To begin with, just as feminist liberalism is not supposed to be a liberalism only for women but rather a liberalism that *all* good liberals, including males, should embrace, so black radical liberalism should be welcomed and endorsed by white liberals also.[2] Black radical liberalism is not intended to be a particularistic and exclusionary political ideology just for blacks, but rather one that fully adheres to the standard liberal ideals—if more often betrayed than realized—of universalism and egalitarianism. It seeks to correct the (anti-universalist, anti-egalitarian) distortions in mainstream white liberalism, whether de jure or de facto, introduced by the complicity of that iteration of liberalism with white supremacy, both nationally and globally. As such, it should be accepted (though not uncritically, of course) by conscientious white liberals who are presumably also committed to such a correction, purging, and reconstruction of liberal theory.

The second point is that—given the different varieties of racism to which other ethnoracial groups have historically been subject—the orientation of my discussion by the African American experience should not be taken as implying that I am putting forward a revisionist black liberalism as coextensive with anti-racist liberalisms in general. Recent work in critical

Black Liberalism vs. Black Radicalism
e.g., black nationalism, black Marxism.

(MAINSTREAM)   (FRINGE)

Figure E.1 Conventional contrast in black political theory

race theory has emphasized the importance of rejecting the black-white paradigm/black-white binary as the all-purpose model of racial domination.[3] So while I expect there will be enough commonalities to render such a liberalism more broadly illuminating for other nonwhite groups, it will also need correction and supplementation from the alternate theorizations by other people of color of their own distinctive experience of racial subordination. Ultimately, of course, what one wants is not an interest-group politics but a principled integration of these various possible revisionist liberalisms, guided by a norm of racial justice rather than determined by an unsavory scrambling for competitive racial advantage.

Let me outline my proposed candidate. In taxonomies of African American/black political thought, the standard contrast would be as in Figure E.1.

Black nationalism, as for example in Kwame Ture (Stokely Carmichael) and Charles V. Hamilton's classic *Black Power*, sees blacks as oppressed by a white power structure that relies on both individual and institutional racism.[4] It locates white oppression in a history of European colonialism and racial slavery and calls for blacks to organize around racial solidarity to struggle for liberation from the legacy of these colonial structures. Black Marxism, whose classic exegesis can be found in Cedric Robinson's book on the subject, agrees on the significance of European colonialism and racial slavery but attempts to situate their dynamic within a modified Marxist framework.[5] So "whites" as a group need to be disaggregated into classes, and the imperative of capital accumulation and the role of different class forces within "races" must be taken into account in explaining the overall trajectory of the system. Thus a more complex political picture is involved, for which struggle against *both* racial and class domination is required.

What I am arguing for is a synthesizing, reconstructed black liberalism that draws upon the most valuable insights of the black nationalist and black Marxist traditions and incorporates them into a dramatically transformed liberalism. So this section of the taxonomies would now be drawn differently (Figure E.2).

My three central theorists for this enterprise are Immanuel Kant (idealist and racist liberal), Karl Marx (materialist but class-reductionist [and racist] class theorist), and W. E. B. Du Bois (critical race theorist). This may seem an unlikely combination until one considers their respective areas of

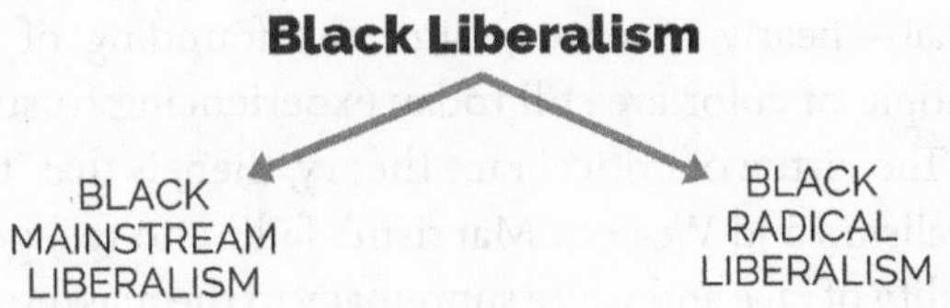

Black Liberalism

BLACK
MAINSTREAM
LIBERALISM

BLACK
RADICAL
LIBERALISM

Figure E.2 Revisionist contrast in black political theory

contribution. Kant is crucial—obviously a Kant purged of the racism I earlier discussed in chapter 6—as the most important theorist of the dominant
variety of contemporary liberalism, "deontological" liberalism. Du Bois is
obviously the most important theorist of race and blackness. And the "radical" reconstructive dynamic by which I hope to transform liberalism will
be supplied by both Du Bois and Marx, in simultaneous cooperation and
contention with each other. Hence each member of the trio provides input
into a proposed combined synthesis: black radical liberalism.

So how does black radical liberalism differ from black mainstream liberalism? By definition they are both "liberal" in endorsing liberalism as a
political philosophy. But black radical liberalism seeks to transform liberalism to make it responsive to the realities of the black diasporic experience in
modernity and the correspondingly necessary reordering of liberal normative priorities. Black radical liberalism both (a) recognizes white supremacy
as central to the making of the United States and (more sweepingly) the
modern world, and (b) seeks to rethink the categories, crucial assumptions,
and descriptive and normative frameworks of liberalism in the light of that
recognition. Black mainstream liberalism either (a) refuses to recognize
white supremacy (for example, by endorsing the "anomaly" view of US racism[6]), or (b) even if it does give lip service to its reality, assumes nonetheless that the categories, crucial assumptions, and descriptive and normative
frameworks of liberalism can be adopted with little change to the task of
getting rid of it.

All three components are therefore crucial. The importance of liberalism is that it is the most successful political philosophy of modernity and
is now globally hegemonic. Liberalism provides the most developed body
of normative theory for understanding the rights of persons and the conceptualization of social justice. Marxism, on the other hand, is the most
developed Western oppositional critique of liberalism and the analysis of
the materialist undermining of liberalism's ideals by the workings of capitalism. It is also, of course, the main ancestor of contemporary "critical
theory." Critical theory should, given its emancipatory pretensions, have
been able on its own to diagnose the importance of race for its "critique"
of modernity. But in fact it was never able to purge itself of its Eurocentric

origins, so that—nearly a century after the founding of the Frankfurt Institute—people of color are still today experiencing frustration with its "whiteness."[7] The virtue of critical race theory, then, is that it corrects both Western liberalism's and Western Marxism's failure to recognize and theorize the centrality of race and white supremacy to the making of the modern world and the implications for normative theory and an expanded vision of what needs to be subjected to liberatory critique to achieve social justice. While liberalism's ideals (the flourishing of the individual and the repudiation of ascriptive hierarchy) are very attractive, they are necessarily undermined by racial/white-supremacist capitalism. The traditional mistake of the white left has been to focus just on capitalism and class exploitation in the shaping of the modern world and not give sufficient attention to race, white supremacy, and racial exploitation. Any serious theorization of social justice needs to correct this omission.

In black radical circles, these claims are, of course, not new but decades (or a century) old. Eric Williams's *Capitalism and Slavery* dates all the way back to 1944; Du Bois's *Black Reconstruction* even further back, to 1935.[8] But the point is that mainstream scholarship is now beginning to catch up with them, as a growing body of work at the most respectable of academic institutions looks at the relationship between African slavery and capitalism.[9] Harvard historian Sven Beckert provides a useful overview of this recent body of work. As he writes:

> The world we live in cannot be understood without coming to terms with the long history of capitalism. . . . And no issue [among US historians of capitalism] currently attracts more attention than the relationship between capitalism and slavery. . . . No other national story raises [the] question with quite the same urgency as the history of the United States. The quintessential capitalist society of our time, it also looks back on long complicity with slavery. But the topic goes well beyond one nation. The relationship of slavery and capitalism is, in fact, one of the keys to understanding the origins of the modern world. . . . And a global perspective allows us to comprehend in new ways how slavery became central to the Industrial Revolution. . . . Europe's ability to industrialize rested at first entirely on the control of expropriated lands and enslaved labor in the Americas. . . . We cannot know if the cotton industry was the only possible way into the modern industrial world, but we do know that it was the path to global capitalism. . . . [W]e need to remember that the world Westerners forged was . . . characterized by . . . vast confiscation of land and labor, huge state intervention in the form of colonialism, and the rule of violence and coercion. . . . The next time we walk the streets of Lower Manhattan or the grounds of Harvard University, we should think at least in passing of the millions of enslaved workers who helped make some of that grandeur possible, and to the ways that slavery's legacy persists today.[10]

In other words, unpaid black slave labor (and colonial exploitation more broadly) is a central foundation of the modern world, not just the abstract "capitalism" targeted by critical theorists. This is the *actual* history and set of historic injustices that is covered up in contemporary justice theory, both American and global, above all in the white fantasy world of Rawlsianism. Hence the imperative of developing a black radical liberalism to challenge white justice theory and its erasure of this history of hundreds of years of racial exploitation.

But a black radical liberalism resting on Kant, Marx, and Du Bois may seem to be based on a very unstable foundation. Here are some obvious objections to this attempt to bring them together, and my replies:

OBJECTIONS AND REPLIES:

(1) How can Marxist and liberal insights be reconciled? Aren't they necessarily opposed?

As emphasized in chapter 2, liberalism comes in different varieties, and black radical liberalism would obviously be a left-wing variety. Liberalism is opposed to state-commandist socialism (what was represented as "Communism"), but state-commandist socialism has proved itself to be a historical failure, both economically and morally. Liberalism is not in principle opposed to social democracy or market socialism.

(2) But how can black nationalist insights be compatible with either liberalism or Marxism?

Black nationalism likewise comes in different varieties. The key insight of the tradition, in my opinion, is the recognition of the reality and centrality of an ontology of race and how it shapes people and their psychology, which can be accommodated in a modified liberalism and Marxism. (Obviously this means rejecting essentialist versions of black nationalism, whether onto-theological or culturalist.) Reconciliations of black nationalism and liberalism have recently been developed by Tommie Shelby and Andrew Valls.[11] And a "black Marxist"/"left nationalist" tradition has long existed that addresses these issues and seeks to resolve the tensions involved in bringing the two together.[12]

(3) But how can even a "black radical liberalism" (assuming it doesn't fly apart from centrifugal forces) deal with the problems identified by, say, Derrick Bell's "racial realism?"[13]

There are no guarantees, but then no other competing ideology can offer them either. Insofar as black radical liberalism is attentive to trends within capitalism (e.g., the forthcoming consolidation and exacerbation of plutocracy in the Western world predicted by Thomas Piketty's *Capital in the Twenty-First Century*),[14] it would hope that an increasing number of the white poor/white working class may begin to wake up to the reality that the prospects for their children and grandchildren under plutocratic capitalism—albeit white-supremacist plutocratic capitalism—are not that great either. As a materialist political philosophy, black radical liberalism does not rest its hopes for social transformation on moral suasion alone but on the mobilization of group interests. The strategy would be to combine the racial justice political project with a larger social justice political project, highlighting the startling fact that the United States has the most unequal distribution of income and wealth of all the Western democracies. Of course, whites may still prefer to hold on to the "psychological wage" (Du Bois) of whiteness if it is going to be jeopardized by such a transracial political alliance. But as emphasized, this will be an obstacle for other anti-racist political programs also. And the impending demographic shift to a nonwhite majority should assist.

So that (very sketchily) would be the real-world agenda. Let us now look at the (academic world) implications for political philosophy, particularly Rawlsian liberalism. Obviously social justice theory does not *have* to be done in a Rawlsian framework, but given its centrality to contemporary Anglo-American political philosophy and to the discussions throughout this book, it seems natural to end by engaging with Rawlsianism.

CHALLENGING MAINSTREAM WHITE POLITICAL PHILOSOPHY

I suggest that the key areas for rethinking would be the following:

- Overarching framework: Non-ideal theory
- Theoretical focus: Ill-ordered societies
- Social ontology: Races in relations of domination/subordination
- Task of social epistemology: Exposing dominant racialized ideologies, whether overt or subtle
- Actual hegemonic variety of liberalism: Racial liberalism
- Normative orientation: Corrective justice
- Key normative tool: Black radical "Kantianism"
- One possible strategy: Adapting Rawls for corrective justice

Let me now go over these briefly, but still (I hope) usefully.

Ideal versus Non-Ideal Theory

As we have seen throughout, Rawls famously focuses in *A Theory of Justice* on "ideal theory," the normative theory of a perfectly just society, characterized by "strict compliance" with its principles of justice. As he acknowledges at the start of the book, "Obviously the problems of partial compliance theory [including "compensatory justice," which I am taking to be corrective justice] are the pressing and urgent matters. These are the things that we are faced with in everyday life."[15] Ideal theory, however, was supposed to be the necessary preliminary to properly doing non-ideal theory. But forty-plus years later, the transition to theorizing "compensatory justice" has still not been made, and contemporary Rawlsian discussions of non-ideal theory are dealing with other senses of the term.

Obviously, for a population historically subordinated in modernity through slavery, colonialism, and Jim Crow, non-ideal theory is the imperative. Afro-modern (as it is now called) political philosophy is centrally shaped by the experience of oppression, domination, and exploitation.[16] So black radical liberalism (like feminist liberalism) is going to be a variety of *non-ideal-theory liberalism*, a liberalism concerned with overcoming group oppression in a nominally liberal society. Indeed, as discussed in chapter 2, we could think of this as a deep theoretical distinction in liberal theory that has not received the attention and formal semantic flagging that it deserves—not merely that there are ideal-theory and non-ideal-theory approaches to justice but that liberalism *itself* should be thought of as coming in ideal-theory and non-ideal-theory variants. Many of the problems standardly attributed by progressives to liberalism as such, liberalism qua liberalism, are really problems distinctive to ideal-theory liberalism, a liberalism abstracting away from social oppression. Once this is recognized, it should immediately be appreciated how different a non-ideal-theory liberalism would have to be, not merely in its approach to justice but in its radically divergent social ontology and social epistemology.

Well-Ordered versus Ill-Ordered Societies

Relatedly, non-ideal-theory liberalism presupposes the ill-orderedness of society. Rawls, as we saw in earlier chapters, directs us to think of societies as "cooperative ventures for mutual advantage," with "well-ordered societies" of "strict compliance" then being a subset of this category.[17] So there is a double idealization involved, bringing home how utterly remote this framework is from even a glancing acquaintance with any actual human social system. But a white-supremacist state is not a cooperative venture for mutual advantage in the first place, let alone a well-ordered one. To assume the cooperative-venture characterization would effectively be to rule racist societies out of normative consideration from the start. So black radical liberalism rejects such a stipulation. Instead, it works with a conception of society broad enough to include ill-ordered societies. Ill-ordered societies are coercive rather than cooperative ventures, characterized by exploitation and systemic disrespect for subordinated groups rather than mutual advantage and reciprocal respect. Ill-ordered societies are, in other words, the world.

Correspondingly, the social ontology of an ill-ordered oppressive society is going to be very different from the social ontology of a well-ordered society. Individuals will be members of dominant and subordinated groups (sometimes at the same time) and this will shape them fundamentally. Races as social constructs will be central social entities that must be theorized by a socially informed metaphysics. Liberal individuals in this non-ideal-theory liberalism will therefore not be atomistic isolates but raced humans interacting with each other in racialized ways, with implications both for their own psychology and for broader cognitive and affective societal patterns. The main obstacles to veridical cognition will, accordingly, not be individually originating bias but dominant-group ideologies (here "whiteness," "white ignorance," etc.). The central liberal contractarian value of what Rawls calls "publicity"—what we would now term "transparency"—will thus need to be fundamentally reoriented by the challenge of overcoming the structural opacities of an ill-ordered (here white-supremacist) society. Racial liberalism—the theme of this book—will have to be exposed for what it is, especially since contemporary versions (as in Rawlsianism itself) will generally be able to fly under the radar through no longer having overt racial identifiers even while continuing to normatively center whites. Black radical liberalism will therefore need to be on the alert for putatively inclusive abstractions that are really color-coded.

Corrective Justice

In more than one chapter, I have mentioned Samuel Fleischacker's important book *A Short History of Distributive Justice*, whose political implications have not, in my opinion, been sufficiently appreciated in the profession.[18] Fleischacker points out that universal distributive justice as a norm in the Western tradition is only slightly more than 200 years old (and of course initially really just extends over the "universe" of white males). Not even white women are included, and certainly not people of color in Western societies.[19] "Corrective justice" as a concept is even *more* undeveloped and

untheorized, especially where groups are concerned. ("Rectificatory justice" in Aristotle presupposes status membership and does not extend to
property rights; "reparations" in Locke are really for individuals.)

The unavoidable implication, it seems to me (even if it *has* been avoided
in the profession), is that Western normative theory in general historically
for most of 2,500 years, and liberalism for most of modernity, has been
complicit with rather than *condemnatory of* group subordination. The under-
theorization in the tradition of corrective justice for subordinated groups,
despite the subordination of most of the population nominally in the theory's ambit, is itself a manifestation of this complicity.[20] Contemporary political philosophy's post-Rawlsian focus on "ideal theory" is thus not aberrant
but completely continuous with this long history of moral evasion.

Black radical liberalism reverses these normative priorities and makes
corrective justice its central concern. Marxism is accurate in seeing exploitation as central to the polity but weak on normative theorization (Marx's
original dismissal of "rights" and "justice" as bourgeois concepts). Hence
the need for a synthesis with liberalism. Also, Marxism's class-reductionism
obscures the reality of *racial* exploitation (as discussed in chapter 7).

Key Normative Tool: Black Radical "Kantianism"

I propose as the key normative tool for achieving this theorization "black
radical 'Kantianism.'" Obviously, given the seemingly oxymoronic character of such a concept, we need once again to go through a list of possible
objections, and my replies.

OBJECTIONS AND REPLIES

(1) But don't mainstream Kantians already (whether aware of Kant's racist
texts or not) use Kantianism in a racially inclusive way? So how would
this be any different?

We need to differentiate nominal racial inclusion from substantive racial
inclusion. (Cf. Susan Moller Okin's famous discussion, in the introduction
to *Justice, Gender, and the Family*, of the difference between false and substantive gender neutrality in the writings of the male justice theorists of her
time.)[21] Substantive theoretical racial inclusion would require that the radically different history and structural positioning of blacks in the polity and
in the normative ontology of the society be taken into account and suitably
incorporated through the appropriate modifications of the apparatus.

(2) But insofar as Kantianism is predicated on our duties to a moral community of "persons," and blacks *are* persons, why do we need any such modification?

Because the history of modernity is one in which most persons, and certainly black persons, have not had their personhood recognized. The moral community has been divided between persons-recognized-as-persons (that is, "persons" as "white men") and persons-not-recognized-as-persons (sub-persons). In particular, white-supremacist societies (such as, but not limited to, the United States) have been founded on a "basic structure" (Rawls) predicated on the racial denial of equal personhood to people of color. So the implications of the categorical imperative in such a society both for individual person-to-person interactions and for our collective duty to transform the *Rassenstaat* into the *Rechtsstaat,* and correct for this past history and its ongoing legacy, are very dramatic indeed.

(3) But then why aren't contemporary Kantian and Rawlsian theory ringing with this revolutionary imperative?

Because of (a) the overwhelmingly white demographic base of the profession, which (b) insulates them experientially from these realities, as well as (c) giving them a vested group interest in ignoring said realities and maintaining the status quo, thereby (d) fostering a preference ("elective affinities") for normative approaches—pre-eminently "ideal theory"—which evade and sidestep all these questions, and which is in keeping with (e) the long history in philosophy earlier mentioned (Cudd, Fleischacker) of conceptual complicity with structural injustice.

Adapting Rawls for Corrective Justice

Let me turn now to corrective justice.[22] In chapter 9, I suggested the following simple way of formulating Rawls's two principles of justice, where the arrows indicate lexical ordering:

$$BL \rightarrow (FEO \rightarrow DP)$$

(The basic liberties principle is lexically dominant over the second principle, in which fair equality of opportunity is lexically dominant over the difference principle.)

Now we need to remind ourselves how very limited (by Rawls's own acknowledgment) the scope of these principles is. As a reminder, let us put them inside identifying and constraining brackets:

$$PDJ\,[BL \rightarrow (FEO \rightarrow DP)]_I$$

That is, these are principles of *distributive justice* for an ideal (I) *well-ordered society*, that being a society which is (a) a cooperative venture for mutual advantage, in which (b) the rules are designed for fair and reciprocal benefit, and (c) people generally follow the rules.

However, we are not, of course, in such a society. We are in a non-ideal (~I) *ill-ordered society*, which was historically established as (a) a coercive and exploitative venture for differential white advantage, and in which (b) the rules are generally designed for white benefit. So how could PDJ_I be the appropriate principles of justice for such a society? Obviously, they cannot. What we want are principles of *corrective justice* that will eliminate *illicit white advantage*. How should they be conceptualized?

In *A Theory of Justice*, in the attempt to establish (problematically, for Fleischacker) the continuity of his approach with the classical, here Aristotelian, tradition, Rawls refers to *pleonexia*, "gaining some [illicit] advantage for oneself by seizing what belongs to another, his property, his reward, his office, and the like, or by denying a person that which is due to him, the fulfilment of a promise, the repayment of a debt, the showing of proper respect, and so on."[23] I suggest we think of illicit white advantage/ white privilege as a form of *racial pleonexia*, historic and current, which needs to be corrected for. Let us call it Δ, the illicit white differential. So what we are seeking are

$$PCJ[P1(\Delta BL) * P2(\Delta EO) * P3(\Delta Respect)]_{\sim I}$$

Translated into prose, these would be principles of corrective justice, P1, P2, P3, for eliminating illicit white advantage/white privilege/racial pleonexia in whites' basic liberties, opportunities, and social respect, in a non-ideal, ill-ordered, white supremacist society.

Some clarificatory points: (a) Respect is included as a basic social good in keeping with both Kantian and Rawlsian norms, and the need for correcting the founding of the polity on the systematic disrespect, dissin', of people of color. (b) The asterisks indicate uncertainty about the principles' ordering; from what Rawls says, P1 → P2, but where would P3 fit? (c) EO is listed rather than FEO, and the DP is not mentioned, because even for whites neither FEO nor the DP were ever institutionalized, and the principles here are principles for correcting *actual* unfair white racial advantage.

Can we arrive at these principles ($PCJ_{\sim I}$) through the utilization of a Rawlsian, or modified Rawlsian, framework? I believe that we can, but it will require a reorientation of Rawls's apparatus as a "device of representation." For we are now trying to represent a different kind of choice situation, a choice sensitized to the historic realities of white racial domination ("white supremacy").

What is the essence, the valuable core, of Rawls? It is, I would claim, the innovation of resurrecting social contract theory in the form of a thought-experiment involving veiled prudential choice within carefully stipulated parameters as a means of generating principles of justice. Despite the criticisms I have made throughout of Rawls, this core still seems to me to be a significant contribution to political philosophy. We can represent it as in Figure E.3.

So for people interested in tackling race within a Rawlsian framework, the strategy has then typically been to work with P1, P2 (as derived in the ideal-theory context), which we can now more precisely and formally identify as $[PDJ1, PDJ2]_I$. One then tries to apply these principles—that is, $[BL \to (FEO \to DP)]_I$—to race. For example, as discussed in chapter 9, Tommie Shelby's attempted appropriation of FEO for this end.

My suggested alternative strategy: Rather than try to tweak PDJ1 and PDJ2 in this way, let us run a *different* thought-experiment custom designed for non-ideal theory. So though in both cases the "contract" as a "device of representation" is being used to derive principles of justice that are consistent with central liberal values, the conceptual difference between the two exercises is made quite explicit. In the first case, we are seeking principles of distributive justice for an ideal society $[PDJ]_I$; in the second case we are

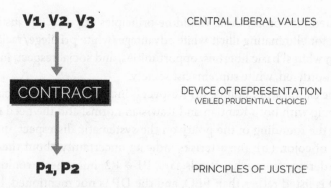

V1, V2, V3   CENTRAL LIBERAL VALUES

CONTRACT   DEVICE OF REPRESENTATION
(VEILED PRUDENTIAL CHOICE)

P1, P2   PRINCIPLES OF JUSTICE

Figure E.3 John Rawls's thought-experiment

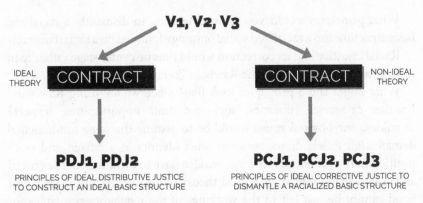

Figure E.4 Expanded thought-experiment

seeking principles of corrective justice for a non-ideal (here racist) society [PCJ]$_{-i}$. See Figure E.4.

My claim is that this is a better strategy for arriving at principles of racial justice than trying to derive them from PDJ1 and PDJ2 (whose moral foundation is *not* the correction of wrongs). The thought experiment (as a "device of representation") is being applied to a different end: not how you would create an ideal basic structure from ground zero but how you would dismantle an *already existing* unjust basic structure. In "contractual" terms, we could think of it as tearing up the "bad" contract that has created the world we live in. (Cf. Rousseau, who described *two* contracts, one non-ideal, one ideal.)[24]

So the thought-experiment plays itself out differently. Self-knowledge is still blocked by the veil (so as to guarantee objectivity). But the veil is thinner on *social* knowledge. We know that we are going to emerge into a society whose basic structure has historically been shaped by white supremacy. *All* the social variants among which we choose will have a white-supremacist state as their ancestor (since an ideal society is not an option for us). So we are making a self-interested choice about different principles of corrective justice that will correct to a greater or lesser degree for this history of racial domination, thereby generating different possible social orders.

The choice then becomes this: What kinds of measures would you select to correct for a history of racial injustice, worried that when the veil lifts, you may turn out to be black or a member of some other historically subordinated race?

What recommendations would you make for altering the legal and political system, the structure of economic opportunities, the dominant cognitive and evaluative norms, the cultural patterns, the somatic ideal, the inherited social ontology of racial superiority and inferiority?

What principles would you choose, in sum, to dismantle a racialized basic structure and a racialized social ontology founded on a racial contract?

Racial injustice and its correction would thus be center stage rather than offstage altogether, as it is in the Rawlsian literature.

What might these principles look like? Since we are using Rawlsian/Kantian categories (liberties, socio-economic opportunities, respect) as guides, one obvious move would be to assume the same fundamental demarcation Rawls draws between one's identity as a citizen and one's position in the economy. However, we also have to include here the crucial addendum that—unlike with ideal theory—"respect" as a primary social good cannot be just left to the workings of the regulatory principles for these two areas, since social "disrespect" for blacks and other subordinated races is an explicit part of the original "contract" and, correspondingly, of the basic structure. Dismantling that structure, voiding the contract, requires a separate principle of justice formally targeting the "expressive harms" of sub-personhood. Thus the critical role of a deracialized Kantianism now grounded in the black experience of the denial of equal humanity: Du Bois's reports from behind the color line. I propose the following three principles (Figure E.5).

I suggest that the plausibility of these three principles is confirmed not merely by their correspondence with Rawls's listing (suitably transmuted for non-ideal conditions) but their resonance with our own everyday moral sense of the major different dimensions of racial injustice. Blacks and other people of color have historically suffered from (a) unequal (zero or second-class) citizenship, without equal status in the civic sphere or pro-portional political input into the governing process, (b) racial exploitation and economic marginalization,[25] and (c) the "ontological" stigmatization of the group as inferior lesser beings because of their "racial" membership.

PDJ1, PDJ2	PCJ1, PCJ2, PCJ3
PRINCIPLES OF IDEAL DISTRIBUTIVE JUSTICE TO CONSTRUCT AN IDEAL BASIC STRUCTURE	PRINCIPLES OF IDEAL CORRECTIVE JUSTICE TO DISMANTLE A RACIALIZED BASIC STRUCTURE
PDJ1 (BL) Regulates ethico-juridical primary goods (one's equal citizenship).	**PCJ1** End racially unequal citizenship.
PDJ2 (FEO→DP) Regulates material primary goods (one's place in the socio-economic system).	**PCJ2** End racial exploitation.
SELF-RESPECT Most important primary social good (underwritten by PDJ1 and PDJ2).	**PCJ3** End racial disrespect.

Figure E.5 Distributive justice versus corrective racial justice

Principles of corrective justice will thus have to target these historic viola-tions of, respectively, the basic rights and liberties, the equal opportunities, and the equal respect that people of color *should* have received, but did not, and the illicit racial edge, Δ, whites have instead had in each sphere.

By contrast with the use of FEO, then, no category mistake or awkward disruption of lexical ordering is involved in this modified Rawlsianism, since in each case it is the *actual* wrong that is being addressed by the appro-priate corrective principle. Obviously, I am not denying that the question of what kind of public policy will in fact be justified by these principles will be a hugely controversial topic. Recall, for example, the outrage generated years ago by Lani Guinier's recommendations to overcome a permanent white majority through cumulative or supermajority voting, or the more recent debate over the weakening of the Voting Rights Act by the Supreme Court's 2013 *Shelby* decision.[26] Consider the effective defeat of affirma-tive action policies and the pre-emptive white rejection of reparations to African Americans.[27] Think of the recent heated disputes over the symbolic significance of the redrafting of high school textbooks to highlight racial oppression (e.g., "Raza Studies"), the flying of the Confederate flag, the use of Native American images and epithets by sports teams, and the naming of buildings and institutions at leading universities after racist white his-torical figures.[28] But the point is that a Rawlsian apparatus that is explic-itly modified to adjudicate matters of non-ideal theory and grounded in the imperative of correcting for the legacy of white supremacy—racially unequal citizenship, racial exploitation, and racial disrespect—could now be an active and valuable contributor to these debates and to the undermin-ing of racial liberalism, not simply a detached spectator or even an actual accomplice to its perpetuation. Rawlsian political philosophy could at last become a real player in the righting of the historic and current white wrongs to black rights. In future work, I hope to develop in greater detail this proj-ect of articulating a black radical liberalism that is true both to the (ideal-ized) liberal tradition, the liberalism that *should have been*, and respectful of the black diasporic experience in modernity, victims of the liberalism that actually was and is.

NOTES

INTRODUCTION

1. Domenico Losurdo, *Liberalism: A Counter-History*, trans. Gregory Elliott (New York: Verso, 2011).
2. For two classic texts here, see C. B. Macpherson, *Democratic Theory: Essays in Retrieval*, with a new introduction (New York: Oxford University Press, 2014; orig. ed. 1973) and Susan Moller Okin, *Justice, Gender, and the Family* (New York: Basic Books, 1989).
3. But compare Jennifer Pitts's "imperial liberalism": Pitts, *A Turn to Empire: The Rise of Imperial Liberalism in Britain and France* (Princeton, NJ: Princeton University Press, 2005).
4. Again, see Okin, *Justice, Gender, and the Family*.
5. Jennifer L. Hochschild, *The New American Dilemma: Liberal Democracy and School Desegregation* (New Haven, CT: Yale University Press, 1984); Rogers M. Smith, *Civic Ideals: Conflicting Visions of Citizenship in U.S. History* (New Haven, CT: Yale University Press, 1997).
6. See, for example, the challenging work of Barnor Hesse, "Racialized Modernity: An Analytics of White Mythologies," *Ethnic and Racial Studies* 30, no. 4 (July 2007): 643–63, and, more recently, "Escaping Liberty: Western Hegemony, Black Fugitivity," *Political Theory* 42, no. 3 (June 2014): 288–313.
7. My thanks to both of the Oxford manuscript reviewers for emphasizing the importance of making this terminological point clear.
8. See Onora O'Neill, "Justice, Gender, and International Relations," in Martha Nussbaum and Amartya Sen, eds., *The Quality of Life* (Oxford: Clarendon Press, 1993).
9. Charles W. Mills, *The Racial Contract* (Ithaca, NY: Cornell University Press, 1997).
10. Consider in this connection the unexpected bestseller success of Thomas Piketty's *Capital in the Twenty-First Century*, trans. Arthur Goldhammer (Cambridge, MA: Belknap Press, 2014).
11. Carole Pateman and Charles W. Mills, *Contract and Domination* (Malden, MA: Polity, 2007).

CHAPTER 1

1. Jennifer Pitts, *A Turn to Empire: The Rise of Imperial Liberalism in Britain and France* (Princeton, NJ: Princeton University Press, 2005).
2. David R. Roediger, *The Wages of Whiteness: Race and the Making of the American Working Class*, rev. and exp. ed. (New York: Verso, 2007; orig. ed. 1991).
3. "The Racial Wealth Gap: Why Policy Matters," online PDF uploaded March 10, 2015; authors: Laura Sullivan, Tatjana Meschede, Lars Dietrich, Thomas Shapiro (Institute for Assets and Social Policy [IASP], Brandeis University) and Amy Traub, Catherine Ruetschlin, Tamara Draut (DEMOS). (This report, based on 2011 figures, is more recent than the one I actually cited in the original 2012 interview.)

CHAPTER 2

1. John Rawls, *A Theory of Justice*, rev. ed. (Cambridge, MA: Harvard University Press, 1999; orig. ed. 1971); Robert Nozick, *Anarchy, State, and Utopia*, with a new foreword (New York: Basic Books, 2013; orig. ed. 1974).
2. But for the problems with such an expansive conception, see Duncan Bell, "What Is Liberalism?" *Political Theory* 42, no. 6 (December 2014): 682–715.
3. John Gray, *Liberalism* (Minneapolis: University of Minnesota Press, 1986), p. x.
4. Karl Marx, *Grundrisse*, excerpted in David McLellan, ed., *Karl Marx: Selected Writings*, 2nd ed. (New York: Oxford University Press, 2000; orig. ed. 1977), pp. 380–81.
5. T. H. Green, *Lectures in the Principles of Political Obligation and Other Writings*, ed. Paul Harris and John Morrow (New York: Cambridge University Press, 1986). I am indebted to Derrick Darby's *Rights, Race, and Recognition* (New York: Cambridge University Press, 2009) for alerting me to the significance of Green's work as an alternative strain within the liberal tradition.
6. Rawls, *Theory of Justice*.
7. Michael J. Sandel, *Liberalism and the Limits of Justice*, 2nd ed. (New York: Cambridge University Press, 1998; orig. ed. 1982); John Rawls, *Political Liberalism* (New York: Columbia University Press, 1993), pp. 22–28.
8. Ann E. Cudd, *Analyzing Oppression* (New York: Oxford University Press, 2006), pp. vii–ix.
9. Cudd, *Analyzing Oppression*, p. viii.
10. Cudd, *Analyzing Oppression*, pp. 34, 26.
11. Cudd, *Analyzing Oppression*, pp. 34–37.
12. Brian Barry, *Why Social Justice Matters* (Malden, MA: Polity, 2005); Lisa H. Schwartzman, *Challenging Liberalism: Feminism as Political Critique* (University Park: Pennsylvania State University Press, 2006); Elizabeth Anderson, *The Imperative of Integration* (Princeton, NJ: Princeton University Press, 2010).
13. Cudd, *Analyzing Oppression*, chs. 3–6.
14. See Louis Althusser, *For Marx*, trans. Ben Brewster (New York: Verso, 2010; orig. ed. 1969), and, for a classic critique, E. P. Thompson, *The Poverty of Theory and Other Essays* (New York: Monthly Review Press, 1978).
15. John Christman, *The Politics of Persons: Individual Autonomy and Socio-Historical Selves* (New York: Cambridge University Press, 2009), p. 48.
16. Michel Foucault, cited in Christman, *Politics of Persons*, p. 55n14.
17. Christman, *Politics of Persons*, p. 10.
18. C. B. Macpherson, *The Political Theory of Possessive Individualism: Hobbes to Locke* (New York: Oxford University Press, 2011; orig. ed. 1962), with a new introduction.
19. Domenico Losurdo, *Liberalism: A Counter-History*, trans. Gregory Elliott (New York: Verso, 2011), pp. vii–viii.
20. Losurdo, *Liberalism*, pp. 340–41.
21. Losurdo, *Liberalism*, pp. 341–43.
22. Losurdo, *Liberalism*, p. 344.
23. Admittedly, Marxism has its own "radical Enlightenment" version of Whiggery, the technological-determinist version of historical materialism revived by G. A. Cohen that vests explanatory primacy in the putative autonomous tendency of the forces of production to develop. See G. A. Cohen, *Karl Marx's Theory of History: A Defence*, exp. ed. (Princeton, NJ: Princeton University Press, 2001; orig. ed. 1978). But alternative interpretations of Marxism existed even at the time that would reject such a reading, and certainly in today's "post-Marxist" world technological inevitabilism has no credibility.
24. See, for example, G. William Domhoff, *Who Rules America? The Triumph of the Corporate Rich*, 7th ed. (Boston: McGraw-Hill, 2013; orig. ed. 1967); Catharine A. MacKinnon, *Toward a Feminist Theory of the State* (Cambridge, MA: Harvard University Press, 1989); Kimberlé Crenshaw, Neil Gotanda, Gary Peller, and Kendall Thomas, eds., *Critical Race Theory: The Key Writings That Formed the Movement* (New York: New Press, 1995).

25. See, for example, Stéphan Courtois et al., *The Black Book of Communism: Crimes, Terror, Repression,* trans. Jonathan Murphy and Mark Kramer (Cambridge, MA: Harvard University Press, 1999).

26. Rawls, *Theory of Justice*; Barry, *Why Social Justice Matters.*

27. John E. Roemer, *A Future for Socialism* (Cambridge, MA: Harvard University Press, 1994); John E. Roemer, ed. *Equal Shares: Making Market Socialism Work* (New York: Verso, 1996); David Schweickart, *After Capitalism,* 2nd ed. (Lanham, MD: Rowman & Littlefield, 2011; orig. ed. 2002).

28. See, for example, Naomi Klein, *This Changes Everything: Capitalism vs. The Climate* (New York: Simon & Schuster, 2014).

29. Karl Marx, "On the Jewish Question," in McLellan, ed., *Karl Marx: Selected Writings,* pp. 46–70, esp. pp. 59–64.

30. Felicia Ann Kornbluh, *The Battle for Welfare Rights: Politics and Poverty in Modern America* (University Park: Pennsylvania State University Press, 2007).

31. Michael T. Martin and Marilyn Yaquinto, eds., *Redress for Historical Injustices in the United States: On Reparations for Slavery, Jim Crow, and Their Legacies* (Durham, NC: Duke University Press, 2007).

32. John M. Hobson, *The Eurocentric Conception of World Politics: Western International Theory, 1760–2010* (New York: Cambridge University Press, 2012).

33. Jennifer Pitts, *A Turn to Empire: The Rise of Imperial Liberalism in Britain and France* (Princeton, NJ: Princeton University Press, 2005); Sankar Muthu, *Enlightenment against Empire* (Princeton, NJ: Princeton University Press, 2003).

34. Losurdo, *Liberalism*; Hobson, *Eurocentric Conception.*

35. Rogers M. Smith, *Civic Ideals: Conflicting Visions of Citizenship in U.S. History* (New Haven, CT: Yale University Press, 1997); Charles W. Mills, "Racial Liberalism," *PMLA (Publications of the Modern Language Association of America)* 123, no. 5 (October 2008): 1380–97 (reprinted as chapter 3 of this book). See also Carol A. Horton, *Race and the Making of American Liberalism* (New York: Oxford University Press, 2005).

36. Martin Gilens, *Why Americans Hate Welfare: Race, Media, and the Politics of Antipoverty Policy* (Chicago: University of Chicago Press, 1999); Deborah E. Ward, *The White Welfare State: The Racialization of U.S. Welfare Policy* (Ann Arbor: University of Michigan Press, 2005).

37. David O. Sears, Jim Sidanius, and Lawrence Bobo, eds., *Racialized Politics: The Debate about Racism in America* (Chicago: University of Chicago Press, 2000).

38. Cited in Hobson, *Eurocentric Conception,* p. 107.

CHAPTER 3

1. Of the "big four" contract theorists (Thomas Hobbes, John Locke, Jean-Jacques Rousseau, Immanuel Kant), Locke and Kant are the most important for liberal theory. Hobbes's *Leviathan* (New York: Cambridge University Press, 1996) conceptualizes morality and justice as conventional and argues for political absolutism, while the radical direct democracy of Rousseau's *Social Contract,* based on the "general will," represents more a challenge to than an endorsement of liberalism: Jean-Jacques Rousseau, *The Social Contract and Other Later Political Writings,* ed. and trans. Victor Gourevitch (New York: Cambridge University Press, 1997).

2. John Rawls, *A Theory of Justice,* rev. ed. (Cambridge, MA: Harvard University Press, 1999; orig. ed. 1971).

3. Curtis Stokes and Theresa Meléndez, eds., *Racial Liberalism and the Politics of Urban America* (East Lansing: Michigan State University Press, 2003).

4. Charles W. Mills, *The Racial Contract* (Ithaca, NY: Cornell University Press, 1997).

5. See Jean Hampton, "The Contractarian Explanation of the State," in Peter A. French, Theodore E. Uehling Jr., and Howard K. Wettstein, eds., *Midwest Studies in Philosophy: The Philosophy of the Human Sciences* (Notre Dame: University of Notre Dame Press,

1990); Jean Hampton, "Feminist Contractarianism," in Louise M. Antony and Charlotte E. Witt, eds., *A Mind of One's Own: Feminist Essays on Reason and Objectivity*, rev. 2nd ed. (Boulder, CO: Westview Press, 2001; orig. ed. 1993); Jean Hampton, "Contract and Consent," in Robert E. Goodin, Philip Pettit, and Thomas Pogge, eds., *A Companion to Contemporary Political Philosophy*, rev. 2nd ed., 2 vols., vol. 2 (Malden, MA: Blackwell, 2007; orig. ed. [1 vol.] 1993).

6. The non-liberal-democratic Hobbesian model is predicated on the approximate physical and mental (rather than moral) equality of self-seeking humans in conflict with one another (the amoral state of nature as a state of war). So Hobbes's solution of a constitutionally unconstrained state—the absolutist sovereign—is obviously uncongenial to those seeking to use the contract model to critique absolutism.

7. Michael J. Sandel, *Liberalism and the Limits of Justice*, 2nd ed. (New York: Cambridge University Press, 1998; orig. ed. 1982), pp. 184–85.

8. John Rawls, *Collected Papers*, ed. Samuel Freeman (Cambridge, MA: Harvard University Press, 1999); John Rawls, *Political Liberalism*, exp. ed. (New York: Columbia University Press, 1996; orig. ed. 1993).

9. Carole Pateman, *The Sexual Contract* (Stanford, CA: Stanford University Press, 1988); Mills, *Racial Contract*.

10. Uday Singh Mehta, *Liberalism and Empire: A Study in Nineteenth-Century British Liberal Thought* (Chicago: University of Chicago Press, 1999); Louis Sala-Molins, *Dark Side of the Light: Slavery and the French Enlightenment*, trans. John Conteh-Morgan (Minneapolis: University of Minnesota Press, 2006).

11. Jennifer Pitts, *A Turn to Empire: The Rise of Imperial Liberalism in Britain and France* (Princeton, NJ: Princeton University Press, 2005).

12. James Tully, *An Approach to Political Philosophy: Locke in Contexts* (New York: Cambridge University Press, 1993); Barbara Arneil, *John Locke and America: The Defence of English Colonialism* (New York: Oxford University Press, 1996); David Armitage, "John Locke, Carolina, and the *Two Treatises of Government*," *Political Theory* 32, no. 5 (October 2004): 602–27; Robert Bernasconi and Anika Maaza Mann, "The Contradictions of Racism: Locke, Slavery, and the *Two Treatises*," in Andrew Valls, ed., *Race and Racism in Modern Philosophy* (Ithaca, NY: Cornell University Press, 2005).

13. Emmanuel Chukwudi Eze, "The Color of Reason: The Idea of 'Race' in Kant's Anthropology," in Eze, ed., *Postcolonial African Philosophy: A Reader* (Cambridge, MA: Blackwell, 1997); Robert Bernasconi, "Who Invented the Concept of Race? Kant's Role in the Enlightenment Construction of Race," in Bernasconi, ed., *Race* (Malden, MA: Blackwell, 2001); Robert Bernasconi, "Kant as an Unfamiliar Source of Racism," in Julie K. Ward and Tommy L. Lott, eds., *Philosophers on Race: Critical Essays* (Malden, MA: Blackwell, 2002); Charles W. Mills, "Kant's *Untermenschen*," in Valls, *Race and Racism*, reprinted as ch. 5 of this book.

14. Michael C. Dawson, *Black Visions: The Roots of Contemporary African-American Political Ideologies* (Chicago: University of Chicago Press, 2001), p. 13.

15. For oral accounts of the African American experience in white philosophy, see George Yancy, ed., *African-American Philosophers: 17 Conversations* (New York: Routledge, 1998), and for the experience of black women in particular, George Yancy, ed., "Situated Voices: Black Women in/on the Profession of Philosophy," *Hypatia: A Journal of Feminist Philosophy* 23, no. 2 (May 2008): 155–89.

16. See, for example, Colin Bird, *An Introduction to Political Philosophy* (New York: Cambridge University Press, 2006); Will Kymlicka, *Contemporary Political Philosophy: An Introduction*, 2nd ed. (New York: Oxford University Press, 2001; orig. ed. 1990); A. John Simmons, *Political Philosophy* (New York: Oxford University Press, 2007); Jonathan Wolff, *An Introduction to Political Philosophy*, rev. ed. (New York: Oxford University Press, 2006; orig. ed. 1996).

17. Steven M. Cahn, ed., *Classics of Political and Moral Philosophy*, 2nd ed. (New York: Oxford University Press, 2012; orig. ed. 2002). Augustine is included in Cahn's anthology and, as a Berber, is a person of color by contemporary standards. But since he wrote at a time when nobody was "raced," he does not count.

18. See Anthony Bogues, *Black Heretics, Black Prophets: Radical Political Intellectuals* (New York: Routledge, 2003) for a valuable reclaiming and reconstruction of the work of some of the key figures in the diasporic black political tradition.
19. Thomas Borstelmann, *The Cold War and the Color Line: American Race Relations in the Global Arena* (Cambridge, MA: Harvard University Press, 2001).
20. Marilyn Lake and Henry Reynolds, *Drawing the Global Colour Line: White Men's Countries and the International Challenge of Racial Equality* (New York: Cambridge University Press, 2008), ch. 12.
21. Andrea Veltman, ed., *Social and Political Philosophy: Classic and Contemporary Readings* (Don Mills, ON: Oxford University Press Canada, 2008); Diane Jeske and Richard Fumerton, eds., *Readings in Political Philosophy: Theory and Applications* (Peterborough, ON: Broadview, 2012); Matt Zwolinski, ed., *Arguing about Political Philosophy*, 2nd ed. (New York: Routledge, 2014; orig. ed. 2009); Omid Payrow Shabani and Monique Deveaux, eds., *Introduction to Social and Political Philosophy: Texts and Cases* (Don Mills, ON: Oxford University Press Canada, 2014).
22. Steven M. Cahn, ed., *Political Philosophy: The Essential Texts*, 3rd ed. (New York: Oxford University Press, 2015; orig. ed. 2002).
23. Rodney C. Roberts, ed., *Injustice and Rectification* (New York: Peter Lang, 2002).
24. Rawls, *Theory of Justice*; John Rawls, *Political Liberalism*, exp. ed. (New York: Columbia University Press, 1996; orig. ed. 1993); John Rawls, *Collected Papers*, ed. Samuel Freeman (Cambridge, MA: Harvard University Press, 1999); John Rawls, *The Law of Peoples, with "The Idea of Public Reason Revisited"* (Cambridge, MA: Harvard University Press, 1999); John Rawls, *Justice as Fairness: A Restatement*, ed. Erin Kelly (Cambridge, MA: Harvard University Press, 2001).
25. Rawls, *Theory of Justice*, p. 8.
26. Mills, *Racial Contract*; Carole Pateman and Charles W. Mills, *Contract and Domination* (Malden, MA: Polity, 2007), chs. 3, 4.
27. David Hume, "Of the Original Contract," in Sir Ernest Barker, ed., *Social Contract: Essays by Locke, Hume, and Rousseau* (London: Oxford University Press, 1960; orig. ed. 1947), p. 154.
28. Jean-Jacques Rousseau, *Social Contract*.
29. Jean-Jacques Rousseau, *The Discourses and Other Early Political Writings*, ed. and trans. Victor Gourevitch (New York: Cambridge University Press, 1997), p. 173.
30. Pateman, *Sexual Contract*.
31. Mills, *Racial Contract*.
32. Onora O'Neill, "Justice, Gender, and International Boundaries," in Martha C. Nussbaum and Amartya Sen, eds., *The Quality of Life* (Oxford: Clarendon Press, 1993); Charles W. Mills, "'Ideal Theory' as Ideology," *Hypatia: A Journal of Feminist Philosophy* 20, no. 3 (August 2005): 165–84, reprinted as ch. 4 of this book.
33. Rawls, *Theory of Justice*, p. 4.
34. Thomas W. Pogge, *Realizing Rawls* (Ithaca, NY: Cornell University Press, 1989), pp. 20, 20n10.
35. Samuel Freeman, *Rawls* (New York: Routledge, 2007), pp. 106, 483.
36. Rawls, *Theory of Justice*, p. 5.
37. Robert Nozick, *Anarchy, State, and Utopia*, with a new foreword (New York: Basic Books, 2013; orig. ed. 1974), chs. 1, 2.
38. Nozick, *Anarchy, State*, pp. 7–9.
39. David Theo Goldberg, *The Racial State* (Malden, MA: Blackwell, 2002), p. 4.
40. Paul Keal, *European Conquest and the Rights of Indigenous Peoples: The Moral Backwardness of International Society* (New York: Cambridge University Press, 2003), pp. 1, 21.
41. George Fredrickson, *White Supremacy: A Comparative Study in American and South African History* (New York: Oxford University Press, 1981), pp. xi–xii.
42. Matthew Frye Jacobson, *Whiteness of a Different Color: European Immigrants and the Alchemy of Race* (Cambridge, MA: Harvard University Press, 1998), p. 25.
43. Judith N. Shklar, *American Citizenship: The Quest for Inclusion* (Cambridge, MA: Harvard University Press, 1991), pp. 2, 15–16.

44. Ian F. Haney López, *White by Law: The Legal Construction of Race*, 10th anniversary rev. ed. (New York: New York University Press, 2006; orig. ed. 1996).

45. Lindsay G. Robertson, *Conquest by Law: How the Discovery of America Dispossessed Indigenous Peoples of Their Lands* (New York: Oxford University Press, 2005), pp. x, 4.

46. Leon F. Litwack, *Trouble in Mind: Black Southerners in the Age of Jim Crow* (New York: Knopf, 1998).

47. Desmond King, *Separate and Unequal: African Americans and the U.S. Federal Government*, rev. ed. (New York: Oxford University Press, 2007; orig. ed. 1995).

48. Cited in King, *Separate and Unequal*, p. 4.

49. King, *Separate and Unequal*, p. 6.

50. Eduardo Bonilla-Silva, *Racism without Racists: Color-Blind Racism and the Persistence of Racial Inequality in the United States*, 4th ed. (Lanham, MD: Rowman & Littlefield, 2013; orig. ed. 2003).

51. Gary Orfield and Susan E. Eaton, *Dismantling Desegregation: The Quiet Reversal of Brown v. Board of Education* (New York: New Press, 1997); Jonathan Kozol, *The Shame of the Nation: The Restoration of Apartheid Schooling in America* (New York: Crown, 2005).

52. Douglas S. Massey and Nancy A. Denton, *American Apartheid: Segregation and the Masking of the Underclass* (Cambridge, MA: Harvard University Press, 1993); Douglas S. Massey, *Categorically Unequal: The American Stratification System* (New York: Sage, 2007).

53. Michelle Alexander, *The New Jim Crow: Mass Incarceration in the Age of Colorblindness* (New York: New Press, 2010).

54. National Criminal Justice Reference Service, NCJ 245032: "Report of the Sentencing Project to the United Nations Human Rights Committee Regarding Racial Disparities in the United States Criminal Justice System" (August 2013), p. 1. The report is available online as a PDF.

55. Derrick Bell, *Faces at the Bottom of the Well: The Permanence of Racism* (New York: Basic Books, 1992).

56. Philip A. Klinkner and Rogers M. Smith, *The Unsteady March: The Rise and Decline of Racial Equality in America* (Chicago: University of Chicago Press, 1999).

57. Dawson, *Black Visions*, p. 14. The very titles of works by black political philosophers show the centrality of race to their normative thinking: Bernard R. Boxill, *Blacks and Social Justice*, rev. ed. (Lanham, MD: Rowman & Littlefield, 1992; orig. ed. 1984); Howard McGary, *Race and Social Justice* (Malden, MA: Blackwell, 1999); Lucius T. Outlaw Jr., *Critical Social Theory in the Interests of Black Folks* (Lanham, MD: Rowman & Littlefield, 2005); Tommie Shelby, *We Who Are Dark: Philosophical Foundations of Black Solidarity* (Cambridge, MA: Harvard University Press, 2005).

58. Stanley Cohen, *States of Denial: Knowing about Atrocities and Suffering* (Malden, MA: Polity, 2001), p. 45.

59. Rogers A. Smith, *Civic Ideals: Conflicting Visions of Citizenship in U.S. History* (New Haven, CT: Yale University Press, 1997).

60. Alexander Saxton, *The Rise and Fall of the White Republic: Class Politics and Mass Culture in Nineteenth Century America* (New York: Verso, 2003; orig. ed. 1990); Fredrickson, *White Supremacy*; Desmond S. King and Rogers M. Smith, "Racial Orders in American Political Development," *American Political Science Review* 99, no. 1 (February 2005): 75–92; Charles W. Mills, "The Racial Polity," in Mills, *Blackness Visible: Essays on Philosophy and Race* (Ithaca, NY: Cornell University Press, 1998). Note, however, that in King and Smith's more recent *Still a House Divided: Race and Politics in Obama's America* (Princeton, NJ: Princeton University Press, 2011), they distance themselves from their previous position, writing "In place of relying on notions of a unitary American 'racial state' or 'racial order,' we employ our novel concept of rival 'racial policy alliances' " (p. 17).

61. Rawls, *Theory*; Nozick, *Anarchy, State*.

62. The book jacket of the new edition of *Anarchy, State* boasts that it has been translated into a hundred languages.

63. Charles W. Mills, "Racial Exploitation and the Wages of Whiteness," in Maria Krysan and Amanda E. Lewis, eds., *The Changing Terrain of Race and Ethnicity* (New York: Russell Sage, 2004), reprinted as ch. 7 of this book.

64. Rawls, *Political Liberalism*, p. liii.

65. Pateman, *Contract and Domination*, p. 77, quoting James Tully.

66. Borstelmann, *Cold War*, p. 10.

67. Massey, *Categorically Unequal*, pp. 56–57. See also Linda Faye Williams, *The Constraint of Race: Legacies of White Skin Privilege in America* (University Park: Pennsylvania State University Press, 2003).

68. Melvin L. Oliver and Thomas M. Shapiro, *Black Wealth/White Wealth: A New Perspective on Racial Inequality*, 10th anniversary ed. (New York: Routledge, 2006; orig. ed. 1995).

69. "The Racial Wealth Gap: Why Policy Matters," PDF uploaded online March 10, 2015 (2011 figures): Laura Sullivan, Tatjana Meschede, Lars Dietrich, Thomas Shapiro (Institute for Assets and Social Policy [IASP], Brandeis University) and Amy Traub, Catherine Ruetschlin, Tamara Draut (DEMOS).

70. Alan Wertheimer, *Exploitation* (Princeton, NJ: Princeton University Press, 1996); Ruth J. Sample, *Exploitation: What It Is and Why It's Wrong* (Lanham, MD: Rowman & Littlefield, 2003).

71. Klinkner and Smith, *Unsteady March*, p. 7.

72. Thomas M. Shapiro, *The Hidden Cost of Being African American: How Wealth Perpetuates Inequality* (New York: Oxford University Press, 2004), p. 26.

73. Shapiro, *Hidden Cost*, p. 5.

74. Shapiro, *Hidden Cost*, p. 13.

75. Cheryl I. Harris, "Whiteness as Property," *Harvard Law Review* 106, no. 8 (June 1993): 1709–91.

76. Michael C. Dawson and Rovana Popoff, "Reparations: Justice and Greed in Black and White," *Du Bois Review: Social Science Research on Race* 1, no. 1 (March 2004), pp. 58–59, 62.

CHAPTER 4

1. James E. Curtis and John W. Petras, eds., *The Sociology of Knowledge: A Reader* (New York: Praeger, 1970).

2. W. V. O. Quine, "Epistemology Naturalized," in Quine, *Ontological Relativity and Other Essays* (New York: Columbia University Press, 1969); Hilary Kornblith, ed., *Naturalizing Epistemology*, 2nd ed. (Cambridge, MA: MIT Press, 1994; orig. ed. 1985).

3. Hilary Kornblith, "A Conservative Approach to Social Epistemology," in Frederick F. Schmitt, ed., *Socializing Epistemology: The Social Dimensions of Knowledge* (Lanham, MD: Rowman & Littlefield, 1994), p. 93.

4. Sandra Harding, ed., *The Feminist Standpoint Theory Reader: Intellectual and Political Controversies* (New York: Routledge, 2004).

5. Steve Fuller, *Social Epistemology*, 2nd ed. (Bloomington: University of Indiana Press, 2002; orig. ed. 1988); Schmitt, *Socializing Epistemology*.

6. Linda Martín Alcoff, *Real Knowing: New Versions of the Coherence Theory* (Ithaca, NY: Cornell University Press, 1996), p. 2n1.

7. Happily, Miranda Fricker's *Epistemic Injustice: Power and the Ethics of Knowing* (New York: Oxford University Press, 2007) would be published the same year as the original version of this essay, stimulating the development within analytic social epistemology of a strain far more sensitive to issues of "social identity and power," in a world where "[epistemic] injustice is normal" (pp. vii–viii).

8. Philip Kitcher, "Contrasting Conceptions of Social Epistemology," in Schmitt, *Socializing Epistemology*, p. 125. That makes it one sentence more than in the more recent collection *Social Epistemology: Essential Readings*, ed. Alvin I. Goldman and Dennis Whitcomb (New York: Oxford University Press, 2011), which has nothing at all.

9. Charles W. Mills, *The Racial Contract* (Ithaca, NY: Cornell University Press, 1997).

10. Alvin I. Goldman, *Knowledge in a Social World* (New York: Oxford University Press, 1999). See also Kitcher, "Contrasting Conceptions," and Kornblith, "Conservative Approach," in Schmitt, *Socializing Epistemology*.

11. Goldman, *Knowledge*, p. 5.

12. Goldman, *Knowledge*, pp. 4–5 (emphasis in original).

13. Kornblith, "Conservative Approach," p. 97.

14. Kornblith, "Conservative Approach," p. 97.

15. Rogers M. Smith, *Civic Ideals: Conflicting Visions of Citizenship in U.S. History* (New Haven, CT: Yale University Press, 1997).

16. Charles W. Mills, "Alternative Epistemologies" (1988), rpt. in Mills, *Blackness Visible: Essays on Philosophy and Race* (Ithaca, NY: Cornell University Press, 1998).

17. David R. Roediger, ed., *Black on White: Black Writers on What It Means to Be White* (New York: Schocken, 1998).

18. Johnson, cited in Roediger, *Black on White*, p. 5.

19. James Baldwin, *Nobody Knows My Name: More Notes of a Native Son* (New York: Vintage International, 1993; orig. ed. 1961), p. 217.

20. Donald B. Gibson, introduction to W. E. B. Du Bois, *The Souls of Black Folk* (New York: Penguin Books, 1989; orig. ed. 1903).

21. Du Bois, *Souls*, p. 4.

22. Ralph Ellison, *Invisible Man* (New York: Vintage, 1995; orig. ed. 1952).

23. Ellison, *Invisible Man*, p. 3.

24. Herman Melville, *Moby-Dick, or, The Whale* (New York: Modern Library, 2000).

25. Herman Melville, "Benito Cereno," in Melville, *Billy Budd, Sailor and Other Stories* (New York: Viking Penguin, 1986).

26. Eric J. Sundquist, *To Wake the Nations: Race in the Making of American Literature* (Cambridge, MA: Belknap Press, 1993), pp. 151–55, 171.

27. Du Bois, *Souls*, p. 5.

28. For the most detailed analysis to date of this famous and oft-cited passage, see Robert Gooding-Williams, *In the Shadow of Du Bois: Afro-Modern Political Thought in America* (Cambridge, MA: Harvard University Press, 2009), ch. 2. In light of Gooding-Williams's reading, I have corrected the relevant sentences of the original (2007) version of this essay, where I mistakenly attributed this enhanced insight to "double-consciousness" itself.

29. But see José Medina's recent *The Epistemology of Resistance: Gender and Racial Oppression, Epistemic Injustice, and Resistant Imaginations* (New York: Oxford University Press, 2013) for a welcome entry in the field, indeed the most thorough attempt I know to bring these issues into the discussion.

30. Lewis R. Gordon, *Bad Faith and Antiblack Racism* (Atlantic Highlands, NJ: Humanities Press, 1995).

31. George M. Fredrickson, *Racism: A Short History* (Princeton, NJ: Princeton Classics, 2015; orig. ed. 2002). But see Benjamin Isaac, *The Invention of Racism in Classical Antiquity* (Princeton, NJ: Princeton University Press, 2004) and Miriam Eliav-Feldon, Benjamin Isaac, and Joseph Ziegler, eds., *The Origins of Racism in the West* (New York: Cambridge University Press, 2009), for an important dissenting view.

32. Nell Irvin Painter, *The History of White People* (New York: W. W. Norton, 2010).

33. Matthew Frye Jacobson, *Whiteness of a Different Color: European Immigrants and the Alchemy of Race* (Cambridge, MA: Harvard University Press, 1998).

34. See, for example, Manning Marable, *Malcolm X: A Life of Reinvention* (New York: Viking Penguin, 2011), pp. 78, 86, 285.

35. Richmond Campbell and Bruce Hunter, eds., *Moral Epistemology Naturalized, Canadian Journal of Philosophy*, supp. vol. 26 (Calgary, AB: University of Calgary Press, 2000).

36. See Nancy Tuana and Shannon Sullivan, eds., *Hypatia: A Journal of Feminist Philosophy*, Special Issue: Feminist Epistemologies of Ignorance, 21, no. 3 (August 2006).

37. This comment was at least partially tongue in cheek—but now there is indeed such work! See Linsey McGoey, ed., *An Introduction to the Sociology of Ignorance: Essays on the Limits*

of Knowing (New York: Routledge, 2014) and Matthias Gross and Linsey McGoey, eds., *Routledge International Handbook of Ignorance Studies* (New York: Routledge, 2015). I have a chapter in the latter extending my claims to the global stage: "Global White Ignorance."

38. Kornblith, "Conservative Approach," p. 97.

39. Marshall G. S. Hodgson, *Rethinking World History: Essays on Europe, Islam, and World History*, ed. Edmund Burke III (New York: Cambridge University Press, 1993), p. 4. In the original appearance of this essay, I had said, mistakenly, that Hodgson invoked the Steinberg *New Yorker* cover itself. But he had died by the time it appeared. He seems actually to have been referring to one of its artistic predecessors (it turns out that the concept was not original to Steinberg), most probably "A New Yorker's Idea of the United States of America" by Daniel K. Wallingford (different versions: 1936, 1937, 1939). See also "The New Yorker's Idea of the Map of the United States" (1922) by John T. McCutcheon. Pictures of both are available online.

40. Hodgson, *Rethinking*, pp. 3–5.

41. Hodgson, *Rethinking*, p. 9.

42. Francis Jennings, *The Invasion of America: Indians, Colonialism, and the Cant of Conquest* (New York: W. W. Norton, 1976; orig. ed. 1975), pp. 12, 10.

43. Jennings, *Invasion*, p. 59.

44. Jennings, *Invasion*.

45. Woody Doane, "Rethinking Whiteness Studies," in Ashley W. Doane and Eduardo Bonilla-Silva, eds., *White Out: The Continuing Significance of Racism* (New York: Routledge, 2003), pp. 13–14.

46. Maurice Halbwachs, *On Collective Memory*, ed. and trans. Lewis A. Coser (Chicago: University of Chicago Press, 1992).

47. John Gillis, "Memory and Identity: The History of a Relationship," in Gillis, ed., *Commemorations: The Politics of National Identity* (Princeton, NJ: Princeton University Press, 1994), p. 3.

48. Adam Hochschild, *King Leopold's Ghost: A Story of Greed, Terror, and Heroism in Colonial Africa* (New York: Houghton Mifflin, 1998), ch. 19.

49. Hochschild, *King Leopold's Ghost*, pp. 293–95, 297. However, Hochschild's book initiated a debate in Belgium that led to a Royal Museum of Central Africa show on the issue: "Memory of Congo: The Colonial Era." Belgian historians dispute his figures and reject the charge of genocide. *New York Times*, February 9, 2005, B3.

50. James W. Loewen, *Lies My Teacher Told Me: Everything Your American History Textbook Got Wrong* (New York: Touchstone/Simon & Schuster, 1996; orig. ed. 1995), p. 133.

51. Loewen, *Lies*, pp. 137–70.

52. W. E. B. Du Bois, "The Souls of White Folk," in David Levering Lewis, ed., *W. E. B. Du Bois: A Reader* (New York: Henry Holt, 1995), p. 459.

53. W. E. B. Du Bois, *Black Reconstruction in America, 1860–1880* (New York: Free Press, 1998; orig. ed. 1935).

54. Kirk Savage, "The Politics of Memory: Black Emancipation and the Civil War Monument," in Gillis, *Commemorations*, pp. 130–31, 134–35, 143.

55. Thomas M. Shapiro, *The Hidden Cost of Being African American: How Wealth Perpetuates Inequality* (New York: Oxford University Press, 2004), pp. 75–76.

56. Shapiro, *Hidden Cost*, pp. 76, 10.

57. Thomas McCarthy, "*Vergangenheitsbewältigung* in the USA: On the Politics of the Memory of Slavery, Part I," *Political Theory* 30, no. 5 (October 2002), p. 641. See also his "Coming to Terms with Our Past: On the Morality and Politics of Reparations for Slavery, Part II," *Political Theory* 32, no. 6 (December 2004): 750–72.

58. C. A. J. Coady, *Testimony: A Philosophical Study* (Oxford: Clarendon Press, 1995; orig. ed. 1992).

59. Immanuel Kant, *Observations on the Feeling of the Beautiful and Sublime*, trans. John T. Goldthwait (Berkeley: University of California Press, 1960), p. 113.

60. Cited in Maureen Konkle, *Writing Indian Nations: Native Intellectuals and the Politics of Historiography, 1827–1863* (Chapel Hill: University of North Carolina Press, 2004), pp. 90, 92.

61. Mark Cocker, *Rivers of Blood, Rivers of Gold: Europe's Conflict with Tribal Peoples* (London: Jonathan Cape, 1998), p. 317.

62. Cited in Leon F. Litwack, *Trouble in Mind: Black Southerners in the Age of Jim Crow* (New York: Knopf, 1998), p. 34.

63. James S. Hirsch, *Riot and Remembrance: The Tulsa Race War and Its Legacy* (New York: Houghton Mifflin, 2002), p. 201.

64. See, for example, J. A. Rogers, *100 Amazing Facts about the Negro with Complete Proof: A Short Cut to the World History of the Negro* (St. Petersburg, FL: Helga M. Rogers, 1985; orig. ed. 1952).

65. Stephen Steinberg, *Turning Back: The Retreat from Racial Justice in American Thought and Policy* (Boston: Beacon Press, 1995), p. ix.

66. W. E. B. Du Bois, *Dusk of Dawn: An Essay toward an Autobiography of a Race Concept* (New York: Oxford University Press, 2007; orig. ed. 1940), p. 66.

67. Steinberg, *Turning Back*, p. 51.

68. Steinberg, *Turning Back*, p. 51. See also Francille Rusan Wilson, *The Segregated Scholars: Black Social Scientists and the Creation of Black Labor Studies, 1890–1950* (Charlottesville, VA: University of Virginia Press, 2006).

69. In his recent *The Scholar Denied: W. E. B. Du Bois and the Birth of Modern Sociology* (Oakland: University of California Press, 2015), Aldon Morris argues that it is Du Bois and his "Atlanta school" rather than Robert E. Park and the "Chicago school" who actually deserve the credit for being the founders of American sociology. But apart from his unacceptable blackness, Du Bois's sociological indictment of white supremacy as the real cause of "the Negro problem" made any such acknowledgment impossible in the Jim Crow academy of the time—or even today, more than a century later.

70. See, for example, Brian P. McLaughlin and Amelie Oksenberg Rorty, eds., *Perspectives on Self-Deception* (Berkeley: University of California Press, 1988) and Alfred R. Mele, *Self-Deception Unmasked* (Princeton, NJ: Princeton University Press, 2001).

71. See Ruth J. Sample, *Exploitation: What It Is and Why It's Wrong* (Lanham, MD: Rowman & Littlefield, 2003), for a Kantian updating of the concept and an argument for bringing it back to the center of our concerns.

72. Du Bois, *Dusk of Dawn*, p. 65.

73. Linda Faye Williams, *The Constraint of Race: Legacies of White Skin Privilege in America* (University Park: Pennsylvania State University Press, 2003).

74. Donald R. Kinder and Lynn M. Sanders, *Divided by Color: Racial Politics and Democratic Ideals* (Chicago: University of Chicago Press, 1996), pp. 33, 85.

75. Stanley Cohen, *States of Denial: Knowing about Atrocities and Suffering* (Malden, MA: Polity, 2001), pp. 10–11, 45.

CHAPTER 5

1. Carol Gilligan, *In a Different Voice: Psychological Theory and Women's Development* (Cambridge, MA: Harvard University Press, 1998; orig. ed. 1982); Nel Noddings, *Caring: A Feminine Approach to Ethics and Moral Education*, 2nd ed. (Berkeley: University of California Press, 2003; orig. ed. 1984).

2. Samantha Brennan, "Recent Work in Feminist Ethics," *Ethics* 109 (July 1999), p. 859.

3. Marilyn Friedman, "Feminism in Ethics: Conceptions of Autonomy," in Miranda Fricker and Jennifer Hornsby, eds., *The Cambridge Companion to Feminism in Ethics* (New York: Cambridge University Press, 2000), p. 211.

4. Alison Jaggar, "Ethics Naturalized: Feminism's Contribution to Moral Epistemology," *Metaphilosophy* 31, no. 5 (October 2000), pp. 452–53.

5. Brennan, "Recent Work," p. 860.

6. Alison Jaggar, *Feminist Politics and Human Nature* (Totowa, NJ: Rowman & Allanheld, 1983); Rosemarie Putnam Tong, *Feminist Thought: A More Comprehensive Introduction*, 4th ed. (Boulder, CO: Westview Press, 2013; orig. ed. 1989).

7. Onora O'Neill, "Abstraction, Idealization and Ideology in Ethics," in J. D. G. Evans, ed., *Moral Philosophy and Contemporary Problems* (Cambridge: Cambridge University Press, 1987); Onora O'Neill, "Justice, Gender, and International Boundaries," in Martha C. Nussbaum and Amartya Sen, eds., *The Quality of Life* (Oxford: Clarendon Press, 1993).

8. O'Neill, "Abstraction, Idealization," p. 56.

9. John Rawls, *A Theory of Justice*, rev. ed. (Cambridge, MA: Harvard University Press, 1999; orig. ed. 1971), p. 8.

10. Jaggar, "Ethics Naturalized," p. 453.

11. Karl Marx and Frederick Engels, *The German Ideology: Collected Works*, vol. 5 (New York: International Publishers, 1976), pp. 35–36.

12. Frederick Douglass, "What to the Slave Is the Fourth July?" in William L. Andrews, ed., *The Oxford Frederick Douglass Reader* (New York: Oxford University Press, 1996), p. 116.

13. In her *Analyzing Oppression* (New York: Oxford University Press, 2006), Ann Cudd points out how under-theorized oppression is in the Western philosophical tradition—despite the obvious (one would think) fact that oppression should be the central concern of a discourse on justice—and links this otherwise puzzling characteristic to the traditional demographic base of the profession. Though he does not draw from it the political conclusions that Cudd and I would, Samuel Fleischacker has documented another striking fact: that contrary to conventional wisdom, distributive justice in our contemporary sense is actually only a bit more than 200 years old. Pre-modern conceptions such as Aristotle's tied justice to social status rather than simple humanity and did not extend to property rights: Samuel Fleischacker, *A Short History of Distributive Justice* (Cambridge, MA: Harvard University Press, 2004). Bluntly stated (by me, not Fleischacker), Western normative theory has for most of its 2,500-year existence been a discourse of complicity with injustice.

14. It can, admittedly, serve the interests of *particular* individuals in these groups, who can then be anointed by the establishment as the female or black dissident "courageous" enough to speak out against the "victim mentality" of his or her peers (with appropriate rewards and recognition for said courage to follow)—but not the interests of the group as a whole. My thanks to Margaret Urban Walker for reminding me of this important point.

15. Here the following obvious objection might be raised: isn't *A Theory of Justice* a work in ideal theory that, especially with the rightward shift in the United States in the four decades since it first appeared, articulates a radical political vision now far outside of the mainstream? My response would be this: (a) To the extent that the radical egalitarian tilt of Rawls's book is justified by advertence to the ways in which people are disadvantaged by their class background, it is drawing precisely on (a subsection of) the *non*-ideal facts that non-ideal theory sees as crucial, and so in this respect is *departing* from pure ideal theory. But even here, Rawls's left-liberalism leaves him open to criticisms from those on the Marxist left with a less sanguine, arguably more realistic, picture of the unjust effects of the class inequalities his theory leaves intact—see, for example, the criticisms of R. G. Peffer, *Marxism, Morality, and Social Justice* (Princeton, NJ: Princeton University Press, 1990). (b) As will be discussed in greater detail later, his idealization of the family and marginalization of the history of US slavery and Jim Crow so shape the book that it does *not* address gender and racial oppression and what measures would be necessary to dismantle them and achieve gender and racial justice. So its radicalism, praiseworthy as it is, is basically restricted to issues along a (white male) class axis.

16. See, for example, Brad Hooker and Margaret Olivia Little, eds., *Moral Particularism* (Oxford: Clarendon Press, 2000).

17. See, for example, the exchange between Susan Moller Okin and Jane Flax: Susan Moller Okin, "Gender Inequality and Cultural Difference," *Political Theory* 22, no. 1 (February 1994): 5–24; Jane Flax, "Race/Gender and the Ethics of Difference," *Political Theory* 23, no. 3 (August 1995): 500–510; Susan Moller Okin, "A Response to Jane Flax," *Political Theory* 23, no. 3 (August 1995): 511–16.

18. Sandra Harding, ed., *The Feminist Standpoint Theory Reader: Intellectual and Political Controversies* (New York: Routledge, 2003).

19. F. James Davis, *Who Is Black? One Nation's Definition* (University Park: Pennsylvania State University Press, 1991).
20. Linda Martín Alcoff, "On Being Mixed," ch. 12 in Alcoff, *Visible Identities: Race, Gender, and the Self* (New York: Oxford University Press, 2006).
21. Catriona MacKenzie and Natalie Stoljar, eds., *Relational Autonomy: Feminist Perspectives on Autonomy, Agency, and the Social Self* (New York: Oxford University Press, 2000).
22. Susan Moller Okin, *Justice, Gender, and the Family* (New York: Basic Books, 1989).
23. Rawls, *Theory of Justice.*
24. Hannelore Schröder, "Kant's Patriarchal Order," trans. Rita Gircour, in Robin May Schott, ed., *Feminist Interpretations of Immanuel Kant* (University Park: Pennsylvania State University Press, 1997).
25. Rawls, *Theory of Justice*, pp. 8–9.
26. Robert Nozick, *Anarchy, State, and Utopia*, with a new foreword (New York: Basic Books, 2013; orig. ed. 1974), pp. 150–53.
27. Nozick, *Anarchy, State*, pp. 152–53.
28. See, for example, the cavalierly dismissive treatment of the issue in David Schmidtz, "The Right to Distribute," in Ralf M. Bader and John Meadowcroft, eds., *The Cambridge Companion to Nozick's Anarchy, State, and Utopia* (New York: Cambridge University Press, 2011).
29. Nozick, *Anarchy, State*, p. 344n2.
30. Rogers M. Smith, *Civic Ideals: Conflicting Visions of Citizenship in U.S. History* (New Haven, CT: Yale University Press, 1997).
31. In the decade since the original version of this chapter was published a growing body of literature has emerged debating the relationship between ideal and non-ideal theory. For some overviews, see, for example, Ingrid Robeyns and Adam Swift, eds., "Social Justice: Ideal Theory, Nonideal Circumstances," Special Issue, *Social Theory and Practice* 34, no. 3 (July 2008); A. John Simmons, "Ideal and Nonideal Theory," *Philosophy and Public Affairs* 38, no. 1 (Winter 2010): 5–36; Laura Valentini, "Ideal vs. Non-Ideal Theory: A Conceptual Map," *Philosophy Compass* 7, no. 9 (September 2012): 654–64.

CHAPTER 6

1. The qualification is necessary because of a crucial point of *disanalogy* between race and gender, that while there is just one female sex (at least in the West), there are several non-white races, and their assigned statuses in racist hierarchies have not historically been the same (as will be seen below for Kant). So while "sub-person" is a useful umbrella term, a more detailed treatment would require additional internal divisions.
2. John Rawls, *A Theory of Justice*, rev. ed. (Cambridge, MA: Harvard University Press, 1999; orig. ed. 1971), p. 24.
3. Allen W. Wood, General Introduction, *Immanuel Kant: Practical Philosophy*, trans. and ed., Mary J. Gregor (New York: Cambridge University Press, 1996), p. xvii.
4. Emmanuel Eze, "The Color of Reason: The Idea of 'Race' in Kant's Anthropology," in Eze, ed., *Postcolonial African Philosophy: A Critical Reader* (Cambridge, MA: Blackwell, 1997); Robert Bernasconi, "Who Invented the Concept of Race? Kant's Role in the Enlightenment Construction of Race," in Bernasconi, ed., *Race* (Malden, MA: Blackwell, 2001); Robert Bernasconi, "Kant as an Unfamiliar Source of Racism," in Julie K. Ward and Tommy L. Lott, eds., *Philosophers on Race: Critical Essays* (Malden, MA: Blackwell, 2002).
5. Quoted in Eze, "Color of Reason," p. 118.
6. Quoted in Eze, "Color of Reason," p. 117.
7. Quoted in Bernasconi, "Kant as an Unfamiliar Source," pp. 147–48.
8. Quoted in Eze, "Color of Reason," p. 117.
9. Quoted in Eze, "Color of Reason," p. 116.
10. Quoted in Eze, "Color of Reason," p. 122.
11. Quoted in Bernasconi, "Kant as an Unfamiliar Source," p. 158.
12. Quoted in Eze, "Color of Reason," p. 116.

13. Quoted in Bernasconi, "Kant as an Unfamiliar Source," p. 148.
14. Quoted in Bernasconi, "Kant as an Unfamiliar Source," p. 152.
15. Quoted in Bernasconi, "Kant as an Unfamiliar Source," p. 158.
16. Quoted in Eze, "Color of Reason," p. 126.
17. Quoted in Bernasconi, "Kant as an Unfamiliar Source," p. 159.
18. Allen W. Wood, *Kant's Ethical Thought* (New York: Cambridge University Press, 1999); Robert B. Louden, *Kant's Impure Ethics: From Rational Beings to Human Beings* (New York: Oxford University Press, 2000); Tsenay Serequeberhan, "The Critique of Eurocentrism and the Practice of African Philosophy," in Eze, ed., *Postcolonial African Philosophy*; Bernasconi, "Who Invented?" and "Unfamiliar Source"; Mark Larrimore, "Sublime Waste: Kant on the Destiny of the 'Races,'" in Catherine Wilson, ed., *Civilization and Oppression, Canadian Journal of Philosophy*, Supplementary Volume 25 (Calgary, AB: University of Calgary Press, 1999); Thomas E. Hill Jr. and Bernard Boxill, "Kant and Race," in Bernard Boxill, ed., *Race and Racism* (New York: Oxford University Press, 2001).
19. Rudolf Malter, "Der Rassebegriff in Kants Anthropologie," in Gunter Mann and Franz Dumont, eds., *Die Natur des Menschen: Probleme der Physischen Anthropologie und Rassenkunde (1750–1850)* (Stuttgart: Gustav Fischer Verlag, 1990); Reinhard Brandt, *D'Artagnan und die Urteilstafel: Über ein Ordnungsprinzip der europäischen Kulturgeschichte* (Stuttgart: Franz Steiner, 1991), pp. 133–36. For these references I am indebted, respectively, to Larrimore and Louden.
20. Emmanuel Chukwudi Eze, *Achieving Our Humanity: The Idea of the Postracial Future* (New York: Routledge, 2001), pp. 104–5.
21. Eze, "Color of Reason," p. 116.
22. Bernasconi, "Unfamiliar Source," pp. 150–52 This claim has been challenged in an important later paper by Pauline Kleingeld: "Kant's Second Thoughts on Race," *Philosophical Quarterly* 57, no. 229 (October 2007): 573–92. Kleingeld also argues (as her title implies) that Kant changed his mind on race, moving from a racist to an anti-racist position in the 1790s. For Bernasconi's reply to both claims, see Bernasconi, "Kant's Third Thoughts on Race," in Stuart Elden and Eduardo Mendieta, eds., *Reading Kant's Geography* (Albany: SUNY Press, 2011).
23. Malter, "Der Rassebegriff," pp. 121–22; cited and translated by Larrimore, "Sublime Waste," pp. 99–100.
24. Wood, *Kant's Ethical Thought*, pp. 7, 5.
25. Louden, *Kant's Impure Ethics*, pp. 105, 177.
26. In a personal communication, Louden has referred me to a conference paper of his, "'The Spreading over All Peoples of the Earth': Kant's Moral Gradualism and the Issue of Race," where he explicitly criticizes Malter and distances himself from his position.
27. Hill and Boxill, "Kant and Race," pp. 449–52.
28. Hill and Boxill, "Kant and Race," pp. 453–55.
29. Louden, *Kant's Impure Ethics*.
30. Eze, "Color of Reason," p. 104.
31. Pauline Kleingeld, "The Problematic Status of Gender-Neutral Language in the History of Philosophy: The Case of Kant," *Philosophical Forum* 25, no. 2 (June 1993): 134–50; Hannelore Schröder, "Kant's Patriarchal Order," trans. Rita Gircour, in Robin May Schott, ed., *Feminist Interpretations of Immanuel Kant* (University Park: Pennsylvania State University Press, 1997).
32. Kleingeld, "Comments."
33. Brandt, *D'Artagnan und die Urteilstafel*, p. 136 (my translation, with help from Ciaran Cronin).
34. George M. Fredrickson, *Racism: A Short History* (Princeton, NJ: Princeton Classics, 2015; orig. ed. 2002), pp. 17–47.
35. See, for example, Immanuel Kant, *The Metaphysics of Morals*, trans. Mary Gregor (New York: Cambridge University Press, 1991), pp. 86–87, 159; Kant, "Perpetual Peace: A Philosophical Sketch," in Hans Reiss, ed., *Kant: Political Writings*, trans. H. B. Nisbet, 2nd ed. (New York: Cambridge University Press, 1991; orig. ed. 1970), pp. 106–7.

36. It is on this basis that Wood argues in *Kant's Ethical Thought* that Kant "declines to infer" differential rights from his racism. But note that Wood does not address the "natural slave" characterization of blacks and Native Americans, which seems a pretty clear statement of inferior rights, especially for a theory founded on autonomy as its central value. Nor (with respect to gender) can he deny that the restriction to "passive citizenship" does indeed follow for Kant from his sexist characterization of women.

37. Bernasconi, "Unfamiliar Source," pp. 152–54.

38. Eze, *Achieving Our Humanity*, pp. 77–80.

39. Kleingeld, "Comments."

40. Maureen Konkle, *Writing Indian Nations: Native Intellectuals and the Politics of Historiography, 1827–1863* (Chapel Hill: University of North Carolina Press, 2004).

41. Konkle, *Writing Indian Nations*, pp. 3, 4, 17, 20–21.

42. The phrase, though not the sentiment, is Robert Bernasconi's.

43. Cf. Bernasconi, "Unfamiliar Source," pp. 160–62.

44. Susan Moller Okin, *Justice, Gender, and the Family* (New York: Basic Books, 1989).

45. Thomas McCarthy's *Race, Empire, and the Idea of Human Development* (New York: Cambridge University Press, 2009) provides a fine example of one possible way of rethinking Kantianism in the light of this history.

46. Since the original (2005) appearance of this essay, a significant amount of new work has been published on Kant and race, some of which critiques the position I develop here: Kleingeld, "Kant's Second Thoughts"; Bernasconi, "Kant's Third Thoughts"; Samuel Fleischacker, *What Is Enlightenment?* (New York: Routledge, 2013). For my reply to these critics, an elaboration of my argument, and an updated bibliography on Kant and race, see Charles W. Mills, "Kant and Race, *Redux*," *Graduate Faculty Philosophy Journal*, "Philosophy and Race," 35, nos. 1–2 (2014): 125–57. I should clarify that (as explained in the final paragraphs of this essay) my criticism of Kant is not at all meant to rule out a revisionist anti-racist appropriation of his thought. On the contrary, in the epilogue of this book I make a case for a "black radical Kantianism," which is intended to retrieve and radicalize Kant's insights on personhood in the context of white supremacy. Compare Carol Hay's *Kantianism, Liberalism, and Feminism: Resisting Oppression* (New York: Palgrave Macmillan, 2013), which shows how a feminist Kantianism can be retrieved in the context of patriarchy despite Kant's own sexism.

CHAPTER 7

1. John Rawls, *A Theory of Justice*, rev. ed. (Cambridge, MA: Harvard University Press, 1999; orig. ed. 1971), p. 4.

2. Rawls, *Theory of Justice*, p. 8.

3. Randall Robinson, *The Debt: What America Owes to Blacks* (New York: Dutton, 2000).

4. Ta-Nehisi Coates's recent article "The Case for Reparations" (*Atlantic* 313, no. 5 [June 2014]: 54–71) sparked another brief revival of interest in the matter, but its shelf life was even shorter.

5. W. E. B. Du Bois, "The Souls of White Folk," in David Levering Lewis, ed., *W. E. B. Du Bois: A Reader* (New York: Henry Holt, 1995).

6. But for a critique of the kind of approach to racial justice that I develop here, see Christopher J. Lebron's recent *The Color of Our Shame: Race and Justice in Our Time* (New York: Oxford University Press, 2013). I hope to answer Lebron's critique in detail at some future date.

7. Stanford M. Lyman, "Race Relations as Social Process: Sociology's Resistance to a Civil Rights Orientation," in Herbert Hill and James E. Jones Jr., eds., *Race in America: The Struggle for Equality* (Madison: University of Wisconsin Press, 1993), pp. 370–71, 397.

8. Rogers M. Smith, *Civic Ideals: Conflicting Visions of Citizenship in U.S. History* (New Haven, CT: Yale University Press, 1997), pp. 15, 17, 27.

9. Elizabeth Anderson, *The Imperative of Integration* (Princeton, NJ: Princeton University Press, 2010).

10. Anderson, *Imperative of Integration*, pp. 3–7.

11. Charles W. Mills, "White Supremacy as Sociopolitical System" and "White Supremacy and Racial Justice," chs. 7 and 8 of Mills, *From Class to Race: Essays in White Marxism and Black Radicalism* (Lanham, MD: Rowman & Littlefield, 2003).

12. See, for example, George Fredrickson, *White Supremacy: A Comparative Study in American and South African History* (New York: Oxford University Press, 1981).

13. But see John Roemer, *A General Theory of Exploitation and Class* (Cambridge, MA: Harvard University Press, 1982).

14. Alan Wertheimer, *Exploitation* (Princeton, NJ: Princeton University Press, 1996), pp. ix, 8.

15. Gary A. Dymski, "Racial Inequality and Capitalist Exploitation," in Kai Nielsen and Robert Ware, eds., *Exploitation* (Atlantic Highlands, NJ: Humanities Press, 1997), pp. 335–47.

16. For a classic discussion, see Cedric J. Robinson's *Black Marxism: The Making of the Black Radical Tradition* (Chapel Hill: University of North Carolina Press, 2000; orig. ed. 1983).

17. See the introductory essays by Ashley ("Woody") Doane and Margaret Anderson in Doane and Eduardo Bonilla-Silva, eds., *White Out: The Continuing Significance of Racism* (New York: Routledge, 2003).

18. Cheryl I. Harris, "Whiteness as Property," *Harvard Law Review* 106 (1993): 1709–91; Melvin L. Oliver and Thomas M. Shapiro, *Black Wealth/White Wealth: A New Perspective on Racial Inequality*, 10th anniversary ed. (New York: Routledge, 2006; orig. ed. 1995); George Lipsitz, *The Possessive Investment in Whiteness: How White People Profit from Identity Politics* (Philadelphia: Temple University Press, 1998); Linda Faye Williams, *The Constraint of Race: Legacies of White Skin Privilege in America* (University Park: Pennsylvania State University Press, 2003); Lindsay G. Robertson, *Conquest by Law: How the Discovery of America Dispossessed Indigenous Peoples of Their Lands* (New York: Oxford University Press, 2005); Ira Katznelson, *When Affirmative Action Was White: An Untold History of Racial Inequality in Twentieth-Century America* (New York: W. W. Norton, 2005); Meizhu Lui et al., *The Color of Wealth: The Story Behind the U.S. Racial Wealth Divide* (New York: New Press, 2006); Douglas A. Blackmon, *Slavery by Another Name: The Re-Enslavement of Black Americans from the Civil War to World War II* (New York: Doubleday, 2008); Daria Roithmayr, *Reproducing Racism: How Everyday Choices Lock in White Advantage* (New York: New York University Press, 2014); Andre L. Smith, *Tax Law and Racial Economic Justice: Black Tax* (Lanham, MD: Lexington Books/ Rowman & Littlefield, 2015).

19. Sally Haslanger, *Resisting Reality: Social Construction and Social Critique* (New York: Oxford University Press, 2012).

20. George M. Fredrickson, *Racism: A Short History* (Princeton, NJ: Princeton Classics, 2015; orig. ed. 2002). For an opposing view, see Benjamin Isaac, *The Invention of Racism in Classical Antiquity* (Princeton, NJ: Princeton University Press, 2004).

21. Karl Marx, *Capital*, vol. I, trans. Ben Fowkes (Harmondsworth, Middlesex: Penguin and New Left Review, 1976), p. 280.

22. See, for example, Marshall Cohen, Thomas Nagel, and Thomas Scanlon, eds., *Marx, Justice and History* (Princeton, NJ: Princeton University Press, 1980); Steven Lukes, *Marxism and Morality* (New York: Oxford University Press, 1985).

23. Noel Ignatiev, *How the Irish Became White* (New York: Routledge, 2008; orig. ed. 1995); Karen Brodkin, *How Jews Became White Folks and What That Says about Race in America* (New Brunswick, NJ: Rutgers University Press, 1998); Matthew Frye Jacobson, *Whiteness of a Different Color: European Immigrants and the Alchemy of Race* (Cambridge, MA: Harvard University Press, 1998); Nell Irvin Painter, *The History of White People* (New York: W. W. Norton, 2010).

24. Slavery in the medieval Islamic world, which some scholars have argued differentiated black from non-black slaves, may be an exception: Bernard Lewis, *Race and Slavery in the Middle East: An Historical Enquiry* (New York: Oxford University Press, 1990).

25. Lipsitz, *Possessive Investment*, p. 5.

26. Oliver and Shapiro, *Black Wealth/White Wealth*, p. 51.

27. See, in this regard, the highly instructive work of Donald R. Kinder and Lynn M. Sanders, *Divided by Color: Racial Politics and Democratic Ideals* (Chicago: University of Chicago Press, 1996).

28. The failure of Bernie Sanders's recent (as I write this in summer 2016) "democratic socialist" campaign for the Democratic presidential nomination can be argued to stem in part from its opting for a putatively "universalist" left approach that *dissolved* racial justice into class justice, without giving sufficient attention to the former's distinctive features. Apart from the African American community's long-standing connection to the Clintons, Bill and Hillary, this political mis-diagnosis contributed significantly, I would suggest, to blacks' general alienation from Sanders's program.

29. Thomas Piketty, *Capital in the Twenty-First Century*, trans. Arthur Goldhammer (Cambridge, MA: Belknap Press, 2014).

30. Derrick Bell, *And We Are Not Saved: The Elusive Quest for Racial Justice* (New York: Basic Books, 1989).

CHAPTER 8

1. John Rawls, *A Theory of Justice*, rev. ed. (Cambridge, MA: Harvard University Press, 1999; orig. ed. 1971); John Rawls, *Political Liberalism* (New York: Columbia University Press, 1993); John Rawls, *Political Liberalism*, exp. ed. (New York: Columbia University Press, 1996); John Rawls, *Collected Papers*, ed. Samuel Freeman (Cambridge, MA: Harvard University Press, 1999); John Rawls, *The Law of Peoples, with "The Idea of Public Reason Revisited"* (Cambridge, MA: Harvard University Press, 1999); John Rawls, *Justice as Fairness: A Restatement*, ed. Erin Kelly (Cambridge, MA: Harvard University Press, 2001).

2. Samuel Freeman, ed., *The Cambridge Companion to Rawls* (New York: Cambridge University Press, 2003).

3. See, for example, the contributions to the "Equal Citizenship: Race and Ethnicity" section of the *Fordham Law Review* 72, no. 5 (April 2004) symposium: Rawls and the Law, and, more recently, Christopher J. Lebron, *The Color of Our Shame: Race and Justice in Our Time* (New York: Oxford University Press, 2013).

4. I mean by this not that other oppressions and injustices do not exist or are unimportant, but, rather, that both gender and class, for example, predate the modern world as social structures and social identities. Race by contrast—at least in the conventional scholarly judgment (but see Benjamin Isaac, *The Invention of Racism in Classical Antiquity* [Princeton, NJ: Princeton University Press, 2004])—is distinctively modern, provides the rationale for the European conquest of the world, and insofar as it has facilitated slavery and genocide at a time when human moral equality was supposed to have been broadly established, it is distinctively horrific in the blatancy of the degree of its oppression.

5. Thomas Nagel, "Rawls and Liberalism," in Freeman, *Cambridge Companion*, p. 84n3.

6. Charles W. Mills, *The Racial Contract* (Ithaca, NY: Cornell University Press, 1997).

7. Charles W. Mills, "'Ideal Theory' as Ideology," *Hypatia: A Journal of Feminist Philosophy* 20, no. 3 (August 2005): 165–84, reprinted as ch. 5 in this book; Carole Pateman and Charles W. Mills, *Contract and Domination* (Malden, MA: Polity Press, 2007).

8. John Rawls, *Lectures on the History of Moral Philosophy*, ed. Barbara Herman (Cambridge, MA: Harvard University Press, 2000); John Rawls, *Lectures on the History of Political Philosophy*, ed. Samuel Freeman (Cambridge, MA: Harvard University Press, 2007).

9. Susan Moller Okin, *Justice, Gender, and the Family* (New York: Basic Books, 1989).

10. In citing possible explanations, Rawls does say "Truman once described the Japanese as beasts and said they should be treated as such." But he then immediately goes on to write "how foolish it sounds now to call the Germans and the Japanese as a whole barbarians and beasts" (Rawls, *Law of Peoples*, p. 100), which makes it doubtful that he saw this epithet as racial on Truman's part. For a more informed discussion of the role of race in the Pacific War, see John Dower, *War without Mercy: Race and Power in the Pacific War* (New York: Pantheon Books, 1986).

11. Thomas Nagel claims ("John Rawls and Affirmative Action," *Journal of Blacks in Higher Education* 39 [Spring 2003], p. 82) that Rawls, in a personal conversation, expressed "his view of the importance of defending the constitutionality of affirmative action," but concedes that "he never referred to it in his writings, so far as I know, except obliquely [in one of the passages cited above from *Justice as Fairness*]." In a comment presumably meant as exculpatory, Nagel points out that affirmative action "only began to be a major issue in the early 1970s . . . and the *Bakke* case was not decided until 1978," well after *Theory* appeared. But he does not answer the obvious question of why Rawls did not address the issue in any of his essays in the 1980s, or in his 1993 book *Political Liberalism*, or, for that matter, why the *Justice as Fairness* reference is "oblique" rather than direct.

12. George M. Fredrickson, *White Supremacy: A Comparative Study in American and South African History* (New York: Oxford University Press, 1981), pp. xi–xii.

13. Rawls, *Law of Peoples*, p. 21.

14. Rawls, *Political Liberalism* (1996), p. lxii.

15. Rawls, *Law of Peoples*, pp. 19–22.

16. David E. Stannard, *American Holocaust: Columbus and the Conquest of the New World* (New York: Oxford University Press, 1992).

17. Francis Jennings, *The Invasion of America: Indians, Colonialism, and the Cant of Conquest* (New York: W. W. Norton, 1976; orig. ed. 1975); Lindsay G. Robertson, *Conquest by Law: How the Discovery of America Dispossessed Indigenous Peoples of Their Lands* (New York: Oxford University Press, 2005).

18. Adam Hochschild, *King Leopold's Ghost: A Story of Greed, Terror and Heroism in Colonial Africa* (New York: Houghton Mifflin, 1998).

19. Richard Gott, *Britain's Empire: Resistance, Repression and Revolt* (New York: Verso, 2011).

20. David Brion Davis, *Inhuman Bondage: The Rise and Fall of Slavery in the New World* (New York: Oxford University Press, 2006).

21. Paul Keal, *European Conquest and the Rights of Indigenous Peoples: The Moral Backwardness of International Society* (New York: Cambridge University Press, 2003), pp. 42, 1, 21, 22, 24.

22. Keal, *European Conquest*, pp. 35, 55. See also, more recently, A. Dirk Moses, ed., *Empire, Colony, Genocide: Conquest, Occupation, and Subaltern Resistance in World History* (New York: Berghahn, 2008).

23. Mark Cocker, *Rivers of Blood, Rivers of Gold: Europe's Conflict with Tribal Peoples* (London: Jonathan Cape, 1998), p. xiii. I would, of course, reject Cocker's "tribal society" category, a manifestation of his own unconscious Eurocentrism.

24. Rawls, *Political Liberalism* (1996), p. xxvi.

25. Marilyn Lake and Henry Reynolds, *Drawing the Global Colour Line: White Men's Countries and the International Challenge of Racial Equality* (New York: Cambridge University Press, 2008); Domenico Losurdo, *Liberalism: A Counter-History*, trans. Gregory Elliott (New York: Verso, 2011); John M. Hobson, *The Eurocentric Conception of World Politics: Western International Theory, 1760–2010* (New York: Cambridge University Press, 2012).

26. Robertson, *Conquest by Law*.

27. Rogers M. Smith, *Civic Ideals: Conflicting Visions of Citizenship in U.S. History* (New Haven, CT: Yale University Press, 1997).

28. Rawls, *Political Liberalism* (1996), p. liii. It is, of course, even more strikingly revealed in his failure, as earlier pointed out, to condemn the *extra*-European conquests of the European empires. Europeans conquering other European nations is bad; Europeans conquering non-European nations is apparently not even seen by Rawls *as* conquest (but, presumably, "discovery," "founding of a New World," etc. etc.).

29. Rawls, *Law of Peoples*, p. 90.

30. Hobson, *Eurocentric Conception*.

31. Rodney Roberts, introduction, to Roberts, ed., *Injustice and Rectification* (New York: Peter Lang, 2002).

32. See, for example, Barbara Arneil, *John Locke and America: The Defence of English Colonialism* (Oxford: Clarendon Press, 1996); Uday Singh Mehta, *Liberalism and Empire: A Study in*

Nineteenth-Century British Liberal Thought (Chicago: University of Chicago Press, 1999); Jennifer Pitts, *A Turn to Empire: The Rise of Imperial Liberalism in Britain and France* (Princeton, NJ: Princeton University Press, 2005); Andrew Valls, ed., *Race and Racism in Modern Philosophy* (Ithaca, NY: Cornell University Press, 2005); Thomas McCarthy, *Race, Empire, and the Idea of Human Development* (New York: Cambridge University Press, 2009); Hobson, *Eurocentric Conception*.

33. Cedric J. Robinson, *Black Marxism: The Making of the Black Radical Tradition* (Chapel Hill, NC: University of North Carolina Press, 2000; orig. ed. 1983); Michael C. Dawson, *Black Visions: The Roots of Contemporary African-American Political Ideologies* (Chicago: University of Chicago Press, 2001); Anthony Bogues, *Black Heretics, Black Prophets: Radical Political Intellectuals* (New York: Routledge, 2003); Tommie Shelby, *We Who Are Dark: The Philosophical Foundations of Black Solidarity* (Cambridge, MA: Harvard University Press, 2005).

34. Rawls, *Theory of Justice*, p. 8.

35. Rawls, *Theory of Justice*, p. 7.

36. Rawls, *Law of Peoples*, pp. 89–90.

37. M. F. Ashley Montagu, *Man's Most Dangerous Myth: The Fallacy of Race*, 7th ed., abridged for students (Walnut Creek, CA: AltaMira Press, 1997; orig. ed. 1942).

38. Rawls, *Theory of Justice*, pp. 8, 309. Neither here nor in any of his later books does Rawls ever provide any discussion of what non-ideal "compensatory justice" (which I am taking to be corrective justice) would require. Moreover, his detailed analysis of the appropriate criteria and justification for civil disobedience and conscientious refusal (*Theory of Justice*, §55–59) presupposes throughout "the special case of a nearly just society, one that is well-ordered for the most part but in which some serious violations of justice nevertheless do occur" (*Theory of Justice*, p. 319). So even this discussion of one kind of non-ideal theory is heavily idealized, and thus of little applicability to ill-ordered white-supremacist societies.

39. Chief Justice John Roberts, quoted in "Justices, 5–4, Limit Use of Race for School Integration Plans," *New York Times*, June 29, 2007, A1.

40. But for an alternative approach (to be discussed in the next chapter), see Tommie Shelby, "Race and Social Justice: Rawlsian Considerations," *Fordham Law Review* 72, no. 5 (April 2004): 1697–714.

41. Jean-Jacques Rousseau, *The Discourses and Other Early Political Writings*, ed. and trans. Victor Gourevitch (New York: Cambridge University Press, 1997).

42. Carole Pateman, *The Sexual Contract* (Stanford, CA: Stanford University Press, 1988); Mills, *The Racial Contract*.

43. Pateman and Mills, *Contract and Domination*, chs. 3, 4, and 8.

CHAPTER 9

1. John Rawls, *A Theory of Justice*, rev. ed. (Cambridge, MA: Harvard University Press, 1999; orig. ed. 1971). I would like to thank the three anonymous referees of the original journal version of this essay for their thoughtful and thorough engagement with my argument. I made various changes in the original draft in response to their comments, which undoubtedly turned it into a better essay than it would otherwise have been. In the pertinent notes below, I explain why, though I took his criticisms seriously, I did not, after reflecting on them, act on all the suggestions of one particular referee.

2. Elizabeth Anderson, *The Imperative of Integration* (Princeton, NJ: Princeton University Press, 2010). See, in particular, pp. 3–7, on the significance for her of racial justice being a matter of "nonideal theory." She gives three reasons there for rejecting ideal theory and Rawlsianism: (a) principles must be tailored "to the motivational and cognitive capacities of human beings"; (b) ideal theory, "founded on inadequate empirical assumptions," occludes crucial distinctions and the possibly new ideals that might be required by altered conceptual maps; (c) ideal theory may be "epistemologically disabling," for example, because the representative cognitive positions of an ideal society will be raceless, thus

justifying color-blindness, whereas our own society requires sensitivity to race-based injustices.

3. See chapters 3, 4, and 8 of my book with Carole Pateman, *Contract and Domination* (Malden, MA: Polity, 2007). My claim there is that we need to run a different thought-experiment custom-designed for generating principles of non-ideal theory rather than trying to turn principles of ideal theory to the remedying of non-ideal problems.

4. Tommie Shelby, "Race and Social Justice: Rawlsian Considerations," *Fordham Law Review* 72, no. 5 (April 2004): Symposium: Rawls and the Law: 1697–1714.

5. For Shelby's reply to my original journal article, see Shelby, "Racial Realities and Corrective Justice: A Reply to Charles Mills," *Critical Philosophy of Race* 1, no. 2 (2013): 145–62. Since I hope to answer Shelby's reply in a future essay, I have not made any major changes to this reprinted version, assuming it would be more helpful for readers interested in our exchange to be able to read substantially the same article he is seeking to rebut in his reply rather than a dramatically modified version.

6. As for Anderson's objections: my belief is that the problems she identifies can be addressed by my revision of the orthodox thought-experiment, but for reasons of space I will not pursue this here. It is possible that Anderson might be sympathetic to my modifications but view them as so transforming the Rawlsian apparatus that it ceases to be Rawlsian, even in a scare-quotes sense, so that in effect my own position should be categorized as rejecting Rawls.

7. One referee, though not the other two, found this opening section of the paper ("the paucity of attention to the issue of racism in mainstream [Rawlsian] political philosophy") "quite misplaced." His argument is that since "principles for rectification of injustice both *depend on* an already worked out theory of justice and, second, are part of a different set of principles that have to be fine tuned to particular societies and hence at a different level of abstraction from the principles contained in justice as fairness," I would have to show that "inattention to (non-ideal) conditions of racism in society *distorts* the principles produced by the theory" for such inattention to be criticized as problematic. Otherwise—if the (ideal-theory) principles are merely incomplete rather than defective—my critique is unjustified. But my response would be that the only way we can find out whether the ideal-theory principles can indeed guide us in constructing the pertinent non-ideal-theory principles (for rectificatory racial justice) is for this to be demonstrated, and the point of the opening section is to document how little effort has been made in the profession to do so. Surely forty years is long enough—especially in a society to whose creation racism has been central—for there to be a significant body of work by now showing *how* one derives principles of rectificatory racial justice (a "pressing and urgent matter" [Rawls, *Theory of Justice*, p. 8] if ever there was one) from the ideal-theory principles! That was, after all, Rawls's own rationale for prioritizing ideal theory in the first place, that in "no other way" can "a deeper understanding" of non-ideal questions like "compensatory justice" be gained (Rawls, *Theory of Justice*, p. 8). So I don't see this opening section as begging the question, as the referee asserts (a "non-starter" as an argument, in his opinion, since I have not proven that Rawls's principles cannot be so applied). All I am trying to show at this stage is that they *have not* (for the most part) been so applied, that this (almost complete) silence is a problem, and—as with the parallel feminist claim—that the natural explanation is the profession's dominant demography.

8. Rawls, *Theory of Justice*.

9. Samuel Freeman, *Rawls* (New York: Routledge, 2007), p. x.

10. Freeman, *Rawls*, pp. xvi, xvii, x.

11. Francis Jennings, *The Invasion of America: Indians, Colonialism, and the Cant of Conquest* (New York: W. W. Norton, 1976; orig ed. 1975); George M. Fredrickson, *White Supremacy: A Comparative Study in American and South African History* (New York: Oxford University Press, 1981); Rogers M. Smith, *Civic Ideals: Conflicting Visions of Citizenship in U.S. History* (New Haven, CT: Yale University Press, 1997); Anthony Marx, *Making Race and Nation: A Comparison of the United States, South Africa, and Brazil* (New York: Cambridge University Press, 1998).

12. See Ruth Abbey, ed., *Feminist Interpretations of John Rawls* (University Park: Pennsylvania State University Press, 2013), both for the collected essays and for Abbey's very useful chronological overview of the feminist literature on Rawls.

13. Norman Daniels, ed., *Reading Rawls: Critical Studies on Rawls' A Theory of Justice* (Stanford, CA: Stanford University Press, 1989; orig. ed. 1975), with a new preface.

14. Hardy Jones, "A Rawlsian Discussion of Discrimination," in H. Gene Blocker and Elizabeth H. Smith, eds., *John Rawls's Theory of Social Justice: An Introduction* (Athens: Ohio State University Press, 1980). In the original journal appearance of this chapter, I had said, falsely, that there was no discussion of race in this book. I was—sloppily—relying on my unreliable memory of a book I had read twenty-five years before rather than re-checking it. My apologies to readers of the original article, to the editors, and to Jones himself, especially since Jones's essay turns out to be not merely the most extensive treatment of the issue in these ten books, but the *only* extensive treatment of the issue in these ten books. (Needless to say, my overall point is unaffected.) Jones concludes that "compensatory treatment in the form of preferential hiring, for example, is surely congenial to the Rawlsian conception of equal opportunity. Even reverse discrimination favoring the somewhat less qualified would seem to be acceptable" (p. 283).

15. Henry Richardson and Paul Weithman, eds., *The Philosophy of Rawls: A Collection of Essays*, 5 vols. (New York: Garland, 1999). My thanks to Anthony Laden for this piece of information.

16. Samuel Freeman, ed., *The Cambridge Companion to Rawls* (New York: Cambridge University Press, 2003).

17. Freeman, *Rawls*, pp. 90–91.

18. Jon Mandle, *Rawls's A Theory of Justice: An Introduction* (New York: Cambridge University Press, 2009); Percy B. Lehning, *John Rawls: An Introduction* (New York: Cambridge University Press, 2009); Paul Voice, *Rawls Explained: From Fairness to Utopia* (Chicago: Open Court, 2011). I dropped Frank Lovett, *Rawls's "A Theory of Justice": A Reader's Guide* (New York: Continuum, 2011) from the list in the original article to make room for Jon Mandle and David A. Reidy's more recent co-edited *A Companion to Rawls* (Malden, MA: Wiley Blackwell, 2014).

19. Sebastiano Maffettone, *Rawls: An Introduction* (Malden, MA: Polity, 2010), pp. 79, 80, 111.

20. Mandle and Reidy, *A Companion to Rawls*.

21. Brooke Ackerley et al., "Symposium: John Rawls and the Study of Justice: Legacies of Inquiry," *Perspectives on Politics* 4, no. 1 (March 2006): 75–133.

22. Leif Wenar, "John Rawls," *Stanford Encyclopedia of Philosophy* (rev. 2012; orig. 2008).

23. Henry S. Richardson, "John Rawls," *Internet Encyclopedia of Philosophy* (n.d.).

24. Laurence Thomas, "Rawlsian Self-Respect and the Black Consciousness Movement" (1978), rpt. in Richardson and Weithman, eds., *Philosophy of Rawls*, vol. 3, "Moral Psychology and Community."

25. Michele M. Moody-Adams, "Race, Class, and the Social Construction of Self-Respect," *Philosophical Forum*, Special Triple Issue: "African-American Perspectives and Philosophical Traditions," ed. John Pittman, Vol. 24, nos. 1–3 (Fall–Spring 1992–93): 251–66.

26. See their interviews with George Yancy in Yancy, ed., *African-American Philosophers: 17 Conversations* (New York: Routledge, 1998).

27. Bernard R. Boxill, *Blacks and Social Justice*, rev. ed. (Lanham, MD: Rowman & Littlefield, 1992; orig. ed. 1984); Howard McGary, *Race and Social Justice* (Malden, MA: Blackwell, 1999).

28. Boxill, *Blacks and Social Justice*, pp. 212–18, 219–25.

29. McGary, *Race and Social Justice*, pp. 13–14, 100, 70, 198, 123n6, 208–13.

30. McGary, *Race and Social Justice*, pp. 119–22.

31. Shelby, "Rawls and Social Justice." Shelby has another article where he claims to be drawing on key Rawlsian ideas: "Justice, Deviance, and the Dark Ghetto," *Philosophy and Public Affairs* 35, no. 2 (Spring 2007): 126–60. However, his primary aim here is not to derive

racial justice prescriptions from Rawls but to make a case for what our appropriate moral perspective should be on the black ghetto poor's "deviant" behavior and attitudes (crime, refusal to work in legitimate jobs, contempt for authority). So though moral issues are involved, remediation of the injustice of the "basic structure" is not the real theme. I would also claim that the central ideas he is using are not really distinctively Rawlsian but rather generic liberal concepts and principles.

32. See Rawls, *Theory of Justice*; John Rawls, *Political Liberalism*, exp. ed. (New York: Columbia University Press, 1996; orig. ed. 1993); John Rawls, *Justice as Fairness: A Restatement*, ed. Erin Kelly (Cambridge, MA: Harvard University Press, 2001).

33. Shelby, "Race and Social Justice."

34. Seana Valentine Shiffrin, "Race, Labor, and the Fair Equality of Opportunity Principle," *Fordham Law Review* 72, no. 5 (April 2004): 1643–75.

35. Shelby, "Race and Social Justice," pp. 1710–11.

36. Shelby, "Race and Social Justice," p. 1711. The Rawls passage cited is from *Theory*, p. 63.

37. Shelby, "Race and Social Justice," pp. 1711–12.

38. They are not mentioned in the list on p. 11 of *Theory* and not formally included until a 1975 essay.

39. Rawls, *Theory of Justice*, pp. 17, 129–30.

40. John Rawls, *Political Liberalism* (New York: Columbia University Press, 1993), p. xxviii.

41. One of the anonymous Oxford referees suggested to me that this didn't follow, since "the validity of Shelby's claim that *Theory*'s principles can be used to deal directly with race is independent of Rawls's *beliefs* about what his principles could or could not do—for it is possible that Rawls's beliefs about what his principles could or could not do are mistaken." Similarly, the referee was dubious about the relevance of my later criticism of Shelby (in the "FEO as lexically subordinate" section) that "he [Shelby] is not entitled" to extrapolate FEO "beyond what Rawls himself intended," since, the referee argues, "once published, the principle is open to anyone's interpretation." However, my reply in both cases would be that such usage of FEO is ruled out a priori by Rawls's explicit stipulation at the beginning of *Theory*, and subsequently throughout the text, that these are principles for a well-ordered society (which excludes a racist society) and that they are principles of distributive (not compensatory) justice. This is why I believe, as I claim later, that Shelby is making a category mistake.

42. Rawls, *Political Liberalism* (1996), p. liii.

43. Rawls, *Justice as Fairness*.

44. Rawls, *Justice as Fairness*, pp. 64–65.

45. Rawls, *Justice as Fairness*, p. 66.

46. The same referee cited in note 7, above, misread me here as imputing to Rawls a "hesitation" about condemning racism, and also of insinuating, quite unfairly to Rawls, "that there is something unsaid or hidden" in these passages. But this is a misinterpretation. As I emphasize myself, Rawls condemns racism unequivocally from the start; I meant a "hesitation" to specify what rectificatory racial justice would require. The point I was making, contra Shelby, was that if Rawls thought his *ideal-theory principles* (here FEO) were the appropriate ones to use to deal with racial injustice, he would just have said so. The fact that he didn't, and refers to "a special form" of the DP instead, shows that he believed *other principles were necessary* (the point the referee himself makes in the quote I cite from his review in note 7).

47. Thanks to Derrick Darby for reminding me of this phrase (though Darby himself does not necessarily endorse my judgment here).

48. Thomas Nagel, "Rawls and Liberalism," in Freeman, ed., *Cambridge Companion to Rawls*, p. 84n3.

49. Freeman, *Rawls*, p. 90.

50. *The Ethics of Aristotle: The Nicomachean Ethics*, trans. J. A. K. Thomson, rev. Hugh Tredennick (New York: Penguin Classics, 1976), book V. However, as noted in an earlier chapter, Samuel Fleischacker has argued that in Aristotle himself neither concept really corresponds to our own contemporary version, since the idea of entitlement to a certain distribution of property and rights merely by virtue of being human is a modern one, first

put forward by François-Nöel ("Gracchus") Babeuf: Samuel Fleischacker, *A Short History of Distributive Justice* (Cambridge, MA: Harvard University Press, 2004).

51. Rawls, *Theory of Justice*, pp. 8, 309.
52. Rawls, *Theory of Justice*; John Rawls, *The Law of Peoples, with "The Idea of Public Reason Revisited"* (Cambridge, MA: Harvard University Press, 1999).
53. At various points in his review, the same referee reminds me that racist discrimination violates FEO. I had not at all meant to deny that, but my focus, as made clear at the start, is corrective racial justice (affirmative action, preferential treatment, etc.), not pre-emptive measures.
54. Rawls, *Theory of Justice*, pp. 215–16.
55. Thomas Nagel, "John Rawls and Affirmative Action," *Journal of Blacks in Higher Education* 39 (Spring 2003), p. 82.
56. Rawls, *Theory of Justice*, p. 309.
57. See, for example, Charles W. Mills, "'Ideal Theory' as Ideology," *Hypatia: A Journal of Feminist Philosophy* 20, no. 3 (August 2005): 165–84 (reprinted as ch. 5 of this book); Colin Farrelly, "Justice in Ideal Theory: A Refutation," *Political Studies* 55, no. 4 (December 2007): 844–64; Ingrid Robeyns and Adam Swift, eds., *Social Theory and Practice* 34, no. 3 (July 2008), Special Issue: Social Justice: Ideal Theory, Nonideal Circumstances; Amartya Sen, *The Idea of Justice* (Cambridge, MA: Harvard University Press, 2009); Anderson, *Imperative of Integration*, pp. 3–7; A. John Simmons, "Ideal and Nonideal Theory," *Philosophy and Public Affairs* 38, no. 1 (Winter 2010): 5–36.
58. Rawls, *Justice as Fairness*, pp. 14, 21.
59. See Lawrie Balfour, "Reparations after Identity Politics," *Political Theory* 33, no. 6 (December 2005): 786–811; Alfred L. Brophy, *Reparations Pro & Con* (New York: Oxford University Press, 2006); Pablo de Greiff, "Justice and Reparations," in Pablo de Greiff, ed., *The Handbook of Reparations* (New York: Oxford University Press, 2006); Lawrie Balfour, "Unthinking Racial Realism: A Future for Reparations?" *Du Bois Review: Social Science Research on Race* 11, no. 1 (Spring 2014): 43–56.
60. Thomas McCarthy, "*Vergangenheitsbewältigung* in the USA: On the Politics of the Memory of Slavery," Part I, *Political Theory* 30, no. 5 (October 2002): 623–48; Thomas McCarthy, "Coming to Terms with Our Past: On the Morality and Politics of Reparations for Slavery," Part II, *Political Theory* 32, no. 6 (December 2004): 750–72.
61. Rawls, *Theory of Justice*, p. 63.
62. Melvin L. Oliver and Thomas M. Shapiro, *Black Wealth/White Wealth: A New Perspective on Racial Inequality*, 10th anniversary ed. (New York: Routledge, 2006; orig. ed. 1995). See also Thomas M. Shapiro, *The Hidden Cost of Being African American: How Wealth Perpetuates Inequality* (New York: Oxford University Press, 2004).
63. Robert Taylor, "Rawlsian Affirmative Action," *Ethics* 119, no. 3 (April 2009): 476–506. See, in particular, pp. 487–90, where Taylor draws on the work of Christine Korsgaard to fill in the gaps in Rawls's account of what non-ideal circumstances would permit.
64. Taylor, "Rawlsian Affirmative Action," pp. 488–91, 485.
65. Taylor, "Rawlsian Affirmative Action," p. 489.
66. Taylor, "Rawlsian Affirmative Action," pp. 492–94.
67. I would contend that Taylor's negative conclusions arise in part out of his decision to utilize a "forward-looking" rather than "backward-looking" rectificatory rationale (Taylor, "Rawlsian Affirmative Action," p. 478), and that the deontological imperative to correct for past injustices and unjust enrichment would trump the considerations he adduces against strong affirmative action. Cf. McGary, note 30. But making this argument would, again, require the reorientation of the Rawlsian apparatus in a fundamental way toward non-ideal theory, so as to generate principles of corrective justice directly rather than derivatively. For my own attempt at such a reorientation, see Charles W. Mills, "Racial Equality," in George Hull, ed., *The Equal Society: Essays on Equality in Theory and Practice* (Lanham, MD: Lexington Books/Rowman & Littlefield, 2015).
68. Rawls, *Justice as Fairness*, p. 51.
69. Rawls, *Theory of Justice*, p. 137.

70. Rawls, *Theory of Justice*, pp. 200–201.
71. Rawls, *Justice as Fairness*, pp. 87, 90.
72. Richard M. Valelly, *The Two Reconstructions: The Struggle for Black Enfranchisement* (Chicago: University of Chicago Press, 2004); Philip A. Klinkner and Rogers M. Smith, *The Unsteady March: The Rise and Decline of Racial Equality in America* (Chicago: University of Chicago Press, 1999).
73. Michael K. Brown et al., *Whitewashing Race: The Myth of a Color-Blind Society* (Berkeley: University of California Press, 2003).
74. Donald R. Kinder and Lynn M. Sanders, *Divided by Color: Racial Politics and Democratic Ideals* (Chicago: University of Chicago Press, 1996), pp. 252, 287.
75. Thomas McCarthy, *Race, Empire, and the Idea of Human Development* (New York: Cambridge University Press, 2009), p. 87.
76. However, as noted at the start of the book, we might now (2016) be witnessing a welcome shift the other way.
77. See again Pateman and Mills, *Contract and Domination*, ch. 3.
78. For an insightful essay on the role of ideology in such circumstances, see the work of one Tommie Shelby, "Ideology, Racism, and Critical Social Theory," *Philosophical Forum* 34, no. 2 (June 2003): 153–88.
79. Robert Nozick, *Anarchy, State, and Utopia*, with a new foreword (New York: Basic Books, 2013; orig. ed. 1974).
80. Nozick, *Anarchy, State, and Utopia*, pp. 152–53, 344n2. For a valuable reconstruction and development of a "Nozickian" theorization of racial corrective justice, see Andrew Valls, "The Libertarian Case for Affirmative Action," *Social Theory and Practice* 25, no. 2 (Summer 1999): 299–323.
81. Here I am, of course, presupposing an ideal liberalism. For the sordid history of actual liberalism (in which racial injustice *is* liberal), see Domenico Losurdo's recently translated *Liberalism: A Counter-History*, trans. Gregory Elliott (New York: Verso, 2011).
82. Taylor, "Rawlsian Affirmative Action," p. 486.
83. Insofar as FEO incorporates formal equality of opportunity, it does (implicitly) have an anti-discrimination component. But this is intended by Rawls as a pre-emptive prohibition under ideal conditions, not as a corrective measure justifying redistributive policies under non-ideal conditions. The substantive core of FEO—which does justify redistribution— is the correction of bad luck in the social lottery of an ideal society, not the redress of the legacy of discrimination in a non-ideal society. And the rationale is the moral *arbitrariness* of the social circumstances into which we are born, not the moral *wrongness* of social (here racial) oppression.
84. See my "Contract of Breach: Repairing the Racial Contract," ch. 4 of Pateman and Mills, *Contract and Domination*.
85. It belatedly occurred to me when doing the final revision of this essay (the journal version) that the question may, for a significant subset of variants, simply be undecidable. In other words, Rawls provides so little guidance on how to derive non-ideal principles of corrective justice from his ideal principles that for many candidates we will simply be unable to judge whether they would count as legitimately Rawlsian or not—thereby fundamentally putting into question (in yet another way) the justification for spending so many decades on ideal theory in the first place.

CHAPTER 10

1. Charles W. Mills, "Red Shift: Politically Embodied /Embodied Politics" (2002), rpt. in Mills, *Radical Theory, Caribbean Reality: Race, Class and Social Domination* (Kingston, Jamaica: University of the West Indies Press, 2010).
2. Leonard Harris, ed., *Philosophy Born of Struggle: Anthology of Afro-American Philosophy from 1917* (Dubuque, IA: Kendall/Hunt 1983). However, there were at least two other earlier collections, Charles A. Frye, ed., *Level Three: A Black Philosophy Reader* (Lanham, MD: University Press of America, 1980) and Percy Edward Johnston, ed., *Afro American*

Philosophies: Selected Readings, from Jupiter Hammon to Eugene C. Holmes (Upper Montclair, NJ: Montclair State College Press, 1970).

3. Leonard Harris, ed., *Philosophy Born of Struggle: Anthology of Afro-American Philosophy from 1917*, 2nd ed. (Dubuque, IA: Kendall/Hunt, 2000).

4. *Philosophical Forum* 9, nos. 2–3 (Winter–Spring 1977–78), special double issue, ed. Jesse McDade and Carl Lesnor, "Philosophy and the Black Experience"; *Philosophical Forum* 24, nos. 1–3 (Fall–Spring 1992–93), special triple issue, ed. John Pittman, "African-American Perspectives and Philosophical Traditions"; John Pittman, ed., *African-American Perspectives and Philosophical Traditions* (New York: Routledge, 1996). As Lucius Outlaw has pointed out, the late Marx Wartofsky, editor of the journal, deserves considerable credit for this generous opening of his pages to African American philosophers, something very few if any other white editors of the time would have been prepared to do.

5. Cornel West, *Prophesy Deliverance! An Afro-American Revolutionary Christianity*, 20th anniversary ed., with a new preface (Philadelphia: Westminster John Knox Press, 2002; orig. ed. 1982); Bernard R. Boxill, *Blacks and Social Justice*, rev. ed. (Lanham, MD: Rowman & Littlefield, 1992; orig. ed. 1984).

6. Lewis R. Gordon, *An Introduction to Africana Philosophy* (New York: Cambridge University Press, 2008); Derrick Darby, *Rights, Race, and Recognition* (New York: Cambridge University Press, 2009); Thomas McCarthy, *Race, Empire, and the Idea of Human Development* (New York: Cambridge University Press, 2009); Christopher J. Lebron, *The Color of Our Shame: Race and Justice in Our Time* (New York: Oxford University Press, 2013); Tommie Shelby, *We Who Are Dark: The Philosophical Foundations of Black Solidarity* (Cambridge, MA: Harvard University Press, 2005); Robert Gooding-Williams, *In the Shadow of Du Bois: Afro-Modern Political Thought in America* (Cambridge, MA: Harvard University Press, 2009); Leonard Harris and Charles Molesworth, *Alain L. Locke: The Biography of a Philosopher* (Chicago: University of Chicago Press, 2008).

7. See, for example, Lucius T. Outlaw Jr., "What Is Africana Philosophy?" in George Yancy, ed., *Philosophy in Multiple Voices* (Lanham, MD: Rowman & Littlefield, 2007).

8. Outlaw, "What Is Africana Philosophy?"

9. Harris, *Philosophy Born of Struggle*, 2nd ed., p. 345. The letter, under the heading "'Believe It or Not' or the Ku Klux Klan and American Philosophy Exposed," originally appeared in the APA *Proceedings and Addresses* 68, no. 5 (May 1995): 133–37. It is reprinted in Harris, *Philosophy Born of Struggle*, 2nd ed.

10. Harris, "'Believe It or Not'" (in *Philosophy Born of Struggle*), p. 346.

11. Kwame Anthony Appiah, New York University website.

12. Shelby, *We Who Are Dark*.

13. Tina Fernandes Botts et al., "What Is the State of Blacks in Philosophy?" *Critical Philosophy of Race* 2, no. 2 (2014): 224–42.

14. Indeed, there is some reason to think that the number of tenured black professors may actually *diminish* in the coming years. Liam Kofi Bright, one of the co-authors of the "What Is the State of Blacks in Philosophy?" article (above), suggests that—based, ceteris paribus, on the current numbers in the pipeline and the current attrition rate—the most likely prognosis is for a future reduction in numbers (personal communication).

15. In the original appearance of this chapter, I had included Souleymane Bachir Diagne as being at Columbia. However Diagne is in the Department of French and Romance Philology, with only a secondary appointment in Philosophy.

16. Because his website made no mention of race, I had in my original chapter excluded Hardimon from the list of black philosophers currently working on race. However, Hardimon has informed me that the website information was dated, and that he is in fact doing a book on race.

17. Kwame Anthony Appiah, *Lines of Descent: W. E. B. Du Bois and the Emergence of Identity* (Cambridge, MA: Harvard University Press, 2014).

18. Admittedly, another route would be to get a PhD in a related area of philosophy and then simply educate oneself through one's own reading—as indeed older figures in the field

(such as myself) perforce had to do, since there were no appropriate courses and mentors at the time.

19. Carole Pateman and Charles W. Mills, *Contract and Domination* (Malden, MA: Polity Press, 2007).

20. Charles W. Mills, *The Racial Contract* (Ithaca, NY: Cornell University Press, 1997).

21. John Rawls, *A Theory of Justice*, rev. ed. (Cambridge, MA: Harvard University Press, 1999; orig. ed. 1971).

22. Matt Zwolinski, ed., *Arguing about Political Philosophy*, 2nd ed. (New York: Routledge, 2014; orig. ed. 2009).

23. Ann Cudd, "Contractarianism," *Stanford Encyclopedia of Philosophy* (rev. 2012; orig. 2000); Carole Pateman, *The Sexual Contract* (Stanford, CA: Stanford University Press, 1988).

24. Celeste Friend, "Social Contract Theory," *Internet Encyclopedia of Philosophy* (n.d.).

25. Cornel West, *Race Matters*, with a new preface by the author (Boston: Beacon Press, 2001; orig. ed. 1993).

26. Fred D'Agostino, Gerald Gaus, and John Thrasher, "Contemporary Approaches to the Social Contract," *Stanford Encyclopedia of Philosophy* (rev. 2011; orig. 1996).

27. Mills, *Racial Contract*, pp. 2–4.

28. Gordon gives an account in his book *Disciplinary Decadence: Living Thought in Trying Times* (Boulder: Paradigm, 2006), pp. 111–12, the point of which is to illustrate "Mr. X"'s (my) failure to recognize that it is through such organization and the building-up of social networks that anti-racist progress is made, rather than trying to "use the liberal discursive practice of writing texts that would stimulate white guilt or simply rely[ing] on the reasonableness of white philosophers." Maybe my confession of failure here is a vindication of his point.

29. "Symposium on Charles Mills's *The Racial Contract*" (Mechthild E. Nagel, Richard Schmitt, Naomi Zack, Charles W. Mills), in Curtis Stokes and Theresa Meléndez, eds., *Racial Liberalism and the Politics of Urban America* (East Lansing: Michigan State University Press, 2003), pp. 11–50.

30. "*The Racial Contract*: A Discussion" (Lewis R. Gordon, Anthony Bogues, Clinton Hutton, and Charles W. Mills), *Small Axe: A Journal of Criticism*, no. 4 (1998): 165–201.

31. "Dialogue: *The Racial Contract* Today" (Jack Turner, Desmond Jagmohan, Anna Marie Smith, Keisha Lindsay, and Charles W. Mills), *Politics, Groups, and Identities* 3, no. 3 (September 2015): 469–557.

32. Jorge Garcia, "The Racial Contract Hypothesis," *Philosophia Africana: Analysis of Philosophy and Issues in Africa and the Black Diaspora* 4, no. 1 (March 2001): 27–42.

33. Stephen C. Ferguson II, "Racial Contract Theory: A Critical Introduction," Ph.D. diss., University of Kansas, 2004.

34. Samuel Freeman, ed., *The Cambridge Companion to Rawls* (New York: Cambridge University Press, 2003); Jon Mandle and David A. Reidy, eds., *A Companion to Rawls* (Malden, MA: Wiley Blackwell, 2014).

35. Brooke Ackerley et al., "Symposium: John Rawls and the Study of Justice: Legacies of Inquiry," *Perspectives on Politics* 4, no. 1 (March 2006): 75–133.

36. Pateman and Mills, *Contract and Domination*. Admittedly, a symposium on this book was organized by the *Journal of Political Ideologies* 13, no. 3 (October 2008). But given Pateman's fame within political theory and her own editorial connection to the journal, I don't see this as a real counterexample to my claim.

37. For an earlier, more detailed attempt, see Charles W. Mills, "Non-Cartesian Sums: Philosophy and the African-American Experience" (1994), rpt. in Mills, *Blackness Visible: Essays on Philosophy and Race* (Ithaca, NY: Cornell University Press, 1998).

38. Joyce A. Ladner, ed., *The Death of White Sociology: Essays on Race and Culture*, with an afterword by Becky Thompson (Baltimore: Black Classic Press, 1998; orig. ed. 1973).

39. Hobbes himself, of course, does not start out from moral equality but from approximate physical and mental equality.

40. Robert E. Goodin, Philip Pettit, and Thomas Pogge, eds., *A Companion to Contemporary Political Philosophy*, 2 vols., 2nd ed. (Malden, MA: Blackwell, 2007; orig. ed. [1 vol.] 1993).

41. Charles W. Mills, "The Racial Polity," in Mills, *Blackness Visible*. It also appeared in Susan Babbitt and Sue Campbell, eds., *Philosophy and Racism* (Ithaca, NY: Cornell University Press, 1999).

42. Mills, "The Racial Polity" (in *Blackness Visible*), pp. 120, 125.

43. Philip Pettit, "Analytical Philosophy," in Goodin, Pettit, and Pogge, eds., *Companion*, vol. 1, p. 6.

44. See, for example, Prasenjit Duara, ed., *Decolonization: Perspectives from Now and Then* (New York: Routledge, 2004).

45. Pettit, "Analytical Philosophy," p. 8.

46. Pettit, "Analytical Philosophy," pp. 22–23.

47. For the fascinating story of this revealing, and now deeply embarrassing to the West, historical episode, see Marilyn Lake and Henry Reynolds, *Drawing the Global Colour Line: White Men's Countries and the International Challenge of Racial Equality* (New York: Cambridge University Press, 2008), ch. 12. The authors' (two Australian historians) title is, of course, a tribute to W. E. B. Du Bois.

48. See the following works (I chose 2005 as a cutoff point, given the 2007 publication date of the second edition of the Blackwell *Companion*): Anthony Pagden, *Lords of All the World: Ideologies of Empire in Spain, Britain, and France, c. 1500–c. 1800* (New Haven, CT: Yale University Press, 1995); James Tully, *Strange Multiplicity: Constitutionalism in an Age of Diversity* (New York: Cambridge University Press, 1995); Barbara Arneil, *John Locke and America: The Defense of English Colonialism* (New York: Oxford University Press, 1996); Uday Singh Mehta, *Liberalism and Empire: A Study in Nineteenth-Century British Liberal Thought* (Chicago: University of Chicago Press, 1999); Jennifer Pitts, *A Turn to Empire: The Rise of Imperial Liberalism in Britain and France* (Princeton, NJ: Princeton University Press, 2005); Emmanuel Chukwudi Eze, ed., *Race and the Enlightenment: A Reader* (Malden, MA: Blackwell, 1997); Andrew Valls, ed., *Race and Racism in Modern Philosophy* (Ithaca, NY: Cornell University Press, 2005); George Fredrickson, *White Supremacy: A Comparative Study in American and South African History* (New York: Oxford University Press, 1981); Matthew Frye Jacobson, *Whiteness of a Different Color: European Immigrants and the Alchemy of Race* (Cambridge, MA: Harvard University Press, 1998); Howard Winant, *The World Is a Ghetto: Race and Democracy since World War II* (New York: Basic Books, 2001); Douglas S. Massey and Nancy A. Denton, *American Apartheid: Segregation and the Making of the Underclass* (Cambridge, MA: Harvard University Press, 1993); Stephen Steinberg, *Turning Back: The Retreat from Racial Justice in American Thought and Policy* (Boston: Beacon Press, 1995); Joe Feagin, *Racist America: Roots, Current Realities and Future Reparations* (New York: Routledge, 2001); Eduardo Bonilla-Silva, *White Supremacy and Racism in the Post-Civil Rights Era* (Boulder, CO: Lynne Rienner, 2001); Michael Brown et al., *Whitewashing Race: The Myth of a Color-Blind Society* (Berkeley: University of California Press, 2005); Melvin L. Oliver and Thomas M. Shapiro, *Black Wealth/White Wealth: A New Perspective on Racial Inequality*, 10th anniversary ed. (New York: Routledge, 2006; orig. ed. 1995); Dalton Conley, *Being Black, Living in the Red: Race, Wealth, and Social Policy in America* (Berkeley: University of California Press, 1999); Thomas M. Shapiro, *The Hidden Cost of Being African American: How Wealth Perpetuates Inequality* (New York: Oxford University Press, 2004); Ira Katznelson, *When Affirmative Action Was White: An Untold History of Racial Inequality in Twentieth-Century America* (New York: W. W. Norton, 2005); Deborah E. Ward, *The White Welfare State: The Racialization of U.S. Welfare Policy* (Ann Arbor: University of Michigan Press, 2005); Desmond King, *Separate and Unequal: African Americans and the U.S. Federal Government*, rev. ed. (New York: Oxford University Press, 2007; orig. ed. 1995); Donald R. Kinder and Lynn M. Sanders, *Divided by Color: Racial Politics and Democratic Ideals* (Chicago: University of Chicago Press, 1996); Michael Goldfield, *The Color of Politics: Race and the Mainsprings of American Politics* (New York: New Press, 1997); Rogers M. Smith, *Civic Ideals: Conflicting Visions of Citizenship in U.S. History* (New Haven, CT: Yale University Press, 1997); Anthony W.

Marx, *Making Race and Nation: A Comparison of the United States, South Africa, and Brazil* (New York: Cambridge University Press, 1998); Michael C. Dawson, *Black Visions: The Roots of Contemporary African-American Political Ideologies* (Chicago: University of Chicago Press, 2001); Anthony Bogues, *Black Heretics, Black Prophets: Radical Political Intellectuals* (New York: Routledge, 2003); Linda Faye Williams, *The Constraint of Race: Legacies of White Skin Privilege in America* (University Park: Pennsylvania State University Press, 2003); Paul Keal, *European Conquest and the Rights of Indigenous Peoples: The Moral Backwardness of International Society* (New York: Cambridge University Press, 2003); Lindsay G. Robertson, *Conquest by Law: How the Discovery of America Dispossessed Indigenous Peoples of Their Rights* (New York: Oxford University Press, 2005); Antony Anghie, *Imperialism, Sovereignty and the Making of International Law* (New York: Cambridge University Press, 2005); Ian F. Haney López, *White by Law: The Legal Construction of Race,* 10th anniversary ed. (New York: New York University Press, 2006; orig. ed. 1996); A. Leon Higginbotham Jr., *In the Matter of Color: Race and the American Legal Process, I: The Colonial Period* (New York: Oxford University Press, 1978) and *Shades of Freedom: Racial Politics and Presumptions of the American Legal Process, II* (New York: Oxford University Press, 1996); Kimberlé Crenshaw, Neil Gotanda, Gary Peller, and Kendall Thomas, eds., *Critical Race Theory: The Key Writings That Formed the Movement* (New York: New Press, 1995); Adam Hochschild, *King Leopold's Ghost: A Story of Greed, Terror, and Heroism in Colonial Africa* (Boston: Houghton Mifflin, 1998).

49. Geoffrey Barraclough, "The Revolt against the West" (orig. 1967), in Duara, ed., *Decolonization,* p. 118.

EPILOGUE

1. Thanks to one of the Oxford University Press referees for suggesting this more fitting conclusion to the book.
2. Left-wing liberals will, of course, be that political constituency most sympathetic to a "black radical liberalism." But I am claiming that even centrist and right-wing liberals, if they are genuinely morally committed to racial justice, and willing to acknowledge how white supremacy has shaped modernity and the historically dominant forms of liberalism, should be open to a corrective black liberalism far more "radical" than the current mainstream variety.
3. See, for example, *Critical Philosophy of Race* 1, no. 1 (2013): Special Issue: Critical Philosophy of Race beyond the Black/White Binary.
4. Kwame Ture (Stokely Carmichael) and Charles V. Hamilton, *Black Power: The Politics of Liberation,* with new afterwords by the authors (New York: Vintage, 1992; orig. ed. 1967).
5. Cedric J. Robinson, *Black Marxism: The Making of the Black Radical Tradition,* with a new preface by the author (Chapel Hill: University of North Carolina Press, 2000; orig. ed. 1983).
6. Rogers M. Smith, *Civic Ideals: Conflicting Visions of Citizenship in U.S. History* (New Haven, CT: Yale University Press, 1997).
7. See Lucius Outlaw's classic 1990 essay "Toward a Critical Theory of 'Race,'" rpt. in Bernard Boxill, ed., *Race and Racism* (New York: Oxford University Press, 2001). Outlaw's piece may be the very first article in philosophy explicitly to call for a "critical" theorization of society that is extended to race.
8. Eric Williams, *Capitalism and Slavery,* with a new introduction (Chapel Hill: University of North Carolina Press, 1994; orig. ed. 1944); W. E. B. Du Bois, *Black Reconstruction in America, 1860–1880* (New York: Free Press, 1998; orig ed. 1935).
9. See, for example, Walter Johnson, *River of Dark Dreams: Slavery and Empire in the Cotton Kingdom* (Cambridge, MA: Belknap Press, 2013); Sven Beckert, *Empire of Cotton: A Global History* (New York: Knopf, 2014); Edward E. Baptist, *The Half Has Never Been Told: Slavery and the Making of American Capitalism* (New York: Basic Books, 2014).

10. Sven Beckert, "Slavery and Capitalism," *Chronicle of Higher Education* 61, no. 16 (December 19, 2014): Chronicle Review, Section B, pp. B6–B9.

11. Tommie Shelby, *We Who Are Dark: The Philosophical Foundations of Black Solidarity* (Cambridge, MA: Harvard University Press, 2005); Andrew Valls, "A Liberal Defense of Black Nationalism," *American Political Science Review* 104, no. 3 (August 2010): 467–81.

12. Robinson, *Black Marxism*; Lucius Outlaw, *Critical Social Theory in the Interests of Black Folks* (Lanham, MD: Rowman & Littlefield, 2005).

13. Derrick Bell, *Faces at the Bottom of the Well: The Permanence of Racism* (New York: Basic Books, 1992).

14. Thomas Piketty, *Capital in the Twenty-First Century*, trans. Arthur Goldhammer (Cambridge, MA: Belknap Press, 2014).

15. John Rawls, *A Theory of Justice*, rev. ed. (Cambridge, MA: Harvard University Press, 1999; orig. ed. 1971), p. 8

16. Robert Gooding-Williams, *In the Shadow of Du Bois: Afro-Modern Political Thought in America* (Cambridge, MA: Harvard University Press, 2009).

17. Rawls, *Theory of Justice*, p. 4.

18. Samuel Fleischacker, *A Short History of Distributive Justice* (Cambridge, MA: Harvard University Press, 2004).

19. Carole Pateman, *The Sexual Contract* (Stanford, CA: Stanford University Press, 1988); Charles W. Mills, *The Racial Contract* (Ithaca, NY: Cornell University Press, 1997).

20. Rodney C. Roberts, introduction to Roberts, ed., *Injustice and Rectification* (New York: Peter Lang, 2002).

21. Susan Moller Okin, *Justice, Gender, and the Family* (New York: Basic Books, 1989).

22. The following page overlaps with the discussion on pp. 60–61 of Charles W. Mills, "Racial Equality," in George Hull, ed., *The Equal Society: Essays on Equality in Theory and Practice* (Lanham, MD: Lexington Books/Rowman & Littlefield, 2015).

23. Rawls, *Theory of Justice*, p. 9.

24. See chs. 3 and 4 of Carole Pateman and Charles W. Mills, *Contract and Domination* (Malden, MA: Polity, 2007).

25. As detailed in ch. 7, an enduring pattern of systemic and unfair white advantage is manifest in numerous ways. Racialized concentrations of wealth and poverty tend to perpetuate themselves intergenerationally, whether through continuing discrimination and "opportunity hoarding" or even without overt discriminatory intent, for example, because of residential segregation, inferior schooling, diminished chances to accumulate social capital, exclusion from white employer networks, and so forth. For more recent work documenting these processes, see, for example, Nancy DiTomaso, *The American Non-Dilemma: Racial Inequality without Racism* (New York: Russell Sage, 2012) and Daria Roithmayr, *Reproducing Racism: How Everyday Choices Lock in White Advantage* (New York: New York University Press, 2014).

26. Lani Guinier, *The Tyranny of the Majority: Fundamental Fairness in Representative Democracy* (New York: Free Press, 1994); Ari Berman, *Give Us the Ballot: The Modern Struggle for Voting Rights in America* (New York: Farrar, Straus and Giroux, 2015).

27. Michael T. Martin and Marilyn Yaquinto, eds., *Redress for Historical Injustices in the United States: On Reparations for Slavery, Jim Crow, and Their Legacies* (Durham, NC: Duke University Press, 2007).

28. Julio Cammarota and Augustine Romero, eds., *Raza Studies: The Public Option for Educational Revolution* (Tucson: University of Arizona Press, 2014); John M. Coski, *The Confederate Battle Flag: America's Most Embattled Emblem* (Cambridge, MA: Harvard University Press, 2005); C. Richard King, ed., *The Native American Mascot Controversy: A Handbook* (Lanham, MD: Rowman & Littlefield, 2015).

REFERENCES

Abbey, Ruth, ed. 2013. *Feminist Interpretations of John Rawls*. University Park: Pennsylvania State University Press.

Ackerley, Brooke, et al. 2006. "Symposium: John Rawls and the Study of Justice: Legacies of Inquiry." *Perspectives on Politics* 4, no. 1 (March): 75–133.

Alcoff, Linda Martín. 1996. *Real Knowing: New Versions of the Coherence Theory*. Ithaca, NY: Cornell University Press.

Alcoff, Linda Martín. 2006. "On Being Mixed." In Alcoff, *Visible Identities: Race, Gender, and the Self*. New York: Oxford University Press.

Alexander, Michelle. 2010. *The New Jim Crow: Mass Incarceration in the Age of Colorblindness*. New York: New Press.

Althusser, Louis. 2010. *For Marx*. Trans. Ben Brewster. Orig. ed. 1969. New York: Verso.

Anderson, Elizabeth. 2010. *The Imperative of Integration*. Princeton, NJ: Princeton University Press.

Anghie, Antony. 2005. *Imperialism, Sovereignty and the Making of International Law*. New York: Cambridge University Press.

Appiah, Kwame Anthony. 2014. *Lines of Descent: W. E. B. Du Bois and the Emergence of Identity*. Cambridge, MA: Harvard University Press.

Aristotle. 1976. *The Ethics of Aristotle: The Nicomachean Ethics*. Trans. J. A. K. Thomson. Revised by Hugh Tredennick. New York: Penguin Classics.

Armitage, David. 2004. "John Locke, Carolina, and the *Two Treatises of Government*." *Political Theory* 32, no. 5 (October): 602–27.

Arneil, Barbara. 1996. *John Locke and America: The Defence of English Colonialism*. New York: Oxford University Press.

Babbitt, Susan, and Sue Campbell, eds. 1999. *Philosophy and Racism*. Ithaca, NY: Cornell University Press.

Baldwin, James. 1993. *Nobody Knows My Name: More Notes of a Native Son*. Orig. ed. 1961. New York: Vintage International.

Balfour, Lawrie. 2005. "Reparations after Identity Politics." *Political Theory* 33, no. 6 (December): 786–811.

Balfour, Lawrie. 2014. "Unthinking Racial Realism: A Future for Reparations?" *Du Bois Review: Social Science Research on Race* 11, no. 1 (Spring): 43–56.

Baptist, Edward E. 2014. *The Half Has Never Been Told: Slavery and the Making of American Capitalism*. New York: Basic Books.

Barraclough, Geoffrey. 2004. "The Revolt against the West." In *Decolonization: Perspectives from Now and Then*, ed. Prasenjit Duara. New York: Routledge.

Barry, Brian. 2005. *Why Social Justice Matters*. Malden, MA: Polity.

Beckert, Sven. 2014. *Empire of Cotton: A Global History*. New York: Knopf.

Beckert, Sven. 2014. "Slavery and Capitalism." *Chronicle of Higher Education* 61, no. 16 (December 19), Chronicle Review, Section B: B6–B9.

Bell, Derrick. 1989. *And We Are Not Saved: The Elusive Quest for Racial Justice.* New York: Basic Books.

Bell, Derrick. 1992. *Faces at the Bottom of the Well: The Permanence of Racism.* New York: Basic Books.

Bell, Duncan. 2014. "What Is Liberalism?" *Political Theory* 42, no. 6 (December): 682–715.

Berman, Ari. 2015. *Give Us the Ballot: The Modern Struggle for Voting Rights in America.* New York: Farrar, Straus and Giroux.

Bernasconi, Robert. 2001. "Who Invented the Concept of Race? Kant's Role in the Enlightenment Construction of Race." In *Race,* ed. Bernasconi. Malden, MA: Blackwell.

Bernasconi, Robert. 2002. "Kant as an Unfamiliar Source of Racism." In *Philosophers on Race: Critical Essays,* ed. Julie K. Ward and Tommy L. Lott. Malden, MA: Blackwell.

Bernasconi, Robert. 2011. "Kant's Third Thoughts on Race." In *Reading Kant's Geography,* ed. Stuart Elden and Eduardo Mendieta. Albany: SUNY Press.

Bernasconi, Robert, and Anika Maaza Mann. 2005. "The Contradictions of Racism: Locke, Slavery, and the *Two Treatises.*" In *Race and Racism in Modern Philosophy,* ed. Andrew Valls. Ithaca, NY: Cornell University Press.

Bird, Colin. 2006. *An Introduction to Political Philosophy.* New York: Cambridge University Press.

Blackmon, Douglas A. 2008. *Slavery by Another Name: The Re-Enslavement of Black Americans from the Civil War to World War II.* New York: Doubleday.

Blocker, H. Gene, and Elizabeth H. Smith, eds. 1980. *John Rawls's Theory of Social Justice: An Introduction.* Athens: Ohio State University Press.

Bogues, Anthony. 2003. *Black Heretics, Black Prophets: Radical Political Intellectuals.* New York: Routledge.

Bonilla-Silva, Eduardo. 2001. *White Supremacy and Racism in the Post–Civil Rights Era.* Boulder, CO: Lynne Rienner.

Bonilla-Silva, Eduardo. 2013. *Racism without Racists: Color-Blind Racism and the Persistence of Racial Inequality in the United States.* 4th ed. Orig. ed. 2003. Lanham, MD: Rowman & Littlefield.

Borstelmann, Thomas. 2001. *The Cold War and the Color Line: American Race Relations in the Global Arena.* Cambridge, MA: Harvard University Press.

Botts, Tina Fernandes, et al. 2014. "What Is the State of Blacks in Philosophy?" *Critical Philosophy of Race* 2, no. 2: 224–42.

Boxill, Bernard R. 1992. *Blacks and Social Justice.* Rev. ed. Orig. ed. 1984. Lanham, MD: Rowman & Littlefield.

Boxill, Bernard R., ed. 2001. *Race and Racism.* New York: Oxford University Press.

Brandt, Reinhard. 1991. *D'Artagnan und die Urteilstafel: Über ein Ordnungsprinzip des europäischen Kulturgeschichte.* Stuttgart: Franz Steiner.

Brennan, Samantha. 1999. "Recent Work in Feminist Ethics." *Ethics* 109, no. 4 (July): 858–93.

Brodkin, Karen. 1998. *How Jews Became White Folks and What That Says about Race in America.* New Brunswick, NJ: Rutgers University Press.

Brophy, Alfred L. 2006. *Reparations Pro & Con.* New York: Oxford University Press.

Brown, Michael K., et al. 2003. *Whitewashing Race: The Myth of a Color-Blind Society.* Berkeley: University of California Press.

Cahn, Steven M. 2012. *Classics of Political and Moral Philosophy.* 2nd ed. Orig. ed. 2002. New York: Oxford University Press.

Cahn, Steven M. 2015. *Political Philosophy: The Essential Texts.* 3rd ed. Orig. ed. 2002. New York: Oxford University Press.

Cammarota, Julio, and Augustine Romero, eds. 2014. *Raza Studies: The Public Option for Educational Revolution.* Tucson: University of Arizona Press.

Campbell, Richmond, and Bruce Hunter, eds. 2000. *Moral Epistemology Naturalized. Canadian Journal of Philosophy*, supp. vol. 26. Calgary, AB: University of Calgary Press.

Christman, John. 2009. *The Politics of Persons: Individual Autonomy and Socio-Historical Selves.* New York: Cambridge University Press.

Coady, C. A. J. 1995. *Testimony: A Philosophical Study.* Orig. ed. 1992. Oxford: Clarendon Press.

Coates, Ta-Nehisi. 2014. "The Case for Reparations." *Atlantic* 313, no. 5 (June): 54–71.

Cocker, Mark. 1998. *Rivers of Blood, Rivers of Gold: Europe's Conflict with Tribal Peoples.* London: Jonathan Cape.

Cohen, G. A. 2001. *Karl Marx's Theory of History: A Defence.* Exp. ed. Orig. ed. 1978. Princeton, NJ: Princeton University Press.

Cohen, Marshall, Thomas Nagel, and Thomas Scanlon, eds. 1980. *Marx, Justice, and History.* Princeton, NJ: Princeton University Press.

Cohen, Stanley. 2001. *States of Denial: Knowing about Atrocities and Suffering.* Malden, MA: Polity.

Conley, Dalton. 1999. *Being Black, Living in the Red: Race, Wealth, and Social Policy in America.* Berkeley: University of California Press.

Coski, John M. 2005. *The Confederate Battle Flag: America's Most Embattled Emblem.* Cambridge, MA: Harvard University Press.

Courtois, Stéphan, et al., eds. 1999. *The Black Book of Communism: Crimes, Terror, Repression.* Trans. Jonathan Murphy and Mark Kramer. Cambridge, MA: Harvard University Press.

Crenshaw, Kimberlé, Neil Gotanda, Gary Peller, and Kendall Thomas, eds. 1995. *Critical Race Theory: The Key Writings That Formed the Movement.* New York: New Press.

Critical Philosophy of Race 1, no. 1 (2013). Special Issue: Critical Philosophy of Race Beyond the Black/White Binary.

Cudd, Ann E. 2006. *Analyzing Oppression.* New York: Oxford University Press.

Cudd, Ann E. 2012. "Contractarianism." *Stanford Encyclopedia of Philosophy*, rev. 2012 (orig. 2000). Online.

Curtis, James E., and John W. Petras, eds. 1970. *The Sociology of Knowledge: A Reader.* New York: Praeger.

D'Agostino, Fred, Gerald Gaus, and John Thrasher. 2011. "Contemporary Approaches to the Social Contract." *Stanford Encyclopedia of Philosophy*, rev. 2011 (orig. 1996). Online.

Daniels, Norman. 1989. *Reading Rawls: Critical Studies in Rawls' A Theory of Justice.* With a new preface. Stanford, CA: Stanford University Press. Orig. ed. 1975.

Darby, Derrick. 2009. *Rights, Race, and Recognition.* New York: Cambridge University Press.

Davis, David Brion. 2006. *Inhuman Bondage: The Rise and Fall of Slavery in the New World.* New York: Oxford University Press.

Davis, F. James. 1991. *Who Is Black? One Nation's Definition.* University Park: Pennsylvania State University Press.

Dawson, Michael C. 2001. *Black Visions: The Roots of Contemporary African-American Political Ideologies.* Chicago: University of Chicago Press.

Dawson, Michael C., and Rovana Popoff. 2004. "Reparations: Justice and Greed in Black and White." *Du Bois Review: Social Science Research on Race* 1, no. 1 (March): 47–91.

De Greiff, Pablo. 2006. "Justice and Reparations." In *The Handbook of Reparations*, ed. De Greiff. New York: Oxford University Press.

DiTomaso, Nancy. 2012. *The American Non-Dilemma: Racial Inequality without Racism.* New York: Russell Sage.

Doane, Ashley ("Woody"). 2003. "Rethinking Whiteness Studies." In *White Out: The Continuing Significance of Racism*, ed. Ashley Doane and Eduardo Bonilla-Silva. New York: Routledge.

Domhoff, G. William. 2013. *Who Rules America: The Triumph of the Corporate Rich.* 7th ed. Orig. ed. 1967. Boston: McGraw-Hill.

Douglass, Frederick. 1996. "What to the Slave Is the Fourth July?" In *The Oxford Frederick Douglass Reader*, ed. William L. Andrews. New York: Oxford University Press.

Dower, John. 1986. *War without Mercy: Race and Power in the Pacific War*. New York: Pantheon.

Duara, Prasenjit, ed. *Decolonization: Perspectives from Now and Then* (New York: Routledge, 2004).

Du Bois, W. E. B. 1989. *The Souls of Black Folk*. Orig. ed. 1903. New York: Penguin.

Du Bois, W. E. B. 1995. "The Souls of White Folk." In *W. E. B. Du Bois: A Reader*, ed. David Levering Lewis. New York: Henry Holt.

Du Bois, W. E. B. 1998. *Black Reconstruction in America, 1860–1880*. Orig. ed. 1935. New York: Free Press.

Du Bois, W. E. B. 2007. *Dusk of Dawn: An Essay toward an Autobiography of a Race Concept*. Orig. ed. 1940. New York: Oxford University Press.

Dymski, Gary. 1997. "Racial Inequality and Capitalist Exploitation." In *Exploitation*, ed. Kai Nielsen and Robert Ware. Atlantic Highlands, NJ: Humanities Press.

Eliav-Feldon, Miriam, Benjamin Isaac, and Joseph Ziegler, eds. 2009. *The Origins of Racism in the West*. New York: Cambridge University Press.

Ellison, Ralph. 1995. *Invisible Man*. Orig. ed. 1952. New York: Vintage.

Eze, Emmanuel Chukwudi. 1997. "The Color of Reason: The Idea of 'Race' in Kant's Anthropology." In *Postcolonial African Philosophy: A Reader*, ed. Eze. Cambridge, MA: Blackwell.

Eze, Emmanuel Chukwudi, ed. 1997. *Race and the Enlightenment: A Reader*. Malden, MA: Blackwell.

Eze, Emmanuel Chukwudi. 2001. *Achieving Our Humanity: The Idea of the Postracial Future*. New York: Routledge.

Farrelly, Colin. 2007. "Justice in Ideal Theory: A Refutation." *Political Studies* 55, no. 4 (December): 844–64.

Feagin, Joe. 2001. *Racist America: Roots, Current Realities and Future Reparations*. New York: Routledge.

Ferguson, Stephen C. II. 2004. "Racial Contract Theory: A Critical Introduction." Ph.D. diss., University of Kansas.

Flax, Jane. 1995. "Race/Gender and the Ethics of Difference." *Political Theory* 23, no. 3 (August): 500–510.

Fleischacker, Samuel. 2004. *A Short History of Distributive Justice*. Cambridge, MA: Harvard University Press.

Fleischacker, Samuel. 2013. *What Is Enlightenment?* New York: Routledge.

Fordham Law Review 72, no. 5 (April 2004): Symposium: Rawls and the Law.

Fredrickson, George. 1981. *White Supremacy: A Comparative Study in American and South African History*. New York: Oxford University Press.

Fredrickson, George. 2015. *Racism: A Short History*. Orig. ed. 2002. Princeton, NJ: Princeton Classics.

Freeman, Samuel, ed. 2003. *The Cambridge Companion to Rawls*. New York: Cambridge University Press.

Freeman, Samuel. 2007. *Rawls*. New York: Routledge.

Fricker, Miranda. 2007. *Epistemic Injustice: Power and the Ethics of Knowing*. New York: Oxford University Press.

Friedman, Marilyn. 2000. "Feminism in Ethics: Conceptions of Autonomy." In *The Cambridge Companion to Feminism in Ethics*, ed. Miranda Fricker and Jennifer Hornsby. New York: Cambridge University Press.

Friend, Celeste. N.d. "Social Contract Theory." *Internet Encyclopedia of Philosophy*. Online.

Frye, Charles A., ed. 1980. *Level Three: A Black Philosophy Reader*. Lanham, MD: University Press of America.

Fuller, Steve. 2002. *Social Epistemology*. 2nd ed. Orig. ed. 1988. Bloomington: University of Indiana Press.

Garcia, Jorge. 2001. "The Racial Contract Hypothesis." *Philosophia Africana: Analysis of Philosophy and Issues in Africa and the Black Diaspora* 4, no. 1 (March): 27–42.

Gibson, Donald B. 1989. Introduction to *The Souls of Black Folk* by W. E. B. Du Bois. New York: Penguin.

Gilens, Martin. 1999. *Why Americans Hate Welfare: Race, Media, and the Politics of Antipoverty Policy*. Chicago: University of Chicago Press.

Gilligan, Carol. 1998. *In a Different Voice: Psychological Theory and Women's Development*. Orig. ed. 1982. Cambridge, MA: Harvard University Press.

Gillis, John. 1994. "Memory and Identity: The History of a Relationship." In *Commemorations*, ed. Gillis. Princeton, NJ: Princeton University Press.

Goldberg, David Theo. 2002. *The Racial State*. Malden, MA: Blackwell.

Goldfield, Michael. 1997. *The Color of Politics: Race and the Mainsprings of American Politics*. New York: New Press.

Goldman, Alvin I. 1999. *Knowledge in a Social World*. New York: Oxford University Press.

Goldman, Alvin I., and Dennis Whitcomb, eds. 2011. *Social Epistemology: Essential Readings*. New York: Oxford University Press.

Goodin, Robert E., Philip Pettit, and Thomas Pogge, eds. 2007. *A Companion to Contemporary Political Philosophy*. 2 vols. 2nd ed. Orig. ed. (1 vol.) 1993. Malden, MA: Blackwell.

Gooding-Williams, Robert. 2009. *In the Shadow of Du Bois: Afro-Modern Political Thought in America*. Cambridge, MA: Harvard University Press.

Gordon, Lewis R. 1995. *Bad Faith and Antiblack Racism*. Atlantic Highlands, NJ: Humanities Press.

Gordon, Lewis R. 2006. *Disciplinary Decadence: Living Thought in Trying Times*. Boulder, CO: Paradigm.

Gordon, Lewis R. 2008. *An Introduction to Africana Philosophy*. New York: Cambridge University Press.

Gordon, Lewis R., et al. 1998. "*The Racial Contract*: A Discussion." *Small Axe: A Journal of Criticism* no. 4: 165–201. Reprinted in Charles W. Mills, *Radical Theory, Caribbean Reality: Race, Class and Social Domination*. Mona, Kingston, Jamaica: University of the West Indies Press, 2010.

Gott, Richard. 2011. *Britain's Empire: Resistance, Repression and Revolt*. New York: Verso.

Gray, John. 1986. *Liberalism*. Minneapolis: University of Minnesota Press.

Green, T. H. 1986. *Lectures in the Principles of Political Obligation and Other Writings*, ed. Paul Harris and John Morrow. New York: Cambridge University Press.

Gross, Matthias, and Linsey McGoey, eds. 2015. *Routledge International Handbook of Ignorance Studies*. New York: Routledge.

Guinier, Lani. 1994. *The Tyranny of the Majority: Fundamental Fairness in Representative Democracy*. New York: Free Press.

Halbwachs, Maurice. 1992. *On Collective Memory*. Ed. and trans. Lewis A. Coser. Chicago: University of Chicago Press.

Hampton, Jean. 1990. "The Contractarian Explanation of the State." In *Midwest Studies in Philosophy: The Philosophy of the Human Sciences*, ed. Peter A. French, Theodore E. Uehling Jr., and Howard K. Wettstein. Notre Dame, IN: University of Notre Dame Press.

Hampton, Jean. 2001. "Feminist Contractarianism." In *A Mind of One's Own: Feminist Essays on Reason and Objectivity*, ed. Louise M. Antony and Charlotte E. Witt. 2nd ed. Orig. ed. 1993. Boulder, CO: Westview Press.

Hampton, Jean. 2007. "Contract and Consent." In *A Companion to Contemporary Political Philosophy*, ed. Robert E. Goodin, Philip Pettit, and Thomas Pogge. 2 vols. 2nd ed. Orig. ed. (1 vol.) 1993. Malden, MA: Blackwell.

Harding, Sandra, ed. 2003. *The Feminist Standpoint Theory Reader: Intellectual and Political Controversies*. New York: Routledge.

Harris, Cheryl I. 1993. "Whiteness as Property." *Harvard Law Review* 106, no. 8 (June): 1709–91.

Harris, Leonard, ed. 1983. *Philosophy Born of Struggle: Anthology of Afro-American Philosophy from 1917*. Dubuque, IA: Kendall/Hunt.

Harris, Leonard. 1995. "'Believe It or Not' or the Ku Klux Klan and American Philosophy Exposed." *American Philosophical Association Proceedings and Addresses* 68, no. 5 (May): 133–37. Reprinted in *Philosophy Born of Struggle: Anthology of Afro-American Philosophy from 1917*. 2nd ed. Orig. ed. 1983. Dubuque, IA: Kendall/Hunt.

Harris, Leonard, ed. 2000. *Philosophy Born of Struggle: Anthology of Afro-American Philosophy from 1917*. 2nd ed. Orig. ed. 1983. Dubuque, IA: Kendall/Hunt.

Harris, Leonard, and Charles Molesworth. 2008. *Alain L. Locke: The Biography of a Philosopher*. Chicago: University of Chicago Press.

Haslanger, Sally. 2012. *Resisting Reality: Social Construction and Social Critique*. New York: Oxford University Press.

Hay, Carol. 2013. *Kantianism, Liberalism, and Feminism: Resisting Oppression*. New York: Palgrave Macmillan.

Hesse, Barnor. 2007. "Racialized Modernity: An Analytics of White Mythologies." *Ethnic and Racial Studies* 30, no. 4 (July): 643–63.

Hesse, Barnor. 2014. "Escaping Liberty: Western Hegemony, Black Fugitivity." *Political Theory* 42, no. 3 (June): 288–313.

Higginbotham, A. Leon Jr. 1978. *In the Matter of Color: Race and the American Legal Process*, Vol. I: *The Colonial Period*. New York: Oxford University Press.

Higginbotham, A. Leon Jr. 1996. *Shades of Freedom: Racial Politics and the Presumptions of the American Legal Process*, Vol. II. New York: Oxford University Press.

Hill, Thomas E. Jr., and Bernard Boxill. 2001. "Kant and Race." In *Race and Racism*, ed. Bernard Boxill. New York: Oxford University Press.

Hirsch, James S. 2002. *Riot and Remembrance: The Tulsa Race War and Its Legacy*. New York: Houghton Mifflin.

Hobbes, Thomas. 1996. *Leviathan*. Ed. Richard Tuck. Rev. student ed. Orig. ed. 1991. New York: Cambridge University Press.

Hobson, John M. 2012. *The Eurocentric Conception of World Politics: Western International Theory, 1760–2010*. New York: Cambridge University Press.

Hochschild, Adam. 1998. *King Leopold's Ghost: A Story of Greed, Terror and Heroism in Colonial Africa*. New York: Houghton Mifflin.

Hochschild, Jennifer L. 1984. *The New American Dilemma: Liberal Democracy and School Desegregation*. New Haven, CT: Yale University Press.

Hodgson, Marshall G. S. 1993. *Rethinking World History: Essays on Europe, Islam, and World History*, ed. Edmund Burke III. New York: Cambridge University Press.

Hooker, Brad, and Margaret Olivia Little, eds. 2000. *Moral Particularism*. Oxford: Clarendon Press.

Horton, Carol. A. 2005. *Race and the Making of American Liberalism*. New York: Oxford University Press.

Hume, David. 1960. "Of the Original Contract." In *Social Contract: Essays by Locke, Hume, and Rousseau*, ed. Sir Ernest Barker. Orig. ed. 1947. London: Oxford University Press.

Ignatiev, Noel. 2008. *How the Irish Became White*. Orig. ed. 1995. New York: Routledge.

Isaac, Benjamin. 2004. *The Invention of Racism in Classical Antiquity*. Princeton, NJ: Princeton University Press.

Jacobson, Matthew Frye. 1998. *Whiteness of a Different Color: European Immigrants and the Alchemy of Race*. Cambridge, MA: Harvard University Press.

Jaggar, Alison. 1983. *Feminist Politics and Human Nature*. Totowa, NJ: Rowman & Allanheld.

Jaggar, Alison. 2000. "Ethics Naturalized: Feminism's Contribution to Moral Epistemology." *Metaphilosophy* 31, no. 5 (October): 452–68.

Jennings, Francis. 1976. *The Invasion of America: Indians, Colonialism, and the Cant of Conquest.* Orig. ed. 1975. New York: W. W. Norton.

Jeske, Diane, and Richard Fumerton, eds. 2012. *Readings in Political Philosophy: Theory and Applications.* Peterborough, ON: Broadview.

Johnson, Walter. 2013. *River of Dark Dreams: Slavery and Empire in the Cotton Kingdom.* Cambridge, MA: Belknap Press.

Johnston, Percy Edward, ed. 1970. *Afro American Philosophies: Selected Readings, from Jupiter Hammon to Eugene C. Holmes.* Upper Montclair, NJ: Montclair State College Press.

Jones, Hardy. 1980. "A Rawlsian Discussion of Discrimination." In *John Rawls's Theory of Social Justice: An Introduction,* ed. H. Gene Blocker and Elizabeth H. Smith. Athens: Ohio State University Press.

Kant, Immanuel. 1960. *Observations on the Feeling of the Beautiful and Sublime.* Trans. John T. Goldthwait. Berkeley: University of California Press.

Kant, Immanuel. 1991. *The Metaphysics of Morals.* Trans. Mary Gregor. New York: Cambridge University Press.

Kant, Immanuel. 1991. "Perpetual Peace: A Philosophical Sketch." In *Kant: Political Writings,* ed. Hans Reiss, trans. H. B. Nisbet. 2nd ed. Orig. ed. 1970. New York: Cambridge University Press.

Kant, Immanuel. 1996. *Practical Philosophy.* Trans. and ed. Mary J. Gregor. New York: Cambridge University Press.

Katznelson, Ira. 2005. *When Affirmative Action Was White: An Untold History of Racial Inequality in Twentieth-Century America.* New York: W. W. Norton.

Keal, Paul. 2003. *European Conquest and the Rights of Indigenous Peoples: The Moral Backwardness of International Society.* New York: Cambridge University Press.

Kinder, Donald R., and Lynn M. Sanders. 1996. *Divided by Color: Racial Politics and Democratic Ideals.* Chicago: University of Chicago Press.

King, C. Richard, ed. 2015. *The Native American Mascot Controversy: A Handbook.* Lanham, MD: Rowman & Littlefield.

King, Desmond. 2007. *Separate and Unequal: African Americans and the U.S. Federal Government.* Rev. ed. Orig. ed. 1995. New York: Oxford University Press.

King, Desmond, and Rogers M. Smith. 2005. "Racial Orders in American Political Development." *American Political Science Review* 99, no. 1 (February): 75–92.

King, Desmond, and Rogers M. Smith. 2011. *Still a House Divided: Race and Politics in Obama's America.* Princeton, NJ: Princeton University Press.

Kitcher, Philip. 1994. "Contrasting Conceptions of Social Epistemology." In *Socializing Epistemology: The Social Dimensions of Knowledge,* ed. Frederick F. Schmitt. Lanham, MD: Rowman & Littlefield.

Klein, Naomi. 2014. *This Changes Everything: Capitalism vs. the Climate.* New York: Simon & Schuster.

Kleingeld, Pauline. 1993. "The Problematic Status of Gender-Neutral Language in the History of Philosophy: The Case of Kant." *Philosophical Forum* 25, no. 2 (June): 134–50.

Kleingeld, Pauline. 2007. "Kant's Second Thoughts on Race." *Philosophical Quarterly* 57, no. 229 (October): 573–92.

Klinkner, Philip A., and Rogers M. Smith. 1999. *The Unsteady March: The Rise and Decline of Racial Equality in America.* Chicago: University of Chicago Press.

Konkle, Maureen. 2004. *Writing Indian Nations: Native Intellectuals and the Politics of Historiography, 1827–1863.* Chapel Hill: University of North Carolina Press.

Kornblith, Hilary. 1994. "A Conservative Approach to Social Epistemology." In *Socializing Epistemology: The Social Dimensions of Knowledge,* ed. Frederick F. Schmitt. Lanham, MD: Rowman & Littlefield.

Kornblith, Hilary, ed. 1994. *Naturalizing Epistemology*. 2nd ed. Orig. ed. 1985. Cambridge, MA: MIT Press.

Kornbluh, Felicia Ann. 2007. *The Battle for Welfare Rights: Politics and Poverty in Modern America*. University Park: Pennsylvania State University Press.

Kozol, Jonathan. 2005. *The Shame of the Nation: The Restoration of Apartheid Schooling in America*. New York: Crown.

Kymlicka, Will. 2001. *Contemporary Political Philosophy: An Introduction*. 2nd ed. Orig. ed. 1990. New York: Oxford University Press.

Ladner, Joyce, ed. 1998. *The Death of White Sociology: Essays on Race and Culture*. With an afterword by Becky Thompson. Orig. ed. 1973. Baltimore: Black Classic Press.

Lake, Marilyn, and Henry Reynolds. 2008. *Drawing the Global Colour Line: White Men's Countries and the International Challenge of Racial Equality*. New York: Cambridge University Press.

Larrimore, Mark. 1999. "Sublime Waste: Kant on the Destiny of the 'Races.'" In *Civilization and Oppression: Canadian Journal of Philosophy*, Supp. Vol. 25, ed. Catherine Wilson. Calgary, AB: University of Calgary Press.

Lebron, Christopher J. 2013. *The Color of Our Shame: Race and Justice in Our Time*. New York: Oxford University Press.

Lehning, Percy B. 2009. *John Rawls: An Introduction*. New York: Cambridge University Press.

Lewis, Bernard. 1990. *Race and Slavery in the Middle East: An Historical Enquiry*. New York: Oxford University Press.

Lewis, David Levering, ed. 1995. *W. E. B. Du Bois: A Reader*. New York: Henry Holt.

Lipsitz, George. 1998. *The Possessive Investment in Whiteness: How White People Profit from Identity Politics*. Philadelphia: Temple University Press.

Litwack, Leon F. 1998. *Trouble in Mind: Black Southerners in the Age of Jim Crow*. New York: Knopf.

Loewen, James W. 1996. *Lies My Teacher Told Me: Everything Your American History Textbook Got Wrong*. Orig. ed. 1995. New York: Touchstone/Simon & Schuster.

López, Ian F. Haney. 2006. *White by Law: The Legal Construction of Race*. Rev. 10th anniversary ed. Orig. ed. 1996. New York: New York University Press.

Losurdo, Domenico. 2011. *Liberalism: A Counter-History*. Trans. Gregory Elliott. New York: Verso.

Louden, Robert B. 2000. *Kant's Impure Ethics: From Rational Beings to Human Beings*. New York: Oxford University Press.

Lovett, Frank. 2011. *Rawls's A Theory of Justice*. New York: Continuum.

Lui, Meizhu et al. 2006. *The Color of Wealth: The Story behind the U.S. Racial Wealth Divide*. New York: New Press.

Lukes, Steven. 1985. *Marxism and Morality*. New York: Oxford University Press.

Lyman, Stanford M. 1993. "Race Relations as Social Process: Sociology's Resistance to a Civil Rights Orientation." In *Race in America*, ed. Herbert Hill and James E. Jones. Madison: University of Wisconsin Press.

MacKenzie, Catriona, and Natalie Stoljar, eds. 2000. *Relational Autonomy: Feminist Perspectives on Autonomy, Agency, and the Self*. New York: Oxford University Press.

MacKinnon, Catharine A. 1989. *Toward a Feminist Theory of the State*. Cambridge, MA: Harvard University Press.

Macpherson, C. B. 2011. *The Political Theory of Possessive Individualism: Hobbes to Locke*. With a new introduction. Orig. ed. 1962. New York: Oxford University Press.

Macpherson, C. B. 2014. *Democratic Theory: Essays in Retrieval*. With a new introduction. Orig. ed. 1973. New York: Oxford University Press.

Maffettone, Sebastian. 2010. *Rawls: An Introduction*. Malden, MA: Polity.

Malter, Rudolf. 1990. "Der Rassebegriff in Kants Anthropologie." In *Die Natur des Menschen: Probleme der Physischen Anthropologie und Rassenkunde (1750-1850)*, ed. Gunter Mann and Franz Dumont. Stuttgart: Gustav Fischer Verlag.

Mandle, Jon. 2009. *Rawls's A Theory of Justice: An Introduction*. New York: Cambridge University Press.

Mandle, Jon, and David A. Reidy, eds. 2014. *A Companion to Rawls*. Malden, MA: Wiley Blackwell.

Marable, Manning. 2011. *Malcolm X: A Life of Reinvention*. New York: Viking Penguin.

Martin, Michael, and Marilyn Yaquinto, eds. 2007. *Redress for Historical Injustices in the United States: On Reparations for Slavery, Jim Crow, and Their Legacies*. Durham, NC: Duke University Press.

Marx, Anthony. 1998. *Making Race and Nation: A Comparison of the United States, South Africa, and Brazil*. New York: Cambridge University Press.

Marx, Karl. 1976. *Capital*, vol. I. Trans. Ben Fowkes. Harmondsworth, Middlesex: Penguin and New Left Review.

Marx, Karl. 2000. "Grundrisse." Excerpted in *Karl Marx: Selected Writings*, ed. David McLellan. 2nd ed. Orig. ed. 1977. New York: Oxford University Press.

Marx, Karl. 2000. "On the Jewish Question." In *Karl Marx: Selected Writings*, ed. McLellan. 2nd ed. Orig. ed. 1977. New York: Oxford University Press.

Marx, Karl, and Frederick Engels. 1976. *The German Ideology: Collected Works*, vol. 5. New York: International Publishers.

Massey, Douglas S. 2007. *Categorically Unequal: The American Stratification System*. New York: Sage.

Massey, Douglas S., and Nancy A. Denton. 1993. *American Apartheid: Segregation and the Making of the Underclass*. Cambridge, MA: Harvard University Press.

McCarthy, Thomas. 2002. "*Vergangenheitsbewältigung* in the USA: On the Politics of the Memory of Slavery," Part I. *Political Theory* 30, no. 5 (October): 623–48.

McCarthy, Thomas. 2004. "Coming to Terms with Our Past: On the Morality and Politics of Reparations for Slavery," Part II. *Political Theory* 32, no. 6 (December): 750–72.

McCarthy, Thomas. 2009. *Race, Empire, and the Idea of Human Development*. New York: Cambridge University Press.

McDade, Jesse, and Carl Lesnor, eds. 1977–78. *The Philosophical Forum*, Special Double Issue: "Philosophy and the Black Experience" 9, nos. 2–3 (Winter–Spring).

McGary, Howard. 1999. *Race and Social Justice*. Malden, MA: Blackwell.

McGoey, Linsey, ed. 2014. *An Introduction to the Sociology of Ignorance: Essays on the Limits of Knowing*. New York: Routledge.

McLaughlin, Brian P., and Amelie Oksenberg Rorty, eds. 1988. *Perspectives on Self-Deception*. Berkeley: University of California Press.

Medina, José. 2013. *The Epistemology of Resistance: Gender and Racial Oppression, Epistemic Injustice, and Resistant Imaginations*. New York: Oxford University Press.

Mehta, Uday Singh. 1999. *Liberalism and Empire: A Study in Nineteenth-Century British Liberal Thought*. Chicago: University of Chicago Press.

Mele, Alfred R. 2001. *Self-Deception Unmasked*. Princeton, NJ: Princeton University Press.

Melville, Herman. 1986. "Benito Cereno." In Melville, *Billy Budd, Sailor, and Other Stories*. New York: Viking Penguin.

Melville, Herman. 2000. *Moby-Dick, or, The Whale*. New York: Modern Library.

Mills, Charles W. 1997. *The Racial Contract*. Ithaca, NY: Cornell University Press.

Mills, Charles W. 1998. "Alternative Epistemologies." In Mills, *Blackness Visible: Essays on Philosophy and Race*. Ithaca, NY: Cornell University Press.

Mills, Charles W. 1998. "Non-Cartesian *Sums*: Philosophy and the African-American Experience." In Mills, *Blackness Visible: Essays on Philosophy and Race*. Ithaca, NY: Cornell University Press.

Mills, Charles W. 1998. "The Racial Polity." In Mills, *Blackness Visible: Essays on Philosophy and Race*. Ithaca, NY: Cornell University Press.

Mills, Charles W. 2003. *From Class to Race: Essays in White Marxism and Black Radicalism*. Lanham, MD: Rowman & Littlefield.

Mills, Charles W. 2003. "White Supremacy and Racial Justice." In Mills, *From Class to Race: Essays in White Marxism and Black Radicalism*. Lanham, MD: Rowman & Littlefield.

Mills, Charles W. 2003. "White Supremacy as Sociopolitical System." In Mills, *From Class to Race: Essays in White Marxism and Black Radicalism*. Lanham, MD: Rowman & Littlefield.

Mills, Charles W. 2004. "Racial Exploitation and the Wages of Whiteness." In *The Changing Terrain of Race and Ethnicity*, ed. Maria Krysan and Amanda E. Lewis. New York: Russell Sage. Reprinted as ch. 7 of this book.

Mills, Charles W. 2005. "'Ideal Theory' as Ideology." *Hypatia: A Journal of Feminist Philosophy* 20, no. 3 (August): 165–84. Reprinted as ch. 5 of this book.

Mills, Charles W. 2005. "Kant's *Untermenschen*." In *Race and Racism in Modern Philosophy*, ed. Andrew Valls. Ithaca, NY: Cornell University Press. Reprinted as ch. 6 of this book.

Mills, Charles W. 2008. "Racial Liberalism." *PMLA (Publications of the Modern Language Association of America)* 123, no. 5 (October): 1380–97. Reprinted as ch. 3 of this book.

Mills, Charles W. 2010. "Red Shift: Politically Embodied/Embodied Politics." In Mills, *Radical Theory, Caribbean Reality: Race, Class and Social Domination*. Mona, Kingston, Jamaica: University of the West Indies Press.

Mills, Charles W. 2014. "Kant and Race, Redux." *Graduate Faculty Philosophy Journal*, "Philosophy and Race," 35, nos. 1–2: 125–57.

Mills, Charles W. 2015. "Global White Ignorance." In *Routledge International Handbook of Ignorance Studies*, ed. Mathias Gross and Linsey McGoey. New York: Routledge.

Mills, Charles W. 2015. "Racial Equality." In *The Equal Society: Essays on Equality in Theory and Practice*, ed. George Hull. Lanham, MD: Lexington Books/Rowman & Littlefield.

Montagu, M. F. Ashley. 1997. *Man's Most Dangerous Myth: The Fallacy of Race*. 7th ed., abridged for students. Orig. ed. 1942. Walnut Creek, CA: AltaMira Press.

Moody-Adams, Michele M. 1992–93. "Race, Class, and the Social Construction of Self-Respect." *Philosophical Forum*, Special Triple Issue: "African-American Perspectives and Philosophical Traditions," ed. John Pittman, 24, nos. 1–3 (Fall–Spring): 251–66.

Morris, Aldon D. 2015. *The Scholar Denied: W. E. B. Du Bois and the Birth of Modern Sociology*. Oakland: University of California Press.

Moses, A. Dirk, ed. 2008. *Empire, Colony, Genocide: Conquest, Occupation, and Subaltern Resistance in World History*. New York: Bergahn.

Muthu, Sankar. 2003. *Enlightenment against Empire*. Princeton, NJ: Princeton University Press.

Nagel, Mechthild E., et al. 2003. "Symposium on Charles Mills's *The Racial Contract*." In *Racial Liberalism and the Politics of Urban America*, ed. Curtis Stokes and Theresa Meléndez. East Lansing: Michigan State University Press.

Nagel, Thomas. 2003. "John Rawls and Affirmative Action." *Journal of Blacks in Higher Education* 39 (Spring): 82–84.

Nagel, Thomas. 2003. "Rawls and Liberalism." In *The Cambridge Companion to Rawls*, ed. Samuel Freeman. New York: Cambridge University Press.

New York Times. June 29, 2007. "Justices, 5-4, Limit Use of Race for School Integration Plans": A1.

Noddings, Nel. 2003. *Caring: A Feminine Approach to Ethics and Moral Education*. 2nd ed. Orig. ed. 1984. Berkeley: University of California Press.

Nozick, Robert. 2013. *Anarchy, State, and Utopia*. With a new foreword. Orig. ed. 1974. New York: Basic Books.

Okin, Susan Moller. 1989. *Justice, Gender, and the Family*. New York: Basic Books.

Okin, Susan Moller. 1994. "Gender Inequality and Cultural Difference." *Political Theory* 22, no. 1 (February): 5–24.

Okin, Susan Moller. 1995. "A Response to Jane Flax." *Political Theory* 23, no. 3 (August): 511–16.

Oliver, Melvin L., and Thomas M. Shapiro. 2006. *Black Wealth/White Wealth: A New Perspective on Racial Inequality*. 10th anniversary ed. Orig. ed. 1995. New York: Routledge.

O'Neill, Onora. 1987. "Abstraction, Idealization and Ideology in Ethics." In *Moral Philosophy and Contemporary Problems*, ed. J. D. G. Evans. Cambridge: Cambridge University Press.

O'Neill, Onora. 1993. "Justice, Gender, and International Relations." In *The Quality of Life*, ed. Martha C. Nussbaum and Amartya Sen. Oxford: Clarendon Press.

Orfield, Gary, and Susan E. Eaton. 1997. *Dismantling Desegregation: The Quiet Reversal of Brown v. Board of Education*. New York: New Press.

Outlaw, Lucius T. Jr. 2001. "Toward a Critical Theory of 'Race.'" In *Race and Racism*, ed. Bernard Boxill. New York: Oxford University Press.

Outlaw, Lucius T. Jr. 2005. *Critical Social Theory in the Interests of Black Folks*. Lanham, MD: Rowman & Littlefield.

Outlaw, Lucius T. Jr. 2007. "What Is Africana Philosophy?" In *Philosophy in Multiple Voices*, ed. George Yancy. Lanham, MD: Rowman & Littlefield.

Pagden, Anthony. 1995. *Lords of All the World: Ideologies of Empire in Spain, Britain, and France, c. 1500–c. 1800*. New Haven, CT: Yale University Press.

Painter, Nell Irvin. 2010. *The History of White People*. New York: W. W. Norton.

Pateman, Carole. 1988. *The Sexual Contract*. Stanford, CA: Stanford University Press.

Pateman, Carole, and Charles W. Mills. 2007. *Contract and Domination*. Malden, MA: Polity.

Peffer, R. G. 1990. *Marxism, Morality, and Social Justice*. Princeton, NJ: Princeton University Press.

Pettit, Philip. 2007. "Analytical Philosophy." In *A Companion to Contemporary Political Philosophy*, ed. Robert E. Goodin, Philip Pettit, and Thomas Pogge. 2 vols. 2nd ed. Orig. ed. (1 vol.) 1993. Malden, MA: Blackwell.

Piketty, Thomas. 2014. *Capital in the Twenty-First Century*. Trans. Arthur Goldhammer. Cambridge, MA: Belknap Press.

Pittman, John, ed. 1992–93. *The Philosophical Forum*, Special Triple Issue: "African-American Perspectives and Philosophical Traditions" 24, nos. 1–3 (Fall–Spring).

Pittman, John, ed. 1996. *African-American Perspectives and Philosophical Traditions*. New York: Routledge.

Pitts, Jennifer. 2005. *A Turn to Empire: The Rise of Imperial Liberalism in Britain and France*. Princeton, NJ: Princeton University Press.

Pogge, Thomas W. 1989. *Realizing Rawls*. Ithaca, NY: Cornell University Press.

Quine, W. V. O. 1969. "Epistemology Naturalized." In Quine, *Ontological Relativity and Other Essays*. New York: Columbia University Press.

Rawls, John. 1993. *Political Liberalism*. New York: Columbia University Press.

Rawls, John. 1996. *Political Liberalism*. Exp. ed. Orig. ed. 1993. New York: Columbia University Press.

Rawls, John. 1999. *Collected Papers*. Ed. Samuel Freeman. Cambridge, MA: Harvard University Press.

Rawls, John. 1999. *The Law of Peoples, with "The Idea of Public Reason Revisited."* Cambridge, MA: Harvard University Press.

Rawls, John. 1999. *A Theory of Justice*. Rev. ed. Orig. ed. 1971. Cambridge, MA: Harvard University Press.

Rawls, John. 2000. *Lectures on the History of Moral Philosophy*. Ed. Barbara Herman. Cambridge, MA: Harvard University Press.

Rawls, John. 2001. *Justice as Fairness: A Restatement*. Ed. Erin Kelly. Cambridge, MA: Harvard University Press.

Rawls, John. 2007. *Lectures on the History of Political Philosophy*. Ed. Samuel Freeman. Cambridge, MA: Harvard University Press.

Richardson, Henry S. N.d. "John Rawls." *Internet Encyclopedia of Philosophy*. Online.

Richardson, Henry, and Paul Weithman, eds. 1999. *The Philosophy of Rawls: A Collection of Essays*. 5 vols. New York: Garland.

Roberts, Rodney C., ed. 2002. *Injustice and Rectification*. New York: Peter Lang.

Robertson, Lindsay G. 2005. *Conquest by Law: How the Discovery of America Dispossessed Indigenous Peoples of Their Lands*. New York: Oxford University Press.

Robeyns, Ingrid, and Adam Swift, eds. 2008. *Social Theory and Practice*, Special Issue: "Social Justice: Ideal Theory, Nonideal Circumstances" 34, no. 3 (July).

Robinson, Cedric J. 2000. *Black Marxism: The Making of the Black Radical Tradition*. Orig. ed. 1983. Chapel Hill: University of North Carolina Press.

Robinson, Randall. 2000. *The Debt: What America Owes to Blacks*. New York: Dutton.

Roediger, David. R., ed. 1998. *Black on White: Black Writers on What It Means to Be White*. New York: Schocken.

Roediger, David R. 2007. *The Wages of Whiteness: Race and the Making of the American Working Class*. Rev. and exp. ed. Orig. ed. 1991. New York: Verso.

Roemer, John E. 1982. *A General Theory of Exploitation and Class*. Cambridge, MA: Harvard University Press.

Roemer, John E. 1994. *A Future for Socialism*. Cambridge, MA: Harvard University Press.

Roemer, John E., ed. 1996. *Equal Shares: Making Market Socialism Work*. New York: Verso.

Rogers, J. A. 1985. *100 Amazing Facts about the Negro with Complete Proof: A Short Cut to the World History of the Negro*. Orig. ed. 1952. St. Petersburg, FL: Helga M. Rogers.

Roithmayr, Daria. 2014. *Reproducing Racism: How Everyday Choices Lock in White Advantage*. New York: New York University Press.

Rousseau, Jean-Jacques. 1997. *The Discourses and Other Early Political Writings*. Ed. and trans. Victor Gourevitch. New York: Cambridge University Press.

Rousseau, Jean-Jacques. 1997. *The Social Contract and Other Later Political Writings*. Ed. and trans. Victor Gourevitch. New York: Cambridge University Press.

Sala-Molins, Louis. 2006. *Dark Side of the Light: Slavery and the French Enlightenment*. Trans. John Conteh-Morgan. Minneapolis: University of Minnesota Press.

Sample, Ruth. 2003. *Exploitation: What It Is and Why It's Wrong*. Lanham, MD: Rowman & Littlefield.

Sandel, Michael J. 1998. *Liberalism and the Limits of Justice*. 2nd ed. Orig. ed. 1982. New York: Cambridge University Press.

Savage, Kirk. 1994. "The Politics of Memory: Black Emancipation and the Civil War Monument." In *Commemorations: The Politics of National Identity*, ed. John Gillis. Princeton, NJ: Princeton University Press.

Saxton, Alexander. 2003. *The Rise and Fall of the White Republic: Class Politics and Mass Culture in Nineteenth Century America*. Orig. ed. 1990. New York: Verso.

Schmidtz, David. 2011. "The Right to Distribute." In *The Cambridge Companion to Nozick's Anarchy, State, and Utopia*, ed. Ralf M. Bader and John Meadowcroft. New York: Cambridge University Press.

Schmitt, Frederick F., ed. 1994. *Socializing Epistemology: The Social Dimensions of Knowledge*. Lanham, MD: Rowman & Littlefield.

Schröder, Hannelore. 1997. "Kant's Patriarchal Order." Trans. Rita Gircour. In *Feminist Interpretations of Immanuel Kant*, ed. Robin May Schott. University Park: Pennsylvania State University Press.

Schwartzman, Lisa H. 2006. *Challenging Liberalism: Feminism as Political Critique*. University Park: Pennsylvania State University Press.

Schweickart, David. 2011. *After Capitalism*. 2nd ed. Orig. ed. 2002. Lanham, MD: Rowman & Littlefield.

Sears, David O., Jim Sidanius, and Lawrence Bobo, eds. 2000. *Racialized Politics: The Debate about Racism in America*. Chicago: University of Chicago Press.

Sen, Amartya. 2009. *The Idea of Justice*. Cambridge, MA: Harvard University Press.

Sentencing Project, The. 2013. "Report of the Sentencing Project to the United Nations Human Rights Committee Regarding Racial Disparities in the United States Criminal Justice System." National Criminal Justice Reference Service, NCJ 245032. Online PDF uploaded August 2013.

Serequeberhan, Tsenay. 1997. "The Critique of Eurocentrism and the Practice of African Philosophy." In *Postcolonial African Philosophy: A Reader*, ed. Emmanuel Chukwudi Eze. Cambridge, MA: Blackwell.

Shabani, Omid Payrow, and Monique Deveaux, eds. 2014. *Introduction to Social and Political Philosophy: Texts and Cases*. Don Mills, ON: Oxford University Press Canada.

Shapiro, Thomas M. 2004. *The Hidden Cost of Being African American: How Wealth Perpetuates Inequality*. New York: Oxford University Press.

Shelby, Tommie. 2003. "Ideology, Racism, and Critical Social Theory." *Philosophical Forum* 34, no. 2 (June): 153–88.

Shelby, Tommie. 2004. "Race and Social Justice: Rawlsian Considerations." *Fordham Law Review* 72, no. 5 (April): 1697–1714.

Shelby, Tommie. 2005. *We Who Are Dark: Philosophical Foundations of Black Solidarity*. Cambridge, MA: Harvard University Press.

Shelby, Tommie. 2007. "Justice, Deviance, and the Dark Ghetto." *Philosophy and Public Affairs* 35, no. 2 (Spring): 126–60.

Shelby, Tommie. 2013. "Racial Realities and Corrective Justice: A Reply to Charles Mills." *Critical Philosophy of Race* 1, no. 2: 145–62.

Shiffrin, Seana Valentine. 2004. "Race, Labor, and the Fair Equality of Opportunity Principle." *Fordham Law Review* 72, no. 5 (April): 1643–75.

Shklar, Judith N. 1991. *American Citizenship: The Quest for Inclusion*. Cambridge, MA: Harvard University Press.

Simmons, A. John. 2007. *Political Philosophy*. New York: Oxford University Press.

Simmons, A. John. 2010. "Ideal and Nonideal Theory." *Philosophy and Public Affairs* 38, no. 1 (Winter): 5–36.

Smith, Andre L. 2015. *Tax Law and Racial Economic Justice: Black Tax*. Lanham, MD: Lexington Books/Rowman & Littlefield.

Smith, Rogers M. 1997. *Civic Ideals: Conflicting Visions of Citizenship in U.S. History*. New Haven, CT: Yale University Press.

Stannard, David E. 1992. *American Holocaust: Columbus and the Conquest of the New World*. New York: Oxford University Press.

Steinberg, Stephen. 1995. *Turning Back: The Retreat from Racial Justice in American Thought and Policy*. Boston: Beacon Press.

Stokes, Curtis, and Theresa Meléndez, eds. 2003. *Racial Liberalism and the Politics of Urban America*. East Lansing: Michigan State University Press.

Sullivan, Laura, et al. (Institute for Assets and Social Policy [IASP], Brandeis University) and Amy Traub et al. (DEMOS). 2015. "The Racial Wealth Gap: Why Policy Matters." Online PDF uploaded March 10, 2015.

Sundquist, Eric J. 1993. *To Wake the Nations: Race in the Making of American Literature*. Cambridge, MA: Belknap Press.

Taylor, Robert. 2009. "Rawlsian Affirmative Action." *Ethics* 119, no. 3 (April): 476–506.

Thomas, Laurence. 1999. "Rawlsian Self-Respect and the Black Consciousness Movement." In *The Philosophy of Rawls: A Collection of Essays,* ed. Henry Richardson and Paul Weithman. 5 vols. New York: Garland.

Thompson, E. P. 1978. *The Poverty of Theory and Other Essays.* New York: Monthly Review Press.

Tong, Rosemarie Putnam. 2013. *Feminist Thought: A More Comprehensive Introduction.* 4th ed. Orig. ed. 1989. Boulder, CO: Westview Press.

Tuana, Nancy, and Shannon Sullivan, eds. 2006. *Hypatia: A Journal of Feminist Philosophy,* Special Issue: "Feminist Epistemologies of Ignorance" 21, no. 3 (August).

Tully, James. 1993. *An Approach to Political Philosophy: Locke in Contexts.* New York: Cambridge University Press.

Tully, James. 1995. *Strange Multiplicity: Constitutionalism in an Age of Diversity.* New York: Cambridge University Press.

Ture, Kwame (Stokely Carmichael), and Charles V. Hamilton. 1992. *Black Power: The Politics of Liberation.* With new afterwords by the authors. Orig. ed. 1967. New York: Vintage.

Turner, Jack, et al. 2015. "Dialogue: The Racial Contract Today." *Politics, Groups, and Identities* 3, no. 3 (September): 469–557.

Valelly, Richard M. 2004. *The Two Reconstructions: The Struggle for Black Enfranchisement.* Chicago: University of Chicago Press.

Valentini, Laura. 2012. "Ideal vs. Non-Ideal Theory: A Conceptual Map." *Philosophy Compass* 7, no. 9 (September): 654–64.

Valls, Andrew. 1999. "The Libertarian Case for Affirmative Action." *Social Theory and Practice* 25, no. 2 (Summer): 299–323.

Valls, Andrew, ed. 2005. *Race and Racism in Modern Philosophy.* Ithaca, NY: Cornell University Press.

Valls, Andrew. 2010. "A Liberal Defense of Black Nationalism." *American Political Science Review* 104, no. 3 (August): 467–81.

Veltman, Andrea, ed. 2008. *Social and Political Philosophy: Classic and Contemporary Readings.* Don Mills, ON: Oxford University Press Canada.

Voice, Paul. 2011. *Rawls Explained: From Fairness to Utopia.* Chicago: Open Court.

Ward, Deborah E. 2005. *The White Welfare State: The Racialization of U.S. Welfare Policy.* Ann Arbor: University of Michigan Press.

Weinar, Leif. 2012. "John Rawls." *Stanford Encyclopedia of Philosophy,* rev. 2012 (orig. 2008). Online.

Wertheimer, Alan. 1996. *Exploitation.* Princeton, NJ: Princeton University Press.

West, Cornel. 2001. *Race Matters.* With a new preface by the author. Orig. ed. 1993. Boston: Beacon Press.

West, Cornel. 2002. *Prophesy Deliverance! An Afro-American Revolutionary Christianity.* 20th anniversary ed., with a new preface by the author. Orig. ed. 1982. Philadelphia: Westminster John Knox Press.

Williams, Eric. 1994. *Capitalism and Slavery.* With a new introduction. Orig. ed. 1944. Chapel Hill: University of North Carolina Press.

Williams, Linda Faye. 2003. *The Constraint of Race: Legacies of White Skin Privilege in America.* University Park: Pennsylvania State University Press.

Wilson, Francille Rusan. 2006. *The Segregated Scholars: Black Social Scientists and the Creation of Black Labor Studies, 1890–1950.* Charlottesville: University of Virginia Press.

Winant, Howard. 2001. *The World Is a Ghetto: Race and Democracy since World War II.* New York: Basic Books.

Wolff, Jonathan. 2006. *An Introduction to Political Philosophy.* Rev. ed. Orig. ed. 1996. New York: Oxford University Press.

Wood, Allen W. 1996. "General Introduction." In *Immanuel Kant: Practical Philosophy.* Trans. and ed. Mary J. Gregor. Cambridge: Cambridge University Press.

Wood, Allen W. 1999. *Kant's Ethical Thought*. New York: Cambridge University Press.

Yancy, George, ed. 1998. *African-American Philosophers: 17 Conversations*. New York: Routledge.

Yancy, George, ed. 2008. "Situated Voices: Black Women in/on the Profession of Philosophy." *Hypatia: A Journal of Feminist Philosophy* 23, no. 2 (May): 155–89.

Zwolinski, Matt, ed. 2014. *Arguing about Political Philosophy*. 2nd ed. Orig. ed. 2009. New York: Routledge.